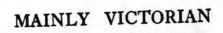

MAINLY VICTORIAN

Thomas Hardy.

S. M. Ellis
Michaelmas: 1922.

E. O. Hoppé

MR. THOMAS HARDY   [_Hoppé_

[_Frontispiece_

MAINLY VICTORIAN

By Stewart Marsh Ellis

With Sixteen Illustrations.

Essay Index Reprint Series

BOOKS FOR LIBRARIES PRESS
FREEPORT, NEW YORK

First Published 1925

Reprinted 1969

STANDARD BOOK NUMBER:
8369-1407-4

LIBRARY OF CONGRESS CATALOG CARD NUMBER:
75-99692

PRINTED IN THE UNITED STATES OF AMERICA

CONTENTS

CONTENTS—*Continued.*

ILLUSTRATIONS

PREFACE

MAINLY ON VICTORIANISM.

MANY friends have expressed the wish that I would reprint in volume form various articles I have contributed, during the past twelve years, to *The Fortnightly Review*, *The Bookman*, and other periodicals, concerning the lives and achievements of certain authors who lived, chiefly, in the Victorian Era. In particular, the late Thomas Seccombe was urgent that I should " make a volume out of the novelists who once were famous. You have," he said, " found a new department of research, and will be another Isaac D'Israeli." Bashfully putting aside his kindly and flattering comparison, it is necessary to point out that this book has outgrown the original intention and contains papers on literary men who are famous for all time in addition to those who " once were famous."

Various circumstances have combined to concentrate my literary interests, and resultant biographical work, on the Victorian period, and more particularly its first thirty years, 1837-1867. The ambit of this book, however, extends over the whole era, with a little overflow at each boundary. But only three or four of the articles—such as those relating to Charles Lamb, Mrs. Radcliffe, and Byron—are concerned with people who lived before the Victorian Era, though the Queen who gave her name to it was born before their lives had ended. At the other end, even the most recent authors I review, such as Miss Sheila Kaye-Smith and Herbert Kennedy, were born before Queen Victoria died. So, by such specious argument and proof, I justify the title of this book, *Mainly Victorian*.

During recent years much controversy has raged on the merits, or, more correctly, the alleged demerits of the Victorians, and much nonsense has been propounded in the course of this would-be intensive criticism. For the critics are really, in a Gilbertian way, attacking themselves, because, in the main, they are Victorian by birth and early environment and education. And so is everybody of any note in contemporary life, whatever his or her art and accomplishment. Even the youngest novelists, such as Mr. Alec Waugh, Mr. Beverley Nichols, Mr. Michael

Arlen, were, I presume, born prior to the golden year of 1901, which the Anti-Victorians no doubt celebrate as the end of The Great Purgatory. The Anti-Victorians find it convenient to forget that Oscar Wilde, Aubrey Beardsley, and all the other pioneers, or " Decadents (so-called) of the 'Nineties,'' were entirely Victorian, however hardly they strove to create a new earth—and a new hell. Oscar Wilde, the Apostle of Beauty, the John Baptist of æsthetic clothing and blue china, spent his youthful and most impressionable years in the early 'Sixties, when crinolines and chignons were most exorbitant, pot-hats and peg-top trousers most pestiferously predominant, in rooms ornate with gilt consoles and glass shades, and hung with heavily corniced and festooned curtains of rep or plush.

In another artistic direction, the Anti-Victorians forget that Thomas Hardy had completed his great series of humanistic novels six years before the close of the era they despise.

Passing to social aspects, the full shaft of disdainful criticism is launched mainly against the women of early and mid Victorian days, the attacks emanating, it would seem, principally from their tube-like and " shingled " successors of to-day, aided by journalistic young men who admire the feminine modes and " manners " of the present period. The grandmothers, or great-grandmothers, of these young persons are stated, without reservation, to have been collectively a poor, anæmic set of girls, who lived mainly by the fireside of airless, sheltered homes; who fainted on every conceivable occasion, ranging from the appearance of a mouse to the proposal of marriage, which was their only aim and object in life. In reply, I would point out that some proportion of women have fainted all through the ages, and—whisper it not!—they do so even in 1924. At the Election in that year it is recorded that several women fainted at a meeting in Edinburgh during the ejectment of a Socialist interrupter; and the heroine of a serial story in a daily illustrated paper was fatuous enough to faint publicly in Piccadilly, though she was supposed to be the last word in modern feminine independence, a young woman who wanted no love or masculine interference in her life.

There were independent women who desired to lead their own life in 1860, and earlier still, as witness Hester Stanhope, Elizabeth Strickland, and Lady Mary Wortley Montagu. The early and mid Victorian girl was not the caricature hothouse plant conceived by those who never knew her. An actual Victorian lady of 1860, Mrs. Hardman, was accustomed to walk, cumbered with crinoline and heavy skirts, for miles over the Surrey hills in the company of her husband and George Meredith—a mighty walker he. Another contemporary, Lady Duff Gordon, smoked cigars. Let it be remembered, too, that well into the middle of the Victorian period every girl of the upper and upper-middle classes was taught to ride on horseback as a matter of course. Read in *Barrington*, by Charles Lever, how Polly Dill swam her horse across a turbulent river with rein and bridle broken, and how bravely Fanny conducted herself when her horse bolted, in *Frank Fairlegh*, by Frank Smedley. These were not considered unusual adventures for the heroine of an early Victorian novel, and the exercise was at least as vigorous as playing tennis or cycling after office hours: the girl of 1854 could dance afterwards until 3 a.m. as strenuously as her descendant of 1924. And what delightful old ladies those girls of 1850-1860 became in after years. I look in vain for any worthy successors to the mothers of my generation—those gracious, dignified women, in their soft silks and laces, possessed of tact and *savoir faire*, a fund of conversation, musical ability, wit and a keen sense of humour: the new old ladies, playing golf by day and losing their money and tempers at bridge by night, are a sorry substitute.

But perhaps it is a work of supererogation to offer any defence of Victorian manners and modes, for I understand it is now *démodé* in the highest circles of the young Intelligentsia of to-day to scoff at these things: it is only penny-a-liners and young women in offices who write letters to the cheap Press that now jeer at and contemn the minds and fashions and furnishings of Queen Victoria's subjects. Mid-Victorian music-hall songs are now sung to the intellectually elect at the latest thing in cabarets; the most up-to-date Oxford undergraduate wears side whiskers, and collects glass lustres, wax fruits, family albums, antimacassars, and other bijoutry of the early Victorian art.

A writer in that super-organ of the youthfully clever, *The London Mercury*, suggested recently that " the revival of interest in the Victorian epoch, a little cult that has been steadily growing for years," has been helped by Mr. Lytton Strachey's " two admirable books." It may be so, but, personally, I do not see much connection between Mr. Strachey's cynical style and mordant comments upon Queen Victoria and some of her great contemporaries and the collecting of daguerreotypes, wool mats, and glass shades. I think it more probable that the observant members of the new generation have been struck by the picturesqueness of the early Victorian period as it recedes more and more into history, just as their immediate predecessors were attracted by the graces of the Stuart period and the romance of Jacobitism. For the earlier Victorian days *were* picturesque in dress. Nothing that women have worn throughout the ages was ever more graceful and distinguished than the crinoline in its first form before it became exaggerated. Examine the exquisite group of the Empress Eugénie and the ladies of her Court as painted by Winterhalter—the flowing lines and beauty of the dresses, the soft grace of the laces and shady hats; and in England any portrait of a great lady about the decade 1848-1858: beauty and stateliness are combined. And even in the 'Sixties, when both male and female fashions had become quaint and exorbitant, the added touch of the bizarre does not lessen the picturesqueness.

To pass to the literary aspect of the new Victorian cult, it was a pleasant shock to me not long ago to find Mr. Michael Sadleir, one of the most modern of the younger school of novelists, stealing my Victorian thunder. He made an excursion into Victorian bibliography, dealing with the works of Captain Marryat, Wilkie Collins, Whyte Melville, Mrs. Gaskell, and other novelists whose stories I fondly believed were read and loved only by dull, middle-aged persons like myself—content, nay proud, to be labelled Victorian and out-of-date. Mr. Sadleir indulged in a rhetorical recantation and confessed how he came to an appreciation of Trollope, Charles Reade, Herman Melville, Disraeli, and the other writers I have just mentioned, after riotous intercourse with the Symbolists, the Gaelic Mystics, the Realists, the Neo-Barbarists, the Cubists, and all the rest of the dreary seekers after something new and startling. He said:—

" Those of an older generation than my own have, perhaps, never betrayed their gentle Victorian heritage. One may envy and applaud their wisdom. But we prodigals, returned from our rioting and sick with the husks of a *démodé* violence, stoop to any self-abasement, to any denial of our own past judgment, so we be allowed entry to the quiet courts and ordered opulence of the age we once affected to despise."

Well, well, there *is* balm in Gilead. I, for one, will not selfishly try to preserve the stately and peaceful pleasances of Victorian literature for my own generation only, nor bar the way to the reformed Young Barbarians who now seek entrance: but I am glad to get this book out before the excited noviciates rush into the Close and seize upon my moss-grown garden gods and paint them pink.

The first thirty years, 1837-1867, of the Victorian Era must ever remain the most attractive to the student of history and modes and manners. And how rich is the illustrative material which can conjure up and revivify that dear, dead world by the Art of Thackeray, Dickens, Surtees, Lever, Frank Smedley, Trollope, Phiz, Cruikshank, Charles Keene, Leech, and others whose names occur in the following pages.

It was a world of women in voluminous, crinolined dresses, poke-bonnets or pork-pie hats, and ringlets or chignons; of hirsute men in pot-hats, paletots, and peg-top trousers; of quaintly-garbed children, the joy of Papa and Mamma; of buxom, bare-bosomed maidservants and tall be-plushed Jeameses. They lived, in London, it is true, in gloomy-looking houses standing in sombre, drab streets: but once within those houses, what cosy warmth, what bright fire-light, and odours of substantial cooking, and unstinted supplies of old Madeira and port and sherry wine. And above, what domestic beatitude and happy nurseries, whence troop the children, all stiff-muslined and tight-suited, yet shouting and rosy, to crowd the ramshackle " growler " cab, with its much be-caped ancient driver, and so off to a jolly night at Astley's or the pantomime (a real one) in conditions of frost and snow, or yellow fog and link-boys, such as we moderns wot not of. Blessed period of peace and prosperity, port and progeny and domesticity *in excelsis* from Buckingham Palace to Bloomsbury Square and brand-new Bayswater. Despite its limitations, it was a good, solid, happy time of English life at its best, and is summed up in the word Victorianism.

S. M. ELLIS.

The Cottage, Mornington Avenue, W.14.
     November 7th, 1924.

ACKNOWLEDGMENTS.

I WISH to express my thanks to the Editors of *The Fortnightly Review, The Bookman, The Saturday Review, The Contemporary Review, The Times Literary Supplement, Chambers's Journal, The Sunday Times*, and other publications duly specified in the following pages, for their permission to reprint articles which appeared originally in the reviews and papers mentioned. *The Bookman* has also kindly lent blocks for several portraits.

The articles of a biographical nature do not profess to be very critical: rather is it their aim to present the actual life and personal aspects of each subject, to point out the influences of heredity and early environment which were reflected in the literary work of the authors in question.

In all the articles, no doubt, the personal aspects will be found predominant.

S. M. E.

MAINLY VICTORIAN.

SOME NEW CHARLES LAMB LETTERS.*

CHARLES LAMB, the ideal bachelor, who might have inspired
Austin Dobson's vignette in rhyme—

> " My brown old books around me wait,
> My pipe still holds, unconfiscate,
>   Its wonted station.
> Pass me the wine.   To those that keep
> The bachelor's secluded sleep
> Peaceful, inviolate, and deep,
>   I pour libation "—

had one romance in his life and made one offer of marriage.
Some letters published twenty-one years ago—1903—made
known the fact that Lamb, at the mature age of forty-four,
proposed marriage to Fanny Kelly, the celebrated actress, who
was fifteen years his junior.   Romance, perhaps, is scarcely the
word to use in connection with this episode, which never ruffled
the calm flow of the Elian river.   There was great friendship and
esteem on either side, but neither Lamb nor Miss Kelly had any
emotion of passionate love one for the other.   Lamb's idea of
matrimony was a household *à trois*—his afflicted sister Mary to
live with them also—and in wording his prosaic proposal of
marriage he first asked Miss Kelly " to consent to take your lot
with us."   He went on to say that it was impossible he should
feel injured or aggrieved by hearing at once that the proposal did
not suit Miss Kelly.   The lady took him at his word, and replied
the same day, July 20th, 1819 : —

" An early and deeply rooted attachment has fixed my heart on one
from whom no worldly prospect can ever induce me to withdraw it, but
while I thus *frankly* and decidedly decline your proposal, believe me, I am
not insensible to the high honour which the preference of such a mind
as yours confers upon me.. . ."

Lamb was not in the least upset by the refusal.   Still on the
same day he wrote again to Miss Kelly in his most characteristic
style : —

---

* The letters of Charles Lamb are printed here by permission of Messrs.
J. M. Dent & Sons, who hold the copyright.   This article appeared originally
in *The Saturday Review*, June 12th and 19th, 1915, which was consequently
the date of the first publication of the Lamb letters in question.

" *Your injunctions shall be obeyed to a tittle.* I feel myself in a lackadaisical no-howish kind of humour. I believe it is the rain or something. . . You will be good friends with us, will you not? "

Good friends they remained, as the later letters, here published for the first time, will demonstrate : —

" C. and M. Lamb have just come from Ware, where they have been confined in a dull Inn for 3 days by wet weather. They will be most happy to see Miss K. and her friends any evening they will name, but should like to know in time, it being C.L.'s holyday, and they purposing to go out here and there for a night or two during the next 3 weeks. Inclosed, or inclosing is a receit for Mrs. Arnold, whom they hope to see too with Mr. A.* or at least the latter. They are sure to be at home before Wednesday."

" Saturday, Islington,
     " June 26th, 1824."

" DEAR MISS KELLY,

" We regret your not being able to come to-morrow, and shall be thankful for the smallest donation of a visit you can spare. Can you name an evening next week towards the end (not Wednesday) in which we may hope you will accompany General and Mrs. Pye, with Mr. Arnold (we hope) to Islington. Pray fix with them if you can, and assure the General, and Mrs. Pye, that it is not from want of respect to them that I leave it to *you* to name an evening, without a formal letter to them first, but simply because we know your many engagements.

" Forward this to them with our best respects *and more.*

                                              " Yours truly,
     " Saturday, April 7th, 1827.   " C. LAMB.
     " Dash barks his compliments to Bluff and congratulates his return."

" DEAR MISS KELLY,

" We are sorry to trouble you at a sad time, but Miss Ibbs, to whom you have been kind, and for whom we are under such obligations to Mr. Arnold, has informed us that at Drury Lane there is a vacancy for a voice in the chorus. The singing master is the same as at your Opera House. Is it in your power to speak a good word for her at that Theatre? It would be a great benefit for the poor girl, and very much bind us to gratitude, if you only tried to do it. But we should be the last to impose an unpleasant task upon you at any time, much less now, when we should be sympathising with you. If you cannot do it pleasantly to yourself, don't cast away a thought upon it, but think us always

              " Your very sincere friends,
                                   " C. AND MARY LAMB.
     " Wednesday morning,
          " Mrs. Leishman's, Chase, Enfield.
               " August 15th, 1827."

The Lambs had just removed from Colebrook Cottage, Islington, to Enfield, where at first they took lodgings before moving into a house of their own.

---

* Mr. Arnold was Miss Kelly's theatrical manager at the English Opera House.

" Enfield, 25th Sept., '27.
" A coach from the Bell, Holborn,
½ past 3, or ½ past 4, to the door.

" DEAR MISS KELLY,
" *Honestly* if you can come down alone, or accompanied with Miss Hamilton or Miss Gray, there is ample accommodation for you either at our lodgings, or in our new House, or elsewhere, for as many hours as Enfield shall be agreeable to you. If this week is most convenient, come this week ; but if you have curiosity to see our new house, it is scarce in order till the next.

" You will find Colebrook Cottage, with its old books, etc., miraculously conveyed to Enfield in the night time. The New River is also come down with it.

" It would give us the greatest gratification to see your party *next Sunday.* We dine *here,* and can go to criticise the *Manor House* after dinner : or Sunday after to dine in the *new House!*

" Our best regards and most earnest wishes to Mr. Arnold to see him with you.

" Our cordial thanks for your kindness to our strange-named friend.*

" Pray let us know if you all come ; but come without that ceremony if alone.

" My sister and Emma send loves, and I respects.

" Yours truly,

" C. LAMB.

" Mary would write, but she is making old carpets look like new."

The tragedy of Mary Lamb is one of the most terrible in the annals of English literature—more terrible than Cowper's. She murdered her mother during one of her fits of insanity. Charles Lamb, who devoted his life to the care of his sister, used to accompany her to the asylum, and fetch her back when she had recovered her reason. One of these recurring mental attacks caused the postponement of Miss Kelly's proposed visit discussed in the last letter, for within a week Lamb had to write : —

" DEAR MISS KELLY,
" All our pleasant prospects of seeing you here are dashed. Poor Mary was taken last night with the beginning of one of her sad illnesses, which last so long. I am here in a new house with her, and without her company. What I expected to be so comfortable has opened gloomily. But I hope she will get through it and enjoy our choice. I hardly know what I write. God bless you and our common friends.

" Yours most truly,

" CH. LAMB.

" Enfield, Chase Side.
" 1st October, 1827."

In about five months' time Mary Lamb was well again, and the invitation to Miss Kelly to come to Enfield was renewed.

---

* Miss Ibbs.

" Dear Miss Kelly,   " Enfield, 10th Mar., 1828.

" Many thanks for your kind consideration about our young friend who is engaged to a clergyman's family near Bury, and it is settled that she goes there in April.   But she and we are equally thankful for the communication.   Emma* has taken the liberty to name the situation to a young friend who will wait upon you immediately, and whom Emma thinks equally qualified with herself in French, and very *superior to her in music,* being a most excellent singer also.   Emma hopes you will pardon her recommendation—from her intimate knowledge of her young friend, whose disposition she describes as excellent, and her parents and connections as most excellent also.   She is about 18, and daughter to Mr. Adams, silversmith, No. 76, Strand, whom I have seen and greatly like.   We think this to be the No.—but it is very near Adam Street, Adelphi ; but she will call and beg to see Mrs. Bryan or you, supposing Mrs. B. to be still with you.   Emma would write, but she is at a school here, where she passes all the time possible in giving a finish to her French and music before her final departure.

" Mary is very well, thank God, and joins in thanks and our friendly remembrances to yourself and our common friends, and above all to good Mrs. Bryan, who has been so thoughtful for Emma.

" We are fixed here at Enfield, on the Chase, next to Mr. Westwood's Insurance Office, where, whenever you can spare a day and a night, it would be most gratifying to see you with Mrs. Bryan.

" Some of us will be in town ere long, and shall try to find you out in your new Old Dean Street, which we hope you find as pleasant as we did Henrietta Street.   I should say something about our not having written to you so long, but I am in haste to get this to the post with some others which must go by it, so pray accept a hasty but warm remembrance from us all.

" Miss Adams has been five years at school at Mrs. Richardson's, Dulwich, with Emma, who is sure that Mrs. R. would give her the best of characters.

" Pray believe us,

" Most truly and affectionately yours,

" Charles and Mary Lamb."

" Mary Lamb sends her love to Miss Kelly, and she and her whole little household will be most glad to see her at Enfield, and still more if she will prevail upon Mrs. Bryan to accompany her ; she has beds at their service, and hopes they will make what stay they can with her.   A coach will bring them from the Bell, corner of Leather Lane, Holborn, we believe, at nine in the morning and set them down at the cottage, on the Chase, next door to Mr. Westwood's Insurance Office.

" Emma joins us in kindest thanks to Mrs. Bryan for the trouble she took so kindly for her young friend, and we all wait in a pleasant expectation of Monday.

" The morning coach, we find, comes at ½ past 8, and the afternoon at ¼ past 3 and ½ past 4, whichever may best suit the ladies.

---

* Emma Isola, Lamb's adopted daughter. She married Edward Moxon in 1833.

" Pray come, it is more than convenient. In my own hand,
Ever yours affectionately,

" March 28th, 1828." " M. LAMB.

" Enfield, May 9th, 1828.

" Miss Lamb rejoices in the hope of seeing Miss Kelly here on Sunday. Cakes and ale at the Barley Mou, as before. Could not Mrs. Bryan accompany her, as we are richer in beds than before by half a bed?

" Charles suggests that perhaps Mr. Arnold will accompany them, which would make a day of it. Do try and persuade him. He shall either have Emma's little bed, and my brother go out, or the latter stay in, and Mr. Arnold *bed* at the Rising Sun. Do come all three.

" This is neither note nor letter, confounding 1st and 3rd persons, and tis Mary's letter, and yet 'tis written by *me*.
" Yours and all yours,

" C. AND M. LAMB.

" Can you extricate this confusion of plurals and singulars? cannot. Who's I? "

" DEAR MISS KELLY,

" In great haste setting out to town I write you lest you should by accident come down to-morrow. We shall see you.
" Yours very truly,

" C. LAMB.

" Enfield,
" August 30th, 1828."

" DEAR MISS KELLY,

" Emma's sister waits upon you to solicit two orders for any night that is convenient, according to your kind promise.

" We are got safe home, rather quiet and rather dull, with a rainy day before us.

" Mary joins in kind love, hoping to see you, with better weather, shortly.
" Yours truly,

" Friday." " C. LAMB.

There only remains the following letter from Mary Lamb, which, although it was written before Charles Lamb's proposal to Miss Kelly, may find a place here, for the rare letters of Mary Lamb are now almost as highly regarded as those of her brother. She taught Miss Kelly Latin.

" MY DEAR MISS KELLY,

" A very pleasant remembrance of you has come to my hands in the shape of a newspaper. The direction is in a good-natured hand-writing, which my brother will have it resembles a hand-writing which he has sometimes seen of yours. Whoever favoured me with it (for there is no name) it has brought you into my mind, with the recollection of the one kind evening which you were able to spare us. You have since been a

B

sad wanderer, and are coming home not exactly, I am afraid, to rest yourself, for labour seems to attend you at home and abroad. Such is the tax which excellence must pay for furnishing an ungrateful world with recreation.

" I have heard, I need not say how painfully, that you have been unwell since you left us. It is some satisfaction that you have been able to appear before the Edinborough audience. If those cold northern people do not appear quite to estimate your powers of giving pleasure, you are soon coming home, where one or two at least know how to value them.

" I feel particularly awkward in writing to you for the first time, but I could not let pass even a direction on a newspaper, which is like yours, without attempting to reply to it.

" I am afraid our poor Latin is at a standstill, but I will not mix the angry jealousy of a schoolmistress with the different feelings with which I have the pleasure to subscribe myself,

 " My dear Miss Kelly,

  " Your sincerely affectionate friend,

   " M. Lamb.

" P.S.—My brother joins in kindest regards to you. By the bye, he does not think the style of the Edinborough newspapers so good as that of some other provincial papers.

" 20, Russel Street, Covent Garden.
 " 6th May, 1819."

In addition to the two letters, already mentioned, which Lamb wrote to Miss Kelly in 1819 on the subject of his proposal of marriage, there are extant also two other communications addressed to the same lady—one from Charles Lamb, dated July 6th, 1825, and the other from Mary Lamb, dated March 27th, 1820. The originals of these two letters were sold at Sotheby's a few years ago, and are not available for this article.

There are, of course, many references to Fanny Kelly in Charles Lamb's letters to other friends, and in his published works, including *The True Story of Barbara S——*, which is based on an incident in the early life of the actress related by her to Lamb.

Charles Lamb lived for fifteen years after the date of his proposal of marriage, and during that remaining period of life, as these letters have shown, he ever found delight in the visits of the woman whose varied gifts had once so greatly charmed him. And when the end came in the little house at Edmonton, as all around grew dim and the fragrant memories of that once-powerful mind were fading fast, perchance " a gleam of Fanny Kelly's divine, plain face " struck the last ray of light through the cruel descending pall of the Great Darkness.

FANNY KELLY

Engraved by Alais
from a painting by
Drummond, 1821.

[*Page* 18.

ANN RADCLIFFE

AND HER LITERARY INFLUENCE.

" Hark ! hollow blasts through empty courts resound
And shadowy forms with staring eyes stalk round !"

CRABBE.

A HUNDRED years ago, on the seventh of this month,* died Mrs. Radcliffe, " The Great Mistress of Romance," as she was styled by one of her disciples, Harrison Ainsworth, who was destined to surpass her in merit as a romance writer. An earlier eulogist, Mathias, in his *Pursuits of Literature*, apostrophised Mrs. Radcliffe as " The mighty magician of *The Mysteries of Udolpho*, bred and nourished by the Florentine Muses in their sacred, solitary caverns, amid the paler shrines of Gothic superstition, and in all the dreariness of enchantment, a poetess whom Ariosto would with rapture have acknowledged. . ."

Setting aside hyperbole, no feminine writer has exercised such a powerful and lasting influence upon literature as Mrs. Radcliffe; and she conquered her particular realm of grim romance without any pronounced hereditary equipment or environment in youth suggestive of her later art. Ann Ward was born in the parish of St. Andrew's, Holborn, on July 9th, 1764, the daughter of William Ward, a bookseller, and a nephew on his mother's side of William Cheselden, the famous surgeon. Mrs. Radcliffe's mother was Ann, daughter of James Oates, of Chesterfield; the future novelist's maternal grandmother being Amelia, daughter of Joshua Jebb, hosier and, for a time, Mayor of Chesterfield; one of his grandsons became Sir Richard Jebb, M.D., physician to King George III. Nothing very suggestive of romance in the family history so far. But some literary influences were to accrue from the marriage, in 1754, of Ann Ward's maternal aunt, Hannah Oates, with Thomas Bentley, the brilliant partner of Josiah Wedgwood, and the friend of Rousseau, John Hunter, Sir Joseph Banks, and many other distinguished people. Smiles thus describes Thomas Bentley : —

" Handsome in person and polished in manners and conversation, he entertained his morning audiences of dukes, duchesses, and other noble personages with great suavity and grace. Bentley could speak most European languages, and descant to his hearers on Greek and

---

* This article appeared in *The Contemporary Review*, February, 1923, the centenary of Mrs. Radcliffe's death.

Etruscan art, or converse with the Foreign Ambassadors in French or
in Italian on the progress of artistic manufactures in their various
countries.''

Although her aunt, Mrs. Bentley, was dead, Ann Ward spent
a good deal of her time in girlhood with Thomas Bentley and his
second wife at Chelsea and Turnham Green. Bentley's residence
in the latter place was Linden House, which fifty years later
became notorious as the scene of the crimes of Thomas Griffiths
Wainewright, the poisoner. Oscar Wilde, in his *Pen, Pencil and
Poison*, states that Wainewright's '' boyhood was passed at
Linden House, Turnham Green, one of those many fine Georgian
mansions that have unfortunately disappeared before the inroads
of the suburban builder, and to its lovely gardens and well-
timbered park he owed that simple and impassioned love of nature
which never left him all through his life.'' It may only be a
coincidence of names that Wainewright's wife was Frances
Ward, daughter by her first husband of Mrs. Abercrombie, of
Mortlake, who was Wainewright's second victim, the first being
his uncle, George Edward Griffiths, whom he poisoned in 1829,
in order to obtain possession of Linden House—'' a place to
which he had always been very much attached.''*

Here, then, at Linden House half a century earlier, Ann Ward
met her uncle's guests, such as Mrs. Thrale, Mrs. Montagu, the
formidable Blue-stocking from Portman Square, '' Athenian ''
Stuart, and William Radcliffe, whom '' the little niece '' was
destined to marry seven years after Thomas Bentley's death. The
wedding took place in 1787 at Bath, where the bride's parents
then lived. It is difficult to recover the aspect and personality of
William Radcliffe. He was M.A. of Oxford, and had studied
for the Law; but he took up journalism and purchased *The
English Chronicle*, for which he paid £1,000 in order to experience
the joys of editorship. He was probably a young man of literary
and artistic tastes, rather a dilettante and delicate in health. After
his wife's rise to fame he seems to have become altogether
eclipsed and was simply '' Mrs. Radcliffe's husband ''—a fate
which generally attaches to a mediocre man who marries a
brilliant and gifted wife; Mr. Arthur Bell Nicholls, Mr. Gaskell,
Mr. Riddell are other cases in point.

Mrs. Radcliffe is described as beautiful, slender, and finely-
proportioned—'' a pretty face '' Farington notes in his diary, in
1797, on the report of his friend, Marchi—and though small in
stature, she was one of those determined, strong-willed little

---

* Charles Dickens's short story, *Hunted Down,* was suggested by an
incident in the career of Wainewright.

women who get their own way in all things matrimonial and otherwise. She was rather formal and stately in her bearing, and in her later years professed to dislike the freer manners and behaviour of Society which developed during the Regency and the reaction following the close of the long Napoleonic wars. Mrs. Radcliffe was exclusive, and on one occasion rather curtly declined a visit from the learned and redoubtable Mrs. Elizabeth Carter, the friend of Johnson. After the publication of *The Mysteries of Udolpho* in 1794, Mrs. Carter pronounced a high opinion in favour of the talents of Mrs. Radcliffe, and five years later she sought to make her acquaintance by means of a letter of introduction from H. M. Bowdler, of Bath. She wrote: " If Mrs. Radcliffe is not engaged, Mrs. Carter will have the pleasure of calling upon her about twelve o'clock to-morrow morning." To which she received the prompt reply: " Mrs. Radcliffe is extremely sorry that an engagement to go into the country to-morrow, for some time, on account of Mr. R.'s state of health, which is very critical, will deprive her of the honour intended her by Mrs. Carter, for which she requests Mrs. C. to believe that she has a full and proper respect."

Mrs. Radcliffe turned her attention to literary composition soon after marriage, for her first book, *The Castles of Athlin and Dunbayne*, appeared in 1789. It was a *ballon d'essai*, and though it did not achieve much, its successor, *A Sicilian Romance*, which followed rapidly in 1790, was a great success. The fame of *The Romance of the Forest*, 1791, was surpassed by the universal acclamation bestowed upon *The Mysteries of Udolpho* in 1794. From a literary point of view, *The Italian*, 1797, is perhaps a better accomplishment, though it never attained to the general notoriety of its predecessor, for the name of Udolpho is indissolubly associated with that of Mrs. Radcliffe. Her final romance, *Gaston de Blondeville*, written in 1803, only appeared posthumously in 1826; it described Kenilworth.

Mrs. Radcliffe reaped both fame and material benefits from her work produced during the last decade of the eighteenth century. The reports of the sums she received for her books are contradictory. One memoir asserts she was paid £2,000 for *The Mysteries of Udolpho*; another places the figure at £1,000; but Sir Walter Scott says it was £500. In the same way, £1,500 and £800 are mentioned as the receipts from *The Italian*. In any case, they were very large for that rather moribund period of literary history. But far more than money, Mrs. Radcliffe appreciated the position she had won. Her name had become a literary symbol—the synonym for the Mysterious and the Glooms of Romance. Thus, Shelley when visiting the picturesque and legend-haunted Cuckfield Place, in Sussex, with its undulating park and dark woods, observed it was " like bits of Mrs. Radcliffe." And writing in June, 1795, about the title of a book, Fanny Burney said: " I like well the idea of giving no name at all—why should not I have my mystery as well as *Udolpho*? " Sir Walter Scott stated: " Mrs. Radcliffe has a title to be considered the first poetess of romantic fiction"; and Hazlitt observed of her style: " In harrowing up the soul with imaginary terrors, and making the flesh creep, and the nerves thrill with fond hopes and fears, she is unrivalled among her countrymen." Byron, too, in the fourth canto of *Childe Harold's Pilgrimage*, when describing Venice, paid a tribute to Mrs. Radcliffe's art in depicting scenery and architecture: —

> " I loved her from my boyhood; she to me
> Was as a fairy city of the heart,
> Rising like water-columns from the sea,
> Of joy the sojourn, and of wealth the mart;
> And Otway, Radcliffe, Schiller, Shakespeare's art
> Had stamped her image in me. . . . ."*

The secret of Mrs. Radcliffe's art is twofold. It is comprised in her vast descriptive power of impressive scenery and storms, and in suggestion of the Unknown: not in depicting actual scenes of horror. Her art found expression in picturing lonely castles and convents situated amid mountain fastnesses or forest glooms; in a narrative of exciting adventures, with danger and possible death ever near, in labyrinthine passages and secret chambers where low sighs and hollow groans are heard, and voices of the unseen; where mysterious lights and shadows flit, and malignant hands cause the arras to move. She could attune the mind to coming terrors by a scenic picture. How graphically the first sight of the sinister castle in *The Mysteries of Udolpho* is presented: —

" Towards the close of the day, the road wound into a deep valley. Mountains, whose shaggy sides appeared to be inaccessible, almost surrounded it. To the east a vista opened and exhibited the Apennines in their darkest horrors; and the long perspective of retiring summits rising over each other, their ridges clothed with pines, exhibited a stronger image of grandeur than any that Emily had yet seen. The sun had just sunk below the top of the mountains . . . but his sloping

---

* The Countess of Blessington, describing the Tuscan Château de Bracciano, noted : " The Gothic towers, formed of black lava, stand boldly out in strong relief against the blue sky that surrounds them; and the whole place forms just such a picture as the pen of a Radcliffe delighted to trace. Nor would the lives of some of its former owners furnish an uninteresting subject for one of those dark romances, the perusal of which so often blanched my cheek with fear in the days of my early youth."—*The Idler in Italy*, Vol 2, p. 544.

rays, shooting through an opening of the cliffs, touched with a yellow gleam the summits of the forest that hung upon the opposite steeps, and streamed in full splendour upon the towers and battlements of a castle that spread its extensive ramparts along the brow of a precipice above. . . . . As she gazed the light died away on its walls, leaving a melancholy purple tint, which spread deeper and deeper as the thin vapour crept up the mountain, while the battlements above were still tipt with splendour. From these, too, the rays soon faded, and the whole edifice was invested with the solemn darkness of evening. Silent, lonely, and sublime . . . as the twilight deepened, its features became more awful in obscurity.''

Once within the castle, a Radcliffe heroine meets with nightly experiences of a terrifying nature. Weird noises and mysterious figures disturb her slumbers: —

" She was soon awakened by a noise, which seemed to arise within her chamber . . . she saw the door move and then slowly opened, and perceived something enter the room . . . it seemed to glide along the remote obscurity of the apartment . . . then, advancing slowly towards the bed, stood silently at the feet. . . .''

Or hearing, perchance, cries in a distant part of the castle, the heroine seizes her dim lamp and proceeds to investigate; passing through devious passages and vaults, she comes to a chamber of mystery consummated, where, if her lamp be not extinguished by some unseen agency, she perceives a black curtain. She draws it aside: —

" Beyond appeared a corpse, stretched on a kind of low couch, which was crimsoned with human blood, as was the floor beneath. The features, deformed by death, were ghastly and horrible, and more than one livid wound appeared in the face. Emily, bending over the body, gazed, for a moment, with an eager, phrensied eye; but, in the next, the lamp dropped from her hand, and she fell senseless at the foot of the couch.''

Such was the climax and *bonne-bouche* of Mrs. Radcliffe's style which caused our great-grandparents to shudder: but not very terrifying or impressive to a later generation accustomed to the ghostly horrors and delicious demonology of Sheridan Le Fanu, Algernon Blackwood, and Montague Rhodes James. For neither the ghosts nor the corpses of Mrs. Radcliffe were the real thing. The scenic and mysterious accessories are admirable, but to read a book of hers to the close breaks the charm, for all her supernatural events are explained by natural causes. Nothing could be more futile and infuriating. A ghost story *is* a ghost story, and it should be treated seriously whether or no the teller believes in the possibility of the materialisation of beings from another plane. To arouse feelings of pleasurable awe and fear in the mind of a reader by a tale of terror, and then at the end to turn on him and cry " April Fool,'' as it were, is literary false pretences, and may cause resentment and dislike to be entertained for the perpetrator of the hoax. Mrs. Radcliffe is beyond any active interest in such penalties, but her erroneous method of treating the supernatural is an indelible blot upon her artistry.

It has been advanced that Mrs. Radcliffe was compelled by the literary conventions of her time to end her stories in a happy and normal way, otherwise the susceptibilities of her female readers would have been shocked and outraged by the machinations and triumphs of real evil spirits in a novel. This argument is not sound. Mrs. Radcliffe did not actually found her particular school of Mysterious Romance, though she brought it to its limited perfection. She was preceded by Horace Walpole with *The Castle of Otranto*, 1764 (the year of Mrs. Radcliffe's birth), wherein demons sport in most fantastic style; and she was contemporary with M. G. Lewis, whose curious book, *The Monk*, published in 1795, was in emulation of her method and unprecedented success. The superimposed " immoralities " were entirely his own. *The Monk*, frank combination of supernatural and sensuality, delighted the ladies in question of the last decade of the eighteenth century. As Byron puts it : —

> " Oh ! wonder-working Lewis, Monk and Bard . . .
> By gibbering spectres hailed, thy kindred band ;
> Who tracest chaste descriptions on thy page
> To please the females of our modest age."

Incidentally it must be noted that even Walpole was preceded by some earlier, though unimportant, writers of supernatural romance. And Smollett in *The Adventures of Ferdinand Count Fathom* had made use of the devices of mysterious and apparently supernatural sounds and events which Mrs. Radcliffe later on adopted so effectively. Still, Horace Walpole is generally regarded as the literary father of Mrs. Radcliffe's romances and the numerous imitations which inevitably succeeded them; but he does not seem to have relished the honour, judging by a disparaging remark in a letter of his to Lady Ossory, dated September 4th, 1794, about " some of the descriptive verbose tales, of which your Ladyship says I was the patriarch by several mothers. All I can say for myself is that I do not think my concubines have produced issue more natural for excluding the aid of anything marvellous."

But it was Mrs. Radcliffe who realised and developed the potentialities of Mysterious Romance from the weakly embryo of Walpole; as Sir Walter Scott said, " she has the most decided claim to take her place among the favoured few who have been distinguished as the founders of a class or school." Despite her faults and limitations, Mrs. Radcliffe's influence can be traced in practically all later romantic and supernatural tales. M. G. Lewis, with *The Monk* and *Tales of Wonder*, has already been mentioned. Next comes C. R. Maturin, whose books appeared during the period 1807-1820. His finest romance, *Melmoth the Wanderer*, is extremely horrific, and he alludes in it to the statement that he had essayed to revive the horrors of Radcliffe Romance. Maturin was the great-grand-uncle of Oscar Wilde, who had a great admiration for his relative's literary work. When Wilde was released from prison he assumed the name " Sebastian Melmoth." It may be that the idea of the supernatural picture in *Dorian Gray* generated from the painted effigy hidden by the black veil in *The Mysteries of Udolpho*.

Mrs. Shelley's *Frankenstein* appeared in 1816. Sir Walter Scott was, of course, strongly influenced by Mrs. Radcliffe. At the outset of his career as a novelist he wrote in the first chapter of *Waverley*, when dealing with the title of his book : " Had I, for example, announced in my frontispiece, *Waverley, a Tale of Other Days*, must not every reader have anticipated a castle scarce less than that of Udolpho. . . . Would not the owl have shrieked and the cricket cried in my very title page ? " Scott was the author of the very sympathetic memoir of Mrs. Radcliffe which was prefixed to the collected edition of her works, 1824.

Harrison Ainsworth stated in his Preface to *Rookwood*, 1834, that the story was in the style of Mrs. Radcliffe, " which had always inexpressible charms for me." Ainsworth being a greater artist than Mrs. Radcliffe, he did not explain away his mysteries : the supernatural events, which are found in all his best romances, remain supernatural. On the other hand, G.P.R. James followed the Radcliffe plan so faithfully that he entirely ruined his otherwise fine romance, *The Castle of Ehrenstein*, 1847. The influence of Mrs. Radcliffe is also found in William Godwin's *St. Leon;* in the works of Lytton, G. W. M. Reynolds, and other English writers too numerous to mention, and also in the great French romancists, Balzac, Hugo, Dumas, and Sue.

Andrew Lang in a most entertaining article, *Mrs. Radcliffe's Novels*, which appeared in *The Cornhill Magazine*, July, 1900, pointed out that Charlotte Brontë borrowed the idea of the hidden mad wife in *Jane Eyre* from a similar incident in *A Sicilian Romance*, and that a situation in R. L. Stevenson's *Kidnapped* emanated from the same work.

Mrs. Radcliffe's most effective piece of character drawing was that of fhe implacable and criminal monk, Schedoni, in *The Italian*, whose face, beneath the cowl, " bore the traces of many passions, which seemed to have fixed the features they no longer

animated." He was the progenitor of the silent relentless villain
who appears so often in Byron : —

> " Dark and unearthly is the scowl
> That glares beneath his dusky cowl ;
> The flash of that dilating eye
> Reveals too much of times gone by."
>> *The Giaour.*

> " That brow in furrow'd lines had fix'd at last,
> And spake of passions, but of passions past."
>> *Lara.*

> " His features' deepening lines and varying hue
> At times attracted, yet perplex'd the view,
> As if within that murkiness of mind
> Work'd feelings fearful, and yet undefined."
>> *The Corsair.*

His descendants developed into such presentments of evil as
Count Fosco and Sheridan Le Fanu's creations, Silas Ruthyn and
Dangerfield; and though the strain of original crime and passion
has become diluted in " the strong, silent men" beloved of
present-day female novelists, they, too, without doubt, can trace
their pedigree back to Schedoni.

It was inevitable, of course, that the notoriety of Mrs.
Radcliffe's romances and her horde of imitators should exercise
the art of contemporary satirists, and it was fortunate indeed that
they generated such a masterpiece as *Northanger Abbey.*
Although not published until 1818, Jane Austen had written this
book in 1798, the year after the publication of *The Italian.* As
is well known, it was acquired by a bookseller of Bath for the
vast sum of £10. Mr. Austin Dobson used to offer the interesting
suggestion that this Bœotian personage hesitated to publish his
purchase by reason of his admiration for *The Mysteries of
Udolpho* and those imitative romances enumerated by Isabella
Thorpe in the sixth chapter of *Northanger Abbey.* The books
in question, *Mysterious Warnings, The Midnight Bell, Horrid
Mysteries,* and the rest, actually existed, and were not titles
invented by Jane Austen. We owe this fact to the research of
the Rev. Montague Summers, author of a valuable paper on
Mrs. Radcliffe, read before the Royal Society of Literature in
1917. Mr. Summers discovered and read the seven " horrid "
romances mentioned by Jane Austen. *Northanger Abbey* is most
excellent burlesque of the Radcliffe School. The absurd blunders
in which Catherine Morland is involved by reason of her
saturation in *The Mysteries of Udolpho* and similar tales; her
certainty that the fate of General Tilney's wife must be on a par
with that of the lady in *A Sicilian Romance;* and the discovery of

the secret manuscript, which proves to be a bundle of old washing bills, all is in the true vein of ironic comedy. Another amusing satire of Radcliffean romance was *The Heroine, or the Adventures of Cherubina*, 1813, by Eaton S. Barrett.

It is curious that Mrs. Radcliffe wrote no more fiction (with the exception of the negligible *Gaston de Blondeville*) after *The Italian*. She and her husband were at this date, 1797 and thereabout, living at No. 7, Medina Place, St. George's Fields—the rural district then still existing between the Borough and Kennington Road.

In 1794 Mrs. Radcliffe and her husband had visited Holland and the Rhine, and the English Lakes. She kept a Journal of the Tour, which was published the following year. It was descriptive rather than personal, and a sublime scene, storms, sullen clouds, a lurid sunset, the mournful soughing of the wind, would cause her to pen a description of the kind that adorn her romances. Her susceptibility to the influences of Nature also found expression in her *Poems*, which were collected, mainly from the romances, and published in 1815.*

There is a curious story, too long to quote here, that when visiting France, in 1795, Mrs. Radcliffe was arrested as a spy, and " cast into a dripping dungeon," but four feet high, in the Conciergerie. She was eventually released by the good offices of Madame Tallien, to whom she confided she was haunted by a spectral illusion, which recurred at every midnight.†

During the years 1797-1802 Mrs. Radcliffe travelled over various parts of England; she was in Derbyshire in 1798 at the time of her father's death, and again in 1800 during her mother's last days, for her parents spent their final years in Mrs. Ward's native county. In the latter part of her life Mrs. Radcliffe gave

---

* The following will serve as an example of Mrs. Radcliffe's poetical style :—

" O'er the dim breast of ocean's wave
　　Night spreads afar her gloomy wings,
　　And pensive thought, and silence brings
Save when the distant waters lave !
　　Or when the mariner's lone voice
Swells faintly in the passing gale;
　　Or when the screaming sea-gulls poise
O'er the tall mast and swelling sail.
　　Bounding the gray gleam of the deep,
Where fancied forms arouse the mind,
　　Dark sweeps the shore; on whose rude steep
Sighs the sad spirit of the wind.
Sweet is its voice upon the air
　　At evening's melancholy close,
　　While the smooth wave in silence flows !
Sweet, sweet, the peace its stealing accents bear.
Blest be thy shades, O night ! and blest the song
Thy low winds breathe the distant shores along."

† See Godey's *Lady's Book*, Vol. 45, p. 225.

up distant excursions and contented herself with drives, accompanied by her husband, to Esher, Stanmore, Richmond, and
Harrow, and other pleasant resorts within easy reach of London,
where they would dine at an inn.   In 1812-1815 they were a good
deal at Windsor.   J. T. Smith, in his entertaining book,
Nollekens and his Times, relates two anecdotes of Mrs.
Radcliffe's humanity in rescuing two wretched dogs, who later
became her well-known pets " Dash " and " Fan."   The latter,
cured of the mange, was

" excessively admired for her great beauty, and being under the tuition
of so amiable a protectress, she so improved in manners as to be often
noticed by the late Queen and the Princesses, when walking with her
mistress in Windsor Park, at the time Mrs. Radcliffe had a small cottage
in the town. . . .   The royal equestrians frequently recognised Mrs.
Radcliffe as the authoress and ' Fanny's ' mistress."

Mrs. Radcliffe's last home in London was No. 5, Stafford
Place, Pimlico—a row of houses situated south of James
Street (now called Buckingham Gate).   A few of the houses in
Stafford Place still stand, but if the numbering remains as it was
a century ago, Mrs. Radcliffe's house was probably demolished
to make way for the Buckingham Palace Hotel.   Here she died
in 1823 : —

" On the 6th of February she did not appear in any immediate danger,
although in a state of great weakness.   At twelve o'clock at night,
Mr. Radcliffe assisted in giving her some nourishment, which she took
with apparent satisfaction, her last words being ' there is some substance
in that.'   She then fell into a slumber ; but when Mr. Radcliffe (who had
been sitting up in the next room) re-entered her apartment, in the course
of an hour or two, she was breathing rather hardly, and neither the nurse
nor himself was able to awake her.   Dr. Scudamore was instantly sent
for, but before his arrival she tranquilly expired at between two and
three o'clock in the morning of the 7th February, 1823, being in the
fifty-ninth year of her age.   Her countenance after death was delightfully placid, and it continued so for several days."

Mrs. Radcliffe was buried on February 15th in the (now long
disused) graveyard of St. George's, Hanover Square, which is
hidden away between the houses of the Bayswater Road, Hyde
Park Place, and Connaught Street.   Some years ago I tried to
identify her grave, but I found all the tombstones (except those
to the memory of Laurence Sterne and a few other people) had
been removed and piled up against the walls of the cemetery, the
burial soil being used for the growing of vegetables.   True, it
was " war time," but that vile excuse for all ills and outrages
scarcely justified the use for eventual edible purposes of " that
rich earth " which concealed the dust of many distinguished
persons.   The custodian of the Macabre Allotment had no
knowledge as to the site of Mrs. Radcliffe's grave amid the

welter of cabbages and potatoes. But as the last red rays of the setting winterly sun touched with a faint hue of blood the sparse snow that lay upon the ground, I thought that the gloomy and desolate spot, within a stone's throw of the site of deathly Tyburn Tree, was, perhaps, not an unfitting resting-place for the great exemplar of the Glooms of Romance and the Tomb.

RICHARD HARRIS BARHAM—
" THOMAS INGOLDSBY."*

THE author of *The Ingoldsby Legends* holds a peculiar and unique position in English literature. He is in the front rank in both a popular and academic sense, although only remembered for one book. His writings make no claim to be superfine in diction or style, and the " Legends " in wonderful rhyme are not great poetry, with the exception of the exquisite *As I laye a-thynkynge*. Nevertheless *The Ingoldsby Legends* and their characters are immortal, and many a line from the inimitable collection has become colloquial and as much a part of allusive and familiar English as the most inspired quotation from the national classics. Truly a triumph for a light versifier. But Barham brought exceptional qualities to the development of his particular art. He was a wit, and his initial success was won by his startling originality. Not only did he adapt the Gallic spirit and *conte* to the exigencies of the English language : his blending of saints and demons, ghosts and abbots, monkish legend and romance, antiquarian lore and classical knowledge, murder and crime, with his own freakish and whimsical sense of humour, his lightning leaps from grave to gay, his quaint verbal quips, his wealth of topical allusion and most bizarre rhymes—all combined to secure him immediate attention and resultant fame. Further, there was—and is—something typically English in the " atmosphere " of the " Legends "; the scenes of many of them are laid in Kent—the most typical of English counties, with its low, wooded hills and smiling valleys, where grow the hops of the national beverage; its two cathedrals entwined with history; its historic houses, such as Knole and Penshurst; and, above all, its share of the great river, where " go the ships," and of the sea and the white chalk cliffs of England. And Barham was by heredity, birth, over thirty years' residence, and life-long sympathy, entirely a Man of Kent.

For many centuries the Barhams had been settled in East Kent, giving their name to a village and range of downs between Canterbury and Dover. It pleased the author of *The Ingoldsby Legends* to claim descent from the brother of that notorious historical personage, Sir Randal—or Reginald—FitzUrse, one of the four knights who murdered Archbishop Becket in

* *The Bookman,* January, 1917.

Canterbury Cathedral on that drear December eve in 1170 when the heavens, in meteorological disorder, thundered and lightened. FitzUrse fled to Ireland, and died in exile, leaving his lands in Kent to his brother Robert, who changed the odious name of FitzUrse—literally Bear's Son (three bears figure in the Barham coat-of-arms)—to its English equivalent of De Bearham, which in course of time became Barham. Until the time of James the First the family lived near the village and downs bearing their name, but about this date the property was sold.

To come to the near ancestry of the legendist, it was his great-grandfather, John Barham, who, in 1686, by his marriage with Mary, daughter and heiress of Thomas Harris, a prosperous tradesman, reacquired some of the property once possessed by earlier members of his family. Miss Harris's dower included the manor of Parmstead (in older days called Barhamstead), and the adjoining one of Tappington—a name which was to figure largely in later years in the literary work of her great-grandson. Her father, Thomas Harris, had also purchased, in 1699, from Captain James Bix, a fine house, No. 61, Burgate, in the city of Canterbury, and this was the home of " Ingoldsby's" immediate ancestors, and his own birthplace. Mr. Harris dying in 1724, the house in time came to his grandson, Richard Barham. He died in 1784, and was succeeded by his son, Richard Harris Barham— the father of the subject of this paper. The elder R. H. Barham was an alderman of Canterbury, and a truly gigantic and genial example of that adipose class of corporation. He was a bon-vivant, drank a bottle of port every day, and when he died at the early age of forty-eight he had attained to immense bulk, and weighed twenty-seven stone. It is said that the spacious doorway of his house in Canterbury had to be widened to permit the removal of his coffin on the occasion of the funeral in 1795. Such a grotesquely macabre incident might have inspired an Ingoldsby Legend in the years to come : but little Dick Barham was only six years old when his father died, and beyond his notes for a story to be called *My Grandfather's Knocker*, and the line telling how " many an aldermanic nose roll'd its loud diapason after dinner," " Ingoldsby's " father remains unsung. It was his mother, Elizabeth Fox, a Kentish woman, too, whom Barham most resembled. From her, no doubt, he inherited both his physical and mental qualities, for judging by her portrait she was a vivacious, humorous woman and much resembled her son in colouring and feature.*

* Miss Fox, it is said, was originally Mr. Barham's housekeeper, and, further, that she dispensed with a marriage ceremony; but, on the other hand, her son always bore the name of Barham.

Richard Harris Barham was born at 61, Burgate, Canterbury, on December 6th, 1788 (the birth year also of Byron and Theodore Hook), and was baptised at the adjoining church of St. Mary Magdalene, where many of his ancestors were buried. He had only a sister, Sara, about whom nothing is known. She is believed to have been born in 1784, and to have died about 1796, and the only tangible relic of her is the name " Sara," together with the initials of her brother, scratched on one of the windows in their home. Consequently, Richard Barham was a solitary little boy, living with his mother in this fine house with its beautiful staircase, panelled rooms, deep cupboards, and all the other suggestive mysteries an old house offers to an imaginative and lonely child. A spacious attic, with a quaint hooded fireplace, is believed to have been his nursery, and his favourite companion was a huge dog, who, in an early portrait, stands as high as his young master.

The influences of his home in historic Canterbury were very strongly reflected in Barham's subsequent literary work, and even more so were those of Tappington, of which he was also the youthful owner, and where many of his holidays were spent. This small picturesque building, of timber and mellow red brick, lattice-windowed and creeper-covered, nestling in a gentle green valley, was destined in future years to be the pivot of *The Ingoldsby Legends*. Here the author placed the abode of the Ingoldsby family, compound of imagination and some traditions in his own family. Barham, of course, greatly idealised and enlarged the place in his literary descriptions, a hoax which he elaborated by appending to the collected editions of the " Legends " a woodcut of his imaginary Tappington Hall. His own little farmstead was no stately Manor House with avenue guarded by heraldic lodge gates. The real Tappington Hall was Broome Park near by, on the way to Canterbury, beneath Barham Downs—that bleak elevated land so impregnated with Roman and Saxon remains, and the actual Tappington Moor of *The Hand of Glory*. Broome Park answers very well to the literary and pictorial details of the " Legends," and Barham's composite mansion was achieved by transplanting the Oxendens' seat to the site of his own property. Broome Park possesses an additional, and pathetic, interest as the estate acquired by the late Lord Kitchener, the place where he had hoped to spend his retirement, surrounded by the porcelain and other works of Art he had collected.

To return to Barham's early days, after some preliminary

education in Canterbury he entered, in 1797, St. Paul's School, London, then located on its ancient site in the precincts of the Cathedral to which he was destined to return in later years a dignitary. Among his school friends was Richard Bentley, the future publisher of *The Ingoldsby Legends*. Barham describes himself as " a fat, little, punchy concern of sixteen " in these days —a description which held good all his life, for he was short in person, broadly built, and deep chested. He became Captain of the school, and in due course went to Brasenose College, where commenced his long friendship with Theodore Hook. Barham seems to have been an average Oxford undergraduate, took merely his B.A. degree (in 1811), was extravagant and certainly not what is euphemistically termed " a good young man." For two years, 1811-1813, he was living in Canterbury again, where he founded the convivial Wig Club, whose members, in masquerade, took part in burlesque debates in the summer-house in Barham's garden. His mother, owing to failing health, had returned to her early home at Minster-in-Thanet some time previously. She died at Thanington about 1815. Barham's substantial patrimony having been much reduced by the malpractices of a certain attorney, one of his three guardians, he had originally decided to adopt the profession of the Law. But during a severe illness his views on Life and conduct changed, and he resolved to enter the Church. He accordingly became curate of Ashford, Kent, in 1813, and of Westwell, in the same county, in 1814—the year in which he married Caroline, third daughter of Captain Smart, Royal Engineers, of Ashford.

Preferment came in 1817 to the Rectory of Snargate together with the curacy of Warehorne, and at the latter place the Barhams lived. These charges were situate in or near the drear, lonely region of Romney Marsh and that relic of French invasion panic, the Royal Military Canal. Snargate, its damp church and unhealthy parsonage hemmed in by trees, was the most dismal of villages; and Warehorne was not much better off, though a mile or so from the actual weird, mist-drenched marshland. And yet " this recondite region," as Barham called it in *The Leech of Folkestone*, has its own peculiar grim fascination, like the Fens of East Anglia and Chat Moss in Lancashire, for those with an imaginative mind and a flair for the supernatural : these vast flat expanses are full of suggestion, aided by the mystery of mist, and atmospheric effects, and fen lights at night. Barham's period in Romney Marsh was not wasted, for its subtly picturesque impressions were stamped upon his plastic mind and re-issued in many of the subsequent " Legends." Whilst still

c

here he took to writing, to beguile the tedium of his very lonely life; and in 1819, being laid up for some weeks as the result of a carriage accident, he produced a novel called *Baldwin* (dealing with the case of a man wrongfully accused of murder), published by the Minerva Press the following year. Barham's parishioners were wild, ignorant, reckless people entirely devoted to smuggling, but as long as their parson did not interfere with their illicit pursuits they were civil to him, even though they commandeered his belfry at Snargate as a store for contraband tobacco. However, release from this uncongenial existence was at hand. In 1821 an unexpected stroke of good fortune brought Barham the appointment of Minor Canon of St. Paul's Cathedral. He accepted with alacrity in the form of a rhyming letter, *An Adieu to the Country:*

> " O, I'll be off ! I will, by Jove . . . .
> Quit . . . . Romney Marsh for Piccadilly."

Some time after arriving in London, the Barhams went to live at No. 53, Great Queen Street, where their family was increased by the birth, in 1823, of their daughter Frances, subsequently Lady Bond. Three elder children, including R. H. Dalton Barham (the eventual biographer of his father), had been born in Kent; and the two youngest children, born later in the City, were Edward—Barham's favourite child—and Mary Anne, the Miss Barham who lived for many years at 73, Gower Street, and died in the summer of 1916, the last of " Ingoldsby's " family.

During his early years in London, Barham occupied his spare time with journalism. He edited *The London Chronicle,* and contributed reviews and light poetical trifles to *John Bull, The Literary Gazette,* and *Blackwood's Magazine* (wherein the first of the " Legends "—*The Ghost*—appeared in 1826). But increasing clerical duties caused him, for a time, to write less. In 1824 he was appointed Priest-in-Ordinary to the Chapels Royal, and soon after received the gift of the livings of St. Mary Magdalene and St. Gregory by St. Paul. There was only one church, however; St. Gregory's, which had been situated close to the south-west wall of the old Cathedral, not being rebuilt after the Great Fire of 1666. St. Mary Magdalene stood in Knightrider Street, and Barham, in consequence, came to live at No. 4, St. Paul's Churchyard, adjoining the entrance to Doctors' Commons. At this house (demolished in 1901) Barham spent fifteen years—the happiest, probably, of his life, tempered though they were by the loss of two of his children, his eldest daughter dying in 1826, and his son George in 1832, during the terrible epidemic of cholera. In this period he, at last, enjoyed the society of cultured people for which he was himself so well adapted by reason of his wit and bonhomie and wealth of anecdote. Now he was able to entertain his friends, dine out, and go frequently to the play: and here he achieved his literary fame. His intimate coterie of friends included Theodore Hook; Edward Cannon, the eccentric and witty priest of the Chapels Royal; Tom Hill; Sydney Smith; Thomas Hood; Lord William Lennox; Harrison Ainsworth; Dr. Hughes, Canon Residentiary of St. Paul's and his accomplished wife.

Mrs. Hughes was a very remarkable woman, strong-minded and clever, yet sympathetic and kind-hearted. Somewhat spartan with her grandchildren (who included Tom Hughes, the future author of *Tom Brown's Schooldays*), to her contemporaries— particularly literary men—she was an invaluable and beloved friend. She knew well Sir Walter Scott, had visited at Abbots- ford, and carried on an interesting correspondence with him and Southey and Harrison Ainsworth and many others. When Barham first met her she was a woman of about fifty years of age, and for nearly a quarter of a century their friendship and animated correspondence continued, till severed by death, and to Mrs. Hughes we owe the stimulus and suggestions that produced *The Ingoldsby Legends*. She began her influence on Barham's literary career by borrowing the unfinished manuscript of his novel, *My Cousin Nicholas*, which he had commenced and laid aside fourteen years earlier. She sent it to Blackwood, and the story being accepted and begun in that publisher's magazine in 1834, the author was compelled to exert himself, and finished the work to the satisfaction of all. Barham was accustomed to assert that he was lacking in the power of literary invention. " Give me a story to tell," he said, " and I can tell it in my own way; but I can't invent one." Consequently when his old school friend, Richard Bentley, commenced, in 1837, his famous monthly, *Bentley's Miscellany*, with Charles Dickens as editor, and applied to him for some contributions, Barham sought the advice of Mrs. Hughes. She, having at the command of her retentive memory a vast store of ghost stories and traditional topographical legends, related to him various tales which he transmuted by the alchemy of his genius into the golden metal of those scintillating " Legends." *Hamilton Tighe*, *Look at the Clock*, *The Dead Drummer*, and *The Hand of Glory* were some of the stories which emanated from the Hughes's house in Amen Court. Very fittingly, Barham inscribed his presentation copy of the collected *Ingoldsby Legends*: —

" To Mrs. Hughes, who made me do 'em ;
   ' Quod placeo (si placeo), Tuum,'

" Thos. Ingoldsby."*

Barham's identity as the author of the " Legends " was
quickly discovered, and he did not disdain the pleasures of
success. He was not immune, of course, from some measure of
hostile criticism, the most pronounced being in that ill-natured
work, *The New Spirit of the Age*, by R. H. Horne. As time
went on, Barham was not confined to Mrs. Hughes for the
source of his stories. He utilised many legends he had heard in
Kent, such as those of *Nell Cook*, *The Smuggler's Leap*, and
Grey Dolphin; and for the series known as " The Golden
Legend " he obtained his ideas and many archæological and
hagiographical details from monkish chronicles—including the
Legenda Aurea—preserved in the Library of Sion College,
where he was a frequent reader. These particular legends in the
Ingoldsby collection have naturally always given great offence
to Roman Catholics by reason of the scant reverence shown to
persons and things held sacred by members of that faith.
Barham's own defence to the charge was that he was moved to
point out the danger to the Church of England by the Romeward
movement of Dr. Pusey and his followers. It was a time of
much agitation in religious matters, and Barham's shafts of
ridicule were aimed to check the increasing use of ritual and
veneration of saints in the Established Church. He was sincere,
though his method was ill-advised.

Curiously enough, though Barham is now only remembered
as the author of *The Ingoldsby Legends*, he and his family
regarded his literary work as the least important avocation of
his busy life. To him, indeed, the writing of these trifles—as he
considered them—was merely a vent for his mental activity, a
recreation, such as other men find in cards or hobbies. He would
jot down the original script in little pocket books (still existing
in the possession of his descendants) at odd moments, waiting for
an appointment or a coach or train, and one " Legend " was
written during a slow walk up Richmond Hill on a hot day. He
was at his best, mentally and creatively, as midnight approached,
when he would pour forth a stream of anecdote and witty
comment; or if alone he was wont to write with an amazing
facility up till 2 a.m. and later. He wrote easily or not at all : if
the slightest hitch occurred, he would often throw the piece aside
and never finish it.

---

* The actual copy with this inscription in Barham's holograph is (1917)
in the possession of Bernard Quaritch, who prices it at £96.

R. H. BARHAM

Surrounded by his creations in " The Ingoldsby Legends."

From the picture by George Cruikshank, reproduced by permission of Macmillan & Co.

[*Page* 36.

Being late to bed he was naturally a late riser. As the bell of St. Paul's was clanging for the service at which he was going to officiate, he would take a hurried breakfast at 9-30, standing up, and sharing the food with a stray cat, who was accustomed to wait outside the dining-room window for this ecclesiastical refection. This cat eventually established himself as a member of the household, and was named " Chance." Barham was devoted to the feline tribe. His son relates: " Next to his wife and children, I verily believe my father loved his cats. One or two would commonly be seen sitting on his table—sometimes on his shoulder—as he wrote. . . . One of my father's last injunctions was: ' Take care of " Chance " (an interloper) for my sake: " Jerry " will be taken care of for his own. ' "
" Jerry," a black cat, was the special pet of Miss Mary Anne Barham, who used to dress him up in a baby's robe and bonnet, and put him to sleep in a cradle by the fire. On one occasion when Mr. Bentley called and was waiting to see Barham he noticed this curious object. Being near-sighted, he put on his glasses and bent forward to examine the black-faced baby more closely. The " infant," greatly annoyed at this examination, sprang from the cradle and dashed across the room, tearing the baby's robe to tatters with its claws, to the amazement and horror of Bentley, who was in doubt if this were not some demoniacally possessed child or a materialised little devil from the Ingoldsby collection.

In the summer of 1839 the Barhams moved into Sydney Smith's residentiary house, in Amen Corner*—that delightful and secluded little City close, where, as " Ingoldsby " humorously wrote, he had a garden " containing three poly-anthus roots, a real tree, a shrub, eight broken bottles, and a tortoise-shell tomcat asleep, with a varied and extensive prospect of the back of the ' Oxford Arms,' and a fine hanging wood (the New Drop at Newgate)." The house, built by Wren in 1684, was cosy and commodious, and with its panelled rooms and beautiful staircase was very similar to Barham's first home at Canterbury in the days of youth. So tender-hearted was Barham that he felt compunction at the necessary destruction of the hordes of rats infesting his new abode. " My heart sickens at the thought of this wholesale slaughter," he wrote to Mrs. Hughes.

One can appreciate how keenly his sensitive nature suffered under his many domestic sorrows. The cruellest blow was now to fall, for in June, 1840, he lost his youngest son—his " little boy

* The first house on the right after passing the gateway from Paternoster Row, and now known as No. 1, Amen Court.

Ned "—who died at the age of twelve years. The father's grief was intense, and he never recovered from the shock. Who can read without emotion that pathetic letter to Mrs. Hughes: " I cannot—I can *not* reconcile myself to my loss. . . . God soften my heart. . . . I have shed scarcely a tear, till now that I am writing to you, when, thank God! they are flowing pretty freely. . . . If I sleep, my dear boy is in all my dreams." Barham's supreme sorrow is reflected in many of the subsequent pieces he wrote, particularly in the sad lines at the end of *The Wedding Day*, and pre-eminently in the beautiful *As I laye a-thynkynge*.

After his son's death Barham was away from London for some time, staying first at 30, Bedford Square, Brighton, and later in the summer at Great Burstead Vicarage, where he wrote *The Black Mousquetaire*. The readers of *Bentley's Miscellany*, at the time, little knew that this gay trifle was the refuge of a breaking heart. As he said: " I find work my best solace, and 1 do work incessantly, though I fear not to the same purpose as I think I could have done had my poor boy lived for me to have worked for." He experienced another severe shock the following year at the sudden death of his greatest friend, Theodore Hook. Edward Cannon, James Smith, and Tom Hill were also dead, so Barham was one of the last left of the coterie of wits who had spent such joyous times together. He did not long survive his friends.

Little remains to be told. In 1842 he exchanged his City livings for the contiguous ones of St. Faith and St. Augustine, his church being in Watling Street. The last years passed, devoted to his clerical work and family, and to his recreations in the way of writing the final *Ingoldsby Legends* and making genealogical research. Barham's health failed, and a violent chill he took on a bleak day in October, 1844, caused acute inflammation of the throat. He never recovered from this painful malady, and though he rallied at times and resumed his occupations, each recurring attack left him weaker. In April, 1845, he had a grave relapse, and increasing pain and a tendency to suffocation brought a realisation of the seriousness of his condition. He was taken to Clifton in May, and it was here, on the 29th, from 9, Dowry Square, that he penned his last communication to Mrs. Hughes in the form of that rhyming epistle (subsequently called *The Bulletin*, when published), wherein he recounted, with all the gaiety of his prime and his most freakish rhymes, the pharmaceutic horrors practised upon him during his illness—certainly the most amazing effusion that ever emanated from a death-bed. His sad situation was intensified by the severe illness of his wife. The responsibility resting upon his daughter Frances was almost overwhelming. It was decided to return home, and Barham's old bizarre humour flashed forth for the last time with the remark—as he was carried into his London house—that he was indeed at Amen Corner.

And then for a fortnight there lasted that wonderful death-bed scene, when a man of but fifty-six years of age, and with his brilliant mental powers at their zenith, calmly faced with the bravest fortitude the most appalling experience of humanity. He made careful and minute arrangements for the disposition of his property, and did not forget even the future of his cats. He partook of the Holy Communion with his family for the last time, and awaited the end. The loss of children and friends, and the wearing effect of pain, had weakened all desire to live longer, he only sought rest:

> " As I laye a-thynkynge, the golden sun was sinking,
>   O merrie sang that Birde as it glitter'd on her breast
>   With a thousand gorgeous dyes,
>   While soaring to the skies
>   'Mid the stars she seemed to rise,
>   As to her nest;
>   As I laye a-thynkynge, her meaning was exprest :—
>   ' Follow, follow me away,
>   It boots not to delay,'—
>   Twas so she seem'd to saye,
>   ' Here is Rest.' "

In these lines of rare loveliness, and throughout " Thomas Ingoldsby's " last poem, how exquisitely are blended strains of romance and mystic symbolism and beauty with the sense of regret and weariness which comes to the pilgrim at the end of Life's Journey.

Barham died on June 17th, 1845. He was buried in the vaults of his former church, St. Mary Magdalene : but in 1886 the building was destroyed by fire. The bodies of Barham and his children were reinterred at Kensal Green Cemetery, and there the author of *The Ingoldsby Legends* rests—near many aforetime " friends hid in Death's dateless night " : but his literary work survives for all time.

NOTE ADDED IN 1920.
" THE DEAD DRUMMER."

The recent murder of a motor-driver at Thruxton, on a remote part of Salisbury Plain, recalls the famous murder by a soldier, Jarvis (or Gervase) Matcham, in the eighteenth century, which is immortalised in the Ingoldsby Legend of *The Dead Drummer*. The genius of Barham has associated the crime for all time with

Salisbury Plain, though, as a matter of fact, it occurred in Huntingdonshire.

To take the facts first, Jarvis Matcham was born at Frodingham, in Yorkshire, and early in life was stable-boy to Captain O'Kelly, owner of the renowned racehorse " Eclipse."

He next entered the Navy, but deserted, and joined the Army. He again became a deserter, but enlisted once more, this time in the 49th Foot. When stationed at Huntingdon with a recruiting party in August, 1780, he was sent with a drummer-boy of his regiment named Benjamin Jones, aged fifteen or sixteen, to Diddington, to obtain some subsistence money. On the return journey, instead of proceeding direct to Huntingdon, Matcham induced the boy to go to Alconbury. There, at a lonely spot, still called " Matcham's Bridge," he knocked the youth down and cut his throat—" without any premeditated design, being instigated by the devil," as he afterwards pleaded.

Actually the victim was murdered for the sake of £7 in his possession. The body was left by the roadside, and Matcham fled to London, where he enlisted once more in the Navy. He took part in much active service under Hood and Rodney. At length, being paid off at Plymouth in 1786, he was proceeding with a shipmate in the direction of Salisbury when, during a violent thunderstorm at night, he thought he saw the apparition of his victim, murdered six years before, beating a spectral drum.

Other phantasms seem to have troubled him, and these, combined with the terrors of the storm, caused him to confess his crime. His companion took him to the Salisbury magistrates, who committed the prisoner for trial. This took place at Huntingdon, and Matcham was executed there on August 2nd, 1786, his body being subsequently gibbeted on Alconbury Hill.

But the story of the crime clung curiously to Wiltshire, and in particular to Salisbury Plain, where the spectre was said to have appeared. Miss Child, the author of an entertaining work in rhyme, *The Spinster at Home in the Close of Salisbury* (1844), wherein she recorded the history and events of the locality, suggested that Matcham saw the apparition of his victim on Harnham Hill, just outside Salisbury, but not on the Plain : —

> " At length, with much labour, he arrived at the crown
> Of Harnham's steep hill, where he sat him adown . . .
> Till loud-pealing thunder, with astonishing din,
> Aroused him on sudden from the mood he was in.
>
> And a flash of the lightning, more startling and bright
> Than all that preceded, seem'd to give to his sight
> The ghost of the murder'd, who before him did stand

In sorrow and anger ;—waving slowly its hand,
Made him signs to begone, and divulge his fell crime,
Expiation to make whilst he yet had the time.

     .   .   .   .   .

Then all madly descending the hill at full speed,
Of the elements' war took he no further heed :
To escape from the spectre was now his sole aim,
Heart-stricken and breathless to this city he came,
And all those whom he met, in their terror and awe,
Made way for that man, when his anguish they saw. . . .
For still he exclaimed, in a voice deep and hollow,
' Even stones from the ground do rise up and follow ;
Oh ! that drummer-boy, saw you his clothes dyed with blood?
That ghastly young drummer, just before me who stood?
To my horror I feel that he follows me still.
It *was I—it was I* who his heart's blood did spill ;
Of this phantom but rid me, and then take my life . . .' "

Harnham Hill would certainly be on the route from Plymouth to Salisbury. But Sir Walter Scott, who related the legend to Mrs. Hughes, who, in turn, passed it on to Barham, seems to have fixed the locality of the ghostly manifestation, perhaps for artistic reasons, on a lonely and desolate part of Salisbury Plain. Barham accepted this definition, and in a note to *The Dead Drummer* stated that the names and localities of the legend had been scrupulously retained. He caused the apparition to appear by a signpost east of Tilshead " Where the Lavington road branch'd off to the left from the one to Devizes."

It may be argued that this is a portion of Salisbury Plain that travellers from Plymouth to London would not traverse. But Matcham and his friend may have lost their way in the darkness of night, and anyway Barham evidently had good reason for his topographical exactitude, for in addition to the text in the legend he wrote the following directions to George Cruikshank, to guide the artist in designing that wonderful illustration which accompanies *The Dead Drummer* : —

" Scene : Salisbury Plain, bare and without trees, a cross-road with a direction post, one index marked ' To Lavington,' the other ' To Devizes '; beneath it the ghost of a drummer-boy beating his drum, with pointed cap, etc., in the costume of the drummer in ' Hogarth's March to Finchley.'

" In the foreground two sailors in Guernsey shirts and large pig-tails looking at him. One tall and thin, aged about fifty, is pointing at the drummer with terror in his countenance, his hair standing on end, his hat having fallen off. The other, short and squat-made, bull-headed, etc., is stooping in an attitude of curiosity, with one arm akimbo, the other raised, and his hand shading his eyes, so as to get a better view of the apparition. Horror the expression of the taller one's countenance, curiosity that of the shorter. The drummer's may be grotesque. A storm, lightning. No house, shrub, tree, nor anything else in sight."

The signpost, bearing the lettering described, is still in existence, or was until lately. How vividly Barham visioned the intense loneliness and bareness of the spot is demonstrated by his opening lines in the legend : —

> " Oh, Salisbury Plain is bleak and bare—
> At least, so I've heard many people declare,
> For I fairly confess I never was there.
> Not a shrub, nor a tree, nor a bush can you see,
> No hedges, no ditches, no gates, no stiles,
> Much less a house or a cottage for miles.
> It's a very sad thing to be caught in the rain
> When night's coming on upon Salisbury Plain."

And similar to this was the scene of the recent dramatic murder at Thruxton, which is some eighteen miles east of Black Down, the locality of the legend of *The Dead Drummer*.

CAPTAIN FREDERICK MARRYAT, R.N.*

ONE would not venture to say at this late date, in view of Mr. Conrad, that Marryat retains his old position as the greatest novelist of the sea: it is more correct now to term the earlier writer the greatest novelist of life in the Royal Navy. That designation Marryat can still claim, despite the fact that the conditions of service afloat have entirely changed in the hundred years and more that have elapsed since he gained the experiences he so faithfully and realistically reflected in his naval romances. Heredity, too, contributed its quota to his particular literary qualifications, for the sea and adventure in far countries were in his blood by reason of the lives of his immediate forebears.

Like most families, the Marryats believed they were descended from knightly ancestors, but it will suffice here to note that in the seventeenth and eighteenth centuries they were of the middle-class in England, several of them doctors, with a partiality for Christian names of biblical origin. Obadiah, Zachariah, Zephaniah, Hephzibah, Josiah, Elyas, Samuel, Benjamin, Joseph, Hannah are of frequent occurrence in the pedigree. The novelist's great-grandfather, Zephaniah Marryat, D.D., author of theological works, lived in Southwark, and as his son Joseph was married in St. Paul's Cathedral, in 1744, to Penelope Reid, the families were presumably of some civic importance.

Zephaniah's fourth son, Thomas Marryat, M.D., born in 1730 (the grandfather of Captain Marryat), was an interesting person. As a youth he acted as lay preacher at Wymondham. He became ordained in 1754 and moved to Southwold, on the coast of Suffolk. He married Sarah, daughter of John Davy of that town, a relative presumably of the artist of the same name who, some sixty years later, published a series of engraved views of Southwold. The two eldest children—one of them destined to be the novelist's father—of Thomas Marryat's marriage were born at Southwold. A few years later, in 1760, he resigned the ministry and went to Edinburgh to study medicine. Later he travelled on the Continent and in America. Returning to England, he practised as a doctor at Shrewsbury and in Ireland, where he was deified by his patients, although he is described as an ugly, morose man, aping the ill manners of Johnson—" a

* *The Bookman*, August, 1922.

perfect hedgehog to strangers and those whom he disliked." He finally settled at Bristol, where he died in 1792. His book, *Therapeutics, or the Art of Healing*, became famous, and ran into thirty-seven editions, or so it is alleged.

His eldest son Joseph (the novelist's father), born in 1757, after spending his early years in Southwold, was trained for a mercantile career and then sent to Grenada. In 1788 he visited the United States, where he became acquainted with the family of Frederick von Geyer, of Boston, a German originally from Frankfort. Marryat married the second daughter, Charlotte von Geyer, and returning to England the following year—1789— he commenced a prosperous career as a merchant in London.

It has hitherto been erroneously stated in memoirs and articles that his second and famous son, Frederick Marryat, the naval novelist, was born in Great George Street, Westminster; but the researches of the late Mr. Cecil Davis, of Wandsworth, have conclusively established the fact that the future author was born on July 10th, 1792, in Catherine Court (near the Tower of London), in the parish of All Hallows Barking. Catherine Court,* which connected Trinity Square with Seething Lane, was unfortunately demolished a few years ago in connection with the new buildings of the Port of London Authority; but it is appropriate to remember that the sea novelist was born in that nautical part of London, near the great river and the wharves of merchandise and within sight of Trinity House and the old Navy Office—the original Admiralty—and Seething Lane, with its memories of Pepys. Later his parents removed to New Bridge Street, Blackfriars, and here, still near the Thames, Frederick Marryat spent his early boyhood.

Joseph Marryat's prosperity continued to increase. He became head of the banking house of Marryat, Kaye, Price & Co.; Chairman of the Committee at Lloyd's; and Colonial Agent for the islands of Grenada and Trinidad. He was elected M.P. for Horsham (1808-1810) and Sandwich (1812-1824), and spoke frequently and with authority in the House on colonial and commercial matters. In 1815 he removed from the City, as a resident, to Wimbledon Park House, but he died very suddenly at his bank office in Mansion House Street in 1824. His widow continued to reside at Wimbledon Park House for thirty years, until her death in 1854; she greatly improved and developed the gardens there, planting many rare trees and shrubs. She was elected a Fellow of the Horticultural Society.

---

* There was a view of Catherine Court in The Gardner Collection, No. 1,977, sold at Sotheby's, May 5th, 1924.

Despite his father's wealth (and that of his childless uncle, Samuel Marryat, K.C., of 41, Russell Square, who left £300,000 at his death), Frederick Marryat was not favoured with a good education. He was merely sent to a private school kept by a man named Freeman, at Ponders End, where he proved to be an idle and troublesome pupil. Babbage was his contemporary here for a time. Much of Marryat's home and school life was reflected in his subsequent novels, and it would seem he was not very happy as a boy. Three times he ran away to sea and was as many times brought back to home or school (and caning). At last, his father, realising that the Navy was the right life for such an exuberant, restless spirit as his second son, secured for the boy a nomination as midshipman. In September, 1806, at the age of fourteen, Frederick Marryat joined the frigate *Impérieuse*, under Captain Lord Cochrane (later Dundonald), and sailed for the Mediterranean.

It was a splendid period of the British Navy. Trafalgar was but a year ago, and Cochrane second only to Nelson in distinction and integrity. His influence upon the youthful Marryat was great. Rugged, fearless, violent in temper, he was the beau-ideal, the model of a frigate captain, and as such he is depicted in *The Naval Officer, or Frank Mildmay*, as Captain Savage in *Peter Simple* and as Captain M. in *The King's Own*. In his own private log Marryat spoke of his first captain's solicitude for his men: " I never knew anyone so careful of the lives of his ship's company as Lord Cochrane, or anyone who calculated so closely the risks attending any expedition."

When only fifteen Marryat took part in a sanguinary little battle off Corsica with a Maltese privateer, when seventeen men were killed on the ship and fifteen killed and wounded on the *Impérieuse*. In 1808 the frigate had an eventful cruise along the Spanish coast, bombarding forts and ports, these events being related later in at least three of Marryat's books. Next, his ship was engaged in frequent attacks on the French transport services which were endeavouring to reach Barcelona; and the defence of Rosas, where Marryat received a bayonet wound, is well described in *The Naval Officer*. Marryat was engaged in the Walcheren expedition, and next served on the *Centaur*, the flagship of Sir Samuel Hood, in the Mediterranean. He was for a short time on the *Namur*, and then, joining the *Æolus*, he went to the West Indies, which provided scenes for many of his subsequent books. After a further period on the *Spartan* and *Indian*, he returned home in 1812 and received his commission as lieutenant. In 1813 he was appointed to the sloop *L'Espiègle*, and cruised along the

coast of South America. The following two years provided a
variety of naval experiences.

The Peace of 1815 found Marryat at the age of twenty-three a
Commander. He visited the Continent, and in 1819 married
Catharine, daughter of Sir Stephen Shairp, Consul-General in
Russia, by whom he had seven children, the best known being his
youngest daughter Florence, who became prominent as a novelist
and investigator of spiritualistic phenomena. Mrs. Marryat
survived her husband for thirty-five years.

When in command of the *Beaver* sloop Marryat saw the end
of Napoleon. An English warship was always kept cruising off
St. Helena to prevent the escape of the fallen Emperor.
Marryat's ship was the last to fulfil this duty; and he himself
made a sketch of Napoleon on his death-bed, for Marryat was a
skilful artist in addition to his literary capabilities.

Being in ill-health, he exchanged to the *Rosario*, and it fell
to him to bring to Spithead the dispatches announcing the
Emperor's death. Soon after—1821—the *Rosario* was ordered
to Harwich to form part of the naval escort which attended the
body of Queen Caroline (wife of George the Fourth) to Stade, *en
route* for interment at Brunswick. The following year Marryat
was engaged in hunting down smugglers, and in 1823 he was
appointed to the *Larne*, which proceeded to India and took part
in the invasion of Burmah. Marryat saw a good deal of active
service there, and his health was further affected by the climate
and the salt food which formed the diet of the Navy. He was
rewarded by the Companionship of the Bath, the thanks of the
Indian Government, and the command of the *Ariadne* (28 guns).
This was his last ship. He resigned in 1830, and he never applied
again for a command except once, perhaps, at the end
of his life.

Marryat had now reached the second phase of his career. He
was a post-captain and C.B. at thirty-eight, and he resolved henceforth to devote himself to his family (from whom he had been
absent continually on service) and a literary career, for which he
had long possessed an inclination. As far back as 1817 he had
published *A Code of Signals for the Use of Vessels Employed in
the Merchant Service*, and in 1822 *Suggestion for the Abolition of
the Present System of Impressment in the Naval Service*. His
first novel, *The Naval Officer, or Scenes and Adventures in the
Life of Frank Mildmay*, appeared in March, 1829, and, as he
stated later, it is largely autobiographical as regards the sea
adventures, though he disclaimed the " vices " of the hero. *The
King's Own* was published in April, 1830, and, like its

predecessor, was anonymous. Nevertheless it achieved immediate success, for six days after its appearance we find Harrison Ainsworth writing to his friend Crossley: "*The King's Own* is excellent, excepting always the catastrophe, which is forced, unnatural and revolting; but there are some spirited descriptive scenes, much acute remark, and much caricature sketching. It will amuse you. I know of nothing else." The character of Willie in this book was drawn from Marryat's little boy of the same name who had died in 1826 at the age of seven.

Marryat returned to London at the close of 1830. He had been appointed Equerry to the Duke of Sussex, one of the fatuous younger brothers of the King (William the Fourth). The Duke lived at Kensington Palace and, presumably in order to be near his duties, Marryat purchased from him Sussex House, Hammersmith, which stood with its large garden on the east side of what is now Fulham Palace Road.* Here, for the first two years, Marryat led a life of continuous social gaiety and extravagance, entertaining people he met at Kensington Palace, mixed with a few literary men, such as Captain Chamier (whose best naval novel, *Ben Brace*, was written a few years later—1836) and Theodore Hook, who would delight the assembled company with his ventriloquial and imitative extravagances.

Marryat said he ran through three fortunes at this period— his shares of the estates of his father, his brother Samuel, and his wealthy uncle Samuel, the K.C., of Russell Square. "The smiles of Princes proving evanescent," Marryat resumed literary work in earnest. He contributed to *The Metropolitan Magazine* at the rate of sixteen pounds a sheet, and became editor of this periodical in 1832. *Newton Forster* was written in 1831. Marryat's industry became amazing. *Peter Simple*, *Jacob Faithful* (the author's favourite book), and parts of *The Pacha of Many Tales* all belong to 1833-1834. There was no doubt financial necessity, to meet the expenses of his lavish hospitality and his unsuccessful attempt to enter the House of Commons as Member for Tower Hamlets. His elder brother, Joseph, author of *Pottery and Porcelain*, had been M.P. for their father's old constituency of Sandwich since 1826.

At this period of rash living, Marryat one night, after dinner and copious champagne, foolishly exchanged Sussex House, Hammersmith, for a smaller dwelling with a thousand acres at Langham, in Norfolk, which proved to be the cause of further

---

* A previous occupant of the house in 1812-1817 was Mrs. Billington, the famous opera singer : it was then described as in " Fulham Fields." Marryat owned for a time 5, Cleveland Row, St. James's, about 1821.

financial troubles, for he was quite ignorant about how to manage farm land. In 1834 Marryat removed to Brighton, where he lived in the house at the south-western corner of Hampton Place and Western Road. Here he wrote *Japhet in Search of a Father*, and probably *The Pirate* and *The Three Cutters* and the early portions of *Mr. Midshipman Easy* (which was published in 1836). In 1835 the novelist and his family went off post-haste to the Continent, probably for monetary reasons, and led a gay life at Brussels. Charles Lever and G. P. R. James, with their respective families, did the same. By the time he got to Spa he found it well to live more quietly. He wrote to Lady Blessington in the summer of 1836 : —

" I was tired of bustle, and noise, and excitement, and here there is room for meditation. . . . I write very little, just enough to amuse me, and make memorandums and think. . . . I never thought that I should feel a pleasure in idleness; but I do now. I had done too much and I required repose, or rather *repose to some portions of my brain*. . . . I believe that this is the first epoch of real quiet that I have had in my stormy life. . . . I walk about and pick early flowers with the children, sit on a bench in the beautiful *allées vertes* which we have here, smoke my cigar, and meditate till long after the moon is in the zenith."

Only for a short time was this quiet, idle life to last, for in 1837 Marryat left for America, and that same year his *Snarleyow, or The Dog Fiend* was published, though it was really written in the previous year. *The Phantom Ship* also belongs to 1837, though it was not issued in book form until two years later. Both these works—though a new departure in style—are among Marryat's best seven books. He successfully presented the supernatural, no easy thing to do, and in the case of *The Phantom Ship* vividly revived the old legends of Vanderdecken and the Werewolf.

Marryat had an eventful two years in America. He visited Canada and took part in the fighting against the rebellious French population in 1838. His experiences were recorded in *A Diary in America*, published in 1839. He returned home in the spring of that year and went to live at 8, Duke Street, St. James's. But, ever restless, a year later found him at his mother's home, Wimbledon Park House. Then he took for a short time Gothic Lodge, Wimbledon, which had a previous literary association in the person of Lady Anne Barnard, author of *Auld Robin Gray*. Next, Marryat occupied chambers at 120, Piccadilly, and thence removed to No. 3, Spanish Place, Manchester Square, where he once more entertained a good deal, his guests now being chiefly literary people, including Dickens, Forster, Bulwer, Ainsworth, D'Orsay, and Lady Blessington. But he was soon in financial

CAPTAIN FREDERICK MARRYAT, R.N.

From a portrait reproduced by the courtesy of Mr. H. W. Belcher.

[*Page* 48.

difficulties again; and beginning to weary of incessant literary work, and, perhaps, longing a little for the old life at sea of his youth, he wrote on one occasion: " If I were not rather in want of money, I certainly would not write any more, for I am rather tired of it. I should like to disengage myself from the fraternity of authors, and be known in future only in my profession as a good officer and seaman."

Yet he had of necessity to write as hard as ever, and *Poor Jack*, the excellent *Masterman Ready*, *Joseph Rushbrook, or The Poacher*, *Percival Keene*, and *Monsieur Violet* followed in rapid succession.

Then suddenly, in 1843, Marryat cut himself adrift from all his friends, left London and settled at Langham, near Holt, in the house he had acquired from its builder, Copland, in exchange for Sussex House, Hammersmith (which would have proved a valuable possession for his heirs to-day in view of the building development of the site). The thousand acres in Norfolk he had endeavoured to farm on his own account, with very grave financial loss—over £1,000 in 1842 alone. He hoped to improve matters by living on the spot, though he was worn out in health and his eyesight failing.

The loss on the land at Langham was not so excessive after he came to reside there, and the Manor Cottage was a picturesque thatched house, covered with roses and ivy, built in imitation of The Cottage, the favourite residence of George the Fourth in Windsor Great Park. Here Marryat adopted the life and appearance in dress of the farmer; he shed the attributes of the literary man and the naval officer—even growing a beard, which would have been an impossible solecism in his service days. He rose at five a.m. and acted as his own farm bailiff, riding round his land on his pony called " Dumpling." At other times he found pleasure in walking the lanes, watching the buds develop in the spring, and the birds and nature in all aspects. In the evenings he would play Blind Man's Buff with his children, and romp and dance with them, as he was wont to do in earlier years. Forster records how Marryat " had a frantic delight in dancing, especially with children, of whom and whose enjoyments he was as fond as it became so thoroughly good-hearted a man to be. . . . He was among the first in Dickens's liking."

Apparently Marryat had no regrets for the social life and all the good friends he had voluntarily abandoned in London. Forster and others wrote to beg him to come up and meet them again in festive symposium, but in vain. He was content with his rural solitude, and perhaps aware of the Shadow of Death.

The books he wrote in his last phase are in no way comparable with his early work. They comprise *The Settlers in Canada, The Mission, or Scenes in Africa, The Children of the New Forest, The Little Savage,* and *Valerie,* which he was too ill to finish. *The Privateersman* (1846) was only partly written by Marryat. The earlier portion was the actual autobiography of Captain Robinson Elsdale, and it was sent to Marryat by Harrison Ainsworth with a request to edit it, and enlarge the narrative for *The New Monthly Magazine,* which was duly done. An earlier novel, *Rattlin the Reefer* (1836), generally attributed to Marryat, was in fact written by Edward Howard, who acted as sub-editor, under Marryat, of *The Metropolitan Magazine.*

In 1847 Marryat suffered further severe financial loss by the failure of his property in West India. He made an effort to re-enter the Navy, but he applied for employment in vain. These worries caused a return of a physical trouble which he had suffered from intermittently since his youth, despite his muscular appearance. It caused the rupture of blood-vessels. During his last year of life Marryat went to Wimbledon, to Hastings, to Brighton, in the hope that a milder climate might restore his health. But a final blow of fate rendered every effort vain, when his eldest son, Lieutenant Frederick Marryat, was drowned in the wreck of the naval steamer " Avenger," in December, 1847. That was the end for the father, too. He had no desire to live, and when his doctors in London, at a final consultation, gave him six months more before the end would come, he announced the sentence to his children with an " undisturbed and half-smiling countenance."

He returned to Langham and waited for death during the summer months : —

> " Ah, sad and strange as in dark summer dawns
> The earliest pipe of half-awaken'd birds
> To dying ears, when unto dying eyes
> The casement slowly grows a glimmering square ;
> So sad, so strange, the days that are no more."

To prevent the rupture of blood-vessels, all food diet was given up and he was only kept alive by lemonade. All through the long summer days he lay in the drawing-room at Langham, while his daughters read aloud to him. Flowers delighted him to the end until consciousness failed. The terrible weakness brought on delirium. Morphia became necessary, and it was at the close of a long period of unconsciousness that final rest and peace came, mercifully, at dawn on August 9th, 1848.

Mr. Conrad has written of Marryat and his work and character : —

" He is the enslaver of youth . . . by the heroic quality of his own unique temperament. . . . His novels are not the outcome of his art, but of his character, like the deeds that make up his record of service. . . . He has created a priceless legend. . . ."

That is a fine tribute from a great writer to a great predecessor.

THACKERAY'S ILLUSTRATIONS:
THEIR PERSONAL AND TOPOGRAPHICAL INTEREST.*

It is very seldom that an author is a successful illustrator of his own works. Lear and W. S. Gilbert drew inimitable sketches of their whimsical and fantastic verbal quips. Du Maurier was, perhaps, a greater artist than author. Thackeray was certainly a greater author than artist; but he remains the most interesting example of a novelist who was able to illustrate his own literary creations with drawings very humorous, quaint, and pathetic: drama and horror and passion were beyond the reach of his pencil in the same successful degree, and when he did essay them, on rare occasions, he treated them with a bizarre touch.

Opinion has always been sharply divided as to the exact merits of Thackeray's pictorial work. Some critics have pronounced it to be merely grotesque caricature of faulty proportions; and others, including Charlotte Brontë, have found in it the perfection of anatomy and form. Technical errors they may often possess, but it is irrefutable that very many of Thackeray's drawings exactly suit and vividly interpret the scenes in the text, not only because they realise his own intentions and conceptions, but for the more artistic reason that they are compact of contemporary detail and accessories, and are permeated with the life and spirit of the period they illuminate. Certainly the author's own illustrations give far more pleasure and amusement than those supplied by other eminent artists to some of the Thackeray novels—always excepting Doyle's delightful drawings in *The Newcomes*, which are, indeed, akin to Thackeray's designs in spirit and execution. Thackeray wrote in April, 1854:—

" I have seen for the first time the engravings of *Newcomes*, some of which I like very much indeed. Why, Doyle ought to bless the day that put the etching-needle in his hand. . . . He does beautifully and easily what I wanted to do and can't."

Thackeray at the outset of his career, before he had found the right *métier* for his literary genius, had serious thoughts of devoting himself to Art alone—" That was the object of my early ambition," he said. When he was twenty-one years of age he wrote from Paris: " I have been thinking very seriously of

---

* Part of this article appeared in *The Athenæum*, September, 1916, and another portion in *The Fortnightly Review*, July, 1923.

turning artist. I think I can draw better than do anything else, and certainly like it better than any other occupation." But in those early days other people did not agree with him. The story has often been told how, in 1836, Thackeray applied to Dickens for the post of illustrator to *The Pickwick Papers*, vacant by the suicide of Seymour, and went to Furnival's Inn with some specimen drawings, which Dickens " did not find suitable." It is not so well known that Thackeray was employed that same year by Harrison Ainsworth to illustrate his romance of *Crichton*. Thackeray was delighted, and in the course of a doggerel letter (August, 1836) to the author, made every line to rhyme with *Crichton :—*

> " Dear Ainsworth, I'll do everything what's possible to heighten
> The charms of your immortal book, the admirable *Crichton,*
> And with this noble purpose this little scrap I write on,
> To say I do you drawings such as never man had sight on."

And so on.

Unfortunately the drawings proved unsatisfactory, the project fell through, and Maclise was engaged as illustrator in Thackeray's place. In letters to his publisher, Macrone, Ainsworth wrote : —

> " I conclude you have written to Thackeray and forwarded him the sheets of vol. iii." " Get me Thackeray's address from the Father [Prout], as I wish to write to him. There is a picture in the Museum at Paris I wish him to see." " I saw the Father this morning. He has heard nothing from Thackeray, and expects to hear nothing : I am not displeased with this, as I am sure Maclise will make admirable illustrations."

But Maclise, in turn, was superseded by Hablot Browne (Phiz), who eventually illustrated *Crichton*.

Though naturally depressed by these and similar rebuffs, which followed fast on the neglect accorded to his published folio of extremely humorous designs entitled *Flore et Zéphyr* (a copy of which can now realise £226), Thackeray continued to draw when so inclined, until at last he set foot in his kingdom by his work for *Punch*, and was finally crowned by the success of *Vanity Fair* in 1847, when his merits as both author and artist were, after long delay and disappointment, fully recognised.

R. S. Surtees was one of the first to appreciate the drawings of Thackeray, and he sought to secure him as illustrator of *Mr. Sponge's Sporting Tour*, but Thackeray, now in a position to please himself, replied (May 30th, 1849) : —

> " I was very much flattered by your proposal to illustrate your tale, but I only draw for my own books, and indeed I am not strong enough as an artist to make designs for anybody else's stories. You

would find my pictures anything but comical, and I have not the slightest idea how to draw a horse, a dog, or a sporting scene of any sort."*

It is not the object of this article to deal with Thackeray's drawings from the critical or technical standpoint; it merely aims at tracing the personal association they often possess with their designer, and to point out their topographical interest—if not value—as views of places now vanished or much changed by the march of " Progress," in London especially.

To begin with *Vanity Fair*, we are at the outset confronted by the vignette and its variable interpretation. I incline to the belief that it has a personal association with the author, and that the figure with the broken nose is more or less an auto-portrait of Thackeray—or at any rate symbolical of him in his rôle of literary showman—gazing into the warped mirror of life, of Vanity Fair; behind him is his box of the puppets who figure in the tale-show. In a letter written in 1848, discussing the characters and object of his great novel, Thackeray said : —

" Don't I see (in that may-be cracked and warped looking-glass in which I am always looking) my own weaknesses, wickednesses, lusts, follies, shortcomings? In company let us hope with better qualities about which we will pretermit discourse."

But why in the background of the vignette should there be a view of a church with *two* towers ? The solution suggested is that, the personal element of the drawing being granted, this building is an adaptation of Ottery St. Mary Church, which *has* two towers at the west end, and the Rectory adjoining, much in the style of the illustration. With this Devonshire parish some of Thackeray's happiest boyhood memories were entwined, for here, at Larkbeare near by, he spent his holidays with his mother and step-father. In *Pendennis* (which is known to he auto-biographical in part) he writes of Ottery St. Mary under the name of Clavering, and recalls how, standing with his mother on their lawn at sunset,

" there was a pretty sight : it and the opposite park of Clavering were in the habit of putting on a rich golden tinge . . . the little river ran off noisily westward, and was lost in a sombre wood, behind which the towers of the old abbey church of Clavering (whereby that town is called Clavering St. Mary's to the present day) rose up in purple splendour."

So, perchance, in the vignette to *Vanity Fair* there is an allegorical fancy that amid all the vanities and sins and turmoil of life there remain in the background of memory scenes from far-off happy days of youth and innocence and peace. If we can take the figure in the vignette to be Thackeray with his box of

* *Robert Smith Surtees,* by Himself and E. D. Cuming.

puppets, then it is legitimate to turn to the tail-piece at the end of the novel and see therein the portraits of the author's two little girls: " Come, children, let us shut up the box and the puppets, for our play is played out." The same little girls acted as models for the children in the plate entitled " Miss Sharp in her Schoolroom," as Lady Ritchie relates.

When about seven years old Thackeray went to a school kept by Dr. Turner on Chiswick Mall, where he remained until January, 1822, and although it is impossible to identify the actual house, owing to the rate books of that date not being available, there is little doubt that Dr. Turner's Academy was located in what is now known as Walpole House. This picturesque, mellow, seventeenth-century building, with its many heavy-framed windows, had been, over a hundred years earlier, the last home of Barbara Villiers, Lady Castlemaine and Duchess of Cleveland, the imperious mistress of Charles the Second, and mother of the first Duke of Grafton. Here she died in 1709, and as another writer, C. J. Hamilton, has observed:—

" It almost seems as if that terribly seductive face would peep out from the top window, and a cry would be heard such as curdled the blood of Ann Radcliffe's heroines. Walpole House looks as if it must be haunted . . . at midnight, perhaps, the tapping of high heels is heard on the worm-eaten staircase or the faint rustle of a silken gown glides mysteriously down a dark passage."

However, no ghosts seem to have troubled the little Thackeray whilst here, though it is very likely the influence of the romantic old house was unconsciously impressed upon that facet of his imagination which, years later, shone forth and sparkled in *Henry Esmond*, and most certainly he recalled Walpole House for *Vanity Fair*. He was not very happy at the school, and on one occasion made an escape up Chiswick Lane as far as the Hammersmith Road, where the traffic to and fro from the great world of London decided him to return to the comparative peace of Dr. Turner's establishment. Miss Pinkerton's Academy was created some quarter of a century later; and that it was Walpole House that Thackeray had in mind when writing the opening chapter of *Vanity Fair* is evidenced by his charming little initial letter-sketch, which gives a view of Chiswick Mall, with the railings and stone balls (still in existence) on each side of the gate of Barbara Villiers's old house; beyond are Bedford House and a distant view of Chiswick Church. The large illustration of " Rebecca's Farewell to Chiswick Mall " is not topographically correct. The picture of Dobbin reading in the playground

(Chapter V) might be construed into a back view of Walpole House; but the actual original of " Dr. Swishtail's Seminary " is not clear; it is probably a combination of impressions of Charterhouse, Dr. Turner's, and that other school where Thackeray was boarded in early childhood and was supremely unhappy, as he recorded towards the end of his life in *The Roundabout Papers—On Letts's Diary* : —

" We Indian children were consigned to a school of which our deluded parents had heard a favourable report, but which was governed by a horrible little tyrant, who made our young lives so miserable that I remember kneeling by my little bed of a night, and saying, ' Pray God I may dream of my mother ! ' "

That shows how lasting were Thackeray's memories of his early days.

The three views of Vauxhall Gardens in Chapter VI may be taken to be fairly accurate representations of that vanished resort near Kennington Lane (the site is now covered by Tyers Street and St. Oswald Place) where, for close on two hundred years, the people found open-air amusement of the kind supplied in later times at Earl's Court and Shepherd's Bush. In passing, one may remark on Thackeray's curious footnote accompanying the last Vauxhall sketch, stating that he found the costumes of the period (1815) he wrote of hideous, and accordingly depicted the characters of his book in the dresses and uniforms of the 'forties. And yet the costumes of the Waterloo era, with officers in gorgeous uniforms and slung jackets, and women in gowns of the Empire style, are now rightly regarded as extremely picturesque, and much favoured in any scheme for fancy dress.

The plate " Rebecca makes Acquaintance with a Live Baronet," a characteristic example of Thackeray's best illustrations, gives a glimpse of Berkeley Square; but this district will be discussed presently when dealing with Gaunt House. In passing it may be noted that Sir Pitt Crawley is said to have had an original in the person of Sir William Chaytor, of Witton Castle, Co. Durham. " A Family Party at Brighton " is scarcely an accurate representation of the situation of the Ship Hotel, where the scene is laid; but a thinly sketched picture in the text of Chapter XXXIII well suggests Clarendon Terrace, Kemp Town. The scenes in Brussels and Paris may pass without comment.

In the second volume, the picture of Lord Steyne (Chapter XIII) and the plate " Colonel Crawley is Wanted " (Chapter XVI) bring us to debatable ground and the vexed questions of the originals of Gaunt House and its owner, Lord Steyne.

Mr. E. Beresford Chancellor in his excellent book, *The London of Thackeray*, has "no doubt whatever" that the original of Gaunt House was Harcourt House in Cavendish Square. That statement, I think, is not susceptible to proof, beyond the fact that Harcourt House had a high blind wall in front, above which only the upper windows of the mansion were visible, and that Thackeray related of Gaunt House : " All I have ever seen of it is the vast wall in front, with the rustic columns at the great gates . . . and over the wall the garret and bedroom windows, and the chimneys." I will present Mr. Chancellor with one other piece of evidence in favour of his claim which he does not himself advance, and that is when Tinker, the charwoman, sallied forth from Sir Pitt Crawley's house in Great Gaunt Street to get a coach, she took " her way into Oxford Street," and secured a vehicle from a stand there " in the neighbourhood of Swallow Street "— Swallow Street being the old thoroughfare which followed nearly the present line of Regent Street, and debouched into Oxford Street opposite Holles Street, leading to Cavendish Square.

Nevertheless, I opine that Gaunt House was a composite picture—just as Lord Steyne was a composite portrait, as I shall endeavour to demonstrate presently—and that it had more of Lansdowne House (with a *soupçon* of Hertford House) than of Harcourt House in its composition. I will allow that the blank screening wall of Harcourt House (now demolished) may have been in Thackeray's mind, though but little of Lansdowne House also was visible from Berkeley Square. Undoubtedly Thackeray intended Gaunt House to be in the heart of fashionable London, which Cavendish Square was not. He describes Gaunt House as occupying " nearly a side of the Square." Lansdowne House answers to that description, and so does Hertford House, in Manchester Square, for that matter. But Harcourt House had other houses adjoining it each side on the western section of Cavendish Square, including No. 20, which in recent years was the home of Mr. Asquith.

One of Mr. Chancellor's arguments in favour of Harcourt House is that the statue of " The Butcher " Duke of Cumberland, which stood in Cavendish Square until 1860, may be taken to agree with Thackeray's description, despite the fact that the Duke was attired in military costume of his period, whereas Thackeray said in the centre of the Square " rises the statue of Lord Gaunt, who fought at Minden, in a three-tailed wig, and otherwise habited like a Roman Emperor." Confirmation of this will be found in the plate, " Colonel Crawley

is Wanted," where Thackeray has drawn an equestrian statue in
the centre of the Square, the man's figure habited in Roman garb,
which is also further proof in favour of Lansdowne House, for
in Berkeley Square stood the statue of George the Third
in the rôle of Marcus Aurelius. It was erected in 1766
by Princess Amelia, and executed by Joseph Wilton,
R.A., from the designs of a French artist named Beaupré.
The statue is alluded to in a letter from William Mason
to Horace Walpole, dated November 12th, 1779, and John
Thomas Smith in *Nollekens and his Times* speaks of " that
miserable specimen of leaden-figure taste, the equestrian statue
of George the Third, lately standing in the centre of Berkeley
Square." It was removed prior to 1827, and as early as 1812
there were reports that the statue was giving way and would have
to be removed. In view of the mental decay of the original,
George the Third, a contemporary newspaper was moved
to observe of the statue's collapse: " This circumstance,
associating itself with the actual state of our beloved Sovereign,
has become the topic of conversation in the neighbourhood."

I think, then, that Thackeray intended Gaunt Square
to be Berkeley Square, and Great Gaunt Street to be
either Hill Street or Charles Street, but to avoid any
actual identification he combined with his description of
Lansdowne House some features of Hertford House and
Harcourt House. For the same reason, he based his portrait of
Lord Steyne—if it was a portrait—on the personalities and
appearance of at least three men: it was not a direct actual
transcription of Francis Charles, third Marquis of Hertford
(1777-1842), as the majority of Thackeray's commentators aver.
The latter seem to have arrived at their decision mainly because
this same nobleman, the third Lord Hertford, was depicted by
Disraeli in *Coningsby* as Lord Monmouth, and because, further,
he had an agent or toady, John Wilson Croker, who suggests
the character of Wenham in *Vanity Fair*. But Disraeli drew his
characters in his political novels very accurately from living or
recently dead people. Thackeray merely took an original,
studied him and probed him with his mental scalpel, and then
adapted the borrowed personality to his own fictional purposes.

As for Lord Steyne, the life and characteristics of Francis,
second Marquis of Hertford (1743-1822), are far more in accord
with Becky Sharp's patron than those of his son, the third
Marquis, who is so generally credited with the Steyne attributes.
It is true that Thackeray's " suppressed " (so-called) woodcut
bears some resemblance to Lawrence's portrait of the third

Marquis, inasmuch as both heads are bald on top and face to the left. For purposes of comparison it is difficult to refer to portraits of the second Marquis, as there appear to be very few extant. He was painted as a boy by Sir Joshua Reynolds; and a bust and recumbent statue, both by Sir Francis Chantrey, are in the Ashmolean Museum; these, however, are stored away in the basement and not usually exhibited.

The details in the novel are all in favour of the second Marquis, who did not die until 1822, which covers the period of *Vanity Fair;* the third Marquis was then about forty years of age, whereas Lord Steyne is described as an old man and a grandfather. Further, in the chapter entitled " Gaunt House," Thackeray says: "The Prince and Perdita have been in and out of that door." The Prince of Wales (George the Fourth) separated finally from Mrs. Robinson in 1783, when the future third Marquis of Hertford was only six years of age. In the same paragraph, Egalité, Duc d'Orleans, is mentioned as a friend of Steyne's. Egalité was executed in 1793, when the future third Marquis of Hertford was sixteen years of age. Thackeray gives Lord Steyne the imaginary Court appointment of " Lord of the Powder Closet." The second Marquis of Hertford was Lord Chamberlain of the King's Household, but his son was not.

There is another unwilling claimant to the dubious honour of being the original of Lord Steyne in the person of the third Marquis of Lansdowne (1780-1863), better known as Lord Henry Petty, the statesman, who seems to have borne some considerable resemblance to the " suppressed " woodcut of Lord Steyne in the novel. In Edward FitzGerald's copy of *Vanity Fair*, now in the possession of Mr. Charles P. Johnson, there is the following note in FitzGerald's holograph opposite an inserted portrait of Lord Lansdowne : —

" W.M.T., when, in 1848, he became a Lion among ye Great Folks, told me that Lord Lansdowne who like ye rest had courted him, cut him when Lord Steyne's portrait came out : W. M. T. having had no idea of making a resemblance.—E. F.-G."

On the other hand, Thackeray's daughter, Lady Ritchie, assured Mr. Johnson that Lord Lansdowne was still her father's good friend in later years, and she went with Thackeray several times to Lansdowne House. It may be that Thackeray unintentionally imparted a likeness to Lord Lansdowne in his drawing of Steyne, and was distressed at finding his friend thought the resemblance intentional. This would account for the withdrawal of the " suppressed " woodcut of Steyne after the first issue of *Vanity Fair*, though it is by no means certain that the picture *was*

" suppressed." The same figure of Lord Steyne was retained in the plate, " The Triumph of Clytemnestra," and the face in the initial letter to Chapter XVII, Volume II; and the actual " suppressed " woodcut reappeared in the collected edition of Thackeray's works in 1869. There really seems to have been no reason for its suppression beyond its possible resemblance to Lord Lansdowne, who died in 1863. It could not have been withdrawn on account of offence to any Lord Hertford, for the second Marquis died in 1822 and the third in 1842. *Vanity Fair* appeared in 1847, and the dead are not subject to libel in law. It is true than an " investigator " once avouched that Richard, fourth Marquis of Hertford (1800-1870), was the original of Lord Steyne! But that assertion does not require serious attention in view of the facts, because the fourth Lord Hertford was a bachelor and a recluse, who spent most of his time in Paris. In appearance he was like a Frenchman his mother was an Italian), with the typical Imperial tuft of beard, as can be seen by his bust at Hertford House: he did not bear the slightest resemblance to Thackeray's drawing. Probably the suggestion of Mr. George Somes Layard in his book, *Suppressed Plates*, is the simple and correct reason for the withdrawal of the picture, namely, that the block got broken, and the woodcut consequently disappeared from *Vanity Fair* until a new block was made for the collected edition of 1869.

It may be concluded, then, that Lord Steyne was a composite portrait—the character and details suggested by the second Marquis of Hertford, and the physical attributes by the third Marquis of Hertford and the third Marquis of Lansdowne. No confirmation of any theories on this question will be found in Thackeray's presentment of the ladies of the Gaunt family. The Marchioness of Steyne in no way suggests the magnificent Isabella Ingram, the wife of the second Marquis of Hertford, she who became the favourite of George the Fourth, and supplanted Mrs. Fitzherbert in his affections.

The third Marquis of Hertford married the vivacious Maria Fagnani, the putative daughter of the Italian Marchese Fagnani by his wife Constanza, who was formerly a ballet dancer. But, as is well known, the credit of Maria's paternity was claimed by the Duke of Queensberry and George Selwyn, who both enriched her with large bequests, amounting in the aggregate to £433,000. The life of Maria Fagnani, Marchioness of Hertford, would present a curious study for biography. An absurd scandal alleged her to be the mother of Sir Richard Wallace, who was, in fact, her grandson. He was the illegitimate son of Richard, fourth Marquis of Hertford, then Lord Yarmouth, who as a boy of seventeen had a *liaison* with a girl some years his senior, Agnes Wallace (or Jackson, as she was called later), a sort of camp-follower of the cavalry regiment in which he was a youthful cornet. The child, Richard Wallace, was born on July 24th, 1818. Some years later the facts became known to his grandmother, Maria Lady Hertford, who sent for the boy and had him brought up in the *conciergerie* of her house in Paris. Hence, probably, the gossip that he was her own son. The youth was known as " Monsieur Richard," and in later years he became the trusted agent of his father, the fourth Lord Hertford, in the purchase of many of the choicest works of art in what is now known as the Wallace Collection. Richard Wallace inherited it and a great fortune in money. He, in turn, left everything to his widow. Lady Wallace desired to make Sir John Scott her heir, in return for the care and devotion with which he had managed her affairs; but he, with a rare self-sacrifice, advised her to leave the greater part of the works of art to the English people. Thus the Wallace Collection became a national asset of incalculable value. A large fortune, however, and many choice works of art at Bagatelle, Lord Hertford's little villa near Paris, passed to Sir John Scott, who at his death bequeathed them to Lady Sackville.

To return to *Vanity Fair* and the question of an original of Becky Sharp, it is not generally remembered that there is an interesting allusion to the matter in Oscar Wilde's *Intentions* : —

" I once asked a lady, who knew Thackeray intimately, whether he had any model for Becky Sharp. She told me that Becky was an invention, but that the idea of the character had been partly suggested by a governess who lived in the neighbourhood of Kensington Square, and was the companion of a very selfish and rich old woman. I inquired what became of the governess, and she replied that, oddly enough, some years after the appearance of *Vanity Fair* she ran away with the nephew of the lady with whom she was living, and for a short time made a great splash in society, quite in Mrs. Rawdon Crawley's style, and entirely by Mrs. Rawdon Crawley's methods. Ultimately she came to grief, disappeared to the Continent, and used to be occasionally seen at Monte Carlo and other gambling places."

This account fits in with Lady Ritchie's description of the " dazzling little lady " who arrived at Young Street one day in a hansom, and greeted Thackeray " with great affection and brilliancy, and . . . gave him a large bunch of fresh violets."

In a letter of the year 1889, Lady Ritchie, describing a party at the Richmonds', says : —

" Henry James was there and the Andrew Langs, who told me, of all the people in the world, that Becky Sharp is still alive, at least Miss Tizzy Revis, who was supposed to be Becky, is, and she is now no less a person than the Countess de la Torre, and her cats one reads of in the police courts."

To pass on to other illustrations in the book, " A Meeting " presents a pretty view of Kensington Palace and Gardens. The delightful picture " Georgy Goes to Church Genteelly" gives a contemporary view of the north side of Russell Square and Bernard Street. The Osbornes, we are told, lived at No. 96, Russell Square. There is, of course, no such number, but the house Thackeray had in mind was on the west side, for that is established by the fact that the Sedleys lived on the east side: " There was a hackney-coach stand hard by in Southampton Row," and when Amelia paid her last visit to No. 96, " she could see over the trees of Russell Square the old house in which she herself was born." Before leaving this book, which has illumined sombre Bloomsbury with romance for all time, let us recall that old John Sedley inspired two of Thackeray's most poignant meditative passages—the one depicting the pathos of an auction in a once familiar house (in the chapter " How Captain Dobbin bought a Piano "), and the other on inevitable death (" In which Two Lights are put out"). Sadly true it all is; the friendliest, brightest homes will one day be empty and dark, and, their former owners gone to the Great Desolation, the once-loved possessions dispersed in the sordid public sale.

Curiously enough, *Pendennis*, though dealing much with London, possesses only a few illustrations which come within the scope of this article, for the scenes are mainly of interiors. The plate " Calm Summer Evenings" shows the view of Ottery St. Mary, previously alluded to when dealing with the vignette of *Vanity Fair*. " Youth between Pleasure and Duty " and " A View from the Dean's Garden " give glimpses of Exeter Cathedral, the former also introducing the first presentment of Foker, who, as is well known, had a very definite original in the person of Andrew Arcedeckne of the Garrick Club. " The Captain won't go Home till Morning " is interesting as proof of Thackeray's habit of inserting little details in his sketches. The scene is Covent Garden, and the—to some—cryptic letters " M M U M S " on the house, to the railings of which the inebriated Costigan clings, prove it to be the Old Hummums Hotel, which stood, until 1881, at the south-east corner of the square, and derived its odd name from a corruption of the Eastern word Humoum, signifying Turkish or hot-air baths, and bagnios of ill-fame, which formerly abounded in this neighbourhood.

In the second volume of *Pendennis* are two more sketches of Vauxhall, and in " Almost Perfect Happiness " a reminiscence of another bygone pleasure of Londoners long since abandoned —a dinner at Greenwich. In the middle of the last century a dinner at the Ship or the Crown and Sceptre or the Trafalgar at Greenwich, or at the Star and Garter, Richmond, was the most usual form for a bachelor's hospitality to his friends of the other sex. But with the advent of motor-cars and trips further afield, and the establishment of large restaurants in London, the old riverside taverns have fallen into desuetude or—as in the case of the Star and Garter—ceased to exist. In the initial letter of Chapter XXXIII, towards the end of *Pendennis*, there is a representation of Thackeray's study at No. 13 (now 16), Young Street, Kensington; the actual armchair depicted is still in the possession of Lady Ritchie, and was the one used constantly by her father.*

The Newcomes and Henry Esmond, being illustrated respectively by Doyle and Du Maurier, do not come within the range of this article, though one would fain linger over both, so suggestive are they of comment: I will only note that Lady Castlewood lived at No. 7, Kensington Square. For the same reason we must pass over Frederick Walker's illustrations to *The Adventures of Philip* and *Denis Duval*, only pausing to record one interesting fact. The frontispiece to *Philip*, entitled " Thanksgiving," was intended to show the interior of the church of St. George the Martyr in Queen Square, Bloomsbury, and the faces of the two children were portraits of Miss Grace Dalziel and Gilbert Dalziel, daughter and son of Edward Dalziel —one of the brothers Dalziel, the famous wood engravers. Mr. Gilbert Dalziel, subsequently the editor of *Judy* and founder of *Ally Sloper*, well remembers going to Frederick Walker's studio to sit for this drawing in *Philip*, and he possesses a very amusing letter from the artist written to him at this time. Frederick Walker was introduced to Thackeray by Joseph Swain, the wood engraver who executed most of the novelist's own drawings.

Though the illustrations in *The Virginians* were drawn by Thackeray, they need not detain us long, for here the artist was not depicting places and streets as they were in his time, but rather his idea of their aspect in the eighteenth century—the period of the story. " A Rencontre in Fleet Street " is good, showing old Temple Bar and the impaled heads of the Jacobites who suffered after " the Forty-five." The initial letter to Chapter XXVII is a free transcription from the third plate of

---

* Lady Ritchie died in 1919.

Hogarth's " Industry and Idleness." The illustration entitled
" Harry is Presented to a Great Personage " causes some
speculation as to what the scene in the background represents,
because in the text Harry Warrington was taken " to Court "
for his introduction to George the Second. But this scene is
not " at Court," neither can it be identified with the neighbourhood of St. James's or Kensington. The church steeple looks
very much like that of St. Martin's-in-the-Fields, so possibly
Thackeray intended the locality of the introduction to be outside
the Royal Mews, which were rebuilt by George the Second
in 1732, almost exactly on the site of the present National
Gallery. " Behind Montagu House " gives a glimpse of
the church of St. George, Bloomsbury, crowned by the
popinjay statue of George the First in Roman fancy dress,
borrowed plumes being, no doubt, considered appropriate
for a masquerading British monarch made in Germany.
" Despondency " and " Hope " present more or less fanciful
views of Tottenham Court Road in the middle of the eighteenth
century, the latter plate including Whitefield's Tabernacle.

That delightful little tale, *The Great Hoggarty Diamond*, was
illustrated by the author in his peculiarly appropriate style at its
best—humour and pathos, and a touch of the bizarre in unison
with the story. The plate " A Coronet, by Jingo," again
illustrates Thackeray's love of little details. Lady Drum and
Titmarsh are driving away from the jeweller's in Coventry Street
by Leicester Square, and the words " Miss Linwood " on one
of the houses recall the fact that it was on the site of the present
Empire that, during the first half of the last century, Miss
Linwood's needlework pictures were exhibited to the number of
sixty or more. This innocuous but dreary show was one of the
staple day-time entertainments to which children were taken in
those days; what the kinema-reared child of 1916 would say to
it had better be left unsaid, even in imagination. The plate
illustrating " Over Head and Ears in Love " gives a sketchy
view of Richmond Bridge and Asgill House.

The *Paris* and *Irish Sketch Books*, and *Cornhill to Cairo*,
contain most entertaining illustrations, but they do not suggest
any special comment; and the same remark applies to the even
more humorous drawings accompanying *The Book of Snobs*,
Travels in London, and *Burlesques*. In *The Book of Snobs*,
however, possibly the presentments of certain club snobs—Spavin
and Captain Shindy—were more or less portraits of their
originals, Mr. Wyndham Smith and Mr. Stephen Price of the
Garrick Club.

The Hogarthian drawings for *Mr. Deuceace* and *Catherine* were intentionally exaggerated, and have a touch of the terrible about them in keeping with those grotesquely sombre tales.

The Roundabout Papers, which contain some of Thackeray's most effective and characteristic writing—kindly rumination and charming little reminiscences of his own early days—have also some interesting illustrations. That introducing *On a Lazy Idle Boy* was drawn at Coire in the Alps; and that illustrating *On Some Late Great Victories* shows No. 52, Brompton Crescent,* then occupied by Major Carmichael Smyth, and the railings are still unchanged (Lady Ritchie says), though newsboy, crossing-sweeper, and orange-girl, if still alive, are now old, and he who sketched them long dead. *Tunbridge Toys* is quite a pretty picture in miniature.† The initial letter to *On Being Found Out* is, perhaps, a reminiscence of Thackeray's early school at Chiswick. *On a Peal of Bells* begins with the words:—

" I am reminded somehow of a July day, a garden, and a great clanging of bells years and years ago, on the very day when George IV. was crowned. I remember a little boy lying in that garden reading his first novel. It was called *The Scottish Chiefs*. The little boy (who is now ancient and not little) read this book in the summer-house of his great-grandmamma. She was eighty years of age then. A most lovely and picturesque old lady."

Wishing to identify the scene of this passage and its accompanying illustration, I referred the question to Lady Ritchie, who stated :—

" My father's great-grandmother was Mrs. Becher. She lived at Fareham, in Hampshire, on the Portsmouth Road. The house is now the Reading-Room; it is in the High Street, and has a garden behind it. This is what my father was alluding to in *On a Peal of Bells*."

So let us regard this little sketch as an auto-portrait of Thackeray at the age of ten, with Fareham Church and Mrs. Becher's summer-house in the background. In the same volume, for the paper *Round about the Christmas Tree*, we find a back view of the former little boy at the age of fifty. Thackeray was fond of introducing portraits of himself. In the Prefatory Remarks to *The Book of Snobs* he is seen pursuing Colonel Snobley with a large fork; in the initial letter of Chapter II of *Lovel the Widower* he is grasping the hair of fleeting Time; and at the beginning of *Christmas Books* is that delightful little figure of a very plaintive Thackeray indeed, with his jester's mask removed. He can be found elsewhere in *Christmas Books;* and throughout other books all the initial letters and tail-pieces

---

* Now called Egerton Crescent.
† This and two other drawings by Thackeray were sold for £25 in 1915.

designed by Thackeray repay study, for they are full of fancy and delicate humour and charm.

The illustrations to *Christmas Books* contain some of the artist-author's best work. What a wealth of humour is here displayed, how well varying types of character are visualised, and with what skill a touch of pathos is imparted. The urchins in *Dr. Birch and his Young Friends* are truly delightful, and were doubtless well-remembered figures from Chiswick and Charterhouse. The mirthful fancy of the sketches in *The Rose and the Ring* is in a distinctly different style, and resembles that of Doyle, and, in later times, W. S. Gilbert. In *Mrs. Perkins's Ball* the presentments of the Mulligan are possibly composite portraits of William O'Connell (cousin of Daniel O'Connell) and the O'Gorman Mahon, from both of whom the character is said to have been drawn. And, finally, *Our Street* brings us to Young Street, Kensington, seen in " A Street Ceremony "; and " The Lady whom Nobody Knows " is walking in Kensington Square: the square tower of the old church is seen in both pictures, for the present Decorated church and spire of St. Mary Abbots date only from 1869. Though it was Lady Ritchie who told me *Our Street* was in Kensington, and this locality answers in many respects, I must confess it does not provide a satisfactory explanation for certain details in the stories and sketches. Perhaps *Our Street*, like so many of Thackeray's scenes, was also a composite picture, and in addition to Young Street, and Kensington, offered some aspects of Great Coram Street (where at No. 13, again, Thackeray lived from 1838 to 1843), hard " by Brunsvick Square."

THACKERAY AND LADY RITCHIE.*

It was very unfortunate that Thackeray, during the last few months of his life, was moved by that strange premonition of his approaching end (though he was but fifty-two years old) to say to his daughter Anne : " When I drop there is to be no ' Life ' written of me; *mind this* and consider it as my last testament and desire." The behest has ever been obeyed to a certain extent, inasmuch as no official " Life and Letters " has appeared. But Lady Ritchie did not feel barred from recording the salient facts of her father's life, and her memories of him, in her own way. She contributed very interesting biographical introductions to the collected editions of Thackeray's works in 1898 and 1911, and elsewhere made mention of her early homes. Thackeray's inhibition was, of course, unreasonable, and literal observance of it impossible. He must have realised that in the course of years it would be disregarded. And it has been, for, in addition to his daughter's recollections, several unofficial biographies have ignored the prohibition, and these would have benefited by the co-operation of his family with letters and memoranda.

Probably Thackeray was constrained originally to ban his own biography by reason of his reluctance for the publication of the sad facts which wrecked his married life; though it can be advanced that the mental illness which removed Mrs. Thackeray from her home and husband and children was no secret at the time to their friends, and after the poor lady's death (in 1894) there could be no objection to a discreet presentation of the story, for it was one of infinite pathos and would show Thackeray in a fine and noble aspect.

The most satisfactory biography of Thackeray would have been one written by a competent man friend, who had known him intimately, with the collaboration of Lady Ritchie to supply the home and family touches. A woman alone can never, it is obvious, be altogether a satisfactory and successful biographer of a man's life with all its varied facets and failings as well as merits. Lady Ritchie was a writer of charming stories, but, despite the fact that she essayed a good deal of biographical work, she was not really equipped with the gifts essential to a great biographer. She was sympathetic but sentimental, meticulous in small details, but vague in details of fact necessary to an accurate

---

* See later, page 226, for a view of Fordhook.

E 2

account of a notable person's life. As she herself admitted: " I can never trust my own impressions of place or of time or quantity —only I can feel the essence which is there and which does not vary . . . my memory is a worry. I remember, but so slowly that it is most provoking and irritating." And she could not have presented successfully the other side of Thackeray's life, so different and distinct from his domesticated aspect—the loose-jesting Thackeray of Bohemia in Paris and of the Garrick Club and Evans's, the Thackeray of whom she knew little or nothing.

It is needless to speculate further on what the ideal biography of Thackeray might have been, a book, unfortunately, now never to be written, because those who knew him well, and were also qualified to write about him, are all gone. One must be thankful for what has been done, and a very welcome addition to the spasmodic biographical contributions which have circumvented Thackeray's " last testament " is a volume edited by Miss Ritchie, the novelist's granddaughter.* It may be described as in two parts; the first, a very interesting series of letters written by Thackeray to his daughter Anne and other relatives; the second, letters written by Lady Ritchie; the whole interspersed with some occasional extracts from a journal she kept in a desultory way. It is matter for regret that this diary was not more regularly written up, for what there is of it suggests it would have provided an excellent record of Thackeray's home and social life during his last years.

The story of Thackeray's brief married life is full of sadness. He was twenty-five and Isabella Shawe twenty when they were married in 1836; the two daughters, Anne Isabella and Minny, were born respectively in 1837 and 1840, and in the latter year Mrs. Thackeray's mental health gave way. It meant the break-up of the home; the children were sent away to their grandparents in Paris, and Thackeray remained to tend his wife with infinite devotion and love amid all the labour attendant on earning a living by means of his then inadequately remunerated literary contributions to the journals and magazines of the time. But as he said: " Though my marriage was a wreck I would do it over again, for behold love is the crown and completion of all earthly good."

Finally, as there was no improvement in health, Mrs. Thackeray was removed to the care of a friend at Epsom, and

---

* *Letters of Anne Thackeray Ritchie, with forty-two additional Letters from her Father, William Makepeace Thackeray.* Selected and Edited by her daughter, Hester Ritchie. With Illustrations. (John Murray, 15s. net.)

Thackeray, in 1846, decided to make a home again for his little girls. He took No. 13, Young Street, Kensington, the house which was soon to become so famous for all time, for there *Vanity Fair* and *Henry Esmond* were written. As Lady Ritchie relates : —

" Once more . . . William Thackeray had a home and a family, if a house, two young children, and a little black cat can be called a family. . . . Everything seemed so strangely delightful. The volumes of *Punch* on the drawing-room table, the delightful *Keepsake* books in their red covers, the old school-room with the book-case and the cupboards, and Papa's room with the vine round about the windows and the sun pouring in. . . . He called Pussy ' Louisa ' and gave her his fish at breakfast, and took her up very gently and put her outside the door when she would not leave him alone. When Papa was a tall young man with black hair and an eyeglass I can remember how we used to hold his forefinger when we walked out with him. . . Papa used to talk to us a great deal and tell us about the Bible and religion. He would talk to us of a morning after breakfast in his study, and of an evening after dinner smoking his cigar, and we generally sat on the floor and listened to him. And then we would give him a chair for his legs and a little table for his candles, and he would presently nod to us and go to sleep."

Thackeray was only about thirty-five at this time, and to see him thus already an instructive and soporific parent is interesting proof of how early the Victorians assumed domestic responsibilities : the modern young man of thirty-five is scarcely contemplating matrimony at that age.

Thackeray, of course, was always devoted to children, both boys (whom he loved to entertain and tip) and girls. Before he rented No. 13, Young Street, and when he was living in " bachelor " lodgings, he often on Sundays walked out to Kensal Manor House, in the Harrow Road, to see his friend, Harrison Ainsworth, who was a widower with three little girls. As I have related elsewhere, after sitting in the garden and an early dinner at four o'clock, Thackeray would accompany the Ainsworths on summer evenings across the fields to service at Willesden Church. In connection with this matter Lady Ritchie observed to me : " I can quite imagine how glad my father must have been to be with kind people, and to join in their family life. He always loved children and peaceful home doings."

Henceforth Thackeray's one aim was to make enough money to leave his children comfortably off, and so he essayed the rather distasteful but profitable line of the public lectures or readings from his works. He wrote to his mother in 1859 : —

" If I can work for three years now, I shall have put back my patrimony and a little over—after 30 years of ups and downs. I made a calculation the other day of receipts in the last 20 years and can only sum up about £32,000 of moneys actually received, for which I have values and disbursement of £13,000, so that I haven't spent at the rate of more than £1,000 a year for 20 years. The profits of the lectures figure as the greatest of the receipts, £9,500—*Virginians* 6—*Vanity Fair* only 2. Three years more, please the Fates, and the girls will then have the 8 or 10,000 apiece that I want for them : and we mustn't say a word against filthy lucre, for I see the use and comfort of it every day more and more."

And again in 1862 :—

"Think of the beginning of the story of the Little Sister in *The Shabby Genteel Story* twenty years ago, and the wife ill and the Publisher refusing me £15 who owes me £13.10, and *The Times*, to which I apply for a little more than 5 guineas for a week's work, refusing to give me more—and all that money difficulty ended. God be praised and an old gentleman sitting in his own house like the hero at the end of the story. . . . We must do some more work. I think the story which I began 20 years ago and then, and then—— Did you read about poor Buckle when he got the fever at Damascus crying out, ' O my book, my book !' I don't care enough about mine to be disquieted when that day comes. Shall I live to do the big history ? Who knows ? But I think I shall like to work on it if the time is left me."

It is curious how Thackeray, though only a middle-aged man, had that constant premonition that his time was short. His daughter tells of one day shortly before his death when she found him sitting looking at the fire. " I do not remember ever to have seen him looking like that before, and he said, ' I have been thinking, in fact, that it will be a very dismal life for you when I am gone.' " Thackeray always gives the impression of an old man, yet he was only fifty-two when the tragically sudden end came.

These new letters of his provide much matter for comment. Writing in December, 1839, he says: " Cruikshank . . . bends all his energies to the illustrations of *Jack Sheppard*—I have not read this latter romance, but one or two extracts are good; it is acted at *four* theatres, and they say that at the Coburg people are waiting about the lobbies selling *Sheppard-bags*—a bag containing a few pick-locks, that is, a screw-driver and iron levers; one or two young gentlemen have already confessed how much they were indebted to Jack Sheppard, who gave them ideas of pocket-picking and thieving which they never would have had but for the play."

Well, no doubt Thackeray read *Jack Sheppard* in its entirety very soon after this, because his article on George Cruikshank, in which he professed to compare Ainsworth's romance with that artist's illustrations (in favour of the latter), appeared in *The Westminster Review*, June, 1840. There were eight, not four, dramatic versions of *Jack Sheppard* produced almost simultaneously in the autumn of 1839. I doubt the authenticity of the *Sheppard-bags*: it was probably a canard invented and circulated by the manager of what is now " The Old Vic " Theatre, and probably it proved a very good advertisement for luring within that Temple of Thespis the youth of the New Cut and neighbourhood.

Vanity Fair, it is pleasant to learn, soon brought the author the material gains it deserved, as well as undying fame, and within two years he was earning nearly £2,000 a year. Thackeray, of course, was fully aware of the merits of his greatest work. One remembers the story told by J. T. Fields, the American publisher, who on passing No. 13, Young Street in later years with the author was admonished playfully by Thackeray, " Down on your knees, sir, before that house, for there *Vanity Fair* was written; and I will go down with you, for I have rather a high opinion of that little work myself."

At the same time he always regarded his work very seriously. When he was concluding *The Newcomes* in July, 1855, he related: "I wrote the last lines of the poor old *Newcomes* with a very sad heart. And afterwards what do you think I did? Suppose I said my prayers, and humbly prayed God Almighty to bless those I love and who love me, and to help me to see and speak the truth and to do my duty. . . . That finis at the end of a book is a solemn word. . . . There go two more years of my life spent over those pages. I was quite sorry to part with a number of kind people with whom I had been living and talking these twenty months past."

To pass to Lady Ritchie's part of this book: she wrote excellent letters—I am not sure that they do not represent her best literary expression, despite the fact that her style was a trifle precious and affected. She could picture a scene vividly. Thus Interlaken : —

" All the stars are rushing in a stream between the Mountain and my window, the music is over. . . . Leslie [Stephen] carried me off to-day for a long agonising delightful toil up a pine wood, through strawberries, tree stems, lake dreams, mountain ranges, to a châlet somewhere high up beyond a raven's haunt . . . where we suddenly saw the great white Monk and Monta Rosa through dappled clouds, as we sat on a little balcony and ate bread and honey and looked over the valleys. . . . How I wish one could send all that one sees to you and to all other hard-worked people who really want it ! I should like to send you a pine tree and a bunch of wild strawberries, a valley of sloping, nodding flowers with thousands of glittering spiders' webs, the high-up snows and far-below lakes, and yesterday's yellow evening, dying rather sadly behind the pine ridge and the misty Stockhorn."

Sometimes she caught the trick of her father's quaint, breathless, *non sequitur* epistolary style. Brighton, 1876 : —

" I am sure you will like to know that the sun began to shine and the dog to bark and the kettle to boil and the children to go down by the sea this afternoon and Leslie found Mr. Morley, and Laura has two red cheeks . . . and I have got the second volume of Heine from Mr. Morley, and the lodgings are still unutterably fusty, but the window is fresh, and the sea was delicious to-day tossing with little sudden fishing boats, and the fat old landlady cooks very nicely, and Louise is in a good temper, and I am so glad yesterday is over, for to-day is so much nicer."

Most of all I like a fragment from her Journal of 1864, when staying with Mrs. Sartoris : —

" Warnford was a great house in a great park, a wide river ran across the meadows with driftwood, bare ash trees and willows everywhere. The drawing-room was a lofty room, lights burning, yellow curtains, tall cabinets, a high chimney-piece and the fire smouldering on the hearth. Mrs. Sartoris singing Gordigiani's passionate complaint. Everything harmonious and bright, except that my heart ached and ached. . . .

" Without the old court. The rooks fly round and round, there are green hills beyond the fields ; one seems stifled and closed in on every side, and I feel as if some day the hills will come rolling down and close in and overwhelm the house. There is a fountain on the terrace, and brick steps wet with rain lead down to the lawn. The rooks are flying in the air, ever so high. I hate them. One little bird trilling freshly in the rain."

This was written soon after Thackeray's death, and there is something of the sadness and unflinching detail of the Pre-Raphaelites in all the clear-cut little pictures it brings to the mind's eye. It may be reminiscent of many things, such as Tennyson in *Maud*, Miss Braddon in *Lady Audley's Secret*, and William De Morgan in *An Affair of Dishonour*, but it has a staccato note of melancholy entirely original.

Lady Ritchie was in sympathy with the tones of the Pre-Raphaelites; Watts and Millais were two of her most valued friends. She always loved the beauty of life to the end, though naturally as age advanced her thoughts went back more and more to old days. In my own conversations with her it was always of her father and his contemporaries that we talked. There are several passages in these letters which finely illuminate her attitude to old age, and regrets for the loss of splendid friends in the long past. Thus in 1905 : —

" My message is nearly over now, but I mean to enjoy old age as much as I can. . . . I still love my own life, and the lives of others very much indeed. . . . It is horrid, being old and remembering all these vanished visions as Ruskin says. . . . My last visit to Leighton was one Sunday, with his beautiful picture on the easel of the Faun teaching the boy to aim his arrow, and Leighton, gay, courteous, laughing. . . . I am glad he never failed, glad his charming looks never left us (for people's looks are for *others*, like their kind welcomes and friendly greetings). I don't think I knew Leighton, but we were always friends and I go on caring for him in that strange medley of death in life, in which elderly people are all living.

" *January*, 1919. All yesterday I was tearing up old letters, and it seemed like living through the past once more and parting from it all again. I felt the beloved rush of the *tempest* of life, to which I still seem to belong, far more than to *now*. Who says, " Youth's a stuff will not endure "? It lasts as long as we do, and is older than age. For those moments of eager life of seeing and being come back to us, and we babble of green fields and live among them to the very end."

A month later she died, at the age of eighty-two.

JOHN MARTIN, PAINTER.*

THERE has never been a satisfactory definition of "genius." The suggestion that it represents " an infinite capacity for taking pains " is the dullest and falsest aphorism ever propounded: rather would one define genius as the exact opposite—an erratic force of personality innately gifted to reach the highest expression of thought or art or music without taking any pains at all, for genius is often allied to madness. Further, there is no certainty that what is considered genius by one generation will be so regarded by another. A case in point is John Martin, the painter of grandiose biblical scenes—The Creation of the World, The Deluge, The Fall of Babylon, Belshazzar's Feast, The Day of Judgment, and the stupendous imaginings of the Apocalypse. His greatest pictures are not to be seen in the public collections, and if they are remembered at all in these days it is by means of engravings of them sometimes found in country houses and inns. They can be recognised instantly by the jagged flash of lightning severing great masses of black storm-clouds overhanging toppling mountain peaks or the towering heights of Assyrian architecture. John Martin undoubtedly was a genius—or at least a sublime visionary—and he was appraised as such in his own time, though forgotten now. *The Magazine of the Fine Arts* described him in 1833 as " among the greatest geniuses of all time." In the same year, Bulwer-Lytton, in his *England and the English*, said: " Martin as a painter is, perhaps, the most original genius of his age. . . . In conception he is more original, more self-dependent than either Raphael or Michael Angelo. They perfected the style of others; Martin has borrowed from none." Charles Lamb, in one of his last essays, *Barrenness of the Imaginative Faculty in the Productions of Modern Art*, devoted a good deal of his thesis to Martin's picture, *Belshazzar's Feast*. He maintained that the writing on the wall was only visible to the King, and that Martin had no biblical justification for depicting the terror of the assembled multitude at the supernatural autography. But Lamb paid high tribute to Martin's vast imagination and his power to express it in terms of paint. Constable was a great admirer of Martin's work, and in the course of conversation with him one day said Martin need not mind being ignored by the Royal Academy, for

* *The Fortnightly Review*, July, 1924.

that institution could not do him any good: " John Martin looks at the Royal Academy from the Plains of Nineveh, from the Destruction of Babylon: I am content to look at the Academy from a gate, and the highest spot I ever aspired to was a wind-mill ! " And the recorder of this conversation, Ralph Thomas, Serjeant-at-Law, relates how Constable " went on comparing himself with Martin, speaking of himself and his work with earnest humility, and of Martin with the highest eulogium."

Even Ruskin, who had no particular regard for Martin's work, wrote of him as a deeply influential artist in *The Stones of Venice* : —

" I believe that the four painters who had, and still have, the most influence on the ordinary Protestant Christian mind are Carlo Dolci, Guercino, Benjamin West, and John Martin. Raphael, much as he is talked about, was, I believe, in fact rarely looked at by religious people. But a Magdalen of Dolci, with a tear on each cheek, or a Guercino Christ and St. John, or a Scripture illustration by West, or a dark cloud with a flash of lightning in it by Martin, rarely fails of being very deeply felt."

It is obvious from these quotations that John Martin deserves some attention and reconsideration in an artistic sense. This is not the place to attempt such an appraisement; but I am glad to find a biography of Martin published at this late date of his posthumous decline in popular favour.* The author, Miss Mary Pendered, has supplied a book that was wanted, and she made a fortunate discovery in the memoir of the artist by his son, Leopold Charles Martin, which was printed in the columns of a provincial newspaper some thirty years ago. Miss Pendered ought to have republished this memoir in its entirety, with necessary editing and correction, for Leopold was careless and often inaccurate; but such passages from this memoir as are now given are often full of interest as pictures of life in London and its environs, during the first half of the nineteenth century, and of the notable people of that time with whom the Martins were acquainted.

Like most other painters of note, John Martin came from the provinces and settled in London. He was a Northumberland boy, born at Haydon Bridge, near Hexham, in 1789, and the twelfth child of his parents' large family. His father was a Borrovian-like character—tanner, soldier, innkeeper, drover, pedlar, everything by turn, and of a roving, adventurous disposition; he married Isabella Thompson, the daughter of a small holder in the neighbourhood of Haydon Bridge. Mrs. Martin's mystic temperament suggests that it was her side of

---

* *John Martin, Painter, His Life and Times* (1789-1854). By Mary L. Pendered. (Hurst and Blackett, 18s. net.)

the pedigree which introduced those wild and grandiose imaginings that characterised her four sons, and in the case of two led to insanity. William, the eldest, was an egregious pamphleteer; he termed himself " Philosophical Conqueror of All Nations," and suffered, like all supreme egoists, from the delusion that his inventions had been stolen from him and exploited by other people. His brother Jonathan, sailor and tanner, was a more dangerous man, a religious fanatic who waged war against the clergy, and ended by nearly burning down York Minster in 1829. Great damage was done, and Jonathan Martin spent his remaining years in a lunatic asylum. The incendiarism in York Minster might have been prevented, because Jonathan had issued preliminary notices and warnings in which he inveighed against his *bêtes-noires*, " those clergymen of England who were going to plays and cards." He used the most delightful and phonetic Yorkshire lingo in warning them that a sign from Heaven would put them to confusion—" Ye Clargy in York, blind Hipacrits, Saarpents and Vipears of Hell, Wine Bibears and Beffe Yeaters, Hear the word of the Lord, oh you Dark and lost Clargmen, you desevers of the People, Jona Martin, a friend of the Sun of Boneypart must conclude by warning you again, Oh, repent ! " Jonathan's son committed suicide.

It will be seen that there is some ground for supposing that John Martin, the painter, with his vast imagination and apocalyptic visions, was by heredity or consanguinity a genius of the genus allied to madness. But he also conceived schemes for the improvement of London—ideas which though they seemed impossible in his time have since been realised and carried out. He planned an underground railway, on the lines of a more extensive Inner Circle with the further improvement of a great central connecting terminus; he drew up designs for a Thames Embankment, of which he claimed to have originated the idea. He died in 1854, and the Victoria Embankment was commenced ten years later.

John Martin came to London to earn his living while still a youth in his teens. He travelled by sea in a Newcastle collier, and being robbed of nearly all the little money he possessed, he had arrived in the great city almost destitute. He was sheltered for a time by an Italian friend, Boniface Musso, an artist who had instructed him in Newcastle. He soon got work as a painter in a china factory, and when still under twenty married Susan Garrett, of Crundal, Hampshire, who was nine years older. The marriage proved a happy one. There were six children. The second daughter, Zenobia, married Peter Cunningham, the antiquarian and author of *The Handbook of London* and *The Story of Nell Gwyn*; and the third daughter, Jessie, married Joseph Bononi, the Egyptologist and Curator of the Soane Museum. Of the sons, Charles Martin was a portrait painter of some merit and a contributor of pictures to *The Illustrated London News*, and Leopold Charles (a godson of Leopold the First, King of the Belgians) married a sister of Sir John Tenniel.

John Martin seems to have exhibited his first picture at the Royal Academy in 1911, and the next year there appeared his first characteristic work on the sublime scale, *Sadak in Search of the Waters of Oblivion*, which was engraved subsequently for *The Keepsake* of 1828. There followed, for forty years, a constant series of his great imaginative pictures, varied by many charming landscapes, such as the beautiful views of Richmond Park, now in the Victoria and Albert Museum. Martin painted a great many pictures of the then rural suburbs of London, districts which have now become urban. If they could have been preserved as one collection they would have formed a very valuable addition to such an assemblage as that of the Gardner Views of London and its suburbs, only recently dispersed by auction—to the lasting shame of the central municipal authorities, who at any cost ought to have secured this unique collection for the London Museum or the Guildhall. One would like to see John Martin's *View of a Lane near Hampstead, 1816*, and *View of a Lane near Holland House, 1839;* his numerous views of the River Brent, Hanger Hill, and Horsingdon Hill, all near Ealing, and of the valley of the Wandle, and Wimbledon—all these pictures were painted in the decade of the 'forties.

Martin became a typical Londoner of his time, delighting—like Dickens and his set—in rural excursions and pleasant Cockney jaunts to Surrey and the sylvan northern heights. His early married life was spent at No. 77, High Street, Marylebone, in Northumberland Street, and at No. 30, Allsop Terrace (or Place, as a map of 1840 has it) in the same locality. In the 'forties he was living at Lindsey House, Cheyne Walk, Chelsea.

As I have indicated, the memoir of John Martin by his son is full of interest by reason of the glimpses it gives of rambles round the country adjoining London and the notable people to be met there. Hampstead, he says, " was at all times a spot much frequented by my father. The walk from town, through fields and wooded lanes, was most pleasant. The Eyre Arms Tavern, now the centre of St. John's Wood district, was then on the outskirts. It was well known as a place for athletic sports and for the annual meetings of the Westmorland and Cumberland wrestlers." They proceeded past Old Belsize House, " a mansion truly interesting and historic," and the adjoining " charming and secluded residence of Mr. Thomas Longman," the publisher, to see Constable, the painter:—

" Mr. Constable was then living temporarily at a part of Hampstead termed ' Holmwood.' . . . He received us in his usual kind-hearted, homely manner. In person, as was his wont, he was untidy, for he lived, like an equally great painter, Salvator Rosa, constantly in the wild, splashy, wet, dripping woods. . . . The house at ' Holmwood ' had lovely surroundings. Mr. Constable's favourite sketching ground, a place that went by the name of Child's Hill, was near at hand. It was a woody spot, distinguished as the semaphore, or telegraph, station, being the first from London to Portsmouth and working directly with the Admiralty at Whitehall."

On another day the Martins would go to Ealing, where there were lanes full of " sweet old-fashioned flowers, wild roses, honeysuckle and the like, leading to the wonderfully rich and beautiful districts of Twyford, Castlebar, and Hanger Hill, the chief sketching place of my father. Hanger Hill House, a charming spot, was then the residence of Lady Byron, the widow of the poet Lady Byron later resided at the foot of the hill in a charming old house named Fordhook, once the residence of Henry Fielding, the author of *Tom Jones*.* . . . Ada, ' sole daughter of my house and heart,' as Byron wrote, then a timid, delicate, but beautiful child-like girl, was often seen by us walking her pony in the rustic lanes of Hanger Hill. She was far too timid to trust without a leader at the bridle to guide. . . . Well do I remember seeing the funeral of her father in 1824. The body lay in state for two days at No. 25, Great George Street, Westminster. The whole place was blocked up from early morning with spectators, and I followed the procession as far as the New Road, near Regent's Park."

And here is a picture of Turner. The Martins had called upon him at his large house in Queen Anne Street:—

" Mr. Turner intimated that, on my father's arrival, he was on the point of walking over to his small place at Chelsea. If inclined for a walk, would he accompany him? This my father willingly agreed to do. Crossing Hyde Park, Brompton, and so on by the footpaths through market gardens to Chelsea—a very pleasant ramble—Mr. Turner introduced us to a small six-roomed house on the banks of the Thames. . . . The only attendant seemed to be an old woman, who got us some porter as an accompaniment to some bread and cheese. The rooms were very poorly furnished, all and everything looking as though it was the abode of a very poor man. Mr. Turner pointed out, with seeming pride, the

---

* See later, page 226, for a view of Fordhook.

splendid view from his single window, saying, ' Here you see my study—
sky and water. Are they not glorious? Here I have my lesson night
and day ! ' "

Somehow, Martin, the Cockney pedestrian, visiting his
notable contemporaries, is more interesting than Martin the
sublime visionary. He was a genius, but one who could unbend.
His friend, Ralph Thomas, relates how he and Martin in their
country rambles would munch quantities of " toffy, brandy balls,
and bull's-eyes," the while they enthused on the glories of the
landscape. Like Cruikshank, John Martin could sing a song
and be merry, despite the sombre " madness " of his artistic side.
His biography is very welcome.

DICKENS AND FORSTER.*

WHEN, during the Christmastide festivities of 1836 at Kensal Lodge, Harrison Ainsworth introduced two of his guests, both young men of twenty-four, to each other, he little thought he was laying the corner-stone of a memorable friendship and for all time coupling together two names—Dickens and Forster. And now, seventy-five years later, what may be termed the coping-stone of that friendship appears in the shape of an elaborate and richly illustrated edition of the oft-reprinted book in which the one friend recorded the life of the other.

Forster's *Life of Dickens* is now generally acknowledged to be one of the few great biographies in the English language, and has a place in the select group which includes Boswell's *Johnson*, Lockhart's *Scott*, Morley's *Gladstone*, and Mrs. Gaskell's *Charlotte Brontë*. And yet no biography has ever been more adversely criticised. Personal friends of Dickens, who had known him intimately, were dissatisfied with it. James Crossley, the famous bibliophile, speaking of Forster, said: "I cannot call him the successful biographer of Dickens." And Ainsworth observed: "I see he only tells half the story."

No doubt the views of Dickens's friends were biased by annoyance at the scant notice they received in the authoritative biography; and this lapse, of course, *is* where the book is most open to effective attack. Forster himself is unduly prominent; but other intimates of Dickens, who very strongly influenced his career and literary work, are relegated to an obscure position, and often their share in the life-story is entirely ignored and omitted. It is the same with the correspondence; the letters quoted are practically all addressed to Forster, and no attempt is made to utilise the many valuable letters written by Dickens to other correspondents. Further, the documents Forster did use in his narrative are inartistically introduced and cruelly mutilated. Indeed, his method of dealing with Dickens's original letters makes the blood of more meticulous biographers run cold, for, as a friend (Mr. Percy FitzGerald) of his has recorded:—

"To save time and trouble—and this I was told by Mr. Forster—he would cut out the passages he wanted with a pair of scissors and paste them on his manuscript. As the portion written on the back was thus lost, the rest became valueless.''

It will ever be matter for regret that Forster, with his unique opportunities for a detailed and intimate picture, has given but an incomplete record of perhaps the most interesting period of Dickens's life, the years 1836-1839, the outset of his literary career, when the early books were written with all the young, fresh brilliancy of their author. The biographer gives an unsatisfactory version of Dickens's relations and quarrels with his first publisher, Macrone; in fact, he suppresses all mention of the important point that the author had signed an agreement to write, for two hundred pounds, a novel—probably *Oliver Twist*—to be published by Macrone; but that, owing to the dispute and ill-feeling which had arisen between Dickens and Macrone concerning the copyright and reissue of *Sketches by Boz*, Dickens absolutely declined to carry out the contract, and disposed of his proposed novel to Richard Bentley for five hundred pounds, thus risking a legal action, which, however, was rendered inoperative by Macrone's sudden death. These events occurred in the late autumn of 1836.

Forster's account of Dickens's quarrel, some two years later, with Bentley is also open to criticism. There were two sides to this historic separation, as in every other dispute, and both Dickens and Bentley were justified in fighting for what they considered their rights. Judging by the expressed views of his contemporaries, Bentley was certainly a hard man to deal with; but it does not follow that he was quite the rapacious taskmaster depicted by Forster in his earlier pages. Here we must make allowance for the biographer's affectionate bias towards his friend-hero.

The real facts of this matter were that when, in 1836, Dickens first entered into his arrangements with Bentley his great success and fame were not as yet; and he, a young man of twenty-four, was glad to undertake the editing of *Bentley's Miscellany* for twenty pounds a month, and also to write two serial stories (*Oliver Twist* and *Barnaby Rudge*) for the sum of five hundred pounds each. But the phenomenal success of *Pickwick* and the increasing public attention now given to *Oliver Twist* naturally changed the situation; and so in 1837 Dickens's editorial salary was increased to thirty pounds a month, and the price for the novels to seven hundred and fifty pounds each. A further increase of remuneration was conceded in 1838; but this did not satisfy Dickens, who in February, 1839, refused to continue the editorship of *Bentley's Miscellany*. However, after much dis-

F

cussion and correspondence, new agreements were entered into
—one for *Oliver Twist* and the *Miscellany*, and a second for
Barnaby Rudge, for which Bentley now consented to pay four
thousand pounds, a large and liberal advance, as all must
acknowledge, on the five hundred pounds originally agreed
upon for the work. Dickens stipulated that he would complete
Barnaby Rudge by the end of the year 1839, and this point proved
to be a *casus belli*. For Dickens soon found the simultaneous
composition of two long novels, combined with the editing of the
Miscellany, an intolerable strain, and, to quote his words to
Forster, he said :—

" I cannot—cannot and will not—distress myself by beginning this
tale until I have had time to breathe. . . . There—for six months
Barnaby Rudge stands over."

So when Bentley announced, in December, 1839, the forth-
coming work, *Barnaby Rudge*, he received a lawyer's letter
stating that Dickens would not be ready for three or four months.
Perhaps Bentley would have consented to the desired postponement had not an announcement appeared that Dickens was about
to publish another work, *Master Humphrey's Clock*, elsewhere.
This Bentley regarded as an aggravated violation of his own
agreement, and resulted in the final separation of publisher and
author. Dickens repurchased the copyright and existing stock
of *Oliver Twist* for two thousand two hundred and fifty pounds,
the existing agreement for *Barnaby Rudge* was cancelled, and
the editorship of *Bentley's Miscellany* passed from Dickens to
Ainsworth.

The rumour soon spread in London and in literary circles
that it was the influence and advice of Forster which had caused
Dickens to break his agreement with Bentley; but Dickens, in a
long and very interesting letter to Ainsworth, warmly repudiated
the charge. This letter, printed *in extenso* in the present writer's
William Harrison Ainsworth and his Friends, would certainly
seem to exonerate Forster from the charge in question. As a
matter of fact, it was against his strongly expressed advice that
Ainsworth afterwards took over the editorship of *Bentley's
Miscellany* just resigned by Dickens. This point is conclusively
established by a still existing letter from Forster to Ainsworth.

Forster, again, makes no reference to an interesting serial
work which Dickens and Ainsworth proposed to write in
collaboration in 1838. Ainsworth had achieved unprecedented
success with his first romance, *Rookwood*, 1834, followed by the
scholarly *Crichton*, 1837; and Dickens had already written
Pickwick, and was evolving in his fertile brain *Oliver Twist*,

Nicholas Nickleby, and *Barnaby Rudge,* more or less at the same productive period. Concerning the new joint scheme, Ainsworth wrote to James Maidment, of Edinburgh, on January 16th, 1838: —

" In conjunction with my friend, Mr. Dickens, the author of *Pickwick Papers,* I am about to start . . . a monthly publication, to be entitled *Ancient and Modern London.* Mr. Dickens will illustrate the metropolis of the present day : I shall endeavour to paint its ancient glories. Cruikshank will furnish the designs."

Ainsworth referred further to what he termed " the grand field for the romance writer "—Old London—on February 8th, 1838, in a letter to James Crossley : —

" I think I told you that Dickens and I are about to illustrate ancient and modern London in a Pickwick form. We expect much from this."

There is no record to tell what caused the abandonment of the collaboration. Ainsworth then proceeded to write *Jack Sheppard* and Dickens his *Oliver Twist*—both romances, be it noted, examples of the Newgate School of Fiction. Probably it was Ainsworth who told Dickens that Jack Sheppard had an actual friend and robber-companion named James Sikes—hence the name of Bill Sikes for the murderer in *Oliver Twist,* and perhaps it was the vast and continuing popularity of *Rookwood* which caused Sam Weller to choose *Bold Turpin, vunce on Hounslow Heath* as a topical ballad when he sang in the legal atmosphere of Portugal Street.

Before dismissing the limitations in Forster's otherwise great biography, one may perhaps express a personal regret that the biographer devotes but a few words to the social or convivial phase of Dickens in these first glorious years of youth and fame. He barely mentions the frequent rides through the lovely country then surrounding the surburbs of London, which Dickens delighted to take in company with his two intimates, Forster and Ainsworth; and the even more frequent dinings and festivities the trio enjoyed go almost unrecorded. Certainly the dinner in celebration of the completion of *Pickwick*—when the *pièce de résistance* was a sugary temple of confectionery, beneath the canopy of which stood a little figure of Mr. Pickwick, gaiters and all complete—deserved one word for pleasant memory's sake. Ainsworth thus described the scene to Crossley : —

" November 22nd, 1837.

" . . . . On Saturday last we celebrated the completion of *The Pickwick Papers.* We had a capital dinner, with capital wine, and capital speeches. Dickens, of course, was in the chair. Talfourd was the Vice, and an excellent Vice he made. He speaks with great fervour and tact, and, being greatly interested on the occasion, exerted himself to the utmost.* Just before he was about to propose *the* toast of the evening, the head waiter—for it was at a tavern that the carouse took place—entered, and placed a glittering temple of confectionery on the table, beneath the canopy of which stood a little figure of the illustrious Mr. Pickwick. This was the work of the landlord. As you may suppose, it was received with great applause. Dickens made a feeling speech in reply to the Serjeant's eulogy. There were present Tom Hill, Jerdan, Forster, Macready, Dickens senr., Hogarth (Dickens's father-in-law), one or two private friends, the printers, publishers, and engraver. The same party were invited to celebrate the christening of the next work. Just before dinner Dickens received a cheque for £750 from his Publishers.''

Forster's all too brief allusion to Dickens's two early visits to Manchester with his friends is a distinct biographical lapse, for these visits were intimately concerned with *Nicholas Nickleby*.

It was in November, 1838, that Dickens and Forster first went to Manchester, and they were accompanied by young Hablot Browne, who had just become famous through the illustrations he had furnished for *Pickwick* and *Nicholas Nickleby*. The party was furnished by Ainsworth with letters of introduction to the most prominent literary men of his native city, and in one of these letters (to Crossley) he observed:—

'' Dickens's object is to see the interior of a cotton-mill—I fancy with reference to some of his publications. . . . I rather suspect that he is reconnoitring for character, and perhaps you may aid his researches; but at all events you can help him to the best glass of wine in Manchester, and that will materially assist his judgment in coming to a favourable conclusion of the habits of my townsmen.''

As a matter of fact, one of the express objects of Dickens's visit was to see two quaint but benevolent merchants of Manchester, William and Daniel Grant, whose qualities had often been described to him by Ainsworth. Another Manchester friend of Ainsworth's, Gilbert Winter, arranged the desired meeting, and it was at a dinner at his residence, Stocks House, on Cheetham Hill, that Dickens and the Grants met. The result was that the Grants in due course made their appearance as the Cheeryble Brothers in *Nicholas Nickleby*. No doubt Phiz's sketches of the brothers were also drawn, *sub rosa*, from the originals. Dr. James Bower Harrison, who met Boz in Manchester, noted:—

'' Mr. Dickens was then writing *Nicholas Nickleby*, and I well remember his reading the proofs of his novel, and smiling at his own writings. He was then a smart-looking young man of rather effeminate

* *Pickwick* had been dedicated two months before to Mr. Serjeant Talfourd, M.P., ''as a memorial of the most gratifying friendship I have ever contracted . . . as a token of my fervent admiration of every fine quality of your head and heart.''

appearance, wearing long hair, very much like the pictures of the hero of his story. . . . I still call to mind his polished boots and drawing-room-like attire."

Dickens, Forster, and Phiz devoted one of their three days in Manchester to an expedition to Cheadle Hall, in Cheshire, to see the three little daughters of Ainsworth, who were at a boarding-school there. The respective parties had not hitherto met, so by way of a peace oblation the three young men, all in their " twenties," took various books to present to the three maidens, whose ages ranged from eight to eleven. The youngest lady had been intentionally misinformed by a mischievous fellow-pupil that the " severe-looking gentleman " —Forster—was the dentist on business intent. Consequently when he stepped forward the little girl uttered an exceeding bitter cry, and it was some time before she could be induced to believe that Forster's intentions were friendly, and that, though he might be a man from *The Examiner*, he was not an examiner of teeth. However, peace was restored, and all spent a very happy time together.

Dickens and Forster were so delighted with their experiences in Manchester that they repeated their visit only two months later, in January, 1839, and this time Ainsworth was able to accompany them; the whole party were the guests of his relative, Hugh Beaver, at The Temple, Cheetham Hill, where a large dinner-party was given on the night of their arrival, Saturday, January 10th. On Sunday the trio attended service in the Collegiate Church (now the Cathedral). On Monday a semi-public dinner was given in honour of Dickens and Ainsworth conjointly; on Tuesday they dined with James Crossley, and on Wednesday with Gilbert Winter, when, no doubt, the Grants again came under the ken of Dickens, the party subsequently attending a public assembly.

It will be remembered that Forster, in the biography, merely alludes to all these pleasant days and convivial nights at Manchester in one short sentence as regards Ainsworth, and in a brief note of memory concerning Gilbert Winter and Stocks House; yet in the later phases of Dickens's career, when the biographer was the one and all-important friend, there is often a prolixity of detail in the narrative.

Granting, then, that Forster's book has faults both of omission and commission, that it is egotistical and at times pre-judiced, that its arrangement is bad and its chronology chaotic, yet, owing to the biographer's whole-hearted admiration and enthusiasm for his subject, and by his sympathetic and vivid presentment of his hero's character and achievements, the final result is a great biography, the greatest, it is safe to say, of its great subject, and one that will never be superseded. Many reasons support this conclusion. Dickens himself wished Forster to be his biographer; and the novelist's near relatives, those best qualified to judge of its claims and merits, have always given their *cachet* of approval to this particular work. Dickens's most trusted friend and the executrix of his last wishes, Miss Georgina Hogarth, has stated to me : —

" Mr. Forster was the only person with the material and authority to write the biography. But it was written very soon after Mr. Dickens's death, and a great deal could not be said *then* which becomes possible as years go on. I always feel that Mr. Forster's book will be more appreciated in years to come than it is now."

The truth of Miss Hogarth's belief (expressed eight years ago) is already becoming justified as the Dickens centenary approaches. The successful consummation of this sumptuous Memorial Edition of *The Life of Charles Dickens* demonstrates the fact. Its most attractive feature, of course, is the unique collection of over five hundred illustrations, gathered together and arranged by Mr. B. W. Matz. Of particular value are the views of the houses and schools associated with the youth of Dickens, for the scenes and surroundings where early and lasting impressions were formed must ever be of supreme biographical importance. Great interest will attach to the portraits reproduced in this edition, notably of Dickens himself, his parents, his wife (who is presented in an exquisitely graceful sketch by Maclise), and children; and to the pictures of family life at Gadshill. Though superior critics may vainly assert that the public has no concern with the private life of a great man, but only with his life's work or contribution to art, the inexorable fact remains that humanity is most interested in the human or domestic side of a genius. A book on Nelson and Lady Hamilton will find twenty readers where a work on Nelson and Trafalgar will find but one, Byron's love affairs are more discussed in these days than his poems, and Napoleon's wives threaten to over-shadow Waterloo.

It is to be regretted that Mr. Matz has not included in his great collection portraits of Macrone and Bentley, and a view of Kensal Lodge, where, as previously stated, Dickens and Forster first met; and that he has left Dickens's visits to Manchester in 1838 and 1839 unillustrated, giving no views of Stocks House and The Temple, or portraits of the Grants, Gilbert Winter, and James Crossley. But the compiler may well say that, as these incidents or people are only noted by a few words in Forster's text, the omissions are justified; nevertheless, as this paper has endeavoured to show, they were either important or interesting factors in the life of Dickens. In other respects Mr. Matz's collection is complete and truly admirable, and both he and the publishers are to be congratulated sincerely on their worthy tribute to the great novelist whose centenary is at hand.

PHIZ—HABLOT K. BROWNE.*

In these days of Dickens devotion, when it is possible to run successfully a monthly magazine dealing entirely with the cult, there is perhaps some danger of forgetting how largely the great Victorian novelist was aided by Hablot K. Browne in the popular immortalisation of that vast gallery of characters created by Dickens, but visualised, nearly all, in the mind's eye by Phiz. The two Wellers, Stiggins, Squeers, Quilp, Mrs. Gamp, Chadband and Joe, Captain Cuttle, Mr. Micawber, and, above all, Mr. Pecksniff—when any of these names are mentioned, how at once there flashes to the brain the figure in one of Phiz's plates rather than any passage from the novels. Of course that is the great advantage an artist always possesses over an author; he is able to convey the desired impression of dramatic or pathetic or humorous momentariness in a few strokes of his pencil, whereas the writer has to prepare the mind of the reader for the climax by wordy toil with description and detail.

The world-known figure of Pickwick was not drawn originally by Phiz; it was the pictorial creation of Robert Seymour, who, discarding his first design of a long, thin man, drew the portrait of a short, stout one from the description by Edward Chapman of an actual person he, the publisher, knew at Richmond. It was the suicide of Seymour in 1836 that gave Phiz his great opportunity, for at the age of twenty-one he was selected (in preference to Thackeray†) to fill the vacant post of illustrator to *Pickwick* (then appearing in monthly parts), mainly on the merits of an excellent and humorous drawing of John Gilpin's Ride, which had won for young Browne a medal from the Society of Arts in 1833. Such was the happy chance (though arising from a tragedy) that brought Dickens and Phiz into a conjunction destined to produce such brilliant and imperishable fruits. Phiz skilfully continued Seymour's conceptions of Pickwick and his three friends and allies, and of Jingle; all the other prominent characters of the book were his pictorial creations.

On Dickens's long and happy association with Browne some interesting and valuable side-lights have recently been thrown

---

* *Chambers's Journal,* August 8th, 1914.
† See *ante* page 53.

by the artist's son, Dr. Edgar Browne, in a pleasant, discursive book called *Phiz and Dickens*. It makes no pretence of being a biography, for a full biography of Phiz would hardly be possible. His life, apart from his work, was uneventful and secluded, and documentary material would be scarce, for Phiz (like Dickens) was guilty of burning all his correspondence and many of his own sketches and memoranda on the occasion of his removal from Croydon. In this appalling auto-bonfire perished invaluable letters from Dickens, Ainsworth, Lever, and many other notable Victorian writers whose works were illustrated by Phiz.

Consequently, Dr. Browne's picture of his father's quiet life at Croydon, which then had all the amenities of country within easy reach of London, in those good, solid, unpretentious, comfortable early-Victorian days, gives much assistance to a comprehension of the artist. Phiz was typical of his time. He delighted in riding, roast beef, and good port, though he lacked the gregariousness appertaining to the authors he most successfully illustrated. Phiz was ever shy of strangers, and did not participate in the conviviality dear to his pictorial compeer, George Cruikshank; his life was spent in his studio, and this, to a great extent, saved him from being involved in the quarrels that so often temporarily rent the loving bonds of camaraderie in the literary circle he worked for. All his authors held him in affectionate regard, and his amicable business relations with those fiery, impetuous spirits preserved an unbroken sequence of satisfaction on all sides. In all the work he executed for Dickens there was only one plate, apparently, that gave real dissatisfaction to the author—that of " Paul and Mrs. Pipchin," in *Dombey and Son*, concerning which Dickens wrote to Forster : —

" I am really distressed by the illustration of Mrs. Pipchin and Paul. It is so frightfully and wildly wide of the mark. Good Heaven ! In the commonest and most literal construction of the text it is all wrong. She is described as an old lady, and Paul's ' miniature arm-chair ' is mentioned more than once. He ought to be sitting in a little arm-chair in the corner of the fireplace, staring up at her."

However, Dickens was just then in a state of nervous irritation and emotion at the approaching death of Little Paul, and his comments on this plate were hypercritical; for, after all, the only divergences from the text are that Paul is seated in a child's high chair with a foot-rest instead of a " little arm-chair," and that the delightful black cat is sitting on the hearthrug instead of being " coiled upon the centre foot of the fender "—but he is " purring egotistically and winking at the fire " all right. And, as Dr. Browne appositely observes : —

" To show that the most intimate acquaintance with the text will not always preserve even the author (let alone the illustrator) from making small slips, we find Dickens himself describing old Sol 'squeezing both the Captain's hands with uncommon fervour.' Well may we say ' in the commonest and most literal construction of the text it is all wrong,' as everybody knows Captain Cuttle had only one hand and a hook."

It is interesting to note that Phiz was indictable of far greater divergences from Boz's text (than in this matter of Paul's arm-chair) which, it would seem, neither he nor Dickens ever noticed. For instance, in *Dombey and Son* also, Susan Nipper, " the short, womanly girl of fourteen," is drawn as a very tall, thin adult. Captain Cuttle's hook was attached to his right arm according to the text, and is so depicted in eight illustrations, but in two others (the vignette and " Solemn reference is made to Mr. Bunsby ") it appears on the left arm. Again, in Chapter LVIII of *Barnaby Rudge*, Joe Willet is described as having lost his left arm, and is so represented in Phiz's drawing in Chapter LXXI; but in Chapter LXXVIII Browne shows Joe embracing Dolly Varden with his left arm, and his right sleeve empty. In the " Consecrated Ground " plate of *Bleak House* it is not clear how the dismal burial-place, would be entered, for the railed " gate " has no hinges. Much controversy has raged over the point whether Peggotty's Hut stood on its head or its heels, so to speak. Phiz drew it with the keel on top, but Dickens speaks of the boat being " roofed in"; the artist's conception was the more picturesque in result. In *Martin Chuzzlewit*, though Dickens laid stress on Pecksniff's " white cravat," Phiz through-out gives him a black one, and advisedly so; Pecksniff is perhaps his most successful creation, the symbolic figure of unctuous humbug which rises to the mental eye when the adjective " Pecksniffian " appears in speech or print.* In the same book occurs Browne's most serious departure from the text. In that magnificent passage of Dickens where Jonas Chuzzlewit and Montague drive out from London into the night and the advanc-ing thunderstorm, when poor Montague feels the premonition of his coming fate in every incident of the journey—their horses, maddened by the storm, finally " dashed off wildly down a steep hill, flung the driver from his saddle, drew the carriage to the brink of the ditch, stumbled headlong down, and threw it crashing over . . . Jonas . . . presently observed that Montague was lying senseless on the road . . . he ran to the horses' heads, and pulling at their bridles with all his force, set them struggling and plunging with such mad violence as brought *their* hoofs at

---

* Certain aspects of Pecksniff are supposed to have been drawn from Samuel Carter Hall. Lady Bulwer-Lytton alludes to S. C. Hall as " Pecksniff " as early as 1855.

every effort nearer to the skull of the prostrate man." And later, " with the aid of his knife they . . . disengaged the horses from the broken chariot, and got them, cut and bleeding, on their legs again." That is Dickens's description. But in Phiz's illustration of the scene, one horse is lying in the ditch, and the other, quite free of the carriage, is rearing and being forced backward by Jonas toward the senseless figure, lying in the road, he seeks to murder. But apart from desire for meticulous accuracy in detail, the plate is fine and dramatic.

I always think that this wonderfully impressive chapter in *Martin Chuzzlewit*, with its presentiment of coming murder and storm, was suggested to Dickens by the famous murder case of Gill's Hill, for just as Jonas and Montague drove out into the night with Death in attendance, so did Thurtell drive his wretched victim, Weare, out into that dark night of late October, 1824, along the Edgware Road, out of London, to the lonely lane where the terrible tragedy was thus enacted in the murderer's own words:—

" When I first shot him he jumped out of the gig, ran like the devil up the lane, singing out that he would deliver all he had won off me if I would only spare his life. I jumped out of the gig and ran after him. I got him down and began to cut his throat, as I thought, about the jugular vein, but could not stop his singing out. I then jammed the pistol into his head. I saw him turn round; then I knew I had done him."

Despite the coarseness of the language it visualises the crime. One can see that poor, terror-stricken figure fleeing down the lane, shrieking for mercy, and only the stars witness of the cruel death that outraged the peace of the countryside. So, too, in the dark wood, did Montague meet his fate.*

I am not aware that the numerous commentators of Dickens have ever settled definitely where the great novelist placed the scene of his poignant description of the doomed man going down into the dell to his death. It was evidently somewhere between Salisbury and Amesbury, for it was in the latter place that Pecksniff lived undoubtedly—Amesbury, which is introduced in that rarely beautiful opening scene of an autumn evening, and the village forge, and the vagaries of the wind coming from the great spaces of Salisbury Plain. Before leaving this district, I should like to point out that when Tom Pinch goes to Salisbury to meet Martin he puts up at a certain inn near the Market Place, and later on, when he had

---

* Incidents of the murder of Weare were utilised by Bulwer-Lytton in *Pelham* (Chapter 83), and there is a good deal about Thurtell in the works of Borrow.

finally left Pecksniff's house, he slept at this same inn, preparatory
to his journey to London, in " a low four-poster shelving down-
ward in the centre like a trough," with pictures of a fat ox and an
ox-like man by way of artistic adornment on the walls. Hitherto
Dickens's commentators have identified this inn as " The
George," in the High Street. That, I think, is an erroneous
conclusion. " The George " was not an inn, being then
unlicensed, at the date Dickens wrote his description, and it was
(and is) situated in the quiet High Street which leads only to the
Cathedral Close. The inn Dickens had in mind was certainly
one of those in the bustling Market Place of Salisbury, for he
refers again and again to the busy market scenes and the farmers
and their customers " standing about in groups, or talking noisily
together on the tavern steps." Tom Pinch " walked into the
market while they were getting breakfast ready for him at the
inn." Dickens's vivid picture of Salisbury Market which follows
must have been drawn from actual observation, for it remains
much the same to-day. And we may be sure Dickens watched
the scene from an inn—I think it was probably " The Ox "—
where he could partake of " a well-cooked steak and smoking
hot potatoes . . . . and a jug of most stupendous Wiltshire
beer." I fancy he stopped at Salisbury on the way back from the
famous trip to Cornwall, in the company of Maclise, Clarkson
Stanfield, and Forster, during the late autumn of 1842, for it
was at this date he decided upon the plan of *Martin Chuzzlewit*.
Originally Dickens intended to locate Pecksniff in Cornwall, but
in the event it proved to be Wiltshire.

One would fain linger over Phiz's illustrations to Dickens,
particularly those shadowed scenes in *Bleak House*—" Sunset
at Chesney Wold," " The Lonely Figure," " The Night," " The
Morning " (with the infinite pathos of the weary figure at rest
at last) and " The Ghost's Walk," which always brings to mind
the lines from George Meredith's early poem, *Autumn
Even Song* : —

> " Pale on the panes of the old hall
>   Gleams the lone space
>   Between the sunset and the squall ;
>   And on its face
>   Mournfully glimmers to the last. . . ."

As good as the Dickens plates were those Phiz executed
for the dashing, yet often pathetic novels of Charles Lever.
Mickey Free, Tipperary Joe, Corney Delany, Darby and Tom
Burke, The O'Donoghue and his brother-in-law Sir Archy
M'Nab, The Knight of Gwynne—how all these figures stand

out from memory's background, and not only amid the rollicking escapades of Lever's merry moods. For terrifying horror, few pictures can equal that of " The Death of Shaun " in *Jack Hinton*—that stark, half-naked, blood-stained body (visualised agony), with the ghastly bandage round the head, falling back upon the wretched bed beside which kneels the priest. And then those wonderful night scenes Phiz drew for *Davenport Dunn*, such as " Going Home " and " A Saunter by Moonlight," which rank with the similar dark or moonlit pictures he designed for *Bleak House* and *Little Dorrit* and Ainsworth's *Mervyn Clitheroe*—" The Duel," " My Adventure in the Haunted Chamber," and " The Stranger at the Grave." Phiz was pre-eminent in presenting the glooms and mysteries of woods and waters by night, and the effect of moonlight on landscape and building or peeping through a wrack of clouds.

Phiz did much other good work for Ainsworth's *Crichton, Old St. Paul's, The Star Chamber, The Spendthrift, Ovingdean Grange*, and, in particular, *Auriol*, that strange fragment of nightmare romance wherein the artist found full opportunity for depicting the bizarre. Some of his plates for this work—" The Elixir of Long Life," " The Ruined House in the Vauxhall Road," " The Seizure of Ebba," and " The Chamber of Mystery "—are certainly the most extraordinary, in the weird sense of the word, that he ever drew. G. P. R. James also furnished Browne with an opportunity for some impressive scenes in his ghostly romance, *The Castle of Ehrenstein*, and others of a more varied nature in *The Commissioner*. For Frank Smedley's *Lewis Arundel* and *Harry Coverdale's Courtship* Phiz designed many delightful plates in his own most characteristic style—country scenes with plenty of horses, and domestic interiors with the characters and their actions skilfully contrasted; the former work also contained some powerful dramatic illustrations, such as those in the Venetian portion of the tale.

It is not possible to notice here all the writers who benefited by Phiz's pencil : but mention must be made of *Torlogh O'Brien* (1847) and the rare little volume of *Ghost Stories and Tales of Mystery* (1851), both by Sheridan Le Fanu; and the now very valuable first edition of *Jorrocks's Jaunts and Jollities*, by R. S. Surtees, for which Phiz supplied twelve engravings in 1838. He also illustrated the same author's *Hawbuck Grange* and, in part, *Mr. Facey Romford's Hounds*. Enough has been said to demonstrate that, with the exception of Thackeray and Lytton, the best of the early-Victorian novelists are indissolubly associated with H. K. Browne. And how pleasant it is, after a surfeit of impressionist fiction and futurist art, to sit down by the fire and glance through a favourite book illustrated by Phiz, and renew old memories and ancient delights with those figures as familiar as friends in the flesh. As *Punch* wrote after Browne's death : —

" The lamp is out that lighted up the text
Of Dickens, Lever—heroes of the pen;
' Pickwick ' and ' Lorrequer ' we love, but next
We place the man who made us see such men.
What should we know of ' Martin Chuzzlewit,'
Stern ' Mr. Dombey ' or ' Uriah Heep '?
' Tom Burke of Ours'? Around our hearths they sit,
Outliving their creators—all asleep.
No sweeter gift e'er fell to man than his
Who gave us troops of friends—Delightful Phiz.

He is not dead ! There in the picture book
He lives with men and women that he drew ;
We take him with us to the cozy nook
Where old companions we can love anew.
Dear boyhood's friend ! We rode with him to hounds ;
Lived with dear ' Peggotty ' in after years ;
Messed in old Ireland where fun knew no bounds ;
At ' Dora's ' death we felt poor ' David's ' tears !
There is no death for such a man ; he is
The spirit of an unclosed book—Immortal Phiz.''

Phiz died on July 8th, 1882. His place as a book illustrator—known equally to fame with the authors interpreted—has never been filled, and his method is a lost art. As a man, his qualities were fine and simple, for though he achieved world-wide celebrity he remained entirely unspoilt. Always unpretentious, his reserve and shyness were lifelong. He was devoted to animals, particularly to horses and cats. He was very independent, disliked being waited upon, and was reluctant to ask for anything. He was influenced by weather—glorying in sunshine, but depressed by gloomy days—and even more so by scenery; he was a great lover of the sea and all that was wild and grand in nature, and this trait was reflected in his art. Such was delightful, immortal Phiz.

R. S. SURTEES.*

ROBERT SMITH SURTEES holds a position peculiarly his own in English literature, for though there have been many delineators of sporting life from Pierce Egan and " Nimrod " (Charles James Apperley) and Whyte Melville to Hawley Smart and Nat Gould, his is a distinct and separate category. Surtees wrote of the humorous side of sport, of contretemps in the hunting field or stubble, of the fun supplied by embryo and indifferent sportsmen—generally Cockneys, as exemplified in particular by his immortal creation, John Jorrocks, grocer, of St. Botolph Lane, in the City, and Great Coram Street, Bloomsbury. Further, Surtees possesses the unusual and doubtful privilege of his works always obtaining a phenomenally high price. The reason for this can hardly be that the supply of his books, in various editions, has been unequal to the demand, for in view of the fact that there are no cheap copies of Surtees his readers are, of necessity, few. He has a special place of joy and honour, garbed in glorious binding, in what the booksellers term " a gentleman's library " at a big country house; but even there, probably, the illustrations are more often looked at than the text. To the general reader, Surtees is merely a name; he may have heard of Mr. Jorrocks and Soapey Sponge, but would find it difficult to explain who these worthies were, and what they did in order to secure the sure place they fill in the great gallery of English fiction.

Why, then, are the works of Surtees always priced at a high figure? The usual answer is " Because of the illustrations by Leech and Alken." That is entirely a fallacious reason. Superb and truly delightful are the plates and woodcuts in question, but they are no better than other examples of the work of these artists which realise a much lower price in the book market. Again, a copy of Surtees's rare first book, *The Horseman's Manual*, which has no illustrations at all, is worth more than one of the novels illustrated by Leech or Alken; and the first edition of *Jorrocks's Jaunts and Jollities*, with twelve mediocre designs by " Phiz," is more valuable than the second edition with Alken's fine coloured engravings, though a copy of the latter was sold recently for a hundred and forty pounds. There is no fixed scale for Surtees prices, and the real reason for the inflated financial value of his books remains a mystery; it is also a matter for regret, because these prohibitive charges militate against the

* *The Bookman*, December, 1922.

author's popularity and prevent him from being read as widely as he deserves.

And now for the man himself and the origin of his curious surname. R. S. Surtees belongs to the county of Durham. His family was of the most remote antiquity in the North, with a pedigree reaching back to Saxon times, when a certain Thane, named Orm, by his wife Ethelritha (daughter of Aldred, Earl of Northumberland) had a daughter, Egfrida, who married Ailsi de Tesia. The name de Tesia was derived from the estates of the family in proximity to the river Tees. In the thirteenth century two of its prominent representatives were known as Ralph and Walter Super Teysam. Later the cognomen was contracted to Sureteys, and in the seventeenth century the novelist's ancestor, Cuthbert of Ebchester, spelt the name Surtees, as it has since remained. Through a long line of descendants, described as of Milkwell Burn, we come to Anthony Surtees (1768-1838), a noted sportsman, of Hamsterley Hall, on the borders of Durham and Northumberland. He married, in 1801, Alice Blackett, of Wylam, and their second son, Robert Smith Surtees, the future novelist, was born in 1803.

The boy was educated at Ovingham, in Northumberland, and Durham Grammar School, and his hunting knowledge was acquired with the foxhounds of Mr. Ralph Lambton, of Merton House, Durham. Being a younger son, however, Surtees had to adopt a profession, and so, on leaving school in 1819, he decided for the Law. He proceeded to London for his training in a solicitor's office. Eventually he bought a partnership in a legal firm at Lincoln's Inn. It proved unsatisfactory, but being fortunate enough to recover his purchase money, Surtees decided to abandon the Law and devote himself to literary pursuits, for his future prospects were considerably changed by the death of his elder brother, Anthony, at Malta, on March 24th, 1831. He was now the prospective heir of Hamsterley, and this same year he started, in conjunction with Rudolph Ackermann, *The New Sporting Magazine*: previously he had contributed in 1830, under the name " Nim South," to the old *Sporting Magazine* some accounts of Mr. Ralph Lambton's foxhounds and other hunting matters. In his new venture, as editor, he eventually secured the aid, as contributor, of the great contemporary sporting writer, " Nimrod."*

---

* *The New Sporting Magazine* was a close imitation, both in style and appearance, of *The Sporting Magazine,* which dated from 1793. The latter regarded its new rival with great dislike, and launched attacks several times on the plea of defending the Surrey Hunt, which had been ridiculed by Surtees in his "Jorrocks" sketches.

In 1831, also, Surtees published his first book, *The Horseman's Manual*, which he dedicated to his old friend and early mentor in the chase, Ralph Lambton. At this date Surtees was living at 27, Lincoln's Inn Fields, and his book was in reality a lawyer's treatise on warranty in relation to horses and on equine law in general. But he was soon to strike upon a new and humorous vein of horse lore. In *The New Sporting Magazine*, May, 1831, he commenced a series of amusing sketches of a Cockney sportsman which developed into *Jorrocks's Jaunts and Jollities*.* The adventures of that great grocer and citizen, with his " large bay-window of a corporation," are for all time—in fact, in the words of his counsel, " Not to know Jorrocks is indeed to argue oneself unknown." Many of Jorrocks's sayings are now classic—" Punctuality is the politeness of princes"; " The Chase—I say, it's one of the balances of the Constitution —I say, it's the sport of kings, the image of war without its guilt "; " To be surrounded by one's friends is in my mind the ' A1 ' of 'uman 'appiness"; " I leaves the flowers of speech to them as is better acquainted with botany. . . I likes plain English, both in eating and talking "; and on the subject of drinks— " Water, a thing I never touch—rots one's shoes, don't know what it would do with one's stomach if it was to get there." It is true, though, that on one occasion Mr. Jorrocks "astonished his stomach " with the Cheltenham waters.

Jorrocks's Jaunts and Jollities were the inspiring origin of *The Pickwick Papers*. It is curious that Forster and other biographers of Dickens make no mention of this obvious fact. Dickens relates that he was approached, in 1835-6, by Chapman and Hall with a scheme that he, in conjunction with Seymour, the artist, should produce a series of sketches relating the adventures of a Nimrod Club (" Nimrod," as we have seen, was a coadjutor with Surtees in *The New Sporting Magazine* wherein Jorrocks had first appeared)—" the members of which were to go out shooting, fishing, and so forth, and getting themselves into difficulties through their want of dexterity." Thus the Pickwick Club replaced the Surrey Hunt and shooting excursions of Jorrocks, and at the outset Dickens followed the proposed plan, though, as he opined would be the case, he eventually broke away on the lines of his own genius " with a freer range of English scenes and people." But Winkle and his adventures with the horse from Rochester and on the ice at Dingley Dell

---

* Jorrocks had an original in the person of a follower of the Surrey Hounds. " He made his début," Surtees relates, " precisely as the original made it to me out hunting with those hounds."

are entirely on the Surtees model. Mr. Jorrocks figured in a legal case like Mr. Pickwick, and it is of interest to compare the two reports, and the similarity of the flowery but violent eloquence of the opposing counsel. Mr. Jorrocks was attacked by Mr. Serjeant Bumptious, Mr. Pickwick by Mr. Serjeant Buzfuz. Later on, Mr. Jorrocks observed, when travelling by " The Age " coach, " there was not even a bit of Christmas at the 'orses' ears "; so with that phrase he was before Mr. Weller, who directed the fat boy, when arranging the mince-pies, " to stick a bit o' Christmas in 'em."

" The outside passengers mounted, the insides took their places, threepences and sixpences were pulled out for the porters, the guard twanged his horn, the coachman turned out his elbow, flourished his whip, caught the point, cried ' All right ! sit tight ! ' and trotted out of the yard."

That is Mr. Jorrocks setting out for Newmarket, not the Pickwickians on the Muggleton coach *en route* for Dingley Dell in the splendid Christmas chapter.

In the character of " The Yorkshireman," who so often accompanies Mr. Jorrocks in his outings and adventures, Surtees probably intended to represent himself, and so was enabled to recount actual experiences of his own. He often, from 1825 onwards, had traversed the Great North Road between London and Durham when coaching was at its highest degree of excellence and the Life of the Road most vivid. Surtees's books are not confined to sport and the humours of country life. They contain many entertaining glimpses of London, Brighton, Margate, and other places. His Londoners, it is interesting to note, talk with their W pronounced as V, and vice versa, in the mode of the Wellers. When Mr. Jorrocks rode forth from Great Coram Street to attend a meet of the Surrey Hunt, the newsboys in the Strand called out : " Crikey, a hunter. . . . Vot a beauty ! Vere do you turn out to-day ? Vere's the stag ? Vot a vip the gemman's got ! " I have never heard it explained how and when this particular flower of Cockney speech faded. If the London boys of 1831 talked like this, why did they not do the same as old men, when they came within our purview or, rather, hearing ? Personally, I only remember meeting one man, a former publican, who spoke in this way of Villiam and so on. Yet, according to Dickens, Surtees, and other contemporary writers, all Londoners of the lower class pronounced the W as V, and V as W, eighty years ago.

Like Dickens, Surtees delighted in the description of gastronomical details and unlimited hospitality, whether at

Christmas or any other time. Witness Mr. Jorrocks's Hunt Breakfast in the kitchen at Great Coram Street. It would have been terrible to read during the food control of a few years ago this menu for a dinner party of eight persons at the same hospitable house : —

" Before both Mr. and Mrs. Jorrocks were two great tureens of mock turtle soup, each capable of holding a gallon, and both full up to the brim. Then there were two sorts of fish ; turbot and lobster sauce, and a great salmon. A round of boiled beef and an immense piece of roast occupied the rear of these . . . . and then came two dishes of grouse, each dish holding three brace. The side dishes consisted of a calf's head hashed, a leg of mutton, chickens, ducks, and mountains of vegetables . . . . plum-puddings, tarts, jellies, pies, and puffs."

Jorrocks's Jaunts and Jollities were not reissued in book form until 1838. This rare first edition with twelve illustrations by " Phiz " is seldom to be seen: it is not in the British Museum Library. The second edition, published in 1843 by Ackermann, contained the fifteen fine aquatints by H. Alken, but not the plate entitled " Jorrocks's Hunt Breakfast." The well-known third edition, also with H. Alken's admirable illustrations in colour, appeared in 1869, long after the author's death. Surtees's friend and chief contributor to *The New Sporting Magazine*, " Nimrod," was also a contributor to *The Quarterly Review* (where his papers on *The Chase, The Turf*, and *The Road* appeared), and the editor of the latter review, John Lockhart, becoming acquainted with Mr. Jorrocks, observed of Surtees : " That fellow could write a good novel if he liked to try." The suggestion was duly passed on by " Nimrod," and acted upon by Surtees, with the result that Mr. Jorrocks reappeared, now as a Master of Foxhounds, in *Handley Cross, or the Spa Hunt*, a novel in three volumes, published by Colburn in 1843. The edition of 1854, with John Leech's famous illustrations, was renamed *Handley Cross, or Mr. Jorrocks's Hunt*. Leech drew his conception of Jorrocks's face and figure from a coachman, named Nicholls, in the service of Lady Louisa Clinton. *Handley Cross* was a very successful work, and Surtees devoted his first substantial literary earnings to building a new bridge in the grounds of Hamsterley Hall; it is still called the Handley Cross Bridge. He had succeeded to the family property in 1838 on the death of his father. He resigned the editorship of *The New Sporting Magazine* in 1836, and after that date lived chiefly in the country, devoting himself to his favourite pursuits of hunting and shooting, but continuing also his literary work.

Mr. Jorrocks reappeared once again—and not quite so successfully as before—as a country gentleman in *Hillingdon Hall, or*

The Cockney Squire (1845). Surtees's next book, *The Analysis of the Hunting Field*, was reprinted from *Bell's Life in London*. These sketches of hunting and hunting characters were intended as a souvenir of the season of 1845-1846— " the best hunting season of modern times." Published in November, 1846, by Rudolph Ackermann at the Eclipse Gallery, 191, Regent Street, this volume was gloriously illustrated by the coloured engravings of Henry Alken—among the finest pictures of hunting ever produced. A magnificent new edition of this book, with all the original illustrations, appeared in 1903.

Surtees's succeeding work, also reprinted from *Bell's Life in London*, was *Hawbuck Grange, or the Sporting Adventures of Thomas Scott, Esq.* (1847), with eight illustrations by " Phiz." It was not so good as his previous stories; but the author was soon to produce his second great creation, *Mr. Sponge's Sporting Tour*. This inimitable work was secured by Harrison Ainsworth for serial issue in *The New Monthly Magazine* (1849-1851). It was not until 1853 that it reappeared in book form with John Leech's illustrations, which show his art at its finest point of humour.*

Mr. Soapey Sponge is as great a triumph of character drawing as Mr. Jorrocks, but of an entirely different psychology. Snob and shifty sportsman, he may be free from the vulgarities of the worthy grocer, but he lacks Jorrocks's hospitable, generous ways, for Mr. Sponge's " dexterity in getting into people's houses was only equalled by the difficulty of getting him out again." This book has the most sustained interest of all Surtees's stories. Its numerous characters—Lord Scamperdale (drawn, like Sir Pitt Crawley, from Sir William Chaytor, of Witton Castle, Co. Durham), Lucy Glitters, the Jawleyfords, the Jozzleburys, Mr. Waffles—are all living creatures. In his amusing account of Mr. Sponge's visit to Jawleyford Court, Surtees successfully challenged Thackeray in the vein of *On Some Country Snobs*. *Mr. Sponge's Sporting Tour* was one of Theodore Roosevelt's favourite books, as he mentions in a letter to Lord Trevelyan (1906).

Surtees's next two books, *Ask Mamma, or the Richest Commoner in England* (1858), and *Plain or Ringlets* (1860), also suggest some comparison with Thackeray. Both are social satires, and sport is not quite so prominent as in the author's other works. Leech furnished most delightful illustrations for

---

* In an interesting letter from Thackeray, published in *Robert Smith Surtees, by Himself* and E. D. Cuming (1924), it is established that Thackeray declined Surtees's proposal to illustrate *Mr. Sponge's Sporting Tour*, and suggested Leech as a suitable artist for the work.

each of these stories. *Plain or Ringlets* describes life at Brighton (where Surtees generally passed part of the winter) at the height of the town's prosperity in the 'fifties. It was dedicated to the author's son. Surtees had married, in 1841, Elizabeth Jane, daughter and co-heir of Addison Fenwick, of Field House, Bishop Wearmouth. She died in 1879. The only son of the marriage, Anthony Surtees, died in 1871, at the age of twenty-three. There were two daughters; the elder, Miss Elizabeth Anne Surtees, died in 1915, and the younger is Eleanor Viscountess Gort, the present owner of Hamsterley Hall.

Surtees was devoted to Hamsterley, and fully realised and carried out his duties as a country gentleman. He was Deputy-Lieutenant for the County of Durham, and High Sheriff in 1856, when he entertained the judges and leading members of the Northern Circuit. He was Chairman of the Shotley Bridge Bench of Magistrates, and frequently presided at the meetings of local agricultural societies. He was a fluent and cultivated speaker. In 1837 he had been a parliamentary candidate for Gateshead. Although he thus undertook many manifold occupations as author, sportsman, and prominent country gentleman, his constitution was never robust. For reasons of health he spent the last winters of his life at Brighton, in rooms at Mutton's famous establishment in the King's Road, and there he died on March 16th, 1864, at the age of sixty-one. His end was sudden. He had been in his usual health, but on the fatal night he was awakened by terrible pain in the region of the heart, and in ten minutes he was dead By a curious coincidence, his father, his elder brother, his only son, and his wife all died in the month of March also. He was buried at Ebchester.

Surtees wrote to the end. His last work, *Mr. Facey Romford's Hounds*, came out in monthly parts, and the first number was published almost simultaneously with the author's death. John Leech was the illustrator, but he, too, died, in October, 1864, before the completion of the serial issue, and so it came about that " Phiz " furnished the remaining illustrations— " Immortal Phiz " who had supplied the first pictures for a Surtees book in 1838. Consequently *Mr. Facey Romford's Hounds* contained designs by both Leech and " Phiz " when published in 1865. Surtees's literary powers suffered no declension as his health failed, and his last book is one of his best.

Surtees is an inimitable delineator of some of the most characteristic, if passing, aspects of English life; and as such he is one of the great band—Thackeray, Dickens, Trollope, Lever, Frank Smedley, Cruikshank, Alken, " Phiz," Leech, and Charles

Keene—who have preserved for all time the life and aspect of those good, solid, comfortable people, who ate and drank freely, rode hard, and had their quivers full, in the first thirty years of the reign of Victoria.

R. S. SURTEES

From a photograph sent by his daughter, Eleanor Viscountess Gort.

[*Page* 102.

WHYTE MELVILLE

From a photograph sent by his daughter, Florence Viscountess Massereene and Ferrard.

WHYTE MELVILLE *

THIS month brings the natal centenary of George John Whyte Melville, novelist and song writer, who was born on June 19th, 1821. On his father's side he was Scotch, the son of John Whyte Melville, of Mount Melville, Strathkinness, Fifeshire, who married Lady Catherine Godolphin Osborne, daughter of the fifth Duke of Leeds. Through his mother the future romance writer was fifth in direct descent from John Churchill, the Duke of Marlborough of military fame and perjured loyalty.

The boy was educated at Eton during the head-mastership of Keate, that preposterous little pedagogue of five feet high whose name is remembered for his brutal flogging powers. The records of Eton would doubtless reveal if Whyte Melville was a pupil there on June 30th, 1832, the day when Keate flogged more than eighty boys and surpassed his own record. It was true the school was very turbulent at that period, and the boys sometimes got even by smashing the head master's desk and giving him a fusillade of rotten eggs. Hawtrey, at that time assistant master at Eton, was tutor to Whyte Melville, who mentions him in his first novel, *Digby Grand* (1853) : —

" No wonder that the old Etonian's heart still warms when he catches sight of the walls of ' College '—no wonder that he remembers, with a vividness after years can never obliterate, each characteristic of the long-past scene. The dreaded Hawtrey, my tutor, by turns loathed and beloved. . . ."

Digby Grand originally appeared in *Fraser's Magazine*, and was written obviously in imitation of the very successful *Pelham* of a good many years earlier. It purported to be the memoirs of a young military gentleman on service abroad and at leisure in town. True enough, assuming the novel to be partly auto-biographical, Whyte Melville on leaving Eton had received a commission in the 93rd Highlanders at the age of eighteen. He exchanged into the Coldstream Guards in 1846, and retired with the rank of Captain three years later.

On the outbreak of the Crimean War he rejoined and volunteered for active service. He was appointed Major of Turkish irregular cavalry. His impressions of the war were given in his fifth novel, *The Interpreter* (1858).

After the conclusion of peace, Whyte Melville settled down to the life of a country gentleman at Boughton, Northampton-shire, where he devoted himself to the sport of fox-hunting, varied by his literary pursuits and golf on occasions at St. Andrews, which was close to his father's estate in Fifeshire.

Whyte Melville had married, in 1847, Charlotte, second daughter of the first Lord Bateman; and the only child of the marriage, Florence, became, in 1870, the wife of the eleventh Viscount Massereene and Ferrard—a great-grandson of John Foster, last Speaker of the Irish House of Commons and subsequently created Lord Oriel.

Sir Herbert Maxwell has stated, in the memoir of his friend he wrote for *The Dictionary of National Biography*, that Whyte Melville's marriage was unhappy and that his resulting disappointment found expression in his literary work, where women are generally pictured in a melancholy and regretful manner. Presumably this statement refers to the novels of modern life, for the trait or reflection in question is not particularly conspicuous in the author's historical and sporting works.

With the publication of *Holmby House* in 1860, Whyte Melville may be said to have attained literary fame. It is still probably his most popular book, and deservedly so, for it is one of the best of the historical romances that have described the great Civil War. It is mainly concerned, of course, with the events that took place in Northamptonshire and Oxford, though it also offers picturesque accounts of the trial and execution of Charles the First. The author wrote of the King sympathetically as

" the ideal of a chivalrous, high-minded monarch, who was worthy of the position he occupied and the devotion he commanded, who was no unfit centre around which grouped themselves the proudest, the bravest, the noblest, the most enthusiastic aristocracy that ever failed to save a sovereign."

Whyte Melville, himself the finest type of aristocrat, a chivalrous and high-souled gentleman, was a cavalier born two centuries out of date. Had he been living in the seventeenth century the Stuarts would have found in him the most devoted of adherents. As it was, he could only express his devotion in narratives of romance. He seems like a reincarnation of those gallant cavaliers he conjures up amid the setting of Holmby House, Boughton Hall, and Naseby Field.

Having paid tribute to the charm of Charles the First in *Holmby House*, Whyte Melville two years later expressed his homage to the White King's unhappy grandmother, Mary Queen of Scots, in *The Queen's Maries* (1862). Here is a characteristic passage from the book illustrating his attitude of romance toward the Stuart Queen:

" But what of the Queen of the Roses, the Mary of Maries, the noblest princess in Europe, the loveliest woman in the world? . . . Still the stately flower bloomed on, fair and fragrant under the pure air of heaven, fair and fragrant in the close confinement and the darkened daylight of a prison-house. But the storm was brewing the while low down in the southern sky; the storm that was about to gather so dark and pitiless, to burst at last in its fury over the Queen of the Roses, and lay that lovely head upon the cold earth, beautiful and majestic even in the pale agony of death."

The Queen's Maries was written at " Bartrams," Hampstead, and from this address, where he lived for two or three years, the author dated, in June, 1862, the dedication of his romance to Agnes Strickland, who fully shared his intense enthusiasm for the ill-fated Queen of Scots.

Three entirely different novels had been produced in 1861 between the two Stuart romances, the best being *Market Harborough*. This work and *Holmby House* form the author's pæan of praise to the county of his adoption—beautiful Northamptonshire, with its sylvan splendours and green undulating expanses of rich pasture. *Holmby House* contains exquisite little pen-pictures of the rich wooded country-side of stately Althorp and Boughton. *Market Harborough* is pre-eminently the novel of the Pytchley Hunt. It contains the memorable description of a hunting morning in the chapter entitled " Hail! Smiling Morn."

Another popular novel, *The Gladiators*, appeared in 1863. Five more books succeeded, and then in 1869 Whyte Melville published his collected *Songs and Verses*. He would have been the last to claim a position in the ranks of authentic poets: nevertheless he had considerable poetical gifts. His lyrical work was as diversified as his prose. He wrote equally well romantic ballads, sad little songs, and gay hunting ditties. And he could paint a picture in a line or two: —

> " 'Twas yet but May, and here and there
>   Pink and white the blossoms fell,
> Quivering down through the summer air
> On the shaven sward so trim and bare.
>   Oh! I remember well
>   The very network of the tree
> And its shadow dancing on her and me,
>   My old love, in the garden chair,
>   Looking upward soft and shy,
> With her oval face and her rippling hair,
> And the rich white dress she used to wear,
>   And her work laid idly by.
> 'Tis strange to think of now, and yet
> 'Twere stranger, harder to forget."
>   .   .   .   .   .   .

" Days and months drag wearily by,
    Scenes and shadows, they haunt me still,
The starlit stream and the wintry sky,
    And the day dying out on the crest of the hill."

Whyte Melville's best-known poem is seldom credited to him.
For the lines were set to music by a talented composer and the
song—ever and still a favourite of Melba's—is known as " Tosti's
Good-bye." Yet it might more reasonably be called " Whyte
Melville's *Good-bye*," for the words were his :—

" Falling leaf and fading tree,
Lines of white in a sullen sea,
Shadows rising on you and me ;
The swallows are making them ready to fly,
Wheeling out on a windy sky,
Good-bye, summer ! Good-bye, good-bye ! " . . .

In the remaining eight years of his life Whyte Melville wrote
eleven more books. His total output during the course of his
literary life was twenty-eight works of widely different subject
and style produced during a quarter of a century. That was a
remarkable achievement, but Whyte Melville always regarded it
lightly and as of no importance in comparison with his life in the
hunting field and as a country gentleman. Literature to him was
a side issue. He never frequented literary circles, but preferred
the society of sporting and military men. He wrote books simply
because the gift was in him and had to find expression. There
was no financial necessity; the money he received from his publications he gave away in charity. An institute for working men
in Northampton, for which he provided five hundred pounds from
this source of revenue, still bears his name. He particularly liked
to provide recreation-rooms for the benefit of grooms and stable-
boys.

Whyte Melville's last years were passed at Tetbury in
Gloucestershire. His house, Barton-Abbotts, was pleasant,
except for the fact that it was rather too near the churchyard. A
friend ventured to remark on this objection one day. " Yes,"
replied Whyte Melville, " perhaps it is for some tastes; but the
closer the better for a hunting man : they will not have so far to
carry him." A strange and fateful remark. Shortly after, on
December 5th, 1878, Whyte Melville went hunting in the Vale
of the White Horse. He was mounted on his favourite old horse,
Shah. During a run there was an accident. The rider was
thrown on his head and instantaneously killed. Whyte Melville's
body was conveyed to his house at Tetbury, and a few days later
was buried in the adjoining churchyard—" not far to carry him,"
as the hunting man had previsioned. His pall-bearers were the

Duke of Beaufort, the Marquis of Worcester, the Earl of Rosslyn, the Earl of Suffolk, Lord Wolverton, and five other friends.

Sir Herbert Maxwell finely remarks upon the passing of Whyte Melville: " There was one high-minded gentleman the less in this world—one generous soul the more among the shades."

JAMES GRANT.*

THIS year marks the birth centenary of James Grant, the military novelist, who was born on August 1st, 1822, in Morningside Road, Edinburgh. He must not be confused with his namesake and contemporary and fellow-Scotsman, James Grant (1802-1879), the editor of *The Morning Advertiser*, and an acquaintance of Dickens in his early days as a parliamentary reporter. During their lifetime there was, inevitably, confusion about the two James Grants, much to their indignation, because both were authors and their styles widely different: the one wrote dashing romances of love and war, the other religious books bearing titles such as *God is Love* and *Grace and Glory*. Consequently the fury of each author can be imagined when some remark was made about the amazing fertility and versatility of James Grant who, within a few days, had produced two widely different works —the first, perchance, relating the reprehensible escapades and amours of a gay young cavalier in the time of Charles the Second, and the second providing devotional solace for people who never read novels.

As Sir Walter Scott said, " Every Scottishman has a pedigree," and that of James Grant, the military novelist, now claims some attention. He was in direct descent from John Grant of Freuchie, the common ancestor also of the Ogilvie-Grants, Earls of Seafield. The novelist's great-grandfather, Alexander Grant, of Corrimony in Urquhart, Inverness, was a Jacobite of 1745; he married Jean Ogilvy of Kempcairn, and their son (the novelist's grandfather), James Grant (1743-1835), became a noted Scotch Advocate, and the author of *Thoughts on the Origin and Descent of the Gael and Observations on the Poems of Ossian*, 1814. He had a gift for friendship, and though he lived to the age of ninety-two, " he retained his faculties to the last, and from the extent and variety of his attainments was a delightful companion." Like his father before him, he was an ardent Jacobite; but he was born too late for any active part in the attempts to restore the Stuarts, and his Jacobitism was probably that of the kind described in Scott's *Redgauntlet*. However, it may be assumed that it was from his lips that James Grant the younger gleaned those Stuart stories and that enthusiasm for the Jacobite cause which recur so constantly in his literary work, for the future romance writer was thirteen by the time his picturesque old grandfather departed this life.

The novelist was the son of Captain John Grant, of the 92nd (Gordon Highlanders), by his marriage with Mary Ann Watson. The mother provided further interesting consanguinity, for her father, Captain Andrew Watson, of the 57th, was a second cousin of Sir Walter Scott; and, through the Veitches of Peeblesshire, James Grant's Border strain of blood was to bring him a distinguished third cousin in the person of the present Earl Haig. Sir Walter Scott, James Grant, and Lord Haig all have a common ancestor in Sir John Swinton of Swinton. It was Mrs. Margaret Swinton who figured in Walter Scott's tale, *My Aunt Margaret's Mirror.*

James Grant's mother died when he was very young, and his father, Captain Grant, being appointed to a command in Newfoundland in 1833, took his three young sons with him. Six years were spent in transatlantic barracks, where no doubt the youthful James acquired much military information which proved useful in later literary work. The family returned to Scotland in 1839, and in the following year, James Grant, at the age of eighteen, was gazetted to an ensigncy in the 62nd Foot on the recommendation of Lord Hill, with whom his father had served in the Napoleonic War. He joined the provisional battalion at Chatham, but his actual experience of the Army lasted but a short time, for he resigned his commission in 1843. He then entered the office of Mr. Rhind, architect, of Edinburgh, where he soon became a skilful draughtsman.

At this same time his literary abilities were developing, and he commenced to write *The Romance of War, or the Highlanders in Spain*, which was largely based on anecdotes related to him by his father, who had fought with the 92nd (Gordon Highlanders) during the Peninsular War. For a narrative at second hand, the work was excellently done, vivacious and picturesque in style, displaying the lights and shades of the ever changing panorama of the great campaign, and incidentally detailing every aspect of active military service of the period described. The book was published in 1846, and though the young author of twenty-four only received, it is said, twenty pounds from the publisher, Colburn, it was very successful, so much so that a continuation was called for, which duly appeared in 1847, relating the services of the Gordon Highlanders in France and Belgium to the time of Waterloo. In 1847 he also published *The Phantom Regiment*, and now successfully started on his literary road, James Grant, during the next fourteen years, produced a series of books of remarkable merit in view of their number. Inevitably he exhausted his vein of talent as time went on; in later life he often wrote three novels a year. His total output in forty years was sixty-one novels and twelve works of historical records. His amount of fiction thus exceeded that written by G. P. R. James, who was the prolific author of fifty-six novels; but James's miscellaneous works bring his total to eighty-seven books, thus beating James Grant's total of seventy-three. These figures may be impressive as evidence of energy, ingenuity, and mental power, but are deplorable from an artistic point of view. No man has it in him to write more than twelve or so superlative books.

To return to Grant's early and best work, perhaps the most characteristic of his dashing style is *Harry Ogilvie, or the Black Dragoons*, a most excellent romance of Edinburgh in 1650-1, when the youthful Charles the Second was in the austere grip of the Covenanters. Equally good is *The Scottish Cavalier* (1850), which pictures Edinburgh nearly forty years later, and relates the adventures of the loyalists who fought for King James the Second (and Seventh of Scotland) after his downfall. This story introduces Annie Laurie (one of the four daughters of Sir Robert Laurie, Bart., of Maxwelton) and Finland, who wrote the beautiful song bearing her name: but alas! for romance, the fickle lady married another, Colonel Craigdarroch, an officer in the service of William the Third. *The Scottish Cavalier* may claim to have influenced the imagination of Mr. Thomas Hardy, for he has told me it was one of his favourite books in boyhood, and seventy years later he still retains vivid memories of the scenes and characters in this picturesque romance. *Jane Séton; Bothwell, or the Days of Mary Queen of Scots*; *The Yellow Frigate*; *Philip Rollo*—a tale of the Thirty Years' War; *Frank Hilton*; *Legends of the Black Watch* were all written in the 'fifties, and represent Grant's best work in fiction. He was also at this time writing books of a more strictly historical nature, such as *The Memoirs and Adventures of Sir J. Hepburn; The Memoirs of Montrose; and Memorials of the Castle of Edinburgh*.

Hollywood Hall, 1857, is a tale of the Jacobite rising of 1715, and incidentally includes the escape of Princess Clementina Sobieski from Innsbruck to Bologna before her marriage to James the Third—an incident which has been utilised in later years by Mr. A. E. W. Mason in his romance, *Clementina*. In *The Adventures of Rob Roy*, 1864, James Grant invaded the realms of his famous cousin, Walter Scott, and, further, provided a ghostly adventure in the style of *Wandering Willie's Tale* from *Redgauntlet*. Grant wrote ghost stories well and impressively, for he treated the supernatural seriously. His best essay of the kind, *The Phantom Regiment*, is wonderfully well done—the storm, the scenic setting prelude the apparitions with a fitting artistry. Two other short tales in this vein, *The Dead Tryst* and *A Haunted Life*, appeared in 1866. James Grant has been compared by some critics to G. P. R. James, but in reality he approximates much more closely to Harrison Ainsworth, both in mentality and style. James was ponderous, pompous, and picturesque; both Ainsworth and Grant were picturesque, but gay and light-hearted; they were both ardent Jacobites; both could write a good ghost story or relate a mysterious incident with the right atmosphere, and both, despite their gaiety, had a taste for depicting the *macabre*, scenes of bloodshed and human suffering.

James Grant married in 1856 a daughter of James Brown, LL.D., well known as the author of *The History of the Highlands and of the Highland Clans*, and editor of *The Scots' Magazine* and *The Encyclopædia Britannica*. There were two sons, James, who died before his father, and Roderick, who became a priest in the Roman Catholic Church.* James Grant himself joined the Church of Rome in 1875. During the more eventful years of his life, Grant lived at 26, Danube Street, Edinburgh, from about 1856 to 1870. At that time he busied himself with many interests in addition to his literary work. He founded in 1852 the National Association for the Vindication of Scottish Rights, which received a good deal of satirical attention from *Punch* and the comic journals. He was one of the earliest and most enthusiastic members of the Volunteers, becoming a lieutenant of the 1st Highland Company. He ardently supported Lord Archibald Campbell's agitation for the retention of the military bonnet as the national head-dress of Scotsmen. He became an authority on matters of military costume, and was consulted by the War Office; many of the facings now worn by the British Army emanate from him, and his suggestions before a committee of the War Office bore fruit years later on the formation of the Territorial system. The plans for the proposed alteration of Edinburgh Castle were also submitted to him for his approval.†

---

* Father Roderick Grant is now Chaplain to Lord Petre at Ingatestone Hall, Essex—the scene of Miss Braddon's *Lady Audley's Secret*.
† His brother, John Grant, was Marchmont Herald, and father of Mr. Francis J. Grant, now Rothesay Herald in the Court of the Lord Lyon, Edinburgh.

James Grant was essentially and entirely a Scotsman, and it is therefore difficult to explain why he decided, in 1870, to leave his native city where he had lived most of his life, and the beauties and antiquities of which he had described in many a book. In Edinburgh he was a notable personality and had hosts of friends. In London he was no one in particular, and seemingly unknown in literary and social circles, for his name does not appear in any memoirs of the period. He settled at 25, Tavistock Road, Westbourne Park, in those days a new and unattractive district arising from rough fields. It was then on the extreme edge of London and remote from the important and interesting centres of the capital. There, however, James Grant lived for the last seventeen years of his life, producing every year two or three books, which could not have been very successful, for even the names of most of them are forgotten now. He saved no money during the days of his prosperity in Edinburgh when his best work was written, and he died, almost in poverty, on May 5th, 1887, at the age of sixty-four, the cause of death being liver trouble and jaundice. He lies buried in the Roman Catholic Cemetery at Kensal Green, far from the romantic scenes of his native land which he had loved lang syne.

FRANK SMEDLEY.*

WITH the passing of the Victorian Era many of the lesser stars which once shone brightly in that great literary epoch have become dim and almost forgotten. It is doubtful if the rising generation reads, to any great extent, G. P. R. James, Charles Lever, Fennimore Cooper, James Grant, Mayne Reid, and Frank Smedley, to mention but a few once popular names. Many elderly and middle-aged persons, however, have friendly memories of these authors' works, and particularly of Frank Smedley's. They recall *Frank Fairlegh* and *Lewis Arundel*, but would be hard put to it to say what manner of man he was who wrote these books, for Frank Smedley, unlike some of his famous literary contemporaries, never figured before the public personally, and his private life was entirely unknown to his readers. And of those readers, then or later, how few were aware that this man who wrote so gaily, and to the life, of hunting and horse-racing, wild escapades in town and country, practical jokes, duels and poaching affrays, love-making and marriage, was a life-long cripple and invalid who never did and never could indulge in any active exercise and adventure, and whose physical afflictions placed a barrier between him and domestic life. Gaiety and activity permeate his novels : sadness, bodily pain, and bitter regrets were the portion of the man. Such a triumph of mind over matter, inasmuch that this man lived entirely in imagination the life he would have led in the flesh had Fate permitted, is surely worthy of attention and some brief record, although the story of his short existence, with its restricted scope and compulsory inaction, can present no very eventful scenes.

Frank Smedley was not one of the great majority of authors who write to make a living or some money—which is by no means the same thing. As some compensation for his bodily ills he was always well endowed with the goods of this world and many valued friends. His family on both sides belonged to the upper middle classes, some of his near relatives were wealthy, and others were scholarly and literary. The novelist's grandfather, the Rev. Edward Smedley (1750-1825), Rector of Powderham and North Bovey, Devon, was for over forty years (1774-1820) a master at Westminster School, where another of the name, his nephew, the Rev. James Smedley, was also an usher, from 1797

---

* *The Fortnightly Review*, February, 1915.

H

to 1804, before removing to Wrexham School. Edward Smedley was the author of *Erin*, a geographical and descriptive poem, 1810. By his wife, Hannah, *née* Bellas* (there is a tablet to the memory of both in the cloisters of Westminster Abbey), he had three sons. The eldest, Edward (1788-1836), like his father, became a clergyman, but more particularly devoted himself to teaching until premature ill-health sapped all his energies. He was a literary man, the author of some histories and of many poems both serious and humorous, and he acted as editor of *The Encyclopædia Metropolitana*. His wife, Mary Hume, was a grand-aunt of " Lewis Carroll," and two of his children attained some literary success: Menella Bute Smedley (1820-1877) wrote both prose and verse, and her sister, Elizabeth, Mrs. Hart, was the author of many books for girls. The sad life of the second Edward Smedley in some respects foreshadowed that of his nephew Frank, the novelist; he was the victim of strange, insidious disease, and produced his literary work often amid conditions of severe physical pain, and, like his nephew, died between forty and fifty years of age. Far more fortunate in matters of health and wealth was his brother, Francis Smedley (1791-1859), a fine, handsome man, who practised successfully as a solicitor at 12, Ely Place, where for some years he and his family resided. He also held the office of High Bailiff of Westminster and other emoluments.

Francis Smedley married, in 1817, Frances Sarah, daughter of George Ellison,† of Alfred House, Marlow, and their only child, Francis Edward—better known as Frank—Smedley, was born on October 4th, 1818. His birth took place in his mother's old home, a spacious house in Marlow High Street, which in recent years has been adapted for the post office, and a fortnight later he was baptised in the parish church of Marlow, situated so picturesquely on the banks of the Thames.

At his birth Frank Smedley was a fine child of normal development, but in his early infancy he was attacked by a strange paralytic disease—one report traces it to a nurse's carelessness in allowing the infant to fall from her arms, and another to a carriage accident—which retarded his growth and eventually affected all his physical faculties. Its progress, if slow, was

---

* She was a daughter of the eccentric George Bellas, Registrar in Doctors' Commons; and a domestic tyrant who treated his wife and daughters as slaves. See Beloe's *The Sexagenarian*, 1817. George Bellas was the ancestor also of George Bellas Greenough, President of the Geological Society, and Guillermo Billinghurst, President of Peru.

† A step-brother of Mrs. Smedley's was the late Canon Ellison, father of the Rev. J. H. Ellison, now Rector of St. Michael's, Cornhill, and of General Ellison, C.B.

insidious, and in time, in addition to being unduly small in figure with some malformation of the spine, he lost the entire use of his legs, and in his latter days was compelled to use a wheeled chair, both indoors and out. From his youth, too, he had to wear, day and night, a sort of undercoat made of steel to support the feeble frame. Smedley's boyhood was consequently a sad period; school was out of the question, and he was debarred from enjoying the vigorous sports for which he yearned. But he was always bright and cheerful, and when he was only six years old and confined to the rather dismal house in Ely Place, an aunt, in a contemporary letter, describes him as " a most excellent companion." He was until the age of fourteen educated privately at home (at first by his mother), and then went to a private tutor, the Rev. George Millett, at 89, Montpelier Road, Brighton. Even here, however, the boy's physical disabilities were found incompatible with active association with companions of his own age, and he was removed after a few months. But during his short stay at Mr. Millett's he made effective use of his powers of observation, and utilised his experiences there very skilfully in *Frank Fairlegh*, as will be seen presently. He was next placed under the tuition of his second cousin, the Rev. Edward Arthur Smedley (1804-1890), Vicar of Chesterton, Cambridge, who, like so many members of the family, indulged in the publication of some of his literary compositions.

His education completed, the next few years were the darkest of Frank Smedley's life. To follow any profession was impossible for him, and the lonely boy was thrown back upon his vivid imagination, romantic and full of unattainable desires. His father was occupied with his business affairs, and his mother, a talented woman, was much addicted to the pleasures of society, in which, of course, her invalid son could take but a very small part. The family now lived alternately at 40, Jermyn Street and Nyn Park, near Northaw, a beautiful place with charming gardens, the house, built in 1774, succeeding the sixteenth-century building occupied by Ambrose, Earl of Warwick. Here Frank Smedley, driving in his pony carriage, was able to enjoy the sight of the country he loved so much, though ever debarred from its sports; a curious pleasure of his always was to purchase the latest thing in sporting guns, fishing rods, and riding accessories, which, of course, were never used. Nyn Park and the surrounding county of Hertfordshire evidently inspired all the country-life scenes of Smedley's books. The " Heathfield Park " of *Frank Fairlegh*, the " Broadhurst Park " of *Lewis Arundel*, and the " Coverdale Park " of *Harry*

Coverdale's Courtship are all in " H-shire." He was beginning to find there were some consolations in his seemingly dark lot—the joy of the beauty of earth was his, and friendship.

It was friendship, indeed, which proved the mental salvation of Frank Smedley and found the right outlet for his abilities and a real interest for his limited life—a literary career. During his early manhood one of his chief pleasures had been to carry on a frequent correspondence with three sympathetic girl cousins, Miss Smedleys, though not sisters. They were all about the same age as himself: Menella Bute Smedley was his chief correspondent, and the other two were Millicent (who later became Mrs. John Crompton) and Fanny, married to William Walton. These young ladies, realising that their cousin wrote an excellent letter, full of graphic description, power of observation, delineation of character, and keen sense of humour, suggested—as an expedient for occupying his enforced leisure and diverting his thoughts from himself—that he should write some sketches of incident and character, utilising his own experiences. These experiences were small, certainly, but the most eventful having occurred during his brief stay at the private tutor's at Brighton, he, on adopting his cousins' suggestion, set about to describe his life there. This was the origin of *Frank Fairlegh*. The sketches, under the title of *Scenes from the Life of a Private Pupil*, commenced to appear in *Sharpe's London Magazine* in May, 1846, and attained immediate success and popularity, for here was something original and lively. As the author pointed out in a later preface to the work, there had been endless books dealing with school and college life, but " the mysteries of that paradise of public-school-fearing mammas—a private tutor's—yet continued unrevealed." And reveal them he did with all the brilliance of his imagination playing upon a substratum of actual experience of that phase of life whereof " ragging " is the Attic savour. At the request of the editor of the magazine the sketches were converted into a tale and extended to a length far beyond the original intention of the author, for, in addition to his chronic debility of health, he was now suffering from rheumatic gout.

The characters of *Frank Fairlegh* were largely drawn from life. Mr. Millett, the private tutor at Brighton, appears under the thinnest of disguises as " Dr. Mildman, of (Bright) Helmstone." And though, later on, Smedley took care to emphasise the fact that the characters of " Cumberland " and " Wilford " were entirely fictitious, he admitted that the other *dramatis personæ* of the work were more or less inspired by living models. The original of Freddy Coleman was Frederick Charsley, Registrar of Eton. The incident of the practical jokers ringing the Curfew bells and alarming the inhabitants of " Hillingford " by false rumours of fire actually occurred at Beaconsfield. Some interesting references to his composition of *Frank Fairlegh* are contained in a letter Smedley addressed at this date, 1846, to his cousin, Mrs. Walton, who, it may be noted in passing, was the sister of the Rev. E. A. Smedley, at whose vicarage at Chesterton, near Cambridge, Frank Smedley, during frequent visits, acquired the material for the scenes of university life which are pictured so well in *Frank Fairlegh*. Writing from 40, Jermyn Street, he tells Mrs. Walton : —

" You are right in your conjecture about the original of 'Clara Saville,' altho' I have gone beyond truth when I talk of faultless features, etc. ; the ' trustful look observable in the eyes of a dog ' was a peculiarity, and a very endearing and touching one, in the expression of the original. The entire character is in great measure sketched from hers, tho' not exclusively, or too closely. I can scarcely say (for I am still at work upon her, and my puppets often slightly alter in the making, assuming, as it were, in spite of me, a sort of individuality of their own) how like or unlike it may turn out, or how I may succeed in drawing a woman's character at all. I ought to do it well, I suppose, if experience is of any use, for even you do not know *all* the romances of my life, or can imagine the strange and unlikely things which have come under my notice : some day, when such events are matters of history, and you and I are growing old and garrulous, you shall own that I have reason for what I say. Sharpe wants me to publish *Frank Fairlegh* in monthly numbers, and Phiz is anxious to illustrate it, but I have as yet come to no decision about it. Everybody tells me my head will be turned by all these fine things, but I do not believe them, for it feels pretty much in the same place as usual."

When *Frank Fairlegh* was reissued complete in sixteen monthly numbers with green covers, now very rare, it was illustrated, not by Phiz, but by George Cruikshank, whose thirty excellent designs also appeared in the first edition in book form, 1850, published by Hall and Virtue, and in many subsequent reprints. The work was naturally dedicated " To M.U.S. and M.B.S."—Millicent and Menella Smedley, the cousins who, as already related, first suggested the idea of the story to the author's mind. To them he paid a warm tribute of acknowledgment in his dedicatory letter, saying therein that by their advice to him to adopt a literary career they had " contributed to the happiness of one whose sphere, both of duties and pleasures, Providence has seen fit to limit."

Upon a literary career he was now definitely and in earnest adventured; and in 1848 he commenced *Lewis Arundel: or the*

Railroad of Life, as a serial in *Sharpe's London Magazine,* of which periodical he became editor in November, 1847, at the request of the proprietors.* The tale was subsequently issued in parts, and published in book form by Hall and Virtue in 1852, with admirable illustrations by Phiz. The latter part of *Lewis Arundel* was written when Smedley was enduring great pain after a serious illness in 1851. Writing to Mrs. Walton he said: —

" After four months' pain and annoyance the said illness is now conquered, and its effects disappearing one by one (except certain ideas which illness puts into one's brain, and which are, perhaps, the reason why such evils are sent at all). . . . The only danger now will be in fancying myself quite well, and doing more than I ought, but as I am aware of this danger, it will be my own fault if I do not guard against it. I am finishing *Lewis,* the end whereof will appear in September, and then what to do I know not. I wish not to write another book yet, but something I must do, or alas! for my independence. Literature is a poor profession as far as money is concerned, unless a man draws a very high prize, but to do that requires the greatest talent of the day."

Lewis Arundel is undoubtedly Smedley's best work, for despite the somewhat too Admirable Crichtonian qualities of the hero, the book contains much excellent humour and clever character drawing—character of its period, be it remembered— and reproduces with almost photographic reality the life and atmosphere of the Early Victorian era. Here we see the social life of the 'forties in town, at opera, dinner-party, and in the park; here, too, is the country-house life of the time, and that abroad, when the travels of the upper classes still retained some of the conditions of Le Grand Tour of the previous century; and here, also, are glimpses of the Chartist unrest at home and the Austrian-Italian complications on the Continent. The book may, indeed, be regarded as a sidelight upon history when the time comes for the social life of the Victorian era to be studied historically and in an impartial manner. It is too much the custom now to regard Early Victorianism as a period when furniture, art, and aspirations were ugly, narrow, and Pecksniffian. It is true that after the laxity of the Georgian era there was a willing reaction to an artificial moral public state of mind, yet the Early Victorian period was a great one inasmuch as it coincided with a remarkable fructification of genius of all kinds among exceptional men and women of the country. In addition, there survived in the 'forties some great names of an earlier time, and many people who remembered the stirring epochs of the French Revolution and of Trafalgar and Waterloo.

---

* Two aunts, Eliza and Anna Smedley, who lived a good deal with Frank and his parents, used to assist the editor in transcribing and other work connected with the Magazine.

Consequently, the social life of the period is of much interest, and a book which reflects its manners, customs, and trend of thought so faithfully as *Lewis Arundel* is certainly not ephemeral. And what a different world from ours it pictures. The very character of the hero, his stilted code of conduct and honour, his sensitive pride (which would be a sad disqualification in these hustling days), his airs and attitudes with folded arms and quivering nostrils (" he is like a bad-tempered horse," as someone observed to the present writer)—all this, which his contemporaries accepted as quite normal, is conclusive evidence of the great gulf that divides us from their day. And those arch young ladies, with their ringlets, voluminous skirts and tiny pert parasols, their flirtations and faints and fragile femininity—what a truly amazing change (and not for the better) to the athletic high-school girl, big-limbed and strident, or the shrieking suffragette of 1914. There is very little doubt but that the three heroines of *Lewis Arundel*—" Annie Grant," " Laura Peyton," and " Rose Arundel "—were drawn in the main from the author's cousins, Millicent,* Fanny, and Menella Smedley before mentioned. It is possible that the amusing incident of the "Persian Prince " hoax in *Lewis Arundel* may have suggested the almost identical and completely successful joke which was perpetrated in real life by a party of young Englishmen upon the officers of H.M.S. " Dreadnought " some years ago.

In 1849 there appeared a volume entitled *Seven Tales by Seven Authors*, edited by Frank Smedley, who, in addition, wrote the story called *The Mysteries of Redgrave Court*; the remaining six contributors comprised G. P. R. James, Martin F. Tupper, Mrs. S. C. Hall, Miss Pardoe, Mrs. Burbury, and the editor's cousin, Menella Smedley. The book was produced for the sole benefit of a literary lady in monetary difficulties—a friend of Smedley's and James's.

In 1852 Smedley resigned the editorship of *Sharpe's London Magazine* owing to ill-health, and was succeeded in that capacity by Mrs. S. C. Hall, who announced that she would commence " a three-part tale from the pen of Frank Fairlegh." This was *The Marrying Man*, the work now known as *Harry Coverdale's Courtship*. But concurrently with the commencement of the tale, in 1853, Mrs. Hall abandoned the editorship of the magazine and the continuation therein of her own serial tale, *Helen Lyndsey*. Frank Smedley then resumed control of the magazine, and the following notice was issued: " Mrs. S. C. Hall having

---

* Frank Smedley was deeply attached to his cousin Millicent. His poem, *For M. S.*, in *Gathered Leaves*, explains all.

adopted the unprecedented step of refusing to continue the story of *Helen Lyndsey* . . . we feel it a duty we owe to the readers of *Sharpe's Magazine* to present them with *Marley*, in order to compensate them, as far as lies in our power, for the abrupt and unceremonious breaking off of the previous narrative." Three chapters of *Marley* followed, but Mrs. Hall threatening legal proceedings (on what grounds is not apparent), this tale also abruptly concluded. The real reason for these commotions in *Sharpe's Magazine* was that Smedley some time earlier had commenced a short novel, advertised for publication under the title of *A Cloud and its Silver Lining*. Illness prevented the author from completing it at the appointed time, Christmas, 1852, and the manuscript had to be laid aside for several months. Just as Smedley resumed his work Mrs. Hall published a story with the same title he had hit upon, and so forestalled him. As she had copyrighted the title in question, Smedley was compelled to change his primary one to *The Fortunes of the Colville Family* when his little book appeared in 1853. In the preface he dealt at some length with this dispute he had had with Mrs. Hall in a humorous manner—though his resentment was keen—concluding with the words: " We hereby make over to the authoress of *A Trap to Catch a Sunbeam* all interest in clouds, mists, fogs, vapours, Wills-o'-the-Wisp, rainbows, halos, and other meteorological phenomena available for the purposes of metaphorical nomenclature."

The continuation of *Harry Coverdale's Courtship* was postponed for a time, as Smedley was now occupied, as much as his health permitted, with editorial work. In addition to *Sharpe's Magazine*, to which he also contributed many short pieces and humorous replies to correspondence, Smedley acted as the editor of *George Cruikshank's Magazine* during its brief career in 1854. This unfortunate speculation was engineered by Bogue, the publisher, who still had great faith in the " drawing " powers of this unique artist. But Cruikshank was now in the most impossible mood of his strange life, and handicapped and sacrificed his art to the fanatical fads and crusades he pursued and waged with the full force of his ardent and unstable temperament. He had just issued his delightful illustrations to *The Fairy Library*, but he had taken the liberty to alter the text of these ancient tales to make them serve as total abstinence tracts exhibiting the dire results and crimes arising from the use of alcohol! Dickens cut up this new and spurious propaganda by the " little people " in a paper in *Household Words* (October, 1853) entitled *Frauds on the Fairies*. This caused the collapse of

Cruikshank's *Fairy Library*, and so when his magazine was started he, following his old custom as in the days of *Ainsworth's Magazine* and the row with Bentley, utilised its pages for a personal and ponderous reply to Dickens's strictures. Fads and feuds, indeed, was the policy of the new periodical. The first number commenced a series of pictorial tirades against tobacco-smoking, and Cruikshank seriously approached " Cuthbert Bede " with a view to his writing up to the artist's designs an article against the evils of sucking the handles of sticks and umbrellas, particularly in public conveyances. Such was the unpromising material Frank Smedley was called upon to edit, and, of course, he found it impossible to make a success of this new phase of journalism, where his own work chiefly consisted in writing up to the cuts supplied to him. Despite the cleverness of the artist's pictures—such as " Passing Events, or the Tail of the Comet of 1853 "—*George Cruikshank's Magazine* only ran to two numbers, January and February, 1854. When the magazine was projected, although Cruikshank had previously illustrated *Frank Fairlegh,* artist and editor had never met, and Smedley gave an amusing account of their first meeting to " Cuthbert Bede."*

George Cruikshank's Magazine was also the cause of Smedley's first meeting with Edmund Yates, who became his intimate friend. Yates, then a young man of about twenty-two, was sent by Bogue to call upon Smedley, to talk over and arrange various matters connected with the projected magazine. Like Cruikshank, Yates was only familiar with Smedley's books, and he expected to find their author a strong, brusque, rather horsey personage. His account of the interview, in addition to being amusing, is of value, for it presents the most intimate first-hand account extant of Smedley's personal appearance and manner, to which is added, by later knowledge, a critical estimate of the novelist's character. Arrived at 40, Jermyn Street, Yates proceeds to narrate : —

" I was ushered into the presence of a gentleman, whom, even in the dim light of a shaded lamp standing on the table by his elbow, I could tell to be suffering under some malformation, as he sat in his wheel-chair —a little man, with a peculiar, clever face ; piercing eyes, never moving from the person he was addressing ; a manner beginning in earnestness, then straying into banter ; a voice beginning in harshness, and modulating into pleasantest cadence ; a bearing which, in its endeavour to be thoroughly independent, seemed leaning towards repulsion, and yet which—spite of itself, as it seemed—was indefinably attractive. . . . I think that this kindness of heart, veiled occasionally under an affecta-

---

* This and "Cuthbert Bede's" history of his relations with the artist will be found in Blanchard Jerrold's *Life of George Cruikshank*.

tion of worldly-mindedness, and a little cynicism very badly sustained, was the ruling spirit of his life. He was never happy save when doing a kindness to someone—never pleased save when he had some little pet scheme of beneficence, which he would bring out as though he were ashamed of it; while his quivering lips and brimming eyes belied the assumed roughness of his voice and manner. He was soft-hearted to a degree; indeed, converse with him had a sanctifying and hallowing influence. His physical malady had kept his intercourse with the world so restricted, that while his mind was full, strong, and manly, his experiences of certain sides of life were as pure and unsullied as those of a young girl. . . . With all the masculinity of his writings (and it is allowed that there are very few writers who, in certain phases of description, notably of the hunting-field and the racecourse, have ever equalled, while certainly none have ever surpassed him), his mind was, to a certain degree, feminine. He had the strong likings and dislikings, petulances, love of small jokes, desire of praise, and irritation at small annoyances, which are frequently found in women; but, on the other hand, he had a magnanimity, an amount of patient long-suffering, and a courage both moral and physical, such as are given to few men. I knew, I believe, most of the secret aspirations of his heart; and I look back upon him as, mentally, a perfect type of the romantic knights of old—capable of a devoted, unselfish love; worshipping woman as a being worthy of all honour, and almost incapable of wrong; delighting in feats of horsemanship and daring; of unsullied honour and unswerving integrity, impatient of double-dealing; impetuous, yet easily guided; simple-minded, and of fervent faith."

Frank Smedley collaborated with Edmund Yates in the publication of a little book of nonsense-verses entitled *Mirth* and *Metre*, issued by Routledge in 1855. Smedley had also contributed to a paper called *The Comic Times* from 1853, and when, in 1856, the size of this journal being greatly reduced, the whole staff resigned and joined a new magazine, *The Train*, directed by Edmund Yates, Smedley transferred his services too, and very ably assisted his friend's venture with some excellent contributions. Writing to his publisher, Virtue, from Tandridge Court, Godstone, in September, 1856, he says:—

" Do you see I am working up my old *Sharpe* P.S.'s as articles for ye *Train*? I fear said *Train* is only a trap for Yates to lose money by. Of course, I only write, or rather patch up, for the sake of saving his pocket, which ye *Trains*, etc., drain pretty fast. My head is still unfit for use, but ye fine air on ye Surrey Hills improves my general health . . . as the doctors deny that I am in a peculiarly express train for the next world, I suppose I may look out for jollier times."

It is scarcely remembered to-day that Smedley was a poet as well as a novelist. His style in verse may be classed with that of Hood and Barham, for like these two writers his poems could be both cleverly comic or sentimentally sad. To Barham, indeed, he most closely approximated, and his facile essays in the quaint metres and bizarre rhymes of *The Ingoldsby Legends* read like

FRANK SMEDLEY
From a contemporary photograph.

[*Page* 122.

genuine extracts from that delightful collection. Take, for
example, the opening lines of Smedley's *Maude Allinghame* : —

> " There is weeping and wailing in Allinghame Hall,
> From many an eye does the tear-drop fall,
> Swollen with sorrow is many a lip,
> Many a nose is red at the tip;
> All the shutters are shut very tight,
> To keep out the wind and to keep out the light;
>> While a couple of mutes,
>> With very black suits,
>> And extremely long faces,
>> Have taken their places,
> With an air of professional *esprit de corps,*
> One on each side of the great hall door.
> On the gravel beyond, in a wonderful state
> Of black velvet and feathers, a grand hearse, and eight
> Magnificent horses, the orders await
>> Of a spruce undertaker,
>> Who's come from Long Acre,
> To furnish a coffin and do the polite
> To the corpse of Sir Reginald Allinghame, Knight."

In his novels Smedley depicted his ideal life, the sports and
adventures he would have enjoyed; but there is no hint in them
of his actual life, with its pains and regrets. It was only in his
serious poems that he sometimes voiced the underlying sadness
of his restricted existence and passionate regret for never-to-be-
realised desires : —

> " Oh give me rest ! for youth is gone,
> And middle-age comes darkly on,
> Experience has been hardly bought,
> Ambition palls, and Fame is nought;
> With chary measure Faith is given,
> And hope is dead, and Love's in heaven.
>> I pant for rest."

> . . . .

> " Alone, dark thoughts assail my breast,
> Wild wishes, sad regrets which tear
> The heartstrings with a fierce unrest
> That mocks the calmness of despair."

> . . . .

> " And it's oh and alas ! for the hopes of youth
> When they for ever depart,
> And it's oh and alas ! for the hopes of youth
> When they come to a broken heart.

> " Too late, too late, what a world of fate
> Do these simple words contain ;
> To strive for years thro' a vale of tears,
> A broken heart to gain."

> . . . . .

" Sleep, thy drowsy pinions
O'er my eyelids move,
Still my throbbing pulses,
Let me dream of love ;
Give me back the seeming
Of the hopes that were,
Thus perchance may dreaming
Calm awhile despair."

Sometimes, too, he alluded to his troubles in a half whimsical, half sad way when writing to his cousins : —

" Ah, Fan, I wonder whether my whole life is to be passed in the mental treadmill I now exist in.   I have more than a fancy that I have pre-existed, and that *this* life is *my* Purgatory; if so, I must have been a very bad boy *somewhere,* at *some time,* to have required so much botheration to make a respectable character of me.   Well, there is a heaven above us, and we shall get there some day I suppose.   Don't *quite* forget me, for my philosophy could not stand that. . . . It is always a pleasure to find that one's faith in one's friends has not been misplaced.   On the whole I have been very fortunate in this respect, and as the affection of the few I love is the one thing in this world which I really care about, I ought to (and in some respect do) consider this a sufficient set-off against some of the evils of life of which I have rather an extra share."

Smedley's last novel, *Harry Coverdale's Courtship,* was, as he put it, a sort of *enfant terrible,* or thankless child to its author, and caused him many troubles and worries.   Originally designed for a short story, it eventually, like *Frank Fairlegh,* grew into a long novel—but only after many delays.   As related earlier, the tale commenced in 1853 in *Sharpe's London Magazine,* but when Smedley's editorship of that periodical ceased at the advent of a new proprietor, his serial was also concluded by the new director in a very summary and original manner.   It was not until 1855 that Smedley resumed the work, and *Harry Coverdale's Courtship* was then issued in the popular mode of monthly parts, with illustrations by Phiz, the whole on conclusion being published in volume form.   Throughout its composition the author was in an ever-failing state of health, as is apparent in his letters to Virtue, the publisher of the work.   Writing from 9, Lower Rock Gardens, Brighton, in December, 1855, he said : —

" The *H. C.* affair must be left thus.   I am still unable to *work,* but I write a few lines every evening.   Whether by this means I shall be able to finish in time for January I cannot yet tell, as my head varies so much from day to day . . . my illness is pronounced irritation of the brain from over-straining of it."

And a little later : —

" Ain't you glad I've finished *H. C.*?   I am, I can tell you.   Wasn't I a brick to get it done in time? but the doing of it has thrown me back —still, I am better.   I exmass here, but not over merrily, as I have to keep quiet."

On January 3rd, 1856, he continued: —

" As soon as the *Coverdales* are bound, please send to 40, Jermyn Street 6 copies, 3 whereof are an order, the other 3 are for myself, and I think you ought to make me a present of them. I was, in my green days, too shy to suggest such a thing to you, but I find that other publishers send other authors sometimes 6, sometimes 12 copies as a present, so I don't see why you should be an exception to what is nearly a general rule, and as my books pay you well, I feel no more *delicacy* in asking than I hope you will in giving. . . . Mind, if you put my name on the binding of *H. C.*, you merely put ' Frank Smedley '—no ' Esq.,' or ' Mr.' It is so snobbish."

The story was warmly received by Press and public, for the author had now an acknowledged position in contemporary literature; but Smedley himself, whose health was worse than ever, was dissatisfied with his work. In his preface to the book he, indeed, apologised for what he considered its " lame and impotent conclusion," which he wrote at a time when suffering from severe nervous headache and under strict orders from his doctor not to compose a line of any description. Smedley was more critical of his story than his readers were. Though not on the same level of merit as *Frank Fairlegh* and *Lewis Arundel*, *Harry Coverdale's Courtship* makes excellent reading, and is full of humour, as witness, for example, Mr. Crane at dinner.* The book, too, is again an interesting picture of its period. The decade of the 'fifties has been richly recorded for our benefit in the pages of Dickens, Thackeray, Lever, and Trollope—social life, London life, Irish life, clerical life, life in all its phases, is to be found there; and Frank Smedley adds inimitable sidelights to the panorama, particularly in relation to the doings of the upper classes in their everyday pursuits—intimate pen-pictures of vanished fashions and pleasures, even if it be merely, say, of the great horticultural *fêtes* which attracted all the fashionable world to the Royal Horticultural Society's grounds near Chiswick House.

In September, 1855, the Smedleys gave up Nyn Park, and Frank went to stay at 1, St. George's Place, Canterbury, for a time, later proceeding to Brighton, where he passed the winter. The Smedley family had now inherited and taken up their residence in Grove Lodge, Regent's Park, one of the most delightful houses in London. The richly-wooded grounds of nearly five acres were originally part of the park, from which they are merely separated by the Regent's Canal. It was when the canal was formed that this north-west corner of the park lands was leased by the Crown to George Bellas Greenough (the

---

* Chapter XLVI.

famous geographer and geologist, and a first cousin of Francis Smedley), the house being built in 1823. The grounds consist mainly of winding woodland walks, and the glimpses of water and park obtained from them are extremely picturesque and romantic.* In this wonderful *rus in urbe* Frank Smedley found intense pleasure, for he was able to take exercise in his wheel chair without going outside the gates of the property. The many seats and arbours placed in the grounds still remain as evidence of the favourite spots he liked to visit and read in. He also appreciated the near proximity of his favourite resort, the Zoological Gardens. Lord's Cricket Ground, too, he often visited. Writing to Virtue, his publisher, he says:—

" Come to lunch at 2 on Monday, and go to Lord's for a good match. You may bring any *really* pretty girl you like with you. . . . Please to read the enclosed and try if you can learn anything of the writer. I take it to be from a woman. I am not aware that my noble works have ever shown in a French garb, and I look upon the matter as a European advertisement gratis—thus, if this proves an opportunity of getting the thing decently translated without trouble or expense to you or me, I vote we do not neglect it. Whether either you or I can concoct any swindle on the subject, and contrive to suck profit therefrom, you can probably inform me. I am quite open to a share in profitable burglary, or any other agreeable infamy you may approve. I am still very seedy, but always yours (and wife's) very tenderly,

" FRANK E. S."

Smedley's literary career was now concluded. In the autumn of 1856, owing to a carriage accident, when he was thrown out and dragged some distance along the ground before the pony could be stopped, his health became very much worse, and the prostration resulting from severe and prolonged headaches rendered all composition impossible. He contented himself henceforth with literary ease, and, when free from pain, read much in every branch of literature. He delighted, too, in seeing his old friends, and enjoying congenial talk.† The library, on the west side of Grove Lodge, was, and is, a fine apartment, and as it communicated with all the other reception rooms of the house, and also with his own bedroom, Smedley was able to take part,

---

* It is interesting to note that Grove Lodge is described by Stevenson, under the name of " Rochester House," in *New Arabian Nights,* when the President of the Suicide Club meets his death in a duel with Prince Florizel in a secluded corner of the grounds, now the site of the Rose Garden.

† " I have many a loving friend,
    With their pleasant voices near me,
    And their sympathy to cheer me,
I will wear life to its end.

" And when death has had his will,
    Sparkling eyes for me will weep,
    Loyal hearts a corner keep
For our friendship's memory still."
    —From *Gathered Leaves,* by Frank Smedley.

as far as he wished, in the entertainments given by his parents.*
But this was only for a few years. In the spring of 1859 his
father, Francis Smedley, died, and a burden of responsibility was
thrown on the invalid son which his own rapidly declining health
ill-fitted him to bear. Writing to his cousin, Mrs. Walton, he
said : —

" Your letter was (like yourself) all that is good and loving. I *knew*
you felt for us ! Some day I hope to tell you, *viva voce,* some of the
many things I felt and suffered during this, *the* most painful event in
my not too happy life. I have been very ill, but am now mending. My
poor mother is well in health, and at times able to throw off her most
heavy sorrow—but it is a grief that only death will end. I have a great
deal on me which *must* be done, and very little strength to meet the
demand; but GOD knows what is best for us, and I am well content to
leave the matter to His will and guidance. . . . Rest assured I care for
my *old* cousin Fan as well as I did when I was a romantic boy, and you
were—well, you can guess what I thought you : angels are not so
easily discovered when one is forty."

Smedley had other bereavements to bear this year. Writing
to Virtue in October, 1859, he states : —

" I am not more bodily ill than is now usual to me, but I have had
two severe mental knock-downs within a fortnight. My aunt, Eliza
Smedley, died after a week's illness, and my dear Cousin Millicent (the
M.U.S. of the *Frank Fairlegh* dedication) also died quite unexpectedly
. . . so I am not over jolly. . . . I have learned to like Marlow, and
have bought a small but pretty place here."

This house, called " Beechwood," was pleasantly situated
under the lea of rising ground.† For four succeeding years
Frank Smedley passed the summer months here, delighting in his
garden and the beautiful surroundings of his native place. He
is still remembered in Marlow, a little man passing through the
streets in his wheeled chair with a nod and bright smile or jest for
everyone who saluted him. The autumn and winter months he
spent with his mother at Grove Lodge in Regent's Park, and
enjoyed the society of congenial relatives and friends. Quickly
the last years speeded. On April 28th, 1864, Edmund Yates dined
with him at Grove Lodge, and thought Smedley seemed
better and brighter than he had been for some time . Yates
records : —

---

* Though a fine house in the Smedleys' time, the place has subsequently
been enlarged and much improved. It is now called Grove House, and
occupied by Mr. Sigismund Goetz, who has converted the former stables into
a studio. Mr. Goetz has decorated the principal drawing-room with a series
of beautiful panel paintings, his own work, illustrating mythological subjects;
the sylvan backgrounds are in several cases sketched from views in the
grounds of Grove House.

† Only part of the house now remains, being used as a gardener's cottage
on the property of the more modern " Beechwood," the residence until her
death in 1912 of Mrs. Cripps, mother of Sir Alfred Cripps, K.C., M.P., now
Lord Parmoor.

" When the other guests left the dinner-table he asked me to remain, and talked to me with the greatest spirit and interest about the work on which I was then engaged, about some horses he had bought, about his desire to get away speedily into the country and enjoy all the beauties of the coming summer—about a dozen little trifles, into all of which he entered with even more than his ordinary zest. I left him, promising to return the next week and settle an early date for visiting him at Beechwood."

Three days later, on May 1st, 1864, Frank Smedley was found by his servant, who came to call him in the morning, in a state of stupor, speedily followed by a succession of epileptic fits, and in the evening he died, at the age of forty-five. He was buried a week later at Marlow, between the church and the river, with the lovely woods and hills beyond. All the shops in the little town were closed, and many inhabitants came to pay their last tribute of respect to one who, born amongst them, had become a familiar personality in his later years; and to these now he returned to take his last and final rest—rest which the frail, afflicted body direly needed, that eternal sleep he craved.

> " The weary heart will ache no more,
> For death is rest."

But he had carried out his own precept: —

> " All true honour lies
> In a life-long sacrifice;
> Stars shine clear above the skies,
> Conquer Fate ! "

NOTE.—In 1865, the year following the author's death, was published *Gathered Leaves*, being a collection of thirty-four poems, both serious and humorous, by Frank Smedley, together with a memorial and biographical preface by Edmund Yates, and a portrait of Smedley and a view of Grove Lodge.

In 1867 there followed another little book, *Last Leaves from Beechwood*, edited by William Brailsford, and published at the Enfield Press, containing twenty-one additional pieces by Frank Smedley, his portrait, and a view of Marlow Church.

G. P. R. JAMES.*

MR. THOMAS SECCOMBE has described G. P. R. James as " one of the mysterious figures in Victorian Literature." To a certain extent that is true: an atmosphere of mystery *has* attached to James—not created by the man himself, who was quite normal and unromantic in character and personal appearance despite his adventurous career and many written romances, but mainly owing to the facts that he was ever an adventurous wanderer and that his last years were spent abroad. Further, he has been singularly unfortunate in his biographers, for most of those who have written brief memoirs of James have known little about his actual life and have even erred as to the years of his birth and death.

G. P. R. James, like the majority of notable English authors, came from the professional middle class. His immediate ancestors were medical men, and he had a celebrated grandfather, Dr. Robert James, compounder of the famous James's Powders, and the friend of Dr. Johnson. Born in 1705, Robert James commenced his friendship with Johnson in school days at Lichfield, and their intimacy lasted all through their time in London. James produced his *A Medicinal Dictionary* in 1743; but Boswell's statement that Johnson " furnished some of the articles " and the Preface is controverted by the doctor's grandson, G. P. R. James, in his manuscript autobiography. Of Dr. James's Fever Powders, and how they were regarded as a sovereign specific by Oliver Goldsmith, Horace Walpole, and Prince Charles Edward Stuart, and how the same Powders were accused of hastening Goldsmith's death, it is impossible to relate here. Dr. James, a self-made man, left at his death, in 1776, a fortune of eight thousand pounds a year; by his wife, a daughter of Sir James Clarke, he had a family of three sons and two daughters (one of whom witnessed all the horrors of the French Revolution and, incidentally, refused an offer of marriage from Robespierre).

The youngest son, Dr. Pinkston James (1766-1830), father of the novelist, in early life served in the English Navy as a midshipman. As a boy of fourteen he fought at the first Battle of Cape St. Vincent, and later took part in the American War. On retiring from the Service he studied medicine in Scotland;

* *The Bookman*, April, 1917.

and it was at Edinburgh, in 1791, that he married Jean Churnside. Returning to London, Pinkston James practised for many years as a physician at No. 12, George Street, Hanover Square, and it was here that his son, George Payne Rainsford James, was born on August 9th, 1801. The child was baptised at St. George's Church, opposite the house, in 1802. Pinkston James was physician to the Prince Regent, and hence arose the absurd canard that the initials of his famous son stood for George Prince Regent James.

G. P. R. James was not very happy in his childhood. His mother died early, and he and his education were neglected. He was thrown back upon his own resources, and became a very observant, sharp, but idle boy. Very early he showed his adventurous, roving disposition, for when only about five years of age he ran away from home to see a review of troops, and after much hue and cry was eventually discovered, black with powder, sitting on a drum, drinking strong liquor with a private, who had picked him up and formed a rapid friendship. After this escapade, the boy was sent to a small school conducted by a French *émigré* at Greenwich, and later to the larger establishment of the Rev. William Carmalt at Putney. Like George Meredith subsequently, James found his chief reading delight, as a youth, in *The Arabian Nights;* and just as that work inspired *The Shaving of Shagpat,* so it induced James to write some half-dozen tales in the same Eastern vein, which were published about fifteen years later, 1832, under the title of *The String of Pearls.* He was, however, an omnivorous reader; and when still a boy acquired, in addition to the usual foreign languages, German and Persian. His reading ranged from Dante to the loose English novelists of the eighteenth century, and from Voltaire to Hobbes's *Leviathan.* Undoubtedly the verbosity and diffuse detail characteristic of the novels of G. P. R. James may be attributed to his early familiarity with the vast number of words he achieved in the course of his rather undigested acquisition of many and various languages.

As a boy, James was acquainted with Byron, to whom he was devoted. The poet used to call him " Little Devil," and was so attracted by this curious lad, whose imaginative, adventurous, lax temperament was somewhat akin to his own, that he wanted to take young James abroad as a companion. But hereupon belated parental conscience was aroused to action, for the boy did not go to the Continent with Byron when the poet left England in 1809, or in 1816, though in the latter year James was abroad.

He was in Belgium in 1815, and he witnessed the horrors of the aftermath of Waterloo. He stated that the dead bodies of men and horses were piled up high above the lofty hedges, and that the French prisoners, as they were brought in, had to be protected by the English from massacre by the Prussians.

After peace was proclaimed, James remained on the Continent, where, to use his own words, " alone, unguided, and undirected I wandered over a considerable portion of Europe, and mingling with many classes and varieties of my fellow-creatures I learned the necessity, and endeavoured to practise the art, of investigating keenly, and judging rapidly, the characters of those with whom I was brought in contact." These " investigations," among many other adventures, involved him in a duel with a French officer, when the youthful James had the satisfaction of disabling his adversary in the sword arm. His travels made him familiar with practically all France, Spain, and Germany, and many of his experiences were introduced later in *Morley Ernstein* and other books.

On his return to England nothing very definite was proposed for him in the way of a profession beyond the suggestion that he should enter political life. This plan, owing to the death of Lord Liverpool, his intended sponsor in politics, was abandoned; and from a period of social pleasure as a young man about town, combined with literary dalliance, James gradually merged into a professional and laborious man of letters. In 1825, when he was twenty-four years old, he wrote his first—and considered by many critics his best—novel, *Richelieu*, but the work was not destined to see publication until some four years later. As so often has been the case with subsequently successful authors, James received no encouragement from his relatives to enter seriously upon a literary career. His father, indeed, descanting upon the horrors of mediocrity, declared that his son was unfitted for long and intricate narrative. But Washington Irving, whom James had met abroad, gave encouraging advice to continue, and so the budding author went on quietly with his romance and other work. In 1826 he was again on the Continent, holding some minor appointment in the Diplomatic Service, and for the next two years was occupied with more than one literary project, though as yet nothing was published in book form. By a happy chance, the first part of *Richelieu*, which the author had thrown aside uncompleted, was sent through the introduction of a mutual friend to Sir Walter Scott for his opinion and advice. Months passed, and James had given up all hope of hearing from the great novelist, when one day he received a letter from Scott, of which he relates: " The opinion expressed in that note was more favourable than I had ever expected, and certainly more favourable than I deserved; for Sir Walter Scott was one of the most lenient of critics, especially to the young. However, it told me to persevere, and I did so."

With this distinguished *cachet* of approval, *Richelieu* found acceptance by Henry Colburn, who just previously, in 1828, had privately printed for James a poem in the Southey style entitled *The Ruined City*, which was consequently his first book. Though entirely unknown to the public as an author, James had an intuition that he was about to make a name and take a prominent place in the literary world, for in a letter written some months prior to the appearance of *Richelieu* he spoke of his coming " fame " and position as an author; and, further, he demanded, and received, five hundred pounds and six hundred pounds for his first novels, no despicable remuneration for a new writer. In anticipation of his approaching literary success he felt in a position to marry, and accordingly on December 3rd, 1828, he was united, in St. George's Church, Hanover Square, to Frances, daughter of Honoratus Leigh Thomas, a well-known London surgeon of that time.

Directly after the marriage, the Jameses went to live abroad, renting the Château du Buisson-Garembourg, Evereux. Here the novelist's father died, during a visit, in 1830. It now became necessary to return to England to settle business affairs, and passing through Paris in July, James and his wife came in for the Revolution of 1830. They witnessed the street fighting, and some of their baggage was seized and utilised in a barricade.

James had now commenced in earnest his astonishingly prolific career as a writer, producing often three or more books each year. *Richelieu*, published in 1829, was followed in 1830 by *Darnley, or the Field of the Cloth of Gold; De L'Orme;* and *The History of Chivalry*. *Philip Augustus*, written in less than seven weeks, succeeded rapidly in 1831. It will be impossible within the restricted space of this article to mention the whole of James's work. It must suffice to state that in the period of thirty odd years that comprised his writing life he produced fifty-six novels; eight additional volumes which may be loosely classified as short stories; five more in the form of poems and plays; several political pamphlets; and twelve works dealing with history, some of these —such as *The History of Chivalry; The Life of Edward the Black Prince; The Life and Times of Louis the Fourteenth*—being studies of considerable research and value. They brought to James the honorary, if resonant, appointment of Historiographer

Royal to William the Fourth and Victoria. Roughly speaking, there are eighty-seven works by James, to say nothing of short stories and contributions to magazines not reprinted. An amazing output truly.*

In all the annals of literature probably no tag has attached more persistently to an author than " the solitary horseman " or " two cavaliers " of G. P. R. James—for the number of equestrians riding along a romantic pass varies in both the novels and the public mind. The man who originally branded this literary trade-mark upon James was Thackeray in his clever burlesque, *Barbazure, By G. P. R. Jeames, Esq., etc.* which is something more than a parody : it is the actual presentment of James's style, where every trick and mannerism and detail is caught and reproduced.

In the popular conception James's " two cavaliers " always appear in the first chapter of his books. How far is this delusion justified ? As already stated, James wrote fifty-six works which may be classified as romances, and in only sixteen of these horsemen—single, or in pairs, or parties—make an early appearance. In five books a " solitary horseman " appears in the first chapter, and in two others he delays his arrival until the second chapter; " two cavaliers " *caracole* in the first chapters of only three books and in the second chapter of another; and " parties of horsemen " prance in, at least, six books during the first chapter. It will thus be seen that " the two cavaliers " are in a minority, and that " the solitary horseman " is the most predominant among James's romantic equestrians. But it is interesting to note that the sixteen works in which the horsemen appear were *all written prior to* 1847, the year when Thackeray's *Barbazure* was first published (in *Punch*). That James took this satire to heart is attested by the fact that in all the eighteen stories he wrote subsequent to 1847, there is never a sign of horsemen at the outset; and in one of these later books, *The Fate* (1851), the author alludes to his formerly ubiquitous cavaliers on white horses, and pleads their cause well in pathetic-humorous style.

In addition to what he suffered from *Punch*, James was the target of some very sharply-pointed barbs, aimed by Albert Smith and Angus B. Reach, in *The Man in the Moon*. He, however, did not mind comic criticism, for he had a good sense of humour, and drew a caricature of himself surrounded by his horses and dogs—all with their tails enlarged—bearing the title,

---

* An accurate list of the novels and short stories of G. P. R. James, compiled by Mr. W. A. Frost, who possesses them all, will be found in *Notes and Queries* for August 26th, 1916.

" The Author of *Richelieu*—and Many Other Tails." But the adverse and superficial reviewer of his books had the power to incite James to frenzy, and his letters are full of amusing, vitriolic expressions of his hatred for the tribe. However, James —or his shade—need never be troubled by the condemnatory critics of his books, for the appreciations in his favour expressed by celebrated men are numerous. It is quite remarkable how many great minds have found pleasure—and not only in their boyhood—in the romances of a writer who, if not in the front rank of merit, was certainly meritorious. In addition to Walter Scott (who wrote of James as " a literary man of great merit ") and Washington Irving, James was highly praised by John Wilson in *Noctes Ambrosianæ;* by Leigh Hunt; by even the generally disgruntled R. H. Horne in *A New Spirit of the Age.* Alan Cunningham, S. C. Hall, and Harrison Ainsworth (who thought James might be the debated author of *Jane Eyre*!) paid him many encomiums. He received a complimentary letter from Gladstone in 1843. Thackeray wrote of him in *Roundabout Papers* as " the veteran from whose flowing pen we had the books which delighted our young days—*Darnley* and *Richelieu* and *De L.'Orme.*" Frank Smedley offered a similar tribute in *Frank Fairlegh.* Walter Savage Landor put Scott and James in conjunction as his favourite romance writers. Robert Louis Stevenson in exile had a longing to re-read " my dear old G. P. R. James "—especially *The Gipsey, The Convict, The Stepmother,* and *The Robber.* J. H. Shorthouse, another mature reader of James, liked *The Woodman* and *Forest Days.* Watts-Dunton regarded *Philip Augustus* as a fine historical novel. Sir Francis Burnand delighted in James's books when a boy, as did Mr. Thomas Hardy, who still recalls them with pleasure, particularly *The Ancient Régime.*

Enough has been said to prove that James has had a brilliant array of cultured admirers, and even if he had done no more than fire the youthful imaginations of Thackeray, Stevenson, and Hardy, he would not have written in vain.

It is, of course, true that James's work has not the same appeal to the rising generation as it possessed for his contemporaries and their sons. The youth of to-day likes to imbibe its romance by the rapid methods of the kinema—crude, direct, and without any dilution or interruption. Except for the few, James's long-winded descriptions of scenery and costume are boring, his immaculate love scenes vapid, and even his deaths and murders feeble in comparison with the delicious brutality

G. P. R. JAMES
From a portrait.

[*Page* 134.

and marvellous mortality of the filmed cowboy and Parisian villain. James's style had many faults—diffuseness and a generally mechanical plot, whose luculent workings could be seen from the outset, and a sort of moralising, sentimental " atmosphere " which stultified any true presentment and analysis of character. But this was the paralysing literary convention of his period, and even Dickens and Thackeray were not free from the artifice of ending a story with marriage bells and virtue triumphant, and the concurrent downfall and extinction of the wicked ones (who in real life, of course, flourish like the green bay tree and die in Park Lane). On the other hand, James told a good, blameless, yet stirring tale with the real aroma of romance and derring-do and chivalry. And, after all, what more is required of an historical novelist? The scalpel of analysis and the probe for erotomania are not necessities in his outfit.

To complete the brief biographical outline of James's career. In the spring of 1831 he returned from France and went to live at Maxpoffle, near Melrose. There he was near Walter Scott, who took much pleasure in his society, as recorded by Lockhart. In 1833 the Jameses were at Heidelberg, and in 1834 they travelled in Italy; 1835 witnessed the publication of three books, including *The Gipsey*, completed at 1, Lloyd's Place, Blackheath. In 1836, James removed to The Cottage, Great Marlow, where *Attila* was written; but the author was a congenital wanderer, and hardly ever lived longer than two years in any particular house. So by the autumn of 1837 he was at Fair Oak Lodge, Petersfield, where he wrote *The Robber*. In 1839 he had published no less than seven works within a year, and was living at The Hermitage, near Trevor Square, Brompton, and at Lyme Regis. In 1840 he was at Brussels, where he saw a good deal of Charles Lever, and was associated with the publication of *Charles O'Malley*—but that is another and long story. Back in England in 1841, he lived at The Shrubbery, in the picturesque village of Upper Walmer, where during the next three years he wrote many novels, including *Forest Days* and *Morley Ernstein*, which has some scenes laid in the adjoining town of Deal. James was on very friendly terms with his neighbour at Walmer Castle, the great Duke of Wellington, whose son, Lord Douro, became the author's most intimate friend. In 1843, James moved to The Oaks, Upper Deal, where five novels were written, and in 1845 he returned to the Continent. The Jameses and Levers were both at Carlsruhe, where they created rather a sensation. James was later at Baden, and the influence of his sojourn in Germany was reflected in his next two romances, *Heidelberg* and *The Castle of Ehrenstein*. The latter is perhaps his best work, despite the inartistic conclusion, where all the supernatural mysteries of the story are accounted for by human agency.

In 1847 James was back at Walmer, and seven books were published. In 1848 the restless author removed to Willey House, near Farnham. He was getting poorer and poorer owing to the expenses of his migratory life. And during these, his last, months in England, he took an active part in politics, and wasted the remnant of his fortune in a crusade against Free Trade. A dispute with his publishers and resultant financial troubles gave the final blow to James's monetary stability, and emigration seemed the best expedient, for the novelist had three sons to start in life.

Accordingly in July, 1850, when nearing the age of fifty, James arrived with his family in America on the most precarious adventure of his eventful life. After a stay in New York and elsewhere, he eventually rented a house at Stockbridge, Massachusetts, where he spent some eighteen happy months engaged in literary work and farming, amid lovely scenery and cultured society, for Stockbridge was the centre of a pleasant literary coterie including the Sedgwicks, Oliver Wendell Holmes, and Nathaniel Hawthorne. With the last named James became very friendly, and he also met, and was appreciated by, Longfellow. In November, 1852, James accepted the appointment of British Consul at Norfolk, Virginia, the most depressing station in the States. His health was ruined by the deleterious climate; fever and ague were engendered by the proximity of the Great Dismal Swamp, and yellow fever was introduced every summer by ships from the West Indies, culminating in the terrible epidemic of 1855, when the Consul's experiences were horrible. Further, James, as a climax to his misfortunes, had to endure unpopularity and calumny in Norfolk owing to the Slave Agitation, for he was reported to be in favour of abolition. Consequently he was hated and attacked by the slave owners; eight incendiary outrages occurred at or near his house, and the usual anonymous letters threatening death were received. However, as time went on and the Consul's merits, both in official and private life, were apparent, persecution died down, and even the slave owners of Norfolk came to like and respect him. When he finally left America he parted on the friendliest terms with his neighbours. They presented him with a punch bowl at a farewell banquet in Richmond (to where the Consulate had been removed), ere he set forth to take up his duties as British Consul at Venice.

So after eight adventurous years in America, James and his family left the New World for its extreme antithesis, Venice— " the only city in Europe," as Thackeray observed, " where the famous ' two cavaliers ' cannot by any possibility be seen riding together." The novelist arrived in the autumn of 1858, and his period in Italy coincided with the very disturbed political situation existing between the Italians and Austrians. When the war broke out and Venice was threatened with siege, James remained to attend to his consular work, though he sent his family to the Tyrol during the summer of 1859. He lived at first in the Palazza Foscolo, opposite the Church of Santa Maria della Salute. His health was broken; he was a martyr to asthma and suppressed gout; and an attack of paralysis caused his mind to be obscured at times. Consequently he did not appreciate society as much as of old, though his polyglot neighbours were an amusing set. He liked Captain Chamier, author of Ben Brace, and was glad to find his old friend, Charles Lever, at Spezzia. There were also many eccentric Irish and English people living in Venice, Jacobites and " exiles " who practised the manners of the eighteenth century. James also visited the ill-fated Maximilian, then Governor of the Lombardo-Venetian kingdom, and subsequently Emperor of Mexico; and the Comte de Chambord, heir of the Bourbons, who lived in Venice with his mother, the Duchesse de Berri, and her second husband, Lucchesi Palli.

The story of the last year of James's life is a very sad one. He was a complete wreck, mentally and bodily; he indulged too much with alcohol; his financial difficulties were great; and a second stroke of paralysis brought him to the verge of the final bourne. He had removed to the Palazzo Ferro, on the Grand Canal, and he found pleasure in being rowed in his gondola to the Lido, whence returning he could see the magic spectacle of Venice silhouetted against the glowing sunset skies. To the last, he— who had depictured in words many a fiery sunset illuminating some wild or romantic scene—preserved the historic sense and the appreciation of beauty. " The legendary splendour of old days, the spirit of Romance, dies not to those who hold a kindred spirit in their souls," and it was well that the romancer's eyes gazed their last and grew dim for ever upon the history-haunted Venetian scene, for he was essentially of the old régime. On the morning of June 8th, 1860, James suddenly fell back into the arms of his man-servant; two hours later he was speechless; insensibility followed, and, without recovering from this state, he died at 4-30 a.m. the following day.

G. P. R. James was buried, in the presence of all the chief officials of Venice, in the Protestant Cemetery on St. Michele— The Island of the Dead. It is a singularly picturesque spot—a garden guarded from the sea by fortress-like walls. Though he died very far away from the English scenes of happier days and old friends, his last resting place—a veritable " tomb by the sounding sea," yet amid a profusion of roses, flowering shrubs, ivy, cypress, and vine—is a fitting one for a chronicler of old romance.

SHERIDAN LE FANU.*

SHERIDAN LE FANU remains one of the most distinguished literary men of Ireland. Unlike many other writers of his period and race, he has suffered no eclipse. Charles Lever, I fear, is now regarded mainly as the perpetrator of exaggerated types of Irish character. Samuel Lover, Lady Morgan, John Banim, Crofton Croker, and Maturin, are almost forgotten in England. But Sheridan Le Fanu retains his own special place and fame as *the* Master of Horror and the Mysterious. *Uncle Silas, The House by the Churchyard,* and the short stories of terror in the volume entitled *In a Glass Darkly* are known to everyone interested in the literature of the supernatural and that misused word—sensational. Le Fanu is more highly regarded to-day than at the time he was alive and producing his fine romances, and his greatest admirers are men of archæological and artistic ability, such as Dr. Montague Rhodes James and Mr. Allan Fea. He was the favourite author also of the late Seymour Lucas, R.A., the distinguished historical painter and a high authority on old furniture and armour. I recall how on one occasion, when we were discussing Le Fanu's masterpiece, *The House by the Churchyard,* Mr. Lucas pointed out how accurate are the archæological details of this book—the costumes, the weapons, the furnishings of the period of the story are all depicted with the knowledge and perception of a connoisseur.

I think, then, one of the reasons for the enduring fame of Sheridan Le Fanu is that he was a fine antiquarian and archæologist, and had the true historic sense in addition to his supreme gifts as a tale-teller. This combination of talents in his romances has attracted readers of the highest taste and held their admiration in a way the ordinary writer of the ghost story or sensational murder tale could never accomplish.

Joseph Sheridan Le Fanu was the descendant of a distinguished Huguenot family (possessing a *titre de noblesse* granted by Henri IV in 1595). His Norman ancestor, Etienne Le Fanu, Sieur de Mondeville, suffered imprisonment in France for the cause of religion. Etienne's son, Philippe, and his grandson, Guillaume—then a child—left France between 1708 and 1713, and lived for some years in London. About 1730 they settled in

* *The Bookman,* October, 1916.

Dublin, where a cousin, Charles Le Fanu de Cresseron (who was a pensioner from the army of William the Third) was already living. Thus was the family established in Ireland. Guillaume Le Fanu married Henrietta Raboteau de Puygibaud, also a Huguenot, and their son Joseph held the appointment of Clerk of the Coast in Ireland. This Joseph Le Fanu and his brother Henry respectively married Alicia and Elizabeth Sheridan, sisters of Richard Brinsley Sheridan.

Joseph and Alicia Le Fanu were the parents of Thomas Philip Le Fanu. He became a clergyman and Dean of Emly, and was the father of Joseph Sheridan Le Fanu, the subject of this memoir. In addition to being the grand-nephew of the author of *The School for Scandal*, the future novelist of mystery had other literary influences in his childhood, for his Sheridan grandmother, Alicia, was the author of *Sons of Erin, or Modern Sentiment*, a comedy, 1812; and his mother (Emma, daughter of the Rev. W. Dobbin, D.D., of Dublin) was a writer of some merit.

Joseph Sheridan Le Fanu was born on August 28th, 1814, at the Royal Hibernian Military School, in Phœnix Park, Dublin, of which his father was at the time Chaplain. The boy, together with his sister Catherine and younger brother William, consequently spent his early years near to Chapelizod, that picturesque suburb of Dublin, whereof he retained many romantic memories that forty years later found vivid expression in his powerful romance, *The House by the Churchyard*.

As in the case of other literary men, Le Fanu very early showed his predilection for writing. When about five years old he was wont to draw little pictures to which he appended a descriptive moral. One of these represented a balloon, with the airmen falling headlong to the ground, and the unorthodox " moral " written below was, " See the effects of trying to go to Heaven." He also composed little songs, which he sang very charmingly; and by the time he was fifteen he had produced some creditable verse in the pensive, melancholy strain to which youthful, imaginative writers are partial. Nevertheless he was a merry, witty boy, much addicted to practical joking and with an apt turn for repartee. For example. He was invariably late for morning prayers, and on one occasion he did not appear till ten o'clock, when breakfast was nearly over. His father, the Dean, taking out his watch, said in his severest voice, " I ask you, Joseph, is this right? " " No, sir," replied the boy glancing at the watch, " I'm sure it must be fast."

It was in 1826, when Le Fanu was twelve years old, that his father became Dean of Emly and Rector of Abington, and to the latter place, in the county Limerick, the family accordingly removed. Abington was a centre of typical Irish rural life of that period, and a most entertaining account of the experiences of the young people at the Rectory will be found in *Seventy Years of Irish Life* by William Le Fanu, the Dean's younger son. The faction fights and the superstitions of the peasantry were of immense interest to the boys, and here they heard much of—and perhaps saw—a famous outlaw named Kirby, whose escapades were the inspiring cause of Sheridan Le Fanu's famous ballad of *Shamus O'Brien* in later years. All through his life he had an innate deep sympathy for the wild, unruly elements of the Irish character, and at heart he was ever a Nationalist, though he deprecated any public movement of reaction tending to violence in political affairs. His interest in the patriots of his native land was fostered in early life by his mother, who gloried in being a " rebel." She had known personally some of those who had been executed for their participation in '98, including the brothers Sheares, and she possessed the actual dagger—venerated by her as a sacred relic— with which Lord Edward FitzGerald had killed Captain Ryan in that terrible scene of his capture in Thomas Street, Dublin. Sheridan Le Fanu was still in his early teens when he wrote his ballad on Lord Edward FitzGerald, which opens with all the poignant pathos of a Jacobite lament: —

" The day that traitors sould him and inimies bought him,
  The day that the red gold and red blood was paid—
Then the green turned pale and thrembled like the dead leaves in
  autumn,
  And the heart an' hope iv Ireland in the could grave was laid."

The education of the Le Fanu boys, with the exception of English and French taught by their father, was at first entrusted to a certain elderly clergyman named Stinson, an eccentric character and quite careless of his duty, for he let his pupils do much as they pleased the while he devoted his own time to preparations for fishing, which was the obsessing mania of his life. Fortunately, Sheridan Le Fanu had a taste for reading on his own account, and made good use of his father's well-stocked library, which contained many books on curious and occult subjects. Here, perhaps, may be traced the source of influence that caused him to discover his real *métier*—the supernatural —for whilst still a student of Trinity College, Dublin, where he entered in 1833, he commenced his literary career by writing ghost stories.

Le Fanu's first published story, entitled *The Ghost and the*

Bone-setter, appeared in *The Dublin University Magazine* for January, 1838, when he was twenty-three years of age. During the next two years the same magazine printed twelve further contributions from his pen. *The Fortunes of Sir Robert Ardagh* and *Schalken the Painter* are very grim and vivid stories of satanic possession, much aided by picturesque detail. *The Last Heir of Castle Connor* contains a powerful description of a fatal duel. *Passage in the Secret History of an Irish Countess* is the original form of his later most famous work, *Uncle Silas*, which was elaborated from this early sketch. In the same way, *A Chapter in the History of a Tyrone Family* was many years later extended into the work now known as *The Wyvern Mystery*.

All these early contributions to *The Dublin University Magazine* appeared anonymously, and purported to be transcripts from actual experiences narrated, in virtue of his ghostly office, to Father Francis Purcell, a parish priest in the south of Ireland, and by him recorded in his private papers. *The Purcell Papers* were collected and published by Bentley in 1880, being prefixed by Mr. Alfred P. Graves's memoir of the author. The original ingenuous deception concerning the authorship was elaborated in the eighth *Purcell Paper—Scraps of Hibernian Ballads*—by the introduction of one Michael Finley, an Irish minstrel, to whom Le Fanu chose to attribute the authorship of his ballads—including the popular *Phaudhrig Crohoore*, which was here printed for the first time (June, 1839). This class of literary hoax was just then much in vogue owing to the brilliant polyglot productions in verse and prose of Francis Mahony, who figured as " Father Prout." In addition to Le Fanu, two other clever Irishmen, William Maginn and Edward Kenealy adopted this form of anonymity; and in England, Thackeray, Ainsworth, and others, wrote under various disguises in their earlier years. In so far as Finley had an original it was Paddy O'Neill, a fiddler and bagpipe-player, who composed his own songs for the amusement of the passengers on the steamer plying between Limerick and Kilrush; and Le Fanu took much pleasure in his society and songs when staying at Kilkee during summer holidays. *Phaudhrig Crohoore* was written at the request of William Le Fanu, who, wishing for a ballad of this description that he could recite, said to his brother, " Give me an Irish *Young Lochinvar*."

> " In his arms he took Kathleen, an' stepped to the door ;
> And he leaped on his horse and flung her before ;
> An' they all were so bothered, that not a man stirred
> Till the galloping hoofs on the pavement were heard.

'Then up they all started, llke bees in the swarm,
An' they riz a great shout, like the burst of a storm,
An' they roared and they ran, an' they shouted galore;
But Kathleen and Phaudhrig they never saw more.

But them days are gone by, an' he is no more;
An' the green grass is growin' o'er Phaudhrig Crohoore,
For he couldn't be aisy or quiet at all;
As he lived a brave boy, he resolved so to fall.

And he took a good pike—for Phaudhrig was great,
And he fought, and he died, in the year 'ninety-eight,
An' the day that Crohoore in the green field was killed,
A sthrong boy was sthretched, and a sthrong heart was stilled."

Sheridan Le Fanu's most famous ballad, *Shamus O'Brien*, was composed in 1840, in a few days, and sent on scraps of paper to his brother, who, after he had learned the song by heart, lost the original script. So when, later on, a copy was required, it rested with him to write out the ballad from memory. It was first published, in July, 1850, in *The Dublin University Magazine*. When Samuel Lover visited America during his reading tour in 1846 he recited *Shamus O'Brien* with the greatest success, and owing to the fact that he added a few lines of his own, wherein he made Shamus emigrate to America, the authorship of the ballad was often attributed to him. The correct version, as written by Le Fanu, ends with the line, " And fined like the devil because Jim done them fairly." As before stated, Shamus O'Brien had his prototype in Kirby of the county Limerick; and Le Fanu placed the outlaw's home in the Glen of Aherlow, a picturesque spot he saw under romantic conditions during a walking tour in the summer of 1838. He and his party got lost at night on the Galtee mountains in a thick mist. Here they encountered a wild, galloping horse, which the peasantry—and no doubt Le Fanu also—believed to be the phooka, the four-footed demon in equine guise, well-known in the superstitions of the south of Ireland. The opera based on *Shamus O'Brien*, with music by Sir Charles Villiers Stanford (a cousin of Mrs. Sheridan Le Fanu) was produced in 1896.

In *Shamus O'Brien*, which was written when Le Fanu was twenty-six, how finely is put the point of view of the young Nationalist when Shamus replies to the judge : —

" My Lord, if you ask me if in my lifetime
I thought any threason or did any crime
That would bring to my cheek as I stand alone here
The hot blush of shame or the coldness of fear,
Though I stood by my grave to receive my death-blow,
Before God and the world I would answer you—No !
But if you would ask me, as I think it is like,
If in the Rebellion I carried a pike,

An' fought for ould Ireland from the first to the close,
An' shed the heart's blood of her bittherest foes,
I answer you—Yes ! An' I tell you again,
Though I stand here to perish, it's my glory that then
In her cause I was willin' my veins should run dhry,
An' now, for her sake, I am ready to die.''

In May, 1838, Le Fanu was in London with a view to entering Lincoln's Inn. He was entertained by his connecti᾽ ᴧ, Sheridan Knowles, and by Mr. and Mrs. S. C. Hall. But his legal project in England was suddenly abandoned, for he was back in Dublin by the end of June; and after taking his B.A. degree at Trinity College, he was called to the Irish Bar in 1839. However, to the disappointment of his friends, Le Fanu abandoned also the Law in Ireland and identified himself with journalism. About 1841 he became the proprietor and editor of *The Warder*, a notable Irish paper; and in 1842 he bought *The Protestant Guardian* and merged it in the former journal. He later owned a third share in *The Statesman*, and *The Dublin Evening Packet* and *Evening Mail*. For this last named paper he wrote some very clever political skits—and his satire was scathing. Although as editor of this paper he advocated High Tory doctrine, at heart, as already related, his sympathies were with the Nationalists who suffered in the manner of his Shamus O'Brien.

In 1844, Le Fanu married Susan, daughter of George Bennett,* Q.C., by whom he had a family of two sons and two daughters. When Mr. Bennett died, he left his house No. 18(now 70), Merrion Square, Dublin, to his son-in-law. Hither Sheridan Le Fanu accordingly removed, and this house was his home for the rest of his life, and the place where most of his literary work was written. His first book, which occupied some years, was published in 1845 and entitled *The Cock and Anchor*—an excellent " costume " romance of old Dublin in the eighteenth century, abounding with exciting adventures, highway robberies, murders, and hair-breadth escapes. It also presents very accurate and picturesque scenic descriptions and some clever characterisation. Blarden was an earlier study of implacable villainy, just as Miss Martha in a way foreran the terrible Frenchwoman in *Uncle Silas;* and Oliver French is quite an original, humorous creation. This book was followed in 1847 by *The Fortunes of Colonel Torlogh O'Brien*, illustrated by Phiz, a Jacobite story dealing with the time when James the Second was in Ireland, in 1689-1690, and the unhappy days after the Battle of

---

* Another of Mr. Bennett's daughters, Jane, married, in 1835, the Rev. Delves Broughton, and became the mother of Rhoda Broughton. Mrs. Wilson (mother of the late Field-Marshal Sir Henry Wilson) is related to the Bennett family.

the Boyne. Many of the scenes were laid in the Limerick district so well known to the author, and the story, despite faults of style, for incident and adventure can hold its own with the best rivals in the same school of romance. Strange to say, these two books were not very successful, and did little to make Le Fanu known in his native country. Somewhat disappointed, he, for the time being, abandoned the composition of romances, and, with the exception of writing a few ghost stories and other short pieces, the next fifteen years were devoted to journalism. It is matter for regret that Le Fanu received no encouragement to continue his series of Irish historical romances, for few writers were so ably equipped to understand and interpret the forces, spiritual and natural, of his romantic native land. He might have done for Ireland what Scott achieved for Scotland.

In 1851, Le Fanu published anonymously a little red volume entitled *Ghost Stories and Tales of Mystery*, with four illustrations by Phiz, and now extremely rare. It contained, in addition to *The Evil Guest* and two other stories reprinted from *The Dublin University Magazine*, one of the author's finest essays in the horrible—*The Watcher* (the title was inappropriately changed to *The Familiar* when the story was reprinted in *In a Glass Darkly*). For sheer terror, the haunting of the unhappy protagonist of this tale has no equal. It is a crescendo of horror. At first he is conscious of footsteps dogging him at lonely spots. They intensify. In time, the malignant Watcher becomes visible; and then that appalling death scene, where the author skilfully leaves to the imagination what supreme terror finally wrested the shuddering soul from poor Barton's body. *The Watcher* was excellently illustrated, together with other early tales, by the author's son, Brinsley Le Fanu, in the editions published by Downey, 1889-1896.

It was the accident of domestic bereavement that caused Le Fanu to turn again to the writing of full-length novels (with only occasional Irish setting). His wife died prematurely in 1858, and her loss was an irreparable grief to Le Fanu. From this date he became a recluse and gave up all society save that of a few relatives and intimate friends. It was during the resulting sad and lonely period that his thoughts reverted to literary composition for solace, and the result was that fine—his finest—romance, *The House by the Churchyard*. Herein he conjured up and related with the flair of a consummate tale-teller all the romantic conditions of Chapelizod familiar to him in his boyhood. Many actual characters he remembered are introduced, and every aspect of the aforetime village minutely described. There is a

K

sense of impending and immutable tragedy that arrests attention throughout the long length of this story. Light scenes may intervene, but ever the motifs of murder and retribution press forward with a sort of stately inevitableness. At the outset, at the very opening of the first chapter, the right key-note is struck with supreme artistry. The influences of Nature are attune with the atmosphere of menace which is to envelop the story : —

"An awfully dark night came down on Chapelizod and all the country round. I believe there was no moon, and the stars had been quite put out under the wet ' blanket of the night,' which impenetrable muffler overspread the sky with a funereal darkness.

"There was a little of that sheet-lightning early in the evening which betokens sultry weather. The clouds, column after column, came up sullenly over the Dublin mountains, rolling themselves from one horizon to the other into one black dome of vapour, their slow but steady motion contrasting with the awful stillness of the air. There was a weight in the atmosphere, and a sort of undefined menace brooding over the little town, as if unseen crime or danger—some mystery of iniquity—was stealing into the heart of it, and the disapproving heavens scowled a melancholy warning."

No need to point out the powerful, grim characterisation that gives life to Dangerfield, Sturk, Black Dillon, and many another. *The House by the Churchyard* was issued first in *The Dublin University Magazine* (which Le Fanu had just purchased) during 1862-3 under the family pseudonym of Charles de Cresseron, and it was published in London by Tinsley in 1863.

Wylder's Hand followed rapidly in 1863-4, and this second grim story of murder and retributive fate was regarded by the author's friend, Charles Lever, as Le Fanu's finest work. Lever wrote to him : " You will never beat it—equal it you may. . . . It is first-rate . . . at my fireside you carry off the palm from all competitors." Yet Lever's kindly estimate was controverted almost ere it was penned, for there followed the same year, 1864, *Uncle Silas*, which is generally held to be Le Fanu's masterpiece. Here, again, it is the sense of impending tragedy and horror long drawn out which is almost overwhelming in its cumulative effect. The imagination is excited and dilated to such a pitch that when the actual scene of the murder is reached it is almost an anticlimax. In the original short form of the story it was the heroine's girl cousin who was murdered in mistake, and hence its title, *The Murdered Cousin*, when reprinted in *Ghost Stories*, 1851. In *Uncle Silas* the victim was changed to Madame de la Rougierre. This terrible, weird Frenchwoman was, perhaps, Le Fanu's most powerful creation, though Silas Ruthyn himself is a most subtle study of cool, calculating, velvet-gloved villainy. Madame de la Rougierre had a prototype for some of her physical and mental characteristics in the person of a Swiss governess who was known to Sheridan Le Fanu in his childhood. His recollections of this woman and his literary art combined to create one of the four supreme governesses of fiction—but as regards the other three, Jane Eyre, Miss Wirt, and Miss Gwilt, only the last named was of criminal quality. Much of *Uncle Silas* was written at Beaumaris, where Le Fanu often took his family for the summer holidays. He had a strong love for the place, as he had stayed there with his wife in the happy days of the past. Another locality he had visited with her soon after their marriage was Buxton; and the fateful house and gloomy domain of Bartram-Haugh in Derbyshire, so minutely pictured in *Uncle Silas*, could be identified with an estate in the neighbourhood of that town.

Le Fanu had now in the course of three years produced three sensational stories of murder, and some public comment on his predilection for mystery and bloodshed no doubt caused him to prefix to *Uncle Silas* his able defence of the sensational novel, wherein he maintained that death, crime, and mystery find a place in all the romances of Walter Scott. During this period also he wrote some fine romantic ballads, including *The Legend of the Glaive*. *Beatrice*, a romantic drama, dates from 1865. These, like most of his novels, appeared first in *The Dublin University Magazine*.

He was a true poet, as is evidenced further by the sad little songs scattered through his novels, such as this:—

" The river ran between them,
　And she looked upon the stream,
　And the soldier looked upon her
　As a dreamer on a dream.
' Believe me—oh, believe,'
　He sighed, ' you peerless maid;
　My honour is pure,
　And my true love sure,
　Like the white plume in my hat,
　And my shining blade.'

" The river ran between them,
　And she smiled upon the stream,
　Like one that smiles at folly—
　A dreamer on a dream.
' I do not trust your promise,
　I will not be betrayed;
　For your faith is light,
　And your cold wit bright,
　Like the white plume in your hat,
　And your shining blade.'

" The river ran between them,
  And he rode beside the stream;
And he turned away and parted,
  As a dreamer from his dream :
And his comrade brought his message
  From the field where he was laid—
    Just his name to repeat,
    And to lay at her feet
  The white plume from his hat,
  And his shining blade."

What simple pathos, but it rings true. In entirely a different
vein is that grim ballad of the ghost of Tim Rooney, who
assures his murderer how he will be with him for evermore : —

" Up through the wather your secret rises;
  The stones won't keep it, and it lifts the mould,
An' it tracks your footsteps, and your fun surprises,
  And it sits at the fire beside you, black and cowld.

An' when the pariod iv your life is over,
  The frightful hour of judgment then will me ;
And, Shamus Hanlon, heavy on your shoulder,
  I'll lay my cowld hand, and you'll go wid me."

The next few years were busy ones for Le Fanu. Between
1865 and 1869 he produced six excellent novels, more or less
sensational—*Guy Deverell*,* *All in the Dark*, *The Tenants of
Malory*. *A Lost Name*, *Haunted Lives*, and *The Wyvern
Mystery*. Although Le Fanu was now a recluse, he still, at
this period, found pleasure in the society of a few valued relatives
and friends. His gifted Sheridan cousins, Mrs. Norton and
Lady Gifford (to whom *Uncle Silas* was dedicated), used to visit
him; and an ever-welcome guest was his late wife's niece, Miss
Rhoda Broughton. Mr. Percy FitzGerald and Mr. Alfred P.
Graves were also much at the house, and when Charles Lever
was in Dublin in 1865, the melancholy author of mysterious tales
found much delight in the boisterous company of rollicking
" Harry Lorrequer." For Le Fanu was a man of moods. At
times he, too, could still be anecdotal and tell an amusing story
as well as any Irishman, for his sense of humour never left him,
though it became—like his love of practical jokes—more and
more suppressed by gloomy fancies as his years drew to an end.

Mr. Percy FitzGerald has drawn a pleasant picture of Le
Fanu's home life, and how of an evening in the old house in
Merrion Square, hung with Sheridan and other family portraits,
Miss Rhoda Broughton used to read aloud her early literary
efforts—tales of rugged heroes and fragile heroines. It was her

---

* Swinburne read Le Fanu. He described *Guy Deverell* as " too hasty,
too blurred and blottesque;" and said of *Uncle Silas* that the hero " would
be more ghastly if he were less ghostly."

SHERIDAN LE FANU

From a contemporary photograph sent by his son, Mr. Brinsley Le Fanu.

[*Page* 148.

uncle, Le Fanu, who established Miss Broughton as a novelist, for he accepted her first stories, *Not Wisely but Too Well* and *Cometh up as a Flower*, for his own magazine, and in due course introduced her to his London publisher, Bentley. Miss Broughton has a very agreeable recollection of Le Fanu as a courteous host and entertaining talker, though by reason of his arduous literary work he only appeared at meals and in the evening.

Le Fanu's method of work was rather peculiar. He wrote much at night, in bed, using bound books of copy-paper for his manuscripts. He always had two candles by his side on a small table; one of these would be left alight when he took a short sleep. Waking again about 2 a.m., he would brew himself some strong tea—which he drank habitually and frequently—and then write for another hour or two in that eerie period of the night when human vitality is at its lowest ebb and occult powers said to be in the ascendant. No wonder, with his brain working so actively, day and night, with his terrible and mysterious mental creations, that in these last years Le Fanu was haunted by horrible dreams, and that his mind became obsessed with phantasms and the supernatural. Probably some of his last horrifying stories—*Green Tea*, the vampire *Carmilla*, and others—came to him in the form of dreams.* But apart from drinking much strong tea, from which he obtained inspiration, he was a most abstemious man, and a non-smoker. Le Fanu always breakfasted in bed, and about mid-day went down to his rather gloomy dining-room at the back of the house, where he would resume work, writing at a little table which had been a favourite possession of his grand-uncle, R. B. Sheridan. This room opened out on a small garden, pleasant in spring with lilac and flowering shrubs and fruit blossom, and in this little monastic-like close he took what exercise he fancied, pacing the paths with pencil and paper in hand. In these last years he rarely left his own boundaries. Only under cover of the darkness of night would he sometimes venture out to the office of his magazine; or to some old bookshop in search of works dealing with demonology or ghost lore, where he would pore over the volumes the booksellers had reserved for him. Although the supernatural was his obsessing passion, he apparently never embraced any of the visionary doctrines concerned with magic and intercourse with spirits. He was deeply learned in the views

---

* It is true Le Fanu used to say he had heard of a case in real life in which a man was haunted by a similar demon or delusion, as is described in *Green Tea*, in the form of a monkey.

of Swedenborg and the other exponents of demoniacal
possession; but the anæmic and mild manifestations of ordinary
Spiritualism had no attraction for him: his imagination soared
to terrific horrors far beyond spirit rappings and writings and
faint materialisations, and lingered with

> " The dark folk who live in souls
>   Of passionate men, like bats in the dead trees;
>   And with the wayward twilight companies."

After le Fanu gave up the editorship of *The Dublin
University Magazine* in 1869, he practically disappeared from
mortal ken for the remaining four years of his life. He would
now see no one, and even his old friend, Charles Lever, was
refused admittance when he called at 18, Merrion Square during
his last visit to Dublin. This Le Fanu soon had cause to regret,
for Lever died shortly after. Such was the state of social
extinction of one who had been in other days, to quote Mr.
A. P. Graves, " the beau ideal of an Irish wit and scholar of the
old school." He still worked as hard and prolifically as ever.
In 1871 he produced three works—*Checkmate*; *The Rose and
the Key*, one of the best of his later sensational novels and
dealing with the horrors of a private asylum; and *Chronicles of
Golden Friars*, which contains some excellent ghost stories. In
1872 was published *In a Glass Darkly*, comprising Le Fanu's
finest short stories—*Green Tea*, *The Familiar* (*The Watcher*),
Mr. Justice Harbottle, *Carmilla*, and *The Dragon Volant*.*
Green Tea had originally appeared in *All the Year Round* in
1869, and was just such a grim tale of the supernatural as Dickens
delighted in.

Shortly before his death Le Fanu finished his last book, to
which by a strange coincidence or premonition he gave the title
of *Willing to Die* He died at 18, Merrion Square on February
7th, 1873, from heart disease, after a long and painful illness.
One of the most persistent of the weird dreams that troubled his
sleeping hours during his last years was of a vast and mysterious
old mansion (such as he had often depicted in his stories) in a
state of decay and threatening imminently to fall upon and crush
the dreamer. So painful was this recurring nightmare that he
would struggle and cry out in his sleep, and he mentioned the
matter to his doctor. When the end came, and the doctor stood
by the bedside of Sheridan Le Fanu and looked at the face of the
dead man, he said: " I feared this—that house fell at last."

I have pointed out the versatility of Le Fanu's work—how he

---

* See later, page 324, for some further mention of Le Fanu's short stories,
collected by Dr. M. R. James.

at different times was a writer of ballads voicing the aspirations and romance of Irish national life; a journalist expressing High Tory views; an historical romance writer; a writer of squibs and satires; a fine poet; and a supreme author of ghost stories and novels of murder and mystery. In these last categories he is pre-eminent, and his success is almost entirely achieved by his art of *suggesting* evil presences and coming horrors. Very rarely is there an actual, visible ghost in his stories. His was not the old school of traditionary apparitions, in white or grey, with blue fire, clanking chain, and wailing cry. His spectres—far more terrible—are in the brain of the haunted. Demoniacal possession, and the resultant delusional apparition, or concrete crime—these are the bases of Le Fanu's finest stories. For the actual details of a murder it is true he had rather a morbid partiality, and spared no particulars about the wounds and blood and the aspect of the mangled or strangled corpse. Like Ainsworth, he was distinctly macaberesque, and both seem to have had a sort of *flair* for scenes of human torture and physical pain. There is a description in *Torlogh O'Brien* of the death of a man by the strapado which makes painful reading, so particular are the details of the agony. But, after all, this is merely realism, and realism is not unknown or unprofitable to romance writers of to-day. However realistic Le Fanu may be, there is over most of his scenes of horror a softening veil of romance and mystery; and if Death is all too prominent in his books and poems—why so it is, unhappily, in real life, and Le Fanu's chief exemplar is but a reminder of that inexorable enemy from whom no poor mortal may escape at the last.

AGNES STRICKLAND.*

ALTHOUGH lacking any very particular distinction in literary style, and not altogether free from bias and partisanship in historical judgment, it will nevertheless be conceded that the sisters Agnes and Elizabeth Strickland were pre-eminent as female historians in their generation. No other writers of their sex could claim to be historians in the real sense of the word: many other women produced excellent memoirs of the " scissors and paste " order, but they made no pretension to research among original and archaic documents. The Stricklands— Agnes in particular—have rarely been surpassed by any historian, of either sex, in diligence of research and a really remarkable *flair* for discovering documentary evidence of historical importance in almost forgotten archives. Even now, Agnes Strickland is not credited sufficiently with the great value of the historical and archæological data she gleaned from ancient French manuscripts concerning the lives of the early Queens Consort of England, of whom practically nothing was known in this country prior to her biographies. Her research among the original material relating to Mary Queen of Scots has, it is true, received more tribute. Whyte Melville, for instance, dedicated his historical novel, *The Queen's Maries*, in 1862, " To a lady whose untiring energy and historical research have added largely to the literature of our country, and whose eloquent defence of a calumniated Queen has identified with Mary Stuart the name of Agnes Strickland."

The very limitations of Agnes Strickland as a stylist add to the charm of her biographies. She is no cold narrator in stately and polished prose of impartial history; warm in partisanship, with feminine sympathy, and an intense realisation of the pathos and tears of Life, she gives the human touch when at her best in the lives of those queens who were most unhappy and the victims of fate—Ann Boleyn, Catherine Howard, Mary Stuart, and Mary Beatrice.

The literary style of Elizabeth Strickland was much more masculine and free from personal sentiment. She was a curious remote woman, who early in life decided to leave her home and live alone in London (an early pioneer of feminine liberty). All her literary work was produced anonymously; she desired no fame or adulation. Although she never allowed her name to

---

* *The Bookman,* April, 1919.

appear in connection with the books she wrote in collaboration with her sister, it must be remembered that to *The Queens of England* alone she contributed twenty of the biographies, including those of Mary Tudor, Mary the Second, and Anne. However, as she ever disliked publicity of any kind, this memoir is confined to the career of her sister historian who was temperamentally her opposite in every way, and enjoyed society and literary fame.

Agnes, born in London on August 19th, 1796, was the second surviving daughter of Thomas Strickland, manager of the Greenland Docks, by his second wife, Elizabeth Homer. Agnes Strickland liked to think that her family was a branch of the Stricklands of Sizergh Castle, Westmorland. There does not seem to be any authentic evidence to establish the point, but in all probability the two families were connected and of the same origin, for both were seated in the same district of the north-west of England.

The first traceable ancestor of the historian was a certain Robert Strickland of Light Haugh—Furness Fells—in the time of Henry the Eighth. His grandson Samuel was buried at Hawks-head in 1687. The latter had two sons. The elder followed the exiled Stuarts to St. Germain (as did many of the Stricklands of Sizergh); he later went to Spain in the cause of the Bourbons and was supposed to have been killed at Almanza. But twenty-eight years afterwards he returned to England and successfully claimed the family property, which had naturally passed to his younger brother. This brother, Thomas, of Colton, had married Agnes Taylor of Finsthwaite Hall, on the west bank of Lake Windermere, and their son Samuel, now portionless, came to London to seek his fortune in business. He in time married Elizabeth Cotterell, a member of a Staffordshire family, also devoted to the cause of the Stuarts, and maternally descended from one of the Penderel brothers, who so materially aided the escape of King Charles the Second at Boscobel. These were the grandparents of Agnes Strickland, who, it will be seen, had a pedigree of some historical interest and romance, whereby she inherited her life-long sentimental sympathy with the Stuarts and Jacobitism.

Agnes Strickland's early years were spent at The Laurels, Thorpe, Norwich, and at Stowe House, near Bungay. In 1808 the family removed to Reydon Hall, about two miles from Southwold on the Suffolk coast. In this ancient and picturesque house of Tudor characteristics, amid a charming rural setting, the young Stricklands—six sisters and two brothers—led a life

somewhat like that of the Brontë children at Haworth a quarter
of a century later. That is to say, they passed their time mainly
in a romantic world of their own imagining, with story-telling
and play-acting and first early attempts at literary composition
in the way of tales and poems. But Reydon Hall was of course a
far happier and more comfortable home than the bleak parsonage
of the Yorkshire moors. The Stricklands were a healthy and
merry little coterie, and their abode a place of romance for
imaginative minds. There were mysterious garrets and cellars
and devious stairways and recesses. Ghost stories innumerable
attached to the Hall; in particular a certain " Old Martin "
haunted a remote garret, and a " Little Woman in Grey "
caused the crank of the great mangle to turn by unseen agency
at dead midnight, together with many other maid-scaring pranks.
The noises of rats and the wailings of the wind in the great
chimneys claimed a supernatural origin. In a huge brass-hinged
chest were preserved old costumes and Court dresses of the time
of Queen Anne—invaluable for purposes of " dressing up ";
there was a fine library containing many books which had
belonged to Sir Isaac Newton (who was a grand-uncle of Thomas
Strickland's first wife); and, finally, a great store of writing
paper and quill pens (once the property of an uncle on the staff
of the Bank of England), which provided the essential materials
for literary lucubration. Five of the Strickland sisters achieved
publication of their efforts a few years afterwards.

In the case of Agnes, her first composition to be printed was
a *Monody upon the Death of Princess Charlotte* in 1817; but
her first publication of note was a metrical tale entitled *Worcester
Field, or The Cavalier* (1826). Other works, such as *Historical
Tales*, followed; and in the decade of 1829-1839 Agnes
Strickland was a frequent contributor of prose and verse to
The Keepsake and other annuals then at the zenith of their
popularity. In 1835 she had some hopes of seeing the production
of a play from her pen, for Macready notes in his Diary
May 8th-10th: " Read three acts of Miss Agnes Strickland's
play; how much time I am forced to expend in this kind of
unprofitable labour. . . . Wrote to Fred. Reynolds on Miss
Strickland's play." And there, apparently, the matter ended.

In the meanwhile Elizabeth Strickland had become editor of
The Court Journal, and for this paper she had written some short
biographies of female sovereigns. These suggested to Agnes
the idea of *The Lives of the Queens of England*, and the vast
work, in collaboration with her sister, was commenced. The first
volume, with preface dated from Reydon Hall, December 16th,

1839, appeared early in 1840, and was dedicated by permission to Queen Victoria. It met with immediate success. But unfortunately Agnes, who had arranged for the publication of the work with Colburn, was ignorant of the peculiarities of publishing, and unfair advantage was taken of the fact. A settlement of the author's share in the receipts from the first volume was long delayed, and when it was proffered it proved to be paltry in amount. Agnes fell ill from the effects of her hard work and disappointment at the financial results. After much wearisome negotiation, Colburn was compelled to make a new agreement with the sisters owing to the fortunate (for them) circumstance that he had hitherto been unaware of Elizabeth as a joint author in the work. For the new third volume a hundred and fifty pounds was paid, and the same sum for each succeeding one of the series. But even this was a ridiculously inadequate remuneration for work involving such tremendous research and labour. And the books were some of the most successful that Colburn ever published.

Although Agnes Strickland received but poor monetary reward for her labours, *The Queens of England* brought her instantly literary fame and social honours. She became a celebrity of the first degree. Everybody sought her acquaintance, and all the great houses of the kingdom were open to her. In those days the great territorial peers preserved a semi-royal state, and Agnes Strickland fully appreciated associating with the Dukes of Norfolk and Devonshire* and Somerset, the Duchess of Sutherland, the Spencers, the Dundonalds, the Seafields, and the Blantyres. She was presented at Court by Lady Stourton (a niece of Edward Weld, the first husband of Mrs. Fitzherbert). The Queen asked for her autograph, as did countless other people. She met every one of note, including the Duke of Wellington, Brougham, Macaulay, Disraeli (who paid her many compliments on her work), and Guizot. Walter Scott and Campbell she had known in earlier years.

Agnes Strickland was fully able to maintain her well-won position. Without being exactly handsome she had a striking and aristocratic face, with fine dark eyes and hair, and an imposing presence. Her conversation of course was intellectual,

---

* Agnes Strickland and her sister received a special invitation to inspect some rare archives at Chiswick House by the courtesy of that truly *grand seigneur*, the sixth Duke of Devonshire :—
 " The Duke came from Brighton to receive them, and opened his stores for their examination. He gave them a delicate French dinner; but he dispensed with the attendance of his servants in the dining-room, summoning them when requisite by striking upon a tumbler. Notwithstanding his deafness they found him a pleasant companion—amiable, manly, and unassuming, though surrounded with splendour on every side."

as befitted one of wide reading and great historical knowledge. Her rather loud, drawling voice was a marked feature in *la parure de la célebrité*; but she was always agreeable, and never didactic and egoistic in the manner of some who have reached that sacred caste. There is interesting confirmation of Agnes Strickland's celebrity as early as 1842 when she was present at the " View " of Horace Walpole's collections at Strawberry Hill, prior to the famous sale by Robins. Referring to some exquisite miniatures there by Peter Oliver, the Whartons relate in their *Wits and Beaux of Society* : —

" How sadly, in referring to these invaluable pictures, does one's mind revert to the day when, before the hammer of Robins had resounded in these rooms—before his transcendent eloquence had been heard at Strawberry—Agnes Strickland, followed by all eyes, pondered over that group of portraits : how, as she slowly withdrew, we of the commonalty, scarce worthy to look, gathered around the spot again, and wondered at the perfect life, the perfect colouring, proportion, and keeping of those tiny vestiges of a bygone generation."

As late as 1867, Agnes Strickland relates how, when she arrived at the Royal Academy Soirée, Lord Houghton gave her his arm to lead her to the President, Sir Francis Grant, the while his daughter, Amicia Milnes, then " a fair Annot-Lyle girl of fourteen," whispered to him: " Papa, is that lady the real Miss Agnes Strickland? "

Amid all this fame it must be stated that certain clever men disliked Agnes Strickland. There is the almost incredible story of George Borrow's insolence to her, of how when she said she would like to send him a set of her *Queens of England*, he replied: " For Heaven's sake don't, Madame, I shouldn't know what to do with them," and then turning to a friend, he added: " What a damned fool that woman is." Lady Ritchie told a rather pointless anecdote of how at a reception at the Bishop of London's house in 1859, Milman, Dean of St. Paul's, asked: " Do you know who the lady behind you is?" " Mrs. Grote," replied Miss Thackeray. " My dear Mrs. Grote," exclaimed the Dean, " Heaven forbid! It's Miss Agnes Strickland in black velvet with a bead *berthe*," and turned his (dis)courteous old back upon her.

Macaulay was probably jealous of her fame as an historian, and when he was assigned as her escort at a dinner, given by the Duke and Duchess of Somerset, they did not get on well together. Miss Strickland thought him pompous, ugly, and vulgar in manners. Opposite to them at dinner was seated a very good-looking but silent young man. Macaulay commenced a tirade on the stupidity of handsome men, but Agnes Strickland

AGNES STRICKLAND

From the portrait by Cruikshank.

[*Page* 156.

observed " it was a consolation for ugly men to consider them so." Whereupon the rival historian became sulky and spake no more to his fair—or, rather, dark—neighbour.

During the thirty years, 1842-1872, life was very pleasant for Agnes Strickland. She was constantly engaged in literary work, varied by visits to France, Holland, and all parts of Britain, when she combined recreation with research for her books. She visited London every season, generally staying at 4, Hyde Park Place, with Mr. W. A. Mackinnon, the father of her great friend, the Duchesse de Gramont, and of Lady Dundonald. Her two other most intimate friends were Jane Porter and Georgina Stuart (Lady Buchanan).

After the completion of *The Queens of England, The Lives of the Queens of Scotland* commenced to appear in 1850. The new work was published by Blackwood, who treated the authors in an honourable and courteous manner throughout. In Mary Queen of Scots, Agnes Strickland found her most congenial subject. *The Bachelor Kings of England* appeared in 1861; and when Agnes Strickland was presented by his request to the youthful Prince of Wales (Edward the Seventh) at a ball in Dublin, he assured her, apropos of this book, that he did not intend to be one of them. She describes the Prince as " a very pretty fellow, small in stature, but very well shaped, and dignified in appearance, though timid in manner. . . He blushed and was a little agitated while speaking with me."

The Lives of the Tudor Princesses and *The Stuart Princesses* followed in 1868 and 1872. Agnes Strickland was the author of other books such as *The Seven Bishops*, 1866; *Old Friends and New Acquaintances*, 1860; and *How Will it End?* 1865. The last named was a novel for which Bentley paid her two hundred and fifty pounds, although it had been commenced far back in her girlhood. She had only mediocre gifts as a tale-teller and a graceful touch in verse: her real talents found expression as an historian, and as such she will be remembered. In 1870 she received a Civil List pension of a hundred pounds a year in recognition of her services to literature, on the recommendation of Gladstone.

In 1865 the old home at Reydon Hall was broken up owing to the death of Mrs. Strickland, and Agnes went to live at Park Lane Cottage, Southwold, a pleasant house adjoining the extensive common and not far from the sea. There her last years were spent.

For a time she was still able to visit London and the Continent and her many friends; but in 1872 she had a serious fall down some stairs from the effects of which she never recovered. Some months later a paralytic stroke affected her speech and clouded her once brilliant intellect. Two years went by. She rallied at times and was able to walk out a little and visit her friends in Southwold. But her literary labours were over, and never again was she to take her place as the guest of honour at a London function or in some great country house. She bore her deprivations bravely and never complained at her changed and restricted existence. The days of celebrity were done, and after a period of terrible pain merciful death came on July 13th, 1874, when she had nearly completed her seventy-eighth year. She was buried in Southwold churchyard.

Thus ended the long and useful life of Agnes Strickland. She was an able historian and a kind-hearted woman, beloved alike by the poor of her locality in Suffolk and by numerous friends in all ranks of society and the world of letters.

RODEN NOEL.*

RODEN NOEL is of that select category termed Poet's Poets, that is to say he is read and appreciated mainly by those who possess some measure of literary expression either creatively or critically. But he deserves to be far more widely known and loved, for his work is of extensive ambit and appeals to many tastes. He pictures in vivid colours the loveliness of Nature and Physical Beauty; he touches the lute of life with delicate little lyrics that transfigure death and sad things; he is the singer of wistful memories; he recovers an echo from the deep woods of pagan joys and the reeden pipes of Pan. His mental development, too, offers as remarkable a contrast as his poetry. Brought up as a Calvinist (so he termed the ultra-Protestant faith of his mother's family), frankly pagan and Hellenic in youth, he next passed through a period of despairing unbelief and hopeless agnosticism, finally, by the way of a great bereavement, finding consolation and peace in Christianity. Though an aristocrat by all lines of descent and laws of heredity, he was not in sympathy with his own order: he leaned to Socialism, and was ever pre-occupied by the sufferings of the poor and the wrongs of the oppressed.

The Honourable Roden Berkeley Wriothesley Noel was the fourth son of Charles Noel, first Earl of Gainsborough (of the second creation) and the only son of his fourth wife, Lady Frances Jocelyn, daughter of Robert, third Earl of Roden (the ardent Protestant and Grand Master of the Orange Society—" bigoted, obstinate, and virtuous," as Greville described him), who married Maria, daughter of Thomas, Lord Le Despencer. Born on August 27th, 1834, Roden Noel's childhood was spent mainly at his father's seats, Exton Park, Rutland, and Barham Court, near Teston, in Kent, which latter property had come to the Noel family from his paternal grandmother, Diana Middleton, Baroness Barham in her own right. He was also a good deal at Tullymore Park, County Down, the seat of his grandfather, Lord Roden; and he travelled abroad with his parents. The happiest recollections of his happy childhood were associated with Barham Court in the company of his mother and his little sister, Lady Victoria Noel. Long years after, when Lady Gainsborough died at Barham Court, in 1885, and was

* The Bookman, December, 1917.

buried at Teston, her son recalled those early memories in one of his most beautiful poems, *To My Mother*.

At the age of twelve Roden Noel went to Harrow, where he remained two years, and then became a pupil of the Rev. Charles Harbin at Hindon, in Wiltshire. In due course he proceeded to Trinity College, Cambridge, where he graduated M.A. in 1858. His most intimate friend at the University was Henry Sidgwick, with whom, later, he carried on an intimate correspondence. As Sidgwick said: " We talked and wrote to each other, in the eagerness of youth, on all things in heaven and earth." Through Sidgwick, Noel became a close friend of John Addington Symonds (with whom he had much in common temperamentally), Frederic Myers, and Thomas Woolner, R.A., the sculptor.

In the spring of 1859 he travelled in Egypt with his friend, Cyril Graham, later proceeding to Syria. Here he was attacked by sunstroke, but managed to ride to Tyre, whence he was taken in a felucca to Beyrout. He was now seriously ill, and the family of M. de Broë, a Swiss and manager of the Ottoman Bank at Beyrout, took compassion on him and nursed him back to health in their own house. There was a romantic and happy sequel, for in 1863 Roden Noel married Miss Alice de Broë, the banker's eldest daughter—a marriage, as Robert Buchanan put it, that proved " to be the crown of a fortunate life." It saved him from the dangers and the sorrows and the vain regrets which menace those who seek to recover Hellas and pagan things. For Roden Noel was a seeker after the Ideal of Beauty, which found wonderful expression in his early poems. As Robert Buchanan said: " Out of the portals of a temple of white marble, glimmering through the fogs and clouds of contemporary literature, Roden Noel stept like a young god, with a message from the old Greek world which is ever new. The joy of earth was with him, the sunlight of a lost Divinity clung around him, and so light was his footstep that he seemed to walk on air. Even so I saw him approaching, many years ago, and my heart went out to meet him, in the full certainty that he could speak to me of the hidden things of Hellas, of the vanished Wonderland where gods were born."

This was the period which generated Roden Noel's poems, *Pan* and *Ganymede*, the latter being described by *The Athenæum* as " an idyll thoroughly Greek, a bit of work which reads like Theocritus in the original "; and by Sainte-Beuve as " ce petit chef-d'œuvre de *Ganymede*."

" Azure the heaven, with rare and feathery cloud;
Azure the sea, far-scintillating light,
Soft, rich, like velvet, yielding to the eye
Horizons haunted with soft dreamlike sails;
A temple hypæthral open to the air
Nigh, on the height, columned with solid flame,
Of flutings and acanthus-work instinct
With lithe green lizards and the shadows sharp
Slant, barring gold floor and inner wall.

   .   .   .   .   .

A youth, bare-limbed, the loveliest in the world,
Gloatingly falling on his lily side,
Smoothing one rounded arm and dainty hand
Whereon his head, conscious and conquering,
All chestnut-curled, rests listless and superb.

   .   .   .   .   .

The bird hath seized him, if it be a bird,
And he, though wildered, hardly seems afraid,
So lightly lovingly those eagle talons
Lock the soft yielding flesh of either flank,
His back so tender, thigh and shoulder pillowed
How warmly, whitely in the tawny down
Of that imperial eagle amorous.

   .   .   .   .

Behold ! he fades, receding evermore
From straining vision misting dim with tears,
Gleaming aloft swan-white into the blue."

These heart-outpoured songs, redolent of Greek atmosphere and superb sensuousness, appeared in the volume entitled *Beatrice, and other Poems*, published in 1868. Noel's first volume, *Behind the Veil, and Other Poems*, had been issued in 1863 by Macmillan in London and Cambridge, but afterwards he tried to suppress it. He wrote of this book: —

" I wanted it forgotten. It is so very crude in style, though it is a quarry for poetry, and I have used some of it, and may use more elsewhere, for poems. . . . Before this I wrote very fluently poetry by the yard, but with no ideas in it. Then I fell back on deep thought and study of prose, and when I tried to embody this in poetry, I made this fiasco of a book. I was brought up a Calvinist. Then, under the religious influence of F. D. Maurice, and philosophers like Swedenborg, I wrote this book, which, on the whole, is religious. Afterwards I gradually lost my beliefs, and became partly agnostic, partly pantheistic."

After travelling further in Greece and Turkey, Roden Noel returned to England in 1864. He had essayed business in Beyrout without much success, and had abandoned his early intention of entering the Church. From 1867 to 1871 he acted as Groom of the Privy Chamber to Queen Victoria, but Court life was not to his taste. He stayed for a time in Onslow Crescent, where his daughter Frances was born; and he also occupied a house near Warlies, Waltham Abbey, the home of his sister, Lady Victoria,

L

who had married Sir Thomas Fowell Buxton in 1862. But during most of this period of his Court duties he lived at Kew Cottage (now known as Royal Cottage) on Kew Green, a house which was lent to him by the widow of his uncle, Viscount Jocelyn.* At Kew, the poet's eldest son, Conrad Le Despencer Noel (now Vicar of Thaxted), was born in July, 1869; and here Roden Noel wrote much of the verse which was published in his next volume, *The Red Flag, and Other Poems*, 1872. Some of these poems reflect the charming surroundings of his home, which at the back communicated by a private gate with Kew Gardens, and in front the Thames was but a few steps away across the Green. Thus in *Early Spring* (Kew, 1870) he interprets the scene as he wanders along the path by the river; *On Richmond Hill* expresses the pantheistic thoughts inspired by that wonderful panorama of Nature; and in *Palingenesis* there is a vignette of Petersham in spring, when hawthorns and chestnut trees " sun-smitten to the core, froth over in dumb ecstasy of bloom," and its " little church, with golden vane aglister in the sun, ancient, rich red, and weather-worn." This book of poems won the admiration of Tennyson, who said *Azrael* was "very lovely," and *A Vision of the Desert* and *The Dweller in Two Worlds* among the finest things he had ever read. Also *The Water-Nymph and the boy*, though he thought it immoral. He sent for Noel, and gave him much advice and encouragement, and concluded by observing, " You don't mind my saying all this? I should not do it if I did not think it worth while. Coleridge did exactly the same for me when I was beginning." Years after, shortly before his death, Tennyson wrote to Noel: " You are no minor poet. Your book is full of true poetry."

In 1874 appeared *Livingstone in Africa*, a long descriptive poem in seven cantos, containing much picturesque diction and vivid imagery; and in 1877 *The House of Ravensburg*, a tragedy, in which the author did not fear to introduce the supernatural in the manner of *Hamlet*. Curiously enough, Noel regarded this play as his finest work. He wrote to Mr. Havelock Ellis: —

" *Ravensburg* is the most human thing I have done, and expresses my pity for all tremendous problems of human destiny. *Ravensburg* expresses the idea of Nemesis or Heredity which so got hold of the Greeks and which I believe in as strongly—adapted to more modern ideas."

And he told his sister: —

" In *Ravensburg* immortality is purely dramatic, and I did not believe in it. I am not the poet of free-will as Browning was."

* Lady Jocelyn, one of the beautiful daughters of that Countess Cowper who subsequently married Palmerston, was also attached to the Household of Queen Victoria.

But a change of views was about to dawn.

In 1871 the Noels had removed to a house (now called Firlands) on Maybury Hill, Woking, which was then a very charming and sequestered place amid the pine woods and heathlands. Here was destined to occur the great joy and the great sorrow of the poet's life; the event which changed his spiritual outlook and brought him, after sore travail, from unbelief to Christianity; the grief which, out of the furnace of suffering, was transmuted into his finest creative work. At Maybury Hill in November, 1871, was born Noel's youngest child, Eric, who became the idol of his father's life and was loved with a devotion beyond all belief. In January, 1877, the boy died at the age of five years, and the world was darkened and all was changed for the desolate father. Plunged in the deeps of the blackest despair, his own bitter grief, and the misery and pain he found in the world everywhere, shattered his belief in all creeds. Faithless, hopeless, and convinced that he would never see his child again, he realised that he was verging on madness.

" For more than a year," he said, " I cared for nothing, not literature, not even Nature. Yet Nature was something to me even then, I suppose, for I went alone to Sark and swam a great deal in the sea among the wonderful caves."

He had always been interested in the doctrines of Swedenborg and in Spiritualism, but he found that these were not able to comfort him in his dire distress or place him in communion with his loved and lost one. Then it came about that he found consolation and hope in the New Testament. His soul-searing experience and mental progress found expression in the series of poems he wrote during the three years following his son's death. They were mainly composed at San Remo, where the winters were passed, and were published in 1881 as *A Little Child's Monument*. He wrote to his sister: —

" After Eric's death a complete revolution took place in my thoughts very gradually. My first book inspired by faith, gradually restored after his death, was the *Monument*. That is the record of doubt and despair at first, and of faith only towards the end."

There are forty-two poems in this volume which reflect Noel's changing moods in turn. Despair is the key-note at first, exemplified most pitifully in *Dead*: —

" Where the child's joy-carol
Rang sweeter than the spheres,
There, centre of deep silence,
Darkness, and tears,
On his bed
The child lay dead.

L 2

There a man sat stolid,
Stupefied and cold,
Save when the lamp's flicker
To poor love told
Some mocking lie
Of quivering eye,
Of lips that said
' *He is not dead.*'

Weary night went weeping,
Moaning long and low,
Till dim Dawn, awaking,
Found them so—
The heart that bled,
And his dim dead.

' *Measure him for his coffin,*'
He heard a stranger say;
And then he broke to laughing,
' *God! measure my poor clay,*
And shut me in my coffin,
A soul gone grey!
For hope lies dead,
Life is fled.' "

What a poignancy of sorrow and mental torture there is in
the line, " A soul gone grey." But gradually grief gives way
to memories of the past, and in *Music and the Child* and *Old
Scenes Revisited* he recalls the boy's brief life at Maybury Hill,
and lingers by his deserted garden beneath the windows of the
nursery in the now empty house: —

" Surely in the dim pinewood,
Or in the garden where he leapt,
In the enchanted solitude
Under the window where he slept.

.   .   .   .   .

Ah ! may I not thy semblance find
In the low light, or the low wind?
Do I not yearn to clasp thy ghost,
My own beloved, O my lost?

.   .   .   .   .

There in the days that are no more
Thy mother sang thee soft to sleep;
There sang thee into rest more deep,
Hushed to sleep for evermore.

.   .   .   .   .

But while bereft of thee we roam,
Thou art more near us, love, indeed,
More near than in thy earlier state,
Although we seem so desolate.
The dead from our wan eyes depart,
Only to nestle in our heart."

Then, step by step, consolation and belief are achieved, culminating in *The Desert Shall Blossom as the Rose* and *That They All May be, One.*

> " Whene'er there comes a little child,
> My darling comes with him;
> Whene'er I hear a birdie wild
> Who sings his merry whim,
> Mine sings with him:
> If a low strain of music sails
> Among melodious hills and dales,
> When a white lamb or kitten leaps,
> Or star, or vernal flower peeps,
> Where rainbow dews are pulsing joy,
> Or sunny waves, or leaflets toy,
> Then he who sleeps
> Softly wakes within my heart. . . . .
>
> .   .   .   .   .
>
> Lo ! an eyelid fluttered;
> I know the bosom heaved;
> Now his arms have uttered
> All I disbelieved.
> Dear eyes, long held in durance,
> For ever open wide,
> To yield my soul assurance
> Of all she hath denied."

A Little Child's Monument ranks with *In Memoriam* as a perfect tribute to one very dearly loved; but it has a more human appeal to the bereaved than Tennyson's great poem, which is always in the lofty regions of restrained thought and cold glittering technique, whereas Roden Noel is unrestrained in his grief and pleads for sympathy with warm, pulsating passion: —

> " I would embalm thee in my verse:
> To loving souls it shall rehearse
> Thy loveliness when I am cold,
> And, fragrant with it, may enfold
> For other hearts in misery
> Faint solace; words were sweet to me
> From hearts, who mourned what seemed to be
> Dear, like thee:
> These are thy swathings of rare spice,
> A golden shrine with gems of price,
> A monument of my device."

On returning to England, the Noels stayed for a time with Lady Gainsborough at 17, Hyde Park Square. In 1882 the poet published *A Philosophy of Immortality*, a prose argument for the permanent reality and survival of human personality, which reveals his interest in the manifestations of spiritualistic agencies. In 1885 appeared *Songs of the Heights and Deeps*, which included several fine poems, particularly *Thalatta* and *Suspiria*, whose metres were suggested by the surge of the sea, and *Melcha*, regarded by the author as the best of his long allegorical poems : " It is the philosophy of my ante-Christian years, a sort of pantheistic evolution philosophy." *Thalatta*, written at Land's End, is as fine as the magnificent sea poems of Swinburne, with an added touch of the " eerie tones of some who passed, wailing in the wind's wail, shadows drifting desolately." It is curious that Roden Noel was not more in sympathy with Swinburne, for both poets shared an intense love for the sea and swimming, Sark, children, and the work of Victor Hugo. But Noel rather resented the popular success which had come to the other and never to him. At this period, 1883-1887, he was living at 57, Anerley Park, and saw a good deal of Havelock Ellis, with whom he carried on an extensive and intimate correspondence. There are some interesting references to Swinburne in Noel's letters.* He writes : —

" I don't think Rossetti and Swinburne nearly so good as Tennyson and Browning. But James Thomson, I should say, was nearly so. He, and Buchanan, and William Morris, and, may I be so conceited as to add, your humble servant, stand reverently (but not abjectly) in their several niches below them, and I think above (but anyhow on a level with) Rossetti and Swinburne. I *do* think Rossetti a genuine and original poet. I only demur to the extravagant over-estimate of him and Swinburne formed by their admirers and disciples. The style in each case seems to me so artificial and fantastic, and the substance so *comparatively* thin. . . . Swinburne's endless strophe and antistrophe rhapsodies are surely very windy and truly of very dubious inspiration as poetry. . . . How few thoughts, how little help for life ! I must, however, except *Songs before Sunrise.* . . . His imitators are absolutely detestable. Never was there so much fatal facility, so much gift of the pure gab, such a hæmorrhage of words ! ' Like a tale of little meaning, though the words are strong,' as Tennyson said of something of Swinburne's. ' Full of sound and fury, signifying nothing.' He is not a master of words, for the words run away with him. However, I don't ask you to agree with me. A poetical young man must have the Swinburne fever now, just as babies must have measles ! "

The poets most admired by Roden Noel were Keats, Shelley, Chatterton, Wordsworth, Hugo, Walt Whitman, and Byron. He wrote for the leading reviews some very illuminating studies of these and other poets which he afterwards elaborated and republished in a volume entitled, *Essays on Poetry and Poets* (1886). For Byron he had an intense sympathy both as a poet and man—" I know I am irrationally fond of Byron, from a certain affinity, I suppose," he wrote. They had both been educated at Harrow and Trinity, Cambridge, and Noel, with his similar temperament, understood and could interpret certain

---

* Kindly placed at my service by Mr. Havelock Ellis.

RODEN NOEL
At the age of thirty-four.
From the portrait by G. Richmond, R.A., in the possession of his son,
the Rev. Conrad Noel.

[*Page* 166.

phases in the life of Byron. He offered a remarkable solution to the mystery of the identity of the person to whom the Thyrza poems were addressed in his *Life of Lord Byron*, published in 1887, one of the most sympathetic and valuable contributions to the literature inspired by that wayward and deeply interesting personality: he suggested it was Edleston.

During Noel's time at Anerley Park he often lectured on Byron and Wordsworth, devoting the receipts mainly to the benefit of a fund for providing poor children of the district with food. His solicitude for the poor, and particularly the children, never abated, though the early ardour of his views on Socialism became modified. As he told Havelock Ellis: —

" I am not a socialist that I know of . . . I suppose I am an advanced liberal with views of my own. *I don't see my way to any great scheme of Socialism,* though I have hankerings that way, and advocate some socialistic views. . . . I know I am a strange compound of aristocrat and democrat, man of culture and man of the people. But I am all for eccentricity, individual idiosyncrasy. Socialism would not allow that."

Roden Noel was inclined to assume the conventional aspect of a poet. He is still remembered, when revisiting the locality of his early home in Kent, standing in a rapt attitude, gazing at the scenery, with a cloak flung in picturesque folds over his shoulder. He wore open Byronic collars, and in the evening a sort of Court dress of black velvet, cut to show the lines of his figure. Discussing costume and " Æsthetics," of the Oscar Wilde style, when those subjects were prominent in 1885, he wrote: —

" My unconventional ' evening dress ' was adopted from an old Catholic family I am intimate with, and was worn by me before ' Oscar ' was born."

In 1866 he was at Davos, and proceeded in the autumn to Stuttgart. In 1887-8 Noel edited new editions of Edmund Spenser and Thomas Otway (the latter for the Mermaid Series), and in 1888 appeared his last volume of collected verse, *A Modern Faust, and Other Poems. Poor People's Christmas* was published separately in 1890. Two little volumes of additional poems were issued posthumously in 1896-7, with introductions by his friends, S. and Percy Addleshaw; and Roden Noel's complete *Collected Poems* (excepting those in *Behind the Veil*) were published in one volume, 1902, edited by Lady Victoria Buxton.

It is not possible here to offer any exposition of Noel's long philosophical poems. They were not his best work. Although he said he had tried all his life to write philosophical and allegorical poetry, he was pre-eminently a poet of Nature. His delicate lyrics and sad, sweet songs will surely survive, whereas his long didactic epics like *The Red Flag* and *A Modern Faust* can well rest in oblivion. It is these long poems which have affected his popularity. Propaganda by means of poetry does not appeal; but in avoiding Noel's heavy work the public has missed the melody and beauty of a rare order to be found in his short poems.

Roden Noel felt keenly the lack of appreciation he met with, and he resented particularly the sparse and incompetent criticism of his work in journals which professed to lead literary opinion. But he went forward on the lines he believed right, and voiced his message in notes harsh or musical as his mood might be. As Henry Sidgwick said after his friend's death: " I have always felt that though he was keenly disappointed by the world's inadequate recognition of his genius, he did his work in life none the less resolutely, and brought out his great gifts, and remained nobly true to his ideal."

In 1889-1890, Noel lived at Livingstone House, Burgess Hill, Sussex, and the last few years of his life were spent at 9, St. Aubyn's, Hove. In 1894 he went to Germany to visit a sister-in-law, and on reaching Mainz railway station he was suddenly prostrated by a fatal heart seizure. He died there in this tragic manner, with no relative or friend beside him, on May 26th, 1894, at the age of fifty-nine. He was buried in the English Cemetery at Mainz.

Thus came death mercifully to Roden Noel, for he was spared that pathetic waiting and longing for release which is the portion of those who are world-weary with pain at the last. He had voiced that desire for rest in one of his most exquisite poems, *Dying*:—

> " They are waiting for the boat,
>   There is nothing left to do;
> What was near them grows remote,
>   Happy silence falls like dew;
> Now the shadowy bark is come,
> And the weary may go home.
>
> By still water they would rest,
>   In the shadow of the tree;
> After battle sleep is best,
>   After noise tranquillity."

And he sums up the sadness of life, its brevity and its loveliness, in *The Pity of It*:—

" Who may dream of all the music
    Only a lover hears,
Hearkening to hearts triumphant?
    Bearing down the years?
Ah ! may eternal anthems dwindle
    To a low sound of tears?

   .   .   .   .   .

And now a few poor moments
    Between life and death,
May be proven all too ample
    For love's breath.

Seed that promised blossom,
    Withered in the mould.
Pale petals overblowing,
    Failing from the gold.

   .   .   .   .   .

An hour may yet be yielded us
    Or a very little more—
Then a few tears, and silence
    For evermore."

So he plays upon the muted strings of memory, and his low haunting strains bring back the sad-joyousness of the past and dim visions of old long-lost days.

BULWER-LYTTON.*

The Tragedy of the Literary Temperament.

It is remarkable that so promising a subject for biography as Bulwer-Lytton should have waited forty years for full and authoritative treatment. But there has been reason for the delay. The task was undertaken originally by the novelist's son, Robert, first Earl of Lytton—the poet "Owen Meredith." He published the first two volumes of his work in 1883, but he postponed its continuance—possibly from a reluctance to deal with the miserable quarrels of his parents which had overshadowed and embittered his own early life—and he died leaving the book unfinished. Thus the duty devolved in turn upon his son, the present Lord Lytton, whom the lapse of years has enabled fully to unveil delicate matters which if published earlier would have given pain to persons then living, for Bulwer-Lytton's unhappy marriage dominated his life. As his grandson remarks:—

" It is one of the advantages which the public derive from waiting many years for the biography of a distinguished man that, when at last the story of his life is told, it is likely to be at once more interesting and more truthful."†

Lord Lytton has adopted a rather unusual arrangement of biographical material. He deals with the various phases of his grandfather's career in separate divisions headed " Personal and Domestic," " Literary," and " Political " in turn. This, of course, militates against an unbroken chronological sequence of narrative and makes retrogression inevitable. On the other hand, it enables the reader to turn at once to the most interesting facts of Bulwer-Lytton's life, and without doubt the personal and literary exceed the political records in interest and value.

Aristocrat always, egotistical, theatrical, flamboyant, irritably sensitive, the personality of Bulwer-Lytton is an intensely interesting psychological study. Born in 1803, he was the youngest son of General Bulwer, of Heydon Hall, Norfolk, by his wife, Elizabeth Lytton, and was destined from his cradle to the inheritance of the Knebworth estate of his maternal grandfather Lytton, a noted bibliophile owning a vast library. Here, then, were two early factors in the evolution of an historical novelist—a romantic house filled with armour and antique furnishings, and familiarity with many books. The boy was

---

* The Guardian, November 21st, 1913.
† The Life of Edward Bulwer, First Lord Lytton. By his grandson, the Earl of Lytton. (Macmillan, 30s. net., two vols.)

badly brought up. His male relatives disliked him, and he seems to have been deficient in moral sense, as exemplified in the story he relates, in his autobiography, of how he stole and hid a sailor's dirk, denied all knowledge of the theft, and was thereupon flogged, *ætat* six, without any explanation of his offence and its necessary punishment. He was extremely precocious; he fell in love at six years of age; he could not recall the time when he was unable to read; and, with great self-esteem, he was fully conscious, in calm confidence, of his coming future distinction. He certainly never needed the capitalised advice of his correspondent, Dr. Samuel Parr—" Be ambitious." His first book—*Ishmael*, written when he was thirteen or so—was published in 1820. Long before this his philosophical speculations suggested the advisability of boarding-school. His schools and tutors were many, and after a period of unhappiness —the usual portion of uncommon boys at school—he developed into an arrogant pupil, the very original, it would seem, of Dickens's " Steerforth," for there was even the similar incident of an usher's humiliation.

At the age of seventeen occurred the great romance of Bulwer's life. He was then at a tutor's at Ealing, and used to meet a girl, a few years older than himself, in the sequestered meadows bordering the little river Brent, by Perivale. He showered all the love of his passionate nature upon this early affection, and no subsequent incident of a similar nature ever approached it in ardour. The girl was compelled to marry another, and three years later was dead. The influences of this tragedy lasted throughout the novelist's life; allusions to it can be traced in many of his books, even in one of the last, *Kenelm Chillingly*, written fifty years later and just before his death.

At twenty-two Bulwer had exhausted the pleasures of life and become *blasé*, and at twenty-four he contracted his disastrous marriage. Rosina Wheeler was a good-looking, witty, Irish girl, with a certain coarseness of mind apparent both in conversation and correspondence, and she had been brought up in a very lax way by an undesirable mother. From the outset Bulwer's mother was opposed to the match, and he himself foresaw its probabilities of future unhappiness, for he wrote to Miss Wheeler : —

" Separate yourself from me before it is too late. . . . I know from the gloom and despondency which have become to me a second nature, I know that I am fated to be wretched; avoid me, shun me, and be happy ! Save yourself from a love from which you yourself only antici- pate disappointment and regret, and where the very passion that can alone afford us the strength to hope may only end in your despair."

It was only too true. Miss Wheeler gave herself illicitly to Bulwer, and when passion was dead the marriage was to him only an inevitable reparation—an act demanded by conscience and honour. Such a marriage was doomed to failure, and though for a few years they were passably happy, Nemesis soon overtook them. Bulwer and his wife were both extravagant, and his stiff-necked mother, who disapproved of Rosina Wheeler from the beginning, having stopped supplies, he was compelled to support his costly establishment by arduous literary labours. During the first decade of his marriage : —

" He completed ten novels, two long poems, one political pamphlet, one play, the political sketches in *England and the English,* three volumes of the *History of Athens* (only two of which were ever published), and all the essays and tales collected in *The Student.* At the same time he was editor of *The New Monthly Magazine,* to which he contributed regularly. He also wrote anonymously in *The Edinburgh Review, The Westminster Review, The Monthly Chronicle, The Examiner, The Literary Gazette,* and other periodicals. In addition to this, from 1831 onwards he was an active member of Parliament."

Such a strain inevitably affected the author's nerves. He became irritable, seeking for his ceaseless work quiet and solitude, which his wife resented. Arguments led to quarrels, bitter reproaches, and separations; then came pathetic letters and apologies and good resolutions—only to be broken when companionship was resumed. Each fresh quarrel dulled the embers of expiring love. In the beginning the husband was most to blame, for he was absurdly egotistical, selfish, and full of unreasonable demands. But after the final separation, in 1835-6, at Berrymead Priory, Acton, Mrs. Bulwer's attitude turned to implacable hatred; for the rest of her life she pursued her husband with virulent abuse and libel, in word and letter and print, even to the extent of publicly outraging him before his electors at Hertford on the occasion of his appointment as Secretary to the Colonies in 1858. Then she was illegally confined for a time in a private asylum, but she soon regained her liberty. The two children of this unhappy marriage were of necessity involved in their parents' misery. The daughter died neglected at the age of twenty, and the son's fine, sensitive nature was harrowed by the part of intermediary between warring husband and wife—but, perhaps, what he learnt in youthful sorrow he expressed in song in after years.

Lord Lytton has on the whole presented impartially the painful facts of his grandfather's history. He is not prejudiced or sentimental, and he brings this same admirable impartiality to the consideration of his grandfather's career in other directions, as author, politician, and friend. Unfortunately the book lacks an intimate, detailed account of Bulwer-Lytton's life at Knebworth, with some description of this famous house, its furnishings and legends—all in keeping with the somewhat bizarre owner, who, when there, lived, as far as he could in prosaic times, in feudal, romantic style. But he had many other subsidiary interests in life in addition to literature and politics. He was an excellent landlord, and was active in warfare against many public abuses. His letters show that he was interested in the occult and supernatural, as was, indeed, already apparent from his most remarkable romance, *A Strange Story*. He experimented in Spiritualism, and believed he was visited by the spirits of his dead daughter and of Shakspere. In other respects his religious beliefs were simple and orthodox, for as he wrote to his son in 1871 : —

" The essential things to hold to—God, soul, hereafter, prayer, reverence for and acceptance of the hopes and ethics of Christianity. . . . I accept the Church to which I belong because I think it immaterial to me here and hereafter whether some of its tenets are illogical or unsound. . . . I take many things in life and in thought as settled, or if to be unsettled, I am not the man to do it."

A sufficient creed, surely. The outstanding quality of Bulwer-Lytton was his universality, the variety of his activities. In the words of his biographer—" Distinguished as a novelist, as a dramatist, and an orator, he was also essentially a man of the world. In business capacity, in judgment, in imagination, in brain power, in industry he was equally remarkable. . . . His life, if not a happy one to himself, was full and useful." Its results to-day are not extensive; yet it seems likely that three or four of his books—*The Caxtons* and *A Strange Story* certainly —will live; and there have been signs of late of a revival of interest in his work. That revival is likely to be materially assisted by this frank revelation of the labour and sorrow of his life.

EDWARD VAUGHAN KENEALY.*

His Centenary and Literary Aspect.

THE name of Dr. Kenealy and his turbulent personality are associated in public memory almost exclusively with the notorious Tichborne case, wherein he acted as counsel for the Claimant. The other events of his life are forgotten, particularly the fact that in his earlier years he was an accomplished author, who—had he so desired—could have attained a very high position in the ranks of literature. He was a profound classical scholar, and his powers of polyglot composition were only equalled by his contemporaries, William Maginn and Francis Mahony (" Father Prout "). But he voluntarily abandoned literature and reverted to the law, thereby reversing the more general procedure, for it is remarkable how many successful literary men were originally destined and trained for the legal profession. The list includes the names of Walter Scott, Disraeli, R. S. Surtees, Harrison Ainsworth, Charles Reade, Sheridan Le Fanu, F. C. Burnand, and George Meredith.

Kenealy was born in Nile Street, Cork, on July 2nd, 1819, the eldest son of William Kenealy, who traced his descent from the O'Kenealys (or Cennfaelad in Gaelic)—a typical Irish family who claimed as ancestors " a splendid roll of monarchs, heroes, saints, and conquerors, in whom the blood and passions of many mighty families were grandly blended." But apart from apocryphal progenitors, Kenealy's pedigree was of much interest. His direct paternal ancestors included soldiers and Irish Jacobites; and his mother, Katherine, daughter of Daniel Vaughan, of Mallow, Co. Cork, was a direct descendant of King Edward the Third, through seventeen generations of Plantagenet blood. On the maternal side, also, Edward Vaughan Kenealy was a direct descendant of the Restoration poet, John Wilmot, Earl of Rochester, whose third daughter, Malet, married John Vaughan, first Viscount Lisburne. A dreamy, sensitive child, Kenealy received his early education at various schools in Cork where flogging and bullying were rampant, and a hard experience it was for one of his introspective temperament. He has related of his boyhood:—

" I was as shy as a young antelope; I avoided strange faces. I preferred the dreams which were my friends in field and forest to inter-

* The Times Literary Supplement, July 3rd, 1910.

course with men or boys of my own age. My ideas were majestic; my temper serious, even sage. I climbed the brown hills, fragrant with heather. I saw the sun ascend in parti-coloured cloud. I lingered until the moon swam through the heavens like a goddess in a lake. The distant prospect of towns or farmhouses filled me with rapture. I loved the trees as cherished friends, and sympathized with every inhabitant of nature, save only with human kind."

He entered Trinity College, Dublin, in 1835, and remained there for the next two years without achieving any particular distinction, though he passed the usual examinations with credit. He decided to enter the law rather than the priesthood (to which his family inclined), and came to London in January, 1838, as a student at Gray's Inn. He was called to the Bar at Dublin in 1840.

But at this date his inclinations were all for literature. Through the introductions of William Maginn (the " Captain Shandon " of *Pendennis*) he became acquainted with the most influential writers of the time when Thackeray and Dickens were rising to fame. It was a period when literary men were very social and gregarious, and Kenealy soon became associated with the famous coterie of *Fraser's Magazine*, and as a contributor he participated in those convivial assemblies at 215, Regent Street, the ambrosial memory of which is preserved in many a record of early Victorian life. It was Harrison Ainsworth who primarily established the young Irishman in literary circles, for he accepted his first compositions for *Ainsworth's Magazine*, and treated him as a guest of honour at the memorable reunions at Kensal Manor House. Kenealy wrote assiduously. He possessed astonishing linguistic gifts, and was familiar with eighteen languages. Consequently his work was of polyglot form. One of his earliest papers appeared in *Ainsworth's Magazine* in 1842; it contained a translation into Greek of Chatterton's *A Bacchanalian*, and later he appended a version in Greek of Shakspere's *Take, oh Take Those Lips Away*. Kenealy's method was thus often of a hoaxing nature. He would take some well-known poem, translate it into Greek, Latin, or archaic French, and propound the theory that the English variant was merely a plagiarism or translation from an ancient original. This, of course, was also the literary method of his fellow townsmen, " Father Prout " and William Maginn.

Kenealy's polyglot contributions to the magazines were collected and published, together with his many charming and original poems in English, in 1845, the volume being entitled *Brallaghan, or the Deipnosophists* (the Supper Philosophers or Sages). It was not very successful, though highly appreciated

by people of culture. " Father Prout " told Gavan Duffy he
had seen the book " remaindered " at twopence a copy.
Kenealy was keenly disappointed at the failure of his firstborn,
and this was, no doubt, the cause of his renunciation of literature
as a profession and his return to the more lucrative emoluments
of the law. He wrote in his autobiography this same year,
1845 : —

" I entertain the same disrelish for literature and literary company
that Pitt did—I was going to add Horace Walpole, but however he
disliked authors, he was certainly vain of his writings. I have had as
much fame as ever magazine writer had. . . . When *Brallaghan*
appeared it was fathered on Maginn by one set of newspapers, on
Thackeray by another set . . . and all through Ireland it was attributed
to Father Prout. Ainsworth used to lionize me at his parties. Well—
what is it all? Vanity of vanities. Pleasant enough, but not worth the
hate and envy it occasions. So says Edward Kenealy."

Nevertheless, in after years he essayed literature at intervals.
Cahier Conri, a Metrical Legend, appeared in 1860. *A New
Pantomime* (an extension of his *Goethe*, a strange poem in
imitation of *Faust*), 1862, produced a very hostile notice in *The
Weekly Review*, a Presbyterian journal, edited by Dr. Peter
Bayne, against whom Kenealy brought an action for criminal
libel. Bayne was committed for trial, but a settlement was
arrived at, thus securing the work a great advertisement. *A New
Pantomime* was dedicated to Disraeli, with whom the author had
been associated in a project for founding a newspaper to be
entitled *The Press, or Anti-Coalition*. Kenealy issued a new
and enlarged edition of his *Poems and Translations* in 1863, and
his amazing linguistical gifts are evidenced by the fact that the
work includes examples of Greek, Latin, Gaelic, German,
French, Persian, Hindustani, Swedish, Danish, Spanish, Italian,
Magyar, Portuguese, Basque, Arabic, Breton, and Bengali.

Kenealy also wrote several theological works such as *The
Book of God*, 1867, and *The Book of Fo*, and *The Book of
Enoch*, 1878. But the most remarkable of his later books was
Edward Wortley Montagu: An Autobiography, published in
three volumes in 1869. This curious novel, which deserves
rescue from oblivion, purporting to be written by the wild and
eccentric son of Lady Mary Wortley Montagu, presents a
graphic picture of eighteenth-century life and vivid delineations
of the prominent social and literary figures of that epoch. It
adheres closely to the actual facts of the Wortley Montagu family
history, but interwoven are personal experiences of Kenealy
himself. Thus he introduces with the actual name, Casey, a
brutal flogging schoolmaster, who tortured young Kenealy in
his schooldays at Cork. The incident of the flogging in *Edward*

Wortley Montagu is almost identical with a passage in Kenealy's own autobiography. The latter lengthy work remains mainly in manuscript and unpublished, though a selection from it was printed in *The Memoirs of Edward Vaughan Kenealy*, by his daughter, Miss Arabella Kenealy. The autobiography gives an entertaining account of the writer's career and personality, and throws many valuable sidelights on the notable people he met in the course of his eventful life.

It is not within the province of this article to detail Kenealy's forensic and political life. Briefly, in 1847 he was called to the English Bar. He became well-known in the Criminal Courts, and was junior counsel for the defence of William Palmer, the Rudgeley poisoner, in 1856. The trials of Burke and Casey in 1867, the Wood Green murder in 1869, and the case of Overend, Gurney and Co. added to his reputation as counsel, which was suddenly wrecked by his extraordinary conduct of the Claimant's case in the Tichborne trial of 1873-1874. For this he was " disbenched and disbarred "—unjustly and without sufficient cause as it seems now that the clamour and prejudice of that amazing *cause célèbre* are ancient history, though the fires of the controversy are not even ashes yet. Kenealy was ruined professionally.* He founded the Magna Charta Association to advance his political and social views, and to voice them a paper called *The Englishman*, which attained a circulation of 160,000 copies. He was elected M.P. for Stoke in 1875, and carried on his fiery campaign in the House of Commons. But his stormy life was nearing the end. He had never recovered from the humiliation and mental torture of his expulsion from the legal profession. An insidious disease and terrible physical pain wore down his once intense vitality. He was defeated at the election of 1880 on April 3rd, and thirteen days later he died of heart failure at his house in Tavistock Square, on April 16th, 1880. Far wiser and better for him if he had chosen a quarter of a century back to continue the tranquil path of literature instead of turning into the tempestuous arenas of the Law Courts and Parliament, for the author of *The Deipnosophists* and *Edward Wortley Montagu* was a happier and a greater man than the counsel for the Claimant.

---

* Kenealy had a narrow escape from the same fate earlier in his career. As a young man he was convicted of cruelty to his illegitimate son (Edward Hyde), and in 1850 suffered a month's imprisonment. He was not disbarred, as his Benchers decided the offence was one arising from sudden loss of temper.

THEODORE WATTS-DUNTON.[*]

It is good, and time well spent, to read again Watts-Dunton's reminiscences of some of his famous friends which he contributed to *The Athenæum* either in the form of obituary memoirs or reviews of books dealing with these particular friends and their life's work; and for those who knew him personally, this book has a special, if sad, interest, for it brings back to memory many pleasant visits to " The Pines," Putney, when Watts-Dunton, in his latter years, was ever ready to talk—a sympathetic listener being, of course, essential—of his great contemporaries who had loved him and valued his friendship pre-eminently. He was indeed " the friend of friends," and few men have had such a unique and intimate acquaintanceship with the most potential literary and artistic forces of their era. Meredith, Swinburne, Tennyson, the Rossettis, Borrow, William Morris—to mention these names from a long list is to recall how supremely interesting was Watts-Dunton when discoursing of them. Much of what he was wont to say is fortunately preserved in these published recollections, but it is a matter for regret that he never wrote similar papers in memory of Meredith and Swinburne.

I often expressed to him the hope that he would write the biography of Swinburne, he being, with the exception of Mr. Gosse, the only man in a position to present both an authoritative and literary picture of the poet : but he stated his objections to the work very cogently, his views being much the same as those he enunciated on the subject of biography which will be found in the articles on Dante Gabriel Rossetti in the volume under review.[†] However, he did at one time contemplate recording his personal reminiscences of Swinburne, but was dissuaded from executing the project by the advice of one whose opinion he valued very highly. I recall one little fact he told me concerning Swinburne and Meredith, which may be mentioned here. There was, in their last years, a coolness in the once warm friendship that had bound the two together for over forty years, and the cause was that Swinburne did not appreciate the later Meredith novels. He frankly said he could not get through—I think—*Lord Ormont and his Aminta.* This Meredith resented, but it did not affect his

[*] *The Bookman,* January, 1916.
[†] *Old Familiar Faces.* By Theodore Watts-Dunton. With portraits. (Herbert Jenkins, 5s. net.)

underlying and long-seated regard for Swinburne; the poet's death—his junior by nine years—came as a great shock, as is so finely evidenced in Meredith's letter—the last he ever wrote—to Watts-Dunton on April 13th, 1909: a month later he lay dead at Box Hill. Watts-Dunton was full of anecdote about Meredith and would lay stress on his friend's astonishing, aristocratic beauty of face and head and hair. Meredith was his ideal of manly beauty, whilst he regarded Mrs. Morris as the perfection of female loveliness.

To pass to the contents of this book, the reminiscences of Borrow are the most valuable contribution, for as Watts-Dunton himself says he was probably the man who best understood him, owing to reasons of temperament and mutual experiences. Borrow, that wayward personality who combined with almost a giant's strength the heart of a child and the superfine qualities of a rare romancist with those of the most bombastic and ridiculous of *poseurs*, does not as a rule make a favourable impression in biography, for his gaucheries and rudenesses were appalling. But Watts-Dunton, having penetrated the hard and prickly shell of the outer man and found the fine soul within, was able to present the Romany Rye in his most favourable aspect, and though a little kind to his friend's faults, he does not seek to palliate them. His interest in Borrow was deep and abiding, and to the end of his life one of his (alas! unfulfilled) projects was to write a romance, on the lines of *Aylwin*, in which Borrow was to appear in scenes laid at Dunwich. He was led to speak much of this to me owing to our mutual interest in Dunwich, which, indeed, was the link that first made me acquainted with him. Watts-Dunton had an extraordinary affection for that lonely spot on the shelving cliffs of Suffolk " where over the grave of a city the ghost of it stands," and not only because it inspired Swinburne's magnificent *By the North Sea*. Before leaving Watts-Dunton's published records of Borrow, let us remember that herein are enshrined that wonderful description of a sunset seen from Waterloo Bridge, and that fine definition of a poet— " a man who, while actually feeling the ineffable pathos of human life, can also feel how sweet a thing it is to live, having so great and rich a queen as Nature for his mother, and for companions any number of such amusing creatures as men and women."

The papers on Dante Gabriel Rossetti are the least satisfactory in the book, and consequently disappointing, for it was about Rossetti that Watts-Dunton would talk most freely and relate many anecdotes. He certainly, in later years, modified the views here expressed as to certain aspects of " popular " biography, and the tone of rather sharp sarcasm he uses towards the reading public in the Rossetti and Tennyson articles now seems foreign to his kindly nature and genial outlook upon all mankind. And further, although he advocated in *The Athenæum* the wisdom of destroying the letters and private papers of a man of genius, to prevent them from feeding the insatiable gorge of this same reading public, he did not practise the precept, for he treasured every fragment of Swinburne's holograph (including many pages of a curious " drama " of a pornographic—or, rather, pathological—nature); and, I fancy, many letters from other friends and correspondents were preserved. One must also take exception to the statement that Dickens wrote colourless, commonplace letters: surely his correspondence was often amusingly suggestive of his literary style, as witness his letter to Edmund Yates elaborating Mrs. Gamp's poignant description of how Mr. Harris's " 'owls was organs."

Far finer is the admirable appreciation of Christina Rossetti, that most lyrical singer whose life of dreams—dreams of human love, religious ideals, and scenic beauty—was passed in sombre quarters of London instead of some convent in a picturesque setting amid the Apennines, which would suggest itself as her natural environment. Watts-Dunton's impressions are of infinite value in forming an estimate of Christina Rossetti's idealistic personality.

Watts-Dunton had a very high regard and appraisement for Tennyson's work—higher, it is to be feared, than a more modern school of criticism, which does not suffer gladly *genre* pieces of *The Gardener's Daughter* and *Enoch Arden* style, would tolerate, though *In Memoriam* and some of the beautiful lyrics will pass the test of all the ages.

Excellent is the sketch of William Morris, whose varied and volcanic energies in the service of Art wore him out before his span had run its course. " I have enjoyed my life—few men more so—and death in any case is sure," he told his friend shortly before the end. Yet for one so keenly sensitive to earthly beauty and the glories and romance of this mundane world, Morris's death still brings a sense of peculiar regret, for he had more to lose than most men in their passing. But those who live to be old have to endure the grief of mourning the friends of their prime. That was Watts-Dunton's sad experience. He outlived all his great friends—great in all senses of the word. And how much friendship meant to him is seen in what he said of his meeting with Lord de Tabley: " In a word, I felt that I had discovered a richer gold-mine than the richest in the world, a new friend." His memories of the past, however, were never allowed to sadden unduly his last years. To the end he thoroughly enjoyed life, and was keenly interested in all the questions of the day and the work of the new generation of literary and artistic men. Watts-Dunton was a kindly critic and a kind friend.

DUNWICH IN LITERATURE.*

FINIS will ere long be written to the grim war which, for nine hundred years and more, Dunwich has waged on the Suffolk coast with her implacable, insatiable enemy, the sea. The final passing of the ruined church (the last of how many!) on the edge of the cliff is near. Great encroachments of the sea have taken place this year, and there remain but two arches on the south side and one on the north, and the crumbling tower—what is left of it, for the west side crashed to ruin in 1902. Neptune's victory is nearly won; his long banquet of bones from the churchyards draws to an end, and he will soon overthrow these fragmentary ruins, almost the last frail token of a once populous, flourishing city, long since destroyed by the sea.

To recount the history of Dunwich would require a volume, and only its briefest outline can be given here. Very considerable Roman and Saxon traditions attach to the place, and one authority has suggested it may be the Sitomagus of Antonine's *Itinerary* (about A.D. 200). The first outstanding fact in the town's history is the arrival of Felix of Burgundy, who, on being appointed Bishop of the East Angles, fixed his see at Dunwich A.D. 630, and he died there in 647.

> " At Donwok then was FELIX first bishop
> Of East Angle, and taught the Chrysten faith
> That is full hye in HEVEN I hope."

Thus wrote John Weever (1576-1632), the first poet, apparently, to mention Dunwich.

Despite the removal of the episcopal see, about 870, Dunwich continued to be a town of great importance to the period of the thirteenth century, and was particularly notable for shipping and the number of its religious houses. Stow, writing about 1562, related that Dunwich in old days was surrounded by stone walls with brazen gates, possessed a King's Court, a Bishop's Palace, a mint, mayor's mansion, fifty-two churches, and as many windmills, together with a spacious harbour, much frequented by great ships. The traditions heard by Stow probably exaggerated the former glories of Dunwich, particularly in the number of its churches, but it is quite evident that the harbour was of considerable importance. For other records state that it was " greatly frequented by marchands and marchandize "; that

* The English Illustrated Magazine, October, 1912.

in the reign of Edward the First the town owned some thirty-six large trading vessels and twenty-four smaller fishing boats; that in 1296 the inhabitants built and equipped at their own cost eleven ships of war, carrying each seventy-two men; and that in 1347 Dunwich sent six warships, with one hundred and two men, to assist in the siege of Calais.

Dunwich was represented by two members in Parliament from the time of Edward the First till 1832. At the latter date the electors numbered thirty-two, and the city had long vanished.

Throughout its lengthy history Dunwich had a never-ceasing war to wage with the encroaching sea, and the plucky manner in which the inhabitants rebuilt their houses and churches and clung to the spot for centuries is an example of splendid spirit and indomitable resolve, only quelled finally by irresistible forces. In defiance of the biblical parable, they had built their house, if not upon the sand, upon a precarious, crumbling cliff of sand and loam, easily undermined by the sea; and so, when the floods came and the winds blew, it fell, and great was the fall of it. As early as 1085 certain land which had been taxable in the reign of Edward the Confessor had disappeared into the sea. In 1286 great damage was done; and by 1350 four hundred houses, and the churches of St. Felix (built by that bishop over seven hundred years earlier), St. Leonard, St. Nicholas, St. Martin, St. Michael, and St. Bartholomew were destroyed; and, worst blow of all, the haven was blocked up by shingle and silt, and rendered useless (1328). As an ancient chronicler pathetically observed, the haven " could never be brought by all the costs and labour Donwich bestowed upon it to continew there againe." The town thus lost for ever the tolls and business from the shipping passing to and from Blythburgh, Walberswick, and Southwold, which of yore " came all downe to Donwich to go into the sea."

From the date of this commercial calamity Dunwich decayed (for, after much conflict with their neighbours, the new haven was eventually cut out and established near Southwold), and its valiant men began to lose heart in their hopeless fight. Primitive barricades, prayers and priestly curses, were all in vain: the triumphant sea redoubled its efforts, and between 1540 and 1570 Dunwich suffered incredible damage, so that not one quarter of the town—city no longer—was left standing. It must have been about this date that a vast number of the inhabitants, rendered homeless, migrated to other parts of the country, for a most curious fact in the history of Dunwich is that no ancient dwellings are found in that part of the place, remote then from the sea, which comprises the hamlet of to-day Evidently the affrighted people resolved to build no more in such a fated district, and shook the dust of it from off them, and departed elsewhere. Many, no doubt, settled at Southwold, for that place increased in prosperity and population as Dunwich declined.

The seventeenth century brought no respite to the moribund town, for the sea destroyed the ancient Temple buildings and the Market Place, to say nothing of numerous houses. Only two parish churches now remained. In 1665 and 1672 the inhabitants had two brief, exciting distractions to take their thoughts for awhile from their ever-present tragedy. On June 1st of the first-mentioned year the English fleet (" the greatest England had ever seen," the Duke of York, himself in command, relates) anchored off Dunwich in Sole Bay. What a glorious sight must those ninety-eight great battleships have presented as they arrived in stately procession, with their grim figure-heads, towering galleries astern, vast sails, gay flags and pennons. A few hours later the Dutch fleet of one hundred and thirteen ships of war came up with the east wind, and two days afterwards the men of Dunwich heard the thunder of the guns from the battle taking place to the north-east of Southwold. On May 28th, 1672, they were actual spectators, as far as the smoke from the firing permitted, of a great naval fight just off their town, for on that day took place the memorable Battle of Sole Bay, when the Duke of York engaged the Dutch fleet under De Ruyter. Previous to the fight, the combined fleets of England and France, comprising one hundred and one battleships and many smaller craft, lay at anchor in the Bay, the long line extending from Minsmere (south of Dunwich) to Easton Ness (north of Southwold); and a great many of the officers and sailors were ashore at Dunwich and the other towns when the battle unexpectedly commenced, and large sums of money were offered to the fishermen to convey the absentees to their ships. An old contemporary song, published in *The Norfolk and Suffolk Garland*, 1680, and sung to the tune of *Suffolk Stiles*, concerns this battle, and marks probably the first appearance of Dunwich in verse (excepting the Weever triplet quoted previously) : —

" One day as I was sitting still
Upon the brow of Dunwich hill,
    And looking on the ocean,
By chance I saw De Ruyter's fleet
With royal James's squadron meet ;
In sooth it was a noble treat
    To see that brave commotion.

" I cannot stop to say the names
Of all the ships that fought with James,
Their number or their tonnage ;
But this I say, the noble host
Right gallantly did take his post,
And covered all the hollow coast
From Walberswyck to Dunwich."

And so on for four more verses.

The excitement of the battle over, poor Dunwich (after this reminder of how she, three hundred years before, sent her own brave little fleet to help fight the French) had to turn once more to the eternal war with the sea. Very likely the tremendous concussion of the cannon at Sole Bay Fight caused many tottering ruins in the town to fall. Fire, too, aided the destruction of doomed Dunwich.

The eighteenth century dawned, and the sea devoured the Town Hall, the Jail, and St. Peter's Church. This last, the penultimate church, stood considerably under a quarter of a mile north-east of the existing ruins of All Saints' Church, and the course of events was just the same as has taken place with the latter edifice in our time. St. Peter's Church* was dismantled in 1702 as the sea approached, and the building tumbled over the cliff as the waves undermined it. Gardner, the historian of Dunwich, writing about 1753, records: " This churchyard was swallowed up by the Sea not more than twenty years ago, when the Last Remains of the Dead were seen sticking on the Sides of the Cliff."

In December, 1740, terrible destruction was caused by strong winds from the north-east hurling great seas on the defenceless cliff. All the marshes and surrounding land were under water, and the final ruin of Dunwich was consummated by further storms in 1746 and 1749. Thomas Gardner, aforementioned, collector of revenues for the Salt Works at Southwold, went over to Dunwich after the storm of 1740 to note the damage done, and he relates that he

" beheld the Remains of the Rampart; some tokens of Middlegate; the Foundations of down-fallen edifices, and tottering Fragments of noble structures; Remains of the Dead exposed . . . . several skeletons on the Ouze, divested of their coverings, some lying in pretty good Order, others interrupted and scattered as the Surges carried them. . . ."

Thomas Gardner was so interested in what he saw that he decided to write the history of the place, and his *An Historical Account of Dunwich* was duly published in 1754. This book, which also dealt with Blythburgh, Southwold, and other parts

---

* John Daye (1518-1584), the printer of Foxe's *Book of Martyrs* and of the works of Latimer, Parker, etc., was a native of St. Peter's parish, Dunwich.

of the locality, though often inaccurate, was a very remarkable production for a humble, provincial man in days when research work was difficult and facilities few. He studied diligently the ancient chronicles of Speed, Stow, Bede, Camden, Holinshed, and all the other records which comprise the earlier appearances of Dunwich in Literature; but he seems to have erred in translating the details of the locality from the Domesday Survey.

At the date Gardner wrote, about 1753, he states the population of Dunwich had dwindled to one hundred souls, so it is very evident that after the disastrous storms of 1740-9 most of the few remaining inhabitants moved to neighbouring towns or villages, and that before the close of the eighteenth century the place took the aspect it bears, more or less, to-day. Dunwich now comprises about one hundred and sixty inhabitants, who dwell in modern cottages; and the only remains of the old town are the ruins of the Chapel of St. James's Hospital (dating from about 1190), of a portion of the Priory of Grey Friars or Franciscans with the outer wall and two fine gateways, and of the church of All Saints on the edge of the cliff. This church, which was erected in the fourteenth century, was still used for divine service in Gardner's time, but before 1780 it was dismantled and fallen into ruin. Then began the same drama which has been enacted to the exit of all its predecessors. The sea attacks the base of the cliffs, the undermined upper portions fall, bringing with them great masses of the building and the grim contents of the crowded graveyard.

Such is Dunwich, and the strange history and influences of this spot, " where over the grave of a city the ghost of it stands," have engendered many fine things in English literature. Particularly and pre-eminently was its message impressed upon the imagination of Swinburne, inspiring some of his most magnificent poems. Let me first quote a few verses from his *Dunwich*,* picturing so vividly this tragedy of the churchyard and the sea :—

> " . . . . One hollow tower and hoary
> Naked in the sea-wind stands and moans,
> Filled and thrilled with its perpetual story;
> Here, where earth is dense with dead men's bones.
>
> Low and loud and long, a voice for ever
> Sounds the wind's clear story like a song.
> Tomb from tomb the waves devouring sever,
> Dust from dust as years relapse along;
> Graves where men made sure to rest, and never
> Lie dismantled by the seasons' wrong.

* The extracts from Swinburne's works in this paper are quoted by kind permission of Messrs. W. Heinemann, Ltd., the owners of the copyrights, who publish the poems in their entirety.

[F. Jenkins, Southwold.

[Page 186.

DUNWICH

As Swinburne knew it,

Now displaced, devoured and desecrated,
  Now by Time's hands darkly disinterred,
These poor dead that sleeping here awaited
  Long the archangel's re-creating word,
Closed about with roofs and walls high-gated
  Till the blast of judgment should be heard.

Naked, shamed, cast out of consecration,
  Corpse and coffin, yea the very graves,
Scoffed at, scattered, shaken from their station,
  Spurned and scourged of wind and sea like slaves,
Desolate beyond man's desolation,
  Shrink and sink into the waste of waves.

Tombs, with bare white piteous bones protruded,
  Shroudless, down the loose collapsing banks,
Crumble, from their constant place detruded,
  That the sea devours and gives not thanks.
Graves where hope and prayer and sorrow brooded
  Gape and slide and perish, ranks on ranks.

Rows on rows and line by line they crumble,
  They that thought for all time through to be.
Scarce a stone whereon a child might stumble.
  Breaks the grim field paced alone of me.
Earth and man, and all their Gods wax humble
  Here, where Time brings pasture to the sea."

Earlier in *By the North Sea* Swinburne was less *macabre* in his presentment of Dunwich's graves by the sea : —

  " A land that is lonelier than ruin ;
    A sea that is stranger than death ;
  Far fields that a rose never blew in,
    Wan waste where the winds lack breath ;
  Waste endless and boundless and flowerless,
    But of marsh-blossoms fruitless as free ;
  Where earth lies exhausted, as powerless
      To strive with the sea.

     ·   ·   ·

  No surety to stand, and no shelter
    To dawn out of darkness but one,
  Out of waters that hurtle and welter
    No succour to dawn with the sun.
  But a rest from the wind as it passes,
    Where, hardly redeemed from the waves,
  Lie thick as the blades of their grasses
      The dead in their graves.

    ·   ·   ·   ·

  As the waves of the numberless waters,
    That the wind cannot number who guides,
  Are the sons of the shore and the daughters
    Here lulled by the chime of the tides :
  And here in the press of them standing
    We know not if these or if we
  Live truliest, or anchored to landing
      Or drifted to sea.

    ·   ·   ·   ·

And gentler the wind from the dreary
    Sea-banks by the waves overlapped,
Being weary, speaks peace to the weary
    From the slopes that the tide-stream hath sapped ;
And sweeter than all that we call so
    The seal of their slumbers shall be,
Till the graves that embosom them also
    Be sapped of the sea.

Equally with Dunwich itself, Swinburne was fascinated by the
lonely marsh country to the north-west of the place. A strangely
fascinating region it is, too, the site, in part, of the ancient forest
of Dunwich—the West Wood (the East Wood went into the sea
long centuries ago). Parallel with the sea run the Reedland and
Dingle salt marshes, reaching to Walberswick. Half a mile or
more inland, still parallel, comes a stretch of rising heathland and
woods comprising Dingle; then another great expanse of marsh,
backed by hillocks, woods, and heath, where stands Westwood
Lodge, built in 1652. This and Dingle Stone House are almost
the only habitations visible, except those of Dunwich to the
south. Hear again what Swinburne sings of this lone land, *In
the Salt Marshes* : —

" Miles, and miles, and miles of desolation !
    Leagues on leagues on leagues without a change !
Sign or token of some eldest nation
    Here would make the strange land not so strange.
Time-forgotten, yea since time's creation,
    Seem these borders where the sea-birds range.

        .   .   .   .   .

Tall the plumage of the rush-flower tosses,
    Sharp and soft in many a curve and line
Gleam and glow the sea-coloured marsh-mosses,
    Salt and splendid from the circling brine.
Streak on streak of glimmering seashine crosses
    All the land sea-saturate as with wine.

        .   .   .   .   .

Far, and far between, in divers orders,
    Clear grey steeples cleave the low grey sky ;
Fast and firm as time-unshaken warders,
    Hearts made sure by faith, by hope made high.
These alone in all the wild sea-borders
    Fear no blast of days and nights that die.

        .   .   .   .   .

Out and in and out the sharp straits wander,
    In and out and in the wild way strives,
Starred and paved and lined with flowers that squander
    Gold as golden as the gold of hives,
Salt and moist and multiform : but yonder,
    See, what sign of life or death survives?

        .   .   .   .   .

What houses and woodlands that nestle
  Safe inland to lee of the hill
As it slopes from the headlands that wrestle
  And succumb to the strong sea's will?
Truce is not, nor respite, nor pity,
  For the battle is waged not of hands
Where over the grave of a city
  The ghost of it stands.

Like ashes the low cliffs crumble,
  The banks drop down into dust,
The heights of the hills are made humble,
  As a reed's is the strength of their trust :
As a city's that armies environ,
  The strength of their stay is of sand :
But the grasp of the sea is as iron,
  Laid hard on the land.

Personally, I always like to believe that Swinburne had
Dunwich again in his mind when penning his wonderful poem,
A Forsaken Garden, though I have to admit that Mr. Watts-
Dunton has stated to me : "*A Forsaken Garden* cannot, I think,
be located; it is not a transcript of any particular place, and has
probably as much to do with the Isle of Wight as anywhere."
Still, Mr. Watts-Dunton agreed with me that Swinburne may
have combined impressions of both localities in the poem. The
situation so lyrically pictured might well be between Dunwich
cliff and the salt marshes : —

" In a coign of the cliff between lowland and highland,
  At the sea-down's edge between windward and lee.

The fields fall southward abrupt and broken
  To the low last edge of the long lone land.

Over the meadows that blossom and wither
  Rings but the note of a sea-bird's song ;
Only the sun and the rain come hither
  All year long."

And, as in all the Dunwich poems, the motive of *A Forsaken
Garden* is the triumph of the Sea over the Land and over Death,
the death of Death : —

" Till the slow sea rise and the sheer cliff crumble,
  Till terrace and meadow the deep gulfs drink,
Till the strength of the waves of the high tides humble
  The fields that lessen, the rocks that shrink,
Here now in his triumph where all things falter,
  Stretched out on the spoils that his own hand spread,
As a god self-slain on his own strange altar,
  Death lies dead."

It was in the 'Seventies that Swinburne first visited Dunwich.
He was lodging in what Mr. Watts-Dunton calls " that
wonderful place, Southwold," at one of the Centre Cliff houses,

now merged into the hotel of that name. Both friends had an
intense mutual love for the coast of East Anglia; Swinburne
dedicated *By the North Sea* to Mr. Watts-Dunton in one of his
finest sonnets; and it can be hoped, perhaps, that the survivor
may add yet another book to the list of those wherein the scene
is laid, wholly or in part, at Dunwich.

Now to note briefly some of these works.

George Crabbe, a native of neighbouring Aldeburgh, pictured
the coast scenery by Dunwich in *The Lover's Journey* and
elsewhere. In *The Suffolk Garland*, 1818, appeared *Verses
Written at Dunwich*, by Henry Dell. Bernard Barton, a
frequent visitor from Woodbridge (as was also FitzGerald),
wrote a poem entitled *Dunwich*.

In 1828 James Bird, of Yoxford, produced his *Dunwich: A
Tale of the Splendid City*, in four cantos. Agnes Strickland,
another resident of the locality, wrote a long ballad of forty
verses entitled *Dunwich*, which was published among the notes
of her book, *Worcester Fight, or the Cavalier*, 1826, and she
was also the author of a story (founded on fact) relating to
Dunwich, and called *The Danger of Doing Wrong*, which will
be found in *Harper's Magazine*, 1851. There is an exciting little
tale of smugglers and murder at Dunwich, *The Borrowed Book*
(in *Household Words*, June, 1853); and Wilkie Collins in *No
Name* (1862) places a good part of his story at Aldeburgh, from
whence his characters go to Dunwich. To come down to more
recent times, Sir Henry Rider Haggard has laid the scene of no
less than three of his novels at Dunwich, namely, in *The Witch's
Head* (1884), *Stella Fregelius* (1903), and *Red Eve* (1911). The
author, of course, often takes advantage of justifiable literary
license to alter and adapt the features of the place and neighbourhood to his fictional purposes; and so does Mr. Bernard Capes
in his capital romance, *The Secret in the Hill* (1903), wherein
there is no lack of stirring adventures at " Dunberry "—
smugglers and buried treasure galore. *This Mortal Coil*, by
Grant Allen, and *The Dust Cloud* (in *The Room in the Tower*),
by E. F. Benson, also picture Dunwich.

In *An Affair of Dishonour* (1910) Mr. William De Morgan
has placed a large portion of his story in the salt marshes north
of Dunwich, the weird region which appealed so strongly to the
imagination of Swinburne. In Mr. De Morgan's book—so
compact of " atmosphere " throughout and so vividly
interpretative of English life after the Restoration—his principal
characters take up their abode at Kips Manor:—

" It lay in the flat country out towards the sea. . . . Once it stood
near a small port with a fishing population. . . . Now it was a little

better than a salt marsh. . . . The easterly wind off the sea blew too
strong o' nights, and no sleep could be in it for the howling thereof and
the sound of waves confronted by a long breastwork of shingle less than
a mile away. Also . . . certain birds that would not be content to fly
across the flats without a strange cry. . . . Nothing against sheer silence
but the life of the night without; the distant thunder of the shore, the
cry of its responsive shingle; the wind that means to find in the hours of
sleep new ways of moaning through the silent house and roaring in its
chimneys, and now is rushing inland with the flying scud of foam. . . ."

The site of Kips Manor seems to be identical with that where
stands Stone House, Dingle, surely the most lonely dwelling
imaginable, backed by woods, overhung by trees, and facing
the great stretch of marsh with the sea beyond. Two or three
hundred years ago the house was an inn, known as " The Three
Rabbits." The cellars suggest an even older building of a
religious description. How powerfully and impressively this
strange desolate country appeals to the imaginative mind is
evidenced by what Mr. De Morgan told me of the history of his
book* How vividly Mr. De Morgan realised the situation of
Stone House, those who are familiar with both the book and the
spot can testify. One of the most effective incidents in *An Affair
of Dishonour* is the realistic presentment of the Battle of Sole
Bay, and the sense of terror that overwhelmed the dwellers in the
lonely house of the marshland when the first thunder of the guns
cut the silence that brooded habitually over them. Miss Marjorie
Bowen also deals with Sole Bay Fight in her novel, *I Will
Maintain*.

Dunwich has figured in many magazine articles, poems, and
other works too numerous to mention here. In conclusion, I am
permitted to quote from some privately-printed verses by Miss
Mary E. Shipley, entitled *At Dunwich*, which epitomise very
gracefully the history and aspect of this memorable place : —

" The heath-lands glow with gorse and purple heather ;
  The Dunwich rose blooms pure-white as of yore ;†
The speedwell sheds its tender smile of greeting
  Above the graves of hearts whose strife is o'er.

And as I sit beneath the church's shadow,
  Of all thy ancient churches left the last,
I close my eyes and fancy calls up visions,
  Of those who dwelt here in the shadowy Past.

The warlike Briton fashions here swift arrows,
  Sweeps in his coracle on thy river's breast,
Hunts through thy forests, drives his furious horses,
  Here rears his wattle hut for nightly rest.

---

* See later, page 199
† Bernard Barton, in a note to his poem of *Dunwich*, states that the
Dunwich Rose was brought thither by the Monks, and that there was a tune
called *Dunwich Roses* sung in Suffolk. James Bird in his *Dunwich* says the
rose grew on the cliff :—
    " This decks the stern and sterile cliff, and throws
      O'er its rough brow new beauty where it grows."

The Roman eagles swoop with restless pinions
   Down on thy sunny weald and heath-crown'd height;
Here hangs their eyrie till, by dark need driven,
   Back to old Rome they wing their sombre flight.

A strong, free race from o'er the Northern waters,
   Fills now with warriors thy forsaken fort;
New pagan shrines rise o'er the ruined altars,
   And fair-haired children with old ocean sport.

But hush! the sound of ocean angry raging,
   Prelude of wreck and loss thy years shall know!
No human strength can stay the waves' swift fury,
   Spent upon church and tower and cliff below.

But still, with dauntless front, retreating gravely,
   Thou hold'st thine own among East Anglian towns,
A losing battle thine! Yet wear'st thou bravely
   A peaceful smile to meet old ocean's frowns.

The centuries pass; and now grey-hooded friars
   Go barefoot over heath and street and lane,
Preaching of Christ's dear Love, and living closely
   To His bright Pattern free from earthly stain.

And still the wintry winds, all fiercely raging,
   Scatter the town's defences one by one,
The ocean, turbulent with wrath, engaging
   In that dread work where wind and sea are one.

And now I raise sad eyes, and fair before me
   The quiet ocean smileth in my face,
For one brief hour the Past has lived before me
   Of which the waves have left us scarce a trace.

Blow softly, winds, and spare the grey old tower,
   Land-mark belov'd upon this treacherous coast;
Bloom sweetly, speedwell, with thy message God-like
   To me and those at rest—a countless host.

And when this last frail tower inevitably falls, it will cause
many a pang of real regret, for around it cluster countless
memories, not only those of the historic past, but personal ones
also. The pathetic message of that lonely church in ruins—"full
of the sound of the sorrow of years"—but a step from the restless,
deadly sea, grows more and more audible as the end approaches.
One would hold awhile longer this token of Romance, this
symbol of the mutability of human things, ere it be " taken
wholly away, made one with death, filled full of the night " by
the Triumph of Time.

NOTE.—The last remains of the tower fell on November 24th,
1919. One buttress survived, and this was removed and re-
erected in the churchyard of St. James's, some distance inland,
on March 23rd, 1923. St. James's Church is a modern building,
built in 1830.

WILLIAM DE MORGAN.*

WHEN Joseph Vance stood outside his house in Cheyne Row and heard again the long silent music of his dead wife's piano, each note seemed to say " that the end of it all was Death. There is no life but dies, no love but ceases, no sun but shall some day grow cold and be left an ash in dark space. I stood and watched the dropping red sail of the boat, and my heart pleaded with the music for a respite. But the music only said it again, if possible more beautifully, all it had said before. . . ."

Death came, suddenly and unexpectedly, to William De Morgan—he whose pen had so vividly pictured the last scene of life, sometimes dramatically, ofttimes with pathos. Only seven weeks before he died I spent an afternoon with him at 127, Church Street, Chelsea, little thinking it was the last time we should ever meet. He was then in the best of health and spirits, and certainly had no premonition of impending death, for he several times, when alluding to his future plans, used the expression " after the war is over." Particularly he applied the words to the autobiography he intended to write, and which now, alas! we shall never see: it would have been of intense interest to those who care for the history of life in London and its ever-changing conditions, social and topographical, for De Morgan, after relating his early days in Gower Street, University College, and St. John's Wood, would have passed on to the full and storied life he spent amid artistic pursuits in Fitzroy Square and Chelsea. But, " while the war continued," he expected to be occupied fully with another lengthy novel, of which he had written a considerable portion. This work is, of course, left unfinished; he told me it was a combination and utilisation of several stories he had commenced and thrown aside in busier years.† It was to be partly autobiographical: "I shall describe Chelsea as it was in 1852, though I did not live there until 1872: my method is to let some locality or person suggest a basis and then work out the idea imaginatively," he said.

During this last visit also, he talked more fully and wistfully than ever before of those dear old days of the middle of the last

---

* *The Fortnightly Review,* February, 1918.
† Two posthumous novels have appeared—*The Old Madhouse* in 1919, and *The Old Man's Youth* in 1921. Both were put into shape, and some notes added, by Mrs. De Morgan, who died, unhappily, in May, 1919, before the books were published. The second was evidently the book he mentioned to me.

century—mid-Victorian days—in which we were both so much interested, he by actual knowledge and many links of personal memories, I merely by the vicarious aid of early friends and associations and later literary interests. In converse De Morgan was ever regretfully reminiscent of the days and fashions of his youth, and the same note runs through nearly all his books. There is a passage in his last novel, *When Ghost Meets Ghost*, which exactly illustrates this attitude, expressed in his own whimsical way:—

" For these were the days of crinolines; of hair in cabbage-nets, packed round rubber inflations; of what may be called proto-croquet, with hoops so large that no one ever failed to get through, except you and me; the days when *Ah che la morte* was the last new tune, and Landseer and Mulready the last words in Art. They were the days when there had been but one Great Exhibition—think of it !—and the British Fleet could still get under canvas. We, being an old fogy, would so much like to go back to those days—to think of daguerreotypes as a stupendous triumph of science, balloons as indigenous to Cremorne, and table-turning as a nine days' wonder; in a word, to feel our biceps with satisfaction in an epoch when wheels went slow, folk played tunes, and nobody had appendicitis. But we can't !

" However, it is those very days into which the story looks back and sees this girl with the golden hair, who has been waiting in that rainbow-glory fifty years ago. . . She comes out on the terrace through the high middle-window that opens on it, and now she stands in the blinding gleam, shading her eyes with her hand. It is late in July, and one may listen for a blackbird's note in vain. That song in the ash that drips a diamond-shower on the soaked lawn, whenever the wind breathes, may still be a thrush; his last song, perhaps, about his second family, before he retires for the season. The year we thought would last us out so well, for all we wished to do in it, will fail us at our need, and we shall find that the summer we thought was Spring's success will be Autumn, much too soon, as usual. Over half a century of years have passed since then, and each has played off its trick upon us. Each Spring has said to us :— ' Now is your time for life. Live ! ' and each Summer has jilted us and left us to be consoled by Autumn, a Job's comforter who only says :— ' Make the best of me while you can, for close upon my heels is Winter.' "

He could touch with romance even the lamplighter of his youth:—

" An early lamplighter—for this was in September, 1853—passed along the street with a ladder, dropping stars as he went. There are no lamplighters now, no real ones that run up ladders. . . . They were cold stars, almost green, that this lamplighter dropped; but this was because the sun had left a flood of orange gold behind it. . . ."

But De Morgan was no prejudiced praiser of past times to the exclusion of the claims and advantages of modernity. He was deeply interested in all questions of the day, in the franchise for women, in modern science, and particularly in aviation, which he was studying intently during the last months of his life. He asked me if I knew of any aviator he could meet and resolve various points which he desired to elucidate in connection with this subject. He was much affected by the war, and its many distractions made it difficult for him to work with his former facility. From various letters to me I take these characteristic sentences : —

" November, 1914. I see I have never thanked you for wishing me *m h r o t d**—only in such a world ought one not to wish annihilation ? "

" May I suspend all engagements until our nervous systems can be at rest ? I will pay you a visit with real pleasure after the Zeppelin raid has come off."

" June, 1916. I am just hoping my efforts to get towards finis in the book I am on will produce a result, and I find the only time I succeed in writing is the afternoon. . . . The War has paralysed my inventive powers, or such as are left of them, and I *can't get ahead.* We *may see* better days soon—let us hope for them."

" November, 1916. I shall be here on Thursday next, and shall not send the book—to compel you to come for it. I shall be glad of a chat. You are right in saying I never go out—I don't, and shan't till the Allies are in Berlin. I may be eighty then, as things seem now ! I was seventy-seven two days ago ! ! ! "

William Frend De Morgan was born on November 16th, 1839, at 69 (now 35), Gower Street. His father, Augustus De Morgan, Professor of Mathematics at University College, was an able and scholarly man, author of many scientific works; and his mother, Sophia Eliza Frend (daughter of William Frend, expelled from Cambridge University in 1787 for heretical opinions), was the author of *From Matter to Spirit* and a memoir of her husband, so the future novelist had an inheritance of culture and science.

In 1844 the family moved to No. 7, Camden Street. As a small child William De Morgan remembered going with his mother to see her friend, Lady Byron, the poet's widow, at Fordhook, Ealing,† and one of his cherished possessions was a fragment of a letter from Lady Byron to Mrs. De Morgan containing words to this effect: " I am certain your little boy will in the years to come be a man among men." An apt prophecy. At the age of ten he was sent to University College School, and at sixteen he entered the College, remaining there for three years. In 1858 the family moved to 41, Chalcot Villas, Adelaide Road (now known as 91, Adelaide Road). An allusion to this period of his life, in St. John's Wood, will be found at the beginning of Chapter IV of *When Ghost Meets Ghost.* This, too, was the period when he began to study art at Carey's

---

* Birthday wishes.
† See later, page 226, for a view of Fordhook.

School in Streatham Street, Bloomsbury; he entered the Royal Academy Schools in 1859.

In 1864 he commenced work as an artist in stained glass, occupying rooms in London Street and Grafton Street, both near Tottenham Court Road, and finally at 40, Fitzroy Square. This is the house, haunted by " the lady with the black spots " and those monstrous area cats, that he describes in *Alice-for-Short*, changing the locality to Soho. Charles Heath is an auto-portrait of the author himself at the time in question. In a letter, December, 1912, to me, he said:—

" I was at 40, Fitzroy Square making stained glass somewhere in the latest sixties. I transcribed the house into *Alice-for-Short*, but called it Soho. At No. 38 (as I recollect) was *Abraham*? Ward,* a very fine old boy with a white beard, who engraved on copper—real line engraving on copper ! . . . I fancy I saw James Ward's great Bull picture at his house. None of the other names you mention were known to me in my time. . . . All my knowledge ends in 1872 when I came to Chelsea. It's very funny ! But I find I am already forgetting the contents of my own books. Let me know Mrs. Ward's correction of my recollections. . . . "

Continuing the subject, he wrote:—

" I wonder what made me translate George Raphael into Abraham ! I think the patriarchal beard must have had something to do with it. I used to meet him at odd moments. and was certainly in his house once or twice, may be more, but how can one tell at the end of forty years? But for all the forty years I remember the old gentleman quite vividly—indeed his striking appearance made that certain—and I individualise my visit when I saw the Bull. I should immensely enjoy an *identification chat* with Mrs. E. M. Ward about our corner of the Square, but must ask for it in the Spring when I come back from Italy. I am much oppressed at present with a book I have to finish before I go. It is funny to me to thing that Fitzroy Square was over five years t'other side of half-way back to my baby recollections of Fordhook—say 1845-1870-1912, very rough figures."

I took Mr. De Morgan to see Mrs. E. M. Ward a few months later, and they had a great exchange of reminiscences of old days in the Square. De Morgan had a wonderful power of reviving in his books the London of his youth, particularly this district of Fitzroy Square and Tottenham Court Road, which had hitherto lacked a special novelist of its own. I don't think Dickens mentions the Square—a curious fact, if true, for there are not many important streets or squares that London's greatest novelist does not allude to somewhere; but Thackeray, of course, in *The Newcomes*, introduces Fitzroy Square at the time when it was a noted quarter for artists. I think the house he had in mind for Colonel Newcome and Clive was No. 37, which

---

* George Raphael Ward, son of James Ward, R.A., and father of Mrs. E. M. Ward, and grandfather of Sir Leslie Ward (" Spy "). He lived at No. 31, Fitzroy Square for many years, and moved to No. 38 after 1860.

WILLIAM DE MORGAN
At about the age of seventy-five.

[*Page* 196.

later on (about 1870) became a centre of artistic interest when it was occupied by Ford Madox Brown. " Gandish's " was no doubt intended for Sass's Art School in Charlotte Street (now Bloomsbury Street), where the youthful Millais, W. P. Frith, and many other famous artists received their early training.

An entire article might be devoted to the artistic associations of Fitzroy Square and the adjoining streets, and the notable people who have resided there. In addition to Ford Madox Brown, George Ward, and William De Morgan, there were Sir Charles Eastlake, P.R.A., at No. 7, Fitzroy Square; S. A. Hart, R.A., at No. 36; and the distinguished miniature painter, Sir William Ross, R.A., at No. 38, where he died in 1860; Thomas Davidson, the marine painter, was at No. 39, in the 'Seventies (after leaving his studio at 21, Fitzroy Street); Sir Frank Dicksee, P.R.A., and James Sant, R.A. (about 1850-1867) lived, at different times, in No. 2, Fitzroy Square; the late Lord and Lady Salisbury made their first home after marriage at No. 21, where the present Lord Salisbury was born in 1861; eighty years ago No. 27 was occupied by some relatives of mine named Elliot, who entertained there many of the famous artists of the period*; Bernard Shaw has lived at No. 29, and Stacy Marks R.A., at No. 40. At No. 35, Upper Charlotte Street lived Joseph Farington, R.A., of the *Diary*, a house occupied later by Constable; at No. 54 was Richard Westall; and at No. 63, Daniel Maclise, R.A., who later removed to No. 14, Russell Place. Richard Wilson was at No. 4, Russell Place, and E. M. Ward, R.A., at No. 13, at the time he wooed Miss Henrietta Ward from No. 31, Fitzroy Square, over seventy years ago. Simeon Solomon lived at No. 12, Fitzroy Street. If one could only recover all the past history of the streets of London probably every house would yield some story of interest or claim a notable occupant. I once heard Augustus John relate a vivid ghost story, which he alleged to be a personal experience in a house on the south side of Fitzroy Square. It took the form of a re-enactment of a murder which had been committed in the house long years before Possibly this was the same house, No. 40, which *is* on the south side of the square, wherein De Morgan placed the ghostly appearances in *Alice-for-Short*.

As stated above, it was in 1872, after setting the roof of No. 40, Fitzroy Square on fire and burning it off, as a result of dabbling in pottery firing, that De Morgan moved to 30, Cheyne

---

* Some mention of the parties given by the Elliots at 27, Fitzroy Square will be found in Mrs. E. M. Ward's *Memories of Ninety Years* (1924). In 1919, the upper part of No. 27 was occupied by Mr. Robert Newbery, artist in stained glass, and the lower floor by Mr. William Archer, the dramatic critic.

Row, Chelsea, where, a few doors away, he had Carlyle for a neighbour. Here he commenced his famous ceramic and lustre-ware work, which attracted considerable attention in artistic circles. It was, in particular, much admired by Holman Hunt, who compared it to the best periods of Italian ware in the same craft. The Chelsea works* were moved to Merton Abbey in 1882, and, again, to near Wandsworth Bridge in 1887.

In 1888 William De Morgan married Miss Evelyn Pickering (daughter of Mr. P. A. Pickering, Q.C.), who is an artist of distinctive originality; and he and his wife remained consistently faithful to Chelsea as a dwelling place. For many years they occupied No. 1, The Vale, that former picturesque retreat off the King's Road. Here they lived till driven forth by *force majeure*. The story goes that De Morgan was the last tenant to leave the doomed houses, and that he gave a large *vale* party to his friends when the house-breakers were actually at their ruthless work of demolition of his home. He had the Sentiment for Place in a marked degree. He once said to me, apropos of Ford-hook, Ealing, where Henry Fielding and Lady Byron had lived: " What a good thing it would be if everyone who leaves a house were to seal up a short account of it in a bottle and bury it in the foundations ! "

No. 127, Church Street, Chelsea, was his last home, and having given up his lustre-ware factory in 1905, he commenced, at the mature age of sixty-six, the second famous phase of his life, his literary career. He has related: " I suppose I had the capacity for writing lying dormant in me. . . . I had a few hours' leisure, and I was curious to see whether I could write in the form of fiction. . . . I wrote the first two chapters of *Joseph Vance*, just to see what I could do, but I was so little impressed with the result that I put the manuscript away and forgot it." It is to Mrs. De Morgan that we owe the completion of the story. She came across the forgotten fragment of manuscript in a desk of her husband's, and having read it said, " You ought to go on with this." The result was that the story was finished, and *Joseph Vance* published in 1906.

Although this " Autobiography " is not, of course, that of the author himself, it contains much autobiographical matter (like his other books) in the way of personal memories and experiences; both Chelsea and Florence, where De Morgan had a residence at one time, are used as background for the story.

Alice-for-Short followed in 1907; *Somehow Good* in 1908; *It*

---

* De Morgan had used an old building called Orange House, now the site of the Roman Catholic Church in Cheyne Row, for his workshop and show-room.

Never Can Happen Again in 1909; and then, in 1910, he attacked a new field with *An Affair of Dishonour*. In the last-named sombre and powerful novel the author departed from London and his presentation of the nineteenth century, and in an entirely different style from his usual philosophic-humorous-reminiscent vein evolved a romance of the seventeenth century. Possibly it is his finest work. It is not an historical romance in the ordinary sense of the phrase, for no historical personages or events— excepting, incidentally, the first Battle of Sole Bay, 1665—are depicted; but it is an historical picture of the time it relates to, and I know of no other work of fiction in this category, except *Esmond*, which has so much " atmosphere " about it, for the characters not only speak and act but *think* in the manner of their period. The plot of the story may be unpleasant. It is rather like a bizarre dream from the past, suggested and accompanied by some electrical storm outside in the night. And how fine are the descriptions of storms in the book. Here is the advent of one : —

" How came that great inky curtain to be hanging still above the distant sea, and never nearing the land? Rank upon rank of great, white-crested breakers, lifting to espy the shore, and falling disappointed, but to rise again, spoke of the great wind that was rushing landward from the black pall of the horizon. And yet the storm itself was slow to come. But those clouds were heralds of it, whose speed across the outer blue made the high moon seem to fly for ever through an endless heaven. It could not be long now.

" Not long ! For through the very heart of its blackness shot a sudden splintered shaft of lightning, all the length of the offing, and left it blacker than before. . . . There is none among us but will pause betwixt the first flash and the first voice of the storm's artillery. . . . It came—a long, continuous roar that neither rose nor fell . . . then, on a sudden came a swift glare of lightning all across the sky, and close upon the heels of it its thunder, climbing sound on sound, culminating in an intolerable peal. The storm had come."

A large portion of the story is placed on the desolate coast of Suffolk, in the salt marshes north of Dunwich—that weird, indeterminate region which appealed so powerfully to the imagination of Swinburne.* The influence of this lone land was equally strong upon De Morgan.

And yet his memory of the locality was an unconscious survival, for, in interesting letters in reply to my suggestion that the situation of Kips Manor was identical with that of a certain lonely dwelling, now called Stone House, in this drear yet fascinating marshland, he stated, in 1912 : —

" Over forty years ago I spent a month at Southwold, and heard all about Dunwich and the ancient port, and saw and enjoyed the neighbour-

---

* See *ante*, pages 186—189.

hood. I must have retained a vivid recollection of what I saw, having not only succeeded in the landscape, but popped a house down in it which is pure invention. . . . I ought to try to identify Kip's Manor. I have no doubt it is somewhere there, and that the whole thing happened. The Stone House, at Dingle, looks so very likely. It is the very place that was hanging in my mind at the time of writing—only I am sure I never visited it."

One of the most realistic incidents of this romance is the sudden commencement of the Battle of Sole Bay and the sense of terror that possessed the inhabitants of this house on the marsh when the echoing thunder of the guns broke upon ears accustomed only to the voices of Nature:—

" It came again, and yet again. And the windows shook and rattled with the crash upon crash, and the birds that lived in the ivy without were all in panic, and the great bloodhounds in the court bayed a deep response to each new word of terror as it came across the water. For Hell had broken loose without, in what had been the sweet silence of the morning. . . . all the ships of either fleet were hidden in an evil cloud of smoke, with evil flashes in the heart of it. . . . And no ear escaped it, and none but a babe could hear it and be deaf to the truth of its boasted messages of death. For not a gun was fired that day (nor is in any battle) but had it in its heart to do murder, and a Devil's confidence in its success."

Since this passage was published the people of the East Coast have heard and experienced hostile guns and bombs of a far more devastating kind than those of the Dutch in the seventeenth century. There were two Battles of Sole Bay, in 1665 and 1672; and De Morgan not being quite clear as to which he intended to refer to in his story, we often discussed the matter. In a later letter, written from Florence, Viale Milton N.31 in February, 1914, he said:—

" Being back here it occurred to me to look up the authority from which I got particulars of the Sole Bay battle. I see it was another battle in 1665; as the real battle, when De Ruyter commanded the Dutch, was in 1672. I think we made that out, didn't we, in conversation? Rapin, giving Bishop Burnet as his chief authority, says that the Dutch, in the battle I describe, were commanded by ' Monsieur d'Obdam de Wassenaar.' Of course, my story used History as it liked, and inaccuracy doesn't matter. As a fact, the battle of 1665 was fought in May, not after midsummer, as in my story.

" The fact is, I have always taken full advantage of the painter's and poet's *quidlibet audendi*—and I shall continue on the same lines. What use is History if one may not pervert it in Fiction? After all, one does the same by fact.

" We are suffering from very severe cold here—frozen mornings and so on—and most seductive tales reach us of warmth in your latitudes.

" I must write to *Notes and Queries* about Kips Manor ! "

In another letter of 1914, concerning a scheme to preserve the Browning letters, he wrote:—

" I have not felt the matter of the Browning letters keenly—not sufficiently so to inspire a letter to the Press. And in my opinion only letters written *con amore* ought to be sent to newspapers—I mean in the interest of the promotion of the subject. So make my excuses in that sense to Miss de Lorey.

" I don't think I saw you since Mrs. Ward called on us, and gave us a very delightful hour of chat. There was a blot in the scutcheon though—a little pitted speck in garnered fruit! Neither of her daughters accompanied her for a very academical reason indeed—*viz.*, that I had taken either or both for granted in not asking for the visit. Did you ever? Why, the idea of Mrs. Ward running about among the motors at her age never crossed my mind. My wife and I were balked of a visit to Chester Houses by influenza—drat flu!

" I suppose it was from Lady B.* that my mother had a story that Bulwer Lytton's wife used to annoy him by directing to him at his club as ' Sir Liar Lytton.' I don't think she ever met her, but she was just acquainted (over psycho-mysteries) with the Bart.—as he was then.

" I will write to Heinemann to send you an advance copy of *When Ghost Meets Ghost*—there is no ghost in it.

" At this moment I am being called to lunch, violently, so remain

" Always yours truly,
" W. De Morgan."

In 1912 was published that curious creation *A Likely Story*, compound of satire and supernatural, where again the scene favoured Chelsea and Florence; and in 1914 appeared De Morgan's last and most characteristic novel, of immense length, *When Ghost meets Ghost*. Herein he returned to his speciality and made veritable romance of the purlieus of Tottenham Court Road in mid-Victorian times. This is no small art. From the very first page, with its picturesque and lovingly-reminiscent description of Sapps Court, the reader's attention is held and progresses with every step of that intricate play of incident and character, all so minutely depicted, which leads to the final situation of the two old sisters, each believing the other dead, meeting again after an interval of half a century. But, for some, the minor characters of the story are of greater interest than the principals. The old ex-pugilist, Uncle Mo; Aunt M'riar; Michael Ragstroar, the delightful urchin of Sapps Court; Miss Hawkins; Percival Pellew, and many another, are real creations. And even those who make but brief appearances are admirable, such as Mr. Bartlett, the jerry-builder (almost as amusing as C. Vance, who induled in his " savoury reverie on Sewage " after that wonderful and momentous inspection of drains at Poplar Villa); Sam, the watchman; and old Billy, the bibulous tavern politician. Hear this last on the iniquities of Louis Napoleon:—

" This afternoon he was eloquent on foreign policy. Closing one eye to accentuate the shrewd vision of the other, and shaking his head continuously to express the steadiness and persistency of his convictions,

---

* Lady Byron.

he indicted Louis Napoleon as the *bête noir* of European politics. . . .
' But this Louis Sneapoleun, he's your sly customer. He's as bad as the
whole lot, all boiled up together in a stoo. Don't you be took in by him,
Mr. Moses.　　Calls hisself a Coodytar!　I call him . . .' *etcetera de
rigueur,* as some of old Billy's comparisons were unsavoury.

" ' Can't foller you all the day down the lane, Willy-um,' said
Uncle Mo, who could hardly be expected to identify Billy's variant of
Coup d'État.　' Ain't he our ally? '

" ' That's the p'int, Mr. Moses, the very p'int to not lose sight on,
or where are we?　He's got hisself made our ally for to get between
him and the Rooshians.　What he's a-drivin' at is to get us to fight his
battles for him, and him to sit snug and accoomulate cucumbers like
King Solomons.'

" Uncle Moses felt he ought to interpose on this revision of the
Authorised Version of Scripture.　' You haven't hit the word in the
middle, mate,' said he, and supplied it, correctly enough.　' You can keep
it in mind by thinking of them spiky beggars at the So-logical Gardens
—porky pines—them as get their backs up when wexed, and bristle.'

" ' Well—corkupines, then!　Have it your own way, old Mo!　My
back'd get up and bristle, if I was some of them.　Only when it's
womankind, the likes of us can't jedge, especially when French. . . .' "

De Morgan had the rare art of irradiating common things,
and raising them from their lowness.　As Richard Ford said to
Borrow: " Things are low in manner of handling.　Draw Nature
in rags and poverty, yet draw her truly, and how picturesque."
So it is with this book.　The life of Sapps Court becomes very
real to us, and the grim incidents which attend the convict
Daverill are vivid drama.　Those scenes of capture in the
Hammersmith Inn, " The Pigeons " (which was intended for
" The Doves "—the little tavern by the river-side, near the creek
and William Morris's famous house), and the death-blow in Sapps
Court stand out with the startling actuality of scenes from
Balzac.

And then with a dip of the pen, De Morgan can change his
scene to the calm atmosphere of Ancester Towers and the
refinements of Society with a big S.　Here there is much
delightful play of character; the Earl and Countess are prolific
of entertainment, and their daughter, Lady Gwendolen Rivers,
is a very brilliant, live creation.　She too plays the most
prominent part in linking up the numerous and minute connections in De Morgan's delicately forged chain of events which
go to make up his plot.　He is a master of ingenuity—a very
spider in the patient evolution of his web of narrative.　But even
more than in his plots one finds supreme pleasure in his little
interludes of philosophic musing and reminiscence—such as
this : —

" Old folk and candles burn out slowly at the end.　But before that
end comes they flicker up, once, twice, and again.　It is even so with the

Old Year in his last hours. Is ever an October so chill that he may not bid you suddenly at midday to come out in the garden and recall, with him, what it was like in those Spring days when the first birds sang; those summer days when the hay-scent was in Cheapside, and a great many roses had not been eaten by blights, and it was too hot to mow the lawn? Is ever a November so self-centred as to refuse to help the Old Year to a memory of the gleams of April, and the nightingale's first song about the laggard ash-buds? Is icy December's self so remorseless, even when the holly-berries are making a parade of their value as Christmas decorations?—even when it's not much use pretending, because the Waits came last night, and you thought, when you heard them, what a long time ago it was that a little boy or girl, who must have been yourself, was waked by them to wonder at the mysteries of Night."

In such passages a comparison with the methods of Thackeray is inevitable. There is the same familiar personal ring, the note of actual talk with his reader. Unlike Dickens, De Morgan does not laugh and weep *with* his characters: rather, as I have said, in the habit of Thackeray, he regards them with analytical interest—amusement and pity—and in what he himself styled his " buttonholy " manner enacts the rôle of showman to his readers, pointing out the varied qualities and actions of his creations in colloquial, first-hand conversation.

But it is also true he resembled Dickens in many ways. There is the same vast expanse of canvas and prodigality of texture used in depicting the story; both introduce a great number of characters and subsidiary plots which, however, are all intertwined and working together towards a powerful *dénouement*, when the straying threads of the tale are skilfully gathered into order and the complete literary tapestry consummated. De Morgan freely acknowledged his indebtedness to his great predecessor. During that last visit of mine we discussed Dickens for some time, agreeing that *David Copperfield* was the best and *The Old Curiosity Shop* the least satisfactory of the novels. De Morgan spoke of his great admiration for *Our Mutual Friend*, and he concluded with the words: " Dickens was the master at whose feet I sat." He also shared Dickens's habit of walking about the streets at night, and a predilection for studying London life in its humbler phases. And like Dickens and Thackeray, he left a novel unfinished when he died.

Though De Morgan's style can be found to bear resemblance to that of both Thackeray and Dickens, it was primarily and essentially his own—original and distinctive, like his philosophic humour and reminiscent sentiment. And peculiarly his own were those exquisite little scenic pictures he would offer so unexpectedly in his text, such as this of autumn: —

" The sun that comes to say good-bye to the apples, that will all be plucked by the end of the month, is so strong that forest trees are duped, and are ready to do their part towards a green Yule. . . . Then, not unfrequently, day falls in love with night for the sake of the moonrise, and dies of its passion in a blaze of golden splendour. But the memory of her does not live long into the heart of the night, as it did in the long summer twilights. Love cools and the dews fall, and the winds sing dirges in the elms through the leaves they will so soon scatter about the world without remorse; and then one morning the grass is crisp with frost beneath the early riser's feet, and he finds the leaves of the ash all fallen since the dawn, a green, still heap below their old boughs stript and cold. . . . ."

So let this beautiful expression of the coming of winter bring us gently to that sad, bleak day of mid-winter, January 20th, 1917, when amid the sleet and gathering gloom of the fog the friends of William De Morgan assembled in the old village church of Chelsea to offer their last and regretful tribute of affection to his kindly memory.

A FEBRUARY REVERIE.*

Henry James—Thomas Moore.

Time fleets very swiftly in these momentous days. It seems but yesterday that Henry James was alive and creating those last polished phrases; yet February 28th is the third anniversary of his death.

Glancing again at his delightful autobiography, *A Small Boy, and Others,* one of his last works, is to recover with undiminished charm the art of this consummate conjurer with words, this master of psychological situations. For him " to knock at the door of the past " was not to evolve the conventional bald summary of dates and events; characteristically—elusively—he states the facts of biography, and it is only " as out of a thin golden haze, with all the charm . . . of pressing pursuit rewarded, of distinctness in the dimness " that the history of his boyhood emerges.

His ancestry was mainly Irish until, in the eighteenth century, his progenitors crossed from the Old World to the New. His grandfather, William James, came from the county Cavan, and his maternal great-grandfather, Hugh Walsh, had arrived earlier, in 1764, from Killyleagh, Co. Down. There was a Scotch ancestor in the person of another great-grandfather, Alexander Robertson. Henry James was not, apparently, related to the older novelist of his name, G. P. R. James, for he once stated to me :—

" I enjoy no traceable relationship to G. P. R. James. . . . Our name, as you know, is a considerably frequent one, and apparently of Welsh, and Welsh-Irish origin ; so that branches and sets of Jameses exist who are without consanguinity. *My paternal great-grandfather* was of Irish birth, and we turned up in America (State of New York), but toward the end of the eighteenth century. We had, as a family, no contact with G. P. R. during his time in the United States, and this in spite of the fact that my father, there, was a constant reader of his novels—one or other of which was generally in view (but without enchaining my own personal young attention)."

It was in 1855 that Henry James paid his first visit to London —his adopted home in the years to come. The London he saw then was still that of Dickens and Thackeray; the types of Phiz, nay, even of Hogarth, were yet visible in the town. Consequently the memories of this " mite of observation " have a valuable and abiding claim to the student of the Victorian epoch, to say nothing of their claim as a subtle presentment of those gossamer impressions and early experiences which formed the mentality and personality of one of the most original and arresting writers of our time.

Personally, I think Henry James was at his best in a short story. His intense and peculiar style made it essential, for me, to get at the heart of his story in one reading. That was impossible in the case of the long novels. To break off one night and resume reading the book a few days later was, sometimes, to find the silver cord of narrative loosed, the golden bowl broken, the charm dissipated. But the short stories are ever a sheer delight. *The Figure in the Carpet, The Way it Came, The Other House, Covering End*, and, best of all, *The Turn of the Screw*: what works of art, what perfect examples of literary skill and craftsmanship.

Henry James had an intense dislike to being lionised, and he suffered ungladly the adoring homage of earnest and intense females. On one occasion he had been caught and attended a tea party given by a well-known authoress. On making his escape he met a friend, and pungently observed, with a typically Jamesian expression of face: " I have been in the clutches of a bevy of cadaverous wantons."

Thomas Moore, the anniversary of whose death, on February 25th, 1852, also occurs this month, has a link with G. P. R. James and America; for when Moore, as a young man of twenty-four, was on his way to Bermuda, in 1803, to take up his sinecure of Registrar of the Court of Vice-Admiralty, he stayed with Colonel Hamilton, the British Consul, at Norfolk, Virginia, in the same house which G. P. R. James occupied fifty years later when he was British Consul in Virginia. It was then that Tom Moore visited the neighbouring Great Dismal Swamp, which inspired his poem, *The Lake of the Dismal Swamp*. It contains a line from whence, perhaps, was perverted the colloquial classicism, " Paddle your own canoe ":—

> " They made her a grave too cold and damp
> For a soul so brave and true,
> And she's gone to the Lake of the Dismal Swamp,
> Where all night long, by a fire-fly lamp,
> She paddles her white canoe."

G. P. R. James described the Dismal Swamp in his romance, *The Old Dominion*.

Tom Moore's brief stay in Bermuda has received particular attention from Mr. J. C. L. Clark, of Lancaster, Massachusetts, who has published his researches, with many interesting

illustrations, in a small book entitled *Tom Moore in Bermuda*.
It is produced and printed in that fine style which seems to wait
on literary Americans when they pursue the biographical bypaths of well-known men. Moore's experiences in Bermuda
found many reflections in his poetical work. In particular, the
Odes to Nea were addressed to Hester Louisa Tucker, of St.
George's, and silhouette portraits of her and a view of her home
are given in Mr. Clark's book. He relates an amusing anecdote
of Moore in Bermuda which will be new over here : —

" He was very inquisitive—and he was morbidly afraid of mice. A
young Bermudian lady, Miss Hinson, whom he often visited, learned his
antipathy—which she evidently did not share !—and decided to use it to
punish him for prying.

" Expecting a call from Mr. Moore, she heroically secured a live
mouse, and locked it up in her work-box. Nor did her plot miscarry.
Her guest was hardly seated when he began trying the lock of the box,
and, on his raising the lid, out jumped the mouse."

This episode is asserted to have ended the friendship, and
to Miss Hinson these lines were addressed : —

" When I loved you, I can't but allow
    I had many an exquisite minute ;
But the scorn that I feel for you now
    Hath even more luxury in it.

" Thus, whether we're on or we're off,
    Some witchery seems to await you ;
To love you is pleasant enough,
    And, oh ! 'tis delicious to hate you."

Tom Moore was petty in both form and character, and he
has fallen from his once high literary estate in England. He
assumed a voluptuous, would-be immoral tone in his poetry ; but
with ridiculous prudery he was a willing consenter to that
lamentable burning of Byron's manuscript autobiography, with
which he had been entrusted for biographical purposes, on the
plea of its immorality or indecency.

Moore is still remembered and admired for his Irish melodies,
and rightly so. Probably his great charm to his contemporaries
lay in the art with which he sang these songs to his own
accompaniment. The sentimental N. P. Willis records an
incident at one of Lady Blessington's receptions : —

" We all sat round the piano, and, after two or three songs of Lady
Blessington's choosing, Moore rambled over the keys awhile, and then
sang *When First I Met Thee* with a pathos that beggars description.
When the last word had faltered out, he rose and took Lady Blessington's
hand, said good night, and was gone before a word was uttered."

The primly respectable regions of Regent's Park Road and
Haverstock Hill hardly now seem to suggest duels and
bloodshed, though a hundred years ago Chalk—or Chalcot—

Farm was the favourite rendezvous for settling affairs of honour. It was here that Tom Moore fought his famous stage " duel " with Francis Jeffrey, in 1806, when unkind report asserted the pistols were unloaded. At any rate, Bow Street officers appeared at the opportune moment as the pistols were raised, and knocked the weapons from the hands of the unsanguinary little antagonists.

> " Can none remember that eventful day,
> That ever-glorious, almost fatal fray,
> When Little's leadless pistol met his eye,
> And Bow Street myrmidons stood laughing by? "

RHODA BROUGHTON.*

THE death of Miss Rhoda Broughton, at the age of seventy-nine, last month, marks the passing of almost the last of the women novelists of the mid-Victorian period. Her contemporaries, Miss Braddon, Mrs. Riddell, Miss Yonge, Miss Middlemass, and many others, are all gone now.

The daughter of a clergyman, the Rev. Delves Broughton, of Broughton Hall, Staffordshire, and granddaughter of Sir H. D. Broughton, eighth baronet, Rhoda Broughton was born in North Wales on November 29th, 1840. Her mother was Irish, a member of the Bennett family of The Grange, Birr, King's County,—Jane, daughter of George Bennett, Q.C., of 18 (now renumbered 70), Merrion Square, Dublin. Mr. Bennett's younger daughter, Susan, married Sheridan Le Fanu, the novelist, author of *Uncle Silas* and many another tale of terror. This literary connection had a good deal to do with Miss Broughton's future career as a writer. As a girl she often stayed with her uncle by marriage and her Le Fanu cousins in Dublin. Encouraged and helped by Sheridan Le Fanu she wrote her first stories, and as they progressed she would read then aloud, in the evenings passed in Merrion Square, to him and a few favoured guests, one of the number being Mr. Percy FitzGerald.

These early romances of rugged heroes and unconventional heroines developed into *Not Wisely, but Too Well* and *Cometh up as a Flower*, both of which were published first by Sheridan Le Fanu, in 1867, in *The Dublin University Magazine*, then his own property. He said to her: " You will succeed, and when you do, remember that I prophesied it." Le Fanu also introduced his niece to his London publisher, Bentley, and her literary position was assured after the success of *Red as a Rose is She* in 1872. It was read and praised by everybody. I remember a friend, who was a member of the same club as W. E. Gladstone, relating that on one occasion he saw the statesman in the library, deep in the perusal of a book. Gladstone read on for a long time, and when he eventually put the book down and left the room, the engrossing volume proved to be not a work of philosophy or classical history but—*Red as a Rose is She*.

From 1878 and during the 'eighties, when her literary reputation was at its highest, Miss Broughton lived with her

* *The Bookman*, July, 1920.

O

several dogs at 27, Holywell Street, Oxford. She much enjoyed the academic society of the place. She was a woman of wit and a brilliant, if somewhat caustic, conversationalist. Jowett used to invite her to dine at Balliol to meet his most distinguished guests. Unlike the majority of Oxford ladies, Miss Broughton was always well dressed. Her novel *Belinda* (1883) was a picture of Oxford society of that period, and it is supposed to include a very acute presentation of Mark Pattison, the Rector of Lincoln.

In 1890 she went to live at 1, Mansfield Place, Richmond Hill, Surrey, but ten years later she returned to Oxford. The rest of her life was passed there, at River View, Headington Hill, with lengthy visits to London, where at one time she occupied a flat at 4, Culford Mansions, Chelsea.

Altogether Miss Broughton was the author of some twenty-one successful novels—one of the best being *A Waif's Progress*, which contains some very humorous character drawing. She wrote one good ghost story, *Mrs. Smith of Langmains*. Her last book was *A Thorn in the Flesh* (1917), though I understand a posthumous novel will be published shortly.

She was a pioneer in one sense among feminine novelists because she introduced the daring unconventional heroine in fiction during a very prim period—the 'Sixties—of Victorian life. She really shocked many readers. There is a pleasing but no doubt invented story that Miss Broughton's father forbade her to read her own books. Her style changed later on. As she herself laughingly put it: "I began life as Zola, I finish it as Miss Charlotte Yonge." That of course is an exaggeration: she never approximated to the crude realism of Zola. What is true is that the outspoken freedom and easy wit of her earlier books were succeeded by a more mordant humour, a keener dissection of the emotions and motives which sway poor humanity, and at the same time a more homely and human sentiment.

As a woman, Miss Broughton's numerous friends termed her delightful, and she held a position peculiarly her own, beloved alike for herself and for her books.

AUSTIN DOBSON.*

" You love, my Friend, with me, I think,
That Age of Lustre and of Link ;
Of Chelsea China and long ' s '-es,
Of Bag-wigs and of flowered Dresses ;
That Age of Folly and of Cards,
Of Hackney Chairs and Hackney Bards. "

In such wise did Austin Dobson depict, as in a vignette, his life-long love for the eighteenth century, or more particularly its picturesque accessories. His name and literary work will be associated always with that era, and yet his interest and delight in his subject must have been, in the main, sentimental or based on archæological and artistic tastes. He could never have been in sympathy with the laxity and corruption of the eighteenth century or with its modes of speech and social habits. For Austin Dobson was a man of high character, sober, and almost puritanical in his code of morals and rules of life. He was abstemious in words, smoking, and eating and drinking. He was not gregarious or fond of club life—which may be regarded as the modern substitute for the coffee-houses of the eighteenth century. He rarely dined out, even before his health failed.

Austin Dobson has been criticised for casting a glamour of romance over the eighteenth century, blotting out all details of its vices and follies and cruelty. But such criticism seems to me both hypercritical and fatuous. An artist has the right to choose his subject and interpret what he finds most beautiful in it, whether it be a portrait or a landscape. And the same canon of selection can be claimed by a literary artist. However, the fact remains that in temperament and character and appearance Austin Dobson did not suggest any affinity or sympathy with the period of which he wrote so delightfully. A similar seeming contradiction could be traced in other aspects of his literary work as opposed to his actual life and tastes. Those only familiar with his books might imagine their author to be the ideal bachelor—one who lived in a " many-gabled Grange," oak-panelled, with wide window-seats above a trim garden close. Here, surrounded by choice furniture of Queen Anne's day, old books, old silver, old china, and old wine in the brass-bound cellarette ready to hand, one would picture the author of *Old-World Idylls* in conclave with a fellow-connoisseur : —

* *The Fortnightly Review*, October, 1921.

O 2

" Assume that we are friends. Assume
    A common taste for old costume—
Old pictures—books. Then dream us sitting—
    Us two—in some soft-lighted room.

Outside, the wind; the ' ways are mire,'
    We, with our faces toward the fire,
Finished the feast not full but fitting,
    Watch the light-leaping flames aspire."

.   .   .   .   .

Well, well, the wisest bend to Fate.
My brown old books around me wait,
My pipe still holds, unconfiscate,
    Its wonted station.

Pass me the wine. To those that keep
The bachelor's secluded sleep
Peaceful, inviolate, and deep,
    I pour libation."

But the real Austin Dobson married as a young man, and he was the father of ten children. His literary pursuits for many years had to be subordinate to his duties as a civil servant, and he could only write when his day of official work was over. His private life was domesticated; he lived in a London suburb, Ealing, and for thirty or forty years travelled daily to and from his office like thousands of other men who, unlike him, will leave no record of their name and fame in after years when their little day of work and endeavour in business is done. There was nothing of the Bohemian literary man in Austin Dobson's composition. His habits were decorous. On Sundays he attended to religious observances; at one time, I think, he held sittings at the Ealing Presbyterian Church, in Mount Park Road, during the ministry of that excellent preacher, the late Dr. Thain Davidson. His house, 75, Eaton Rise, was a roomy, double-fronted abode with a pleasant garden behind; but there was nothing to suggest the idyllic settings of his poems. His old-world scenes and picturesque fancies were born in his brain, and I imagine he drew but little from actual experiences. His life, apart from his work, was singularly uneventful—as is, indeed, the case with most literary men.

Henry Austin Dobson was born at Plymouth on January 18th, 1840, the eldest son of George Clarisse Dobson. His paternal grandmother was French, and he considered this fact accounted for his own love of French literature and Gallic forms of verse, such as the rondeau, triolet, and villanelle. His father was a civil engineer, and when Austin was still quite young the family removed to Holyhead, where Mr. Dobson, senior, was in charge of the great breakwater under the direction of his relative, Mr.

Rendel, President of the Institution of Civil Engineers, and father of the late Lord Rendel. It thus came about that the future poet was educated first at a school near by, Beaumaris Grammar School, where he was not very happy. At the age of fourteen he was sent to a school at Coventry kept by Mr. J. W. Knight, another pupil there at the time being John Fisher, just about to enter the Navy and in later years to become Admiral Lord Fisher of Kilverstone. Austin Dobson finished his education at the Gymnase, Strassburg, where, he related, he was the only English boy : —

" The other boys were mostly French with German names. One of them, I remember, bore the rather incongruous appellation of Napoleon Koenig. Strassburg, I need hardly say, at that time was the chief town of a French Department. What I learned at the Gymnase chiefly was French and a little German. Latin I made no great progress with, as I was not sufficiently proficient in French for some time to take advantage of the teaching, which, of course, was all in that language. The teaching, however, was excellent."*

He returned to England when sixteen years of age, and it was proposed that he should enter the Armstrong Works at Newcastle, Mr. (later Lord) Armstrong being a great friend of Dobson's relative, Mr. Rendel. But, though the boy was a good mechanical draughtsman, he disliked mathematics, and consequently he accepted instead the offer of a Government clerkship. There were no competitive examinations in those days, and he secured a nomination through Mr. Owen Stanley, of Penrhos, Holyhead, brother of Lord Stanley of Alderley, President of the Board of Trade. Austin Dobson accordingly entered that office in 1856. He became a first-class clerk in 1874, and a principal one in 1884, eventually retiring in 1901 after forty-five years' service. He related of his official experiences : —

" There is, I believe, an impression that work in a Government Department is of an extremely monotonous character. I cannot say that I found it so. On the contrary, my duties were of the most varied character. At the Board of Trade I was successively in the Draughtsmen's department, the Railway department, the Library, the Marine department, and the Harbour department. . . . I must say I did not find the work of a public office at all irksome, even though it did keep me from my literary studies. My official labours, I consider, tended to inculcate in me qualities in which literary men—the literary men of former ages, at all events—have been rather notoriously deficient. They taught me habits of punctuality and regularity. A man who has been a Government clerk is not likely to say, as some poets have done, ' I must wait for inspiration.' Rather does he do as did Anthony Trollope, who was always at work, even when he was on a journey. His *Life of Cicero* he wrote while on board a steamer on his way to India. I visited Trollope at his house in Montagu Square, and saw the little room where

---

* Interview with representative of *The Morning Post,* January 17th, 1914.

he wrote so many of his novels. It was up a flight of stairs, and it looked on nothing. Every morning his mother called him and gave him a cup of coffee, and Trollope, as soon as he was dressed, went into his study and wrote a certain fixed number of pages before he left for the Post Office. As a Post Office official he showed great energy, as he did in every other capacity. To him we owe the pillar-boxes which are so great a convenience. It was very largely through Trollope's encouragement that I first became engaged in literary pursuits. I did think of doing something in the way of book illustration, and became a student at South Kensington, but was deterred when I found that there were around me, at the Board of Trade, men who were much cleverer artists than myself. I came to the conclusion that I could never hope to be anything more than a fairly successful copyist."*

Austin Dobson's first poem, *A City Flower*, was accepted by Edmund Yates for *Temple Bar*, where it appeared in December, 1864, the editor welcoming it with extreme cordiality as " fresh, original, and very pretty." Soon after, when *St. Paul's Magazine* made its appearance, with Anthony Trollope as editor, Dobson's *Une Marquise* marked the initiation of a long series of contributions from his muse. When he published his first volume of collected poems, entitled *Vignettes in Rhyme and Vers de Société*, Austin Dobson naturally dedicated the work to Trollope. This was in 1873, and directly after the book appeared Frederick Locker called at the Board of Trade and introduced himself to the author with the plea of desiring to compliment him sincerely on *Vignettes in Rhyme*. A warm friendship resulted, and Dobson dedicated his second volume of verse, *Proverbs in Porcelain*, 1877, to the author of *London Lyrics* : —

> " Is it to kindest friend I send
> This nosegay gathered new ?
> Or is it more to critic sure—
> To singer clear and true ?
> I know not which, indeed, nor need ;
> All three I found—in You."

In addition to the literary influence of Mackworth Praed Austin Dobson owed a good deal to Locker. He gave the sub-title of *Vers de Société* to his first book because of the popularity that form of verse was enjoying, mainly through the impulses given to it by Frederick Locker. But, as he said, " Unlike Locker, I did not claim to be a distinguished member of society. In fact, I have been more or less of a bookworm and a recluse all my life. Public dinners I dislike, and I have never made a practice of going out much."

Locker introduced Dobson to many notable people, but he was a man who cared only for a circle of a few choice friends, though

---

* Interview in *The Morning Post,* January 17th, 1914.

when he did form a friendship it was fine and lasting. This
he exemplified admirably in " A Greeting " (to W. C.) : —

" But once or twice we met, touched hands,

Time like a despot speeds his sands :
A year he blots, a day he brands;
We walked, we talked by Thamis' side
But once or twice.

What makes a friend? What filmy strands
Are these that turn to iron bands?
What knot is this so firmly tied
That naught but Fate can now divide?
Ah, these are things one understands
But once or twice."

The small, select circle of Austin Dobson's friends included
Cosmo Monkhouse, Andrew Lang, W. E. Henley, George
Saintsbury, Hugh Thomson (the artist most gifted by temperament and similarity of taste to interpret Dobson's work), Arthur
Waugh, and Edmund Gosse. The last-named was the most
favoured of all, for it became Austin Dobson's pleasant custom
when presenting a book, whether one of his own or a choice copy
of an eighteenth-century classic, to this friend to inscribe a few
lines of original verse in the volume, such as this : —

" Gossip, may we live as now,
Brothers ever, I and thou;
Us may never Envy's mesh hold,
Anger never cross our threshold ;
Let our modest Lares be
Friendship and urbanity."

The friendship between the two commenced in the far-away
days when Mr. Gosse was also employed at the Board of Trade.
One of Max Beerbohm's most delightful caricatures depicted a
scene at the Board of Trade in the early 'Eighties with Mr.
Austin Dobson and Mr. Edmund Gosse, in the guise of two
schoolboy figures, caught in the act of composing a romantic
ballad during office hours by their sleuth-like President, Mr.
Joseph Chamberlain.

Austin Dobson married Frances Mary, daughter of Nathaniel
Beardmore, also a civil engineer, of Broxbourne, Hertfordshire.
Their first home at Ealing was in Tranquil Terrace, The Grove,
near the Common; and Mr. Dobson told me the poems he wrote
at that period were literal lucubrations, composed by the light of
midnight oil (or perhaps gas!) after a hard day's work at the
Board of Trade. And yet how good the poems of this date were
—*The Ladies of St. James's, The Sundial, The Forgotten Grave,
The Curé's Progress, The Masque of the Months,* and many

another: they show no trace of a tired brain. All are touched
with the delicate art of a miniature, with polished phrasing. And
with what tender pathos he could present some little tragedy of
poor humanity, as in " The Cradle " : —

> " How steadfastly she'd worked at it !
> How lovingly had drest
> With all her would-be-mother's wit
> That little rosy nest.
>
> .　　　.　　　.　　　.　　　.
>
> He came at last, the tiny guest,
> Ere bleak December fled ;
> That rosy nest he'd never prest . . .
> Her coffin was his bed."

Again, in *Before Sedan*, with those exquisite last lines, the
truth of which so many mourners must sorrowfully have
echoed : —

> " Ah, if beside the dead
> Slumbered the pain !
> Ah, if the hearts that bled
> Slept with the slain !
> If the grief died ;—But no ;—
> Death will not have it so."

And yet again in *Good-night, Babette!* where the old, old
man dimly recognises the shadows from the past that bend over
his bed, the while Babette sings the Norman *chansonnette* : —

> " Once at the Angelus
> (Ere I was dead),
> Angels all glorious
> Came to my bed :
> Angels in blue and white,
> Crowned on the head.
>
> One was the Friend I left
> Stark in the snow ;
> One was the Wife that died
> Long—long ago ;
> One was the Love I lost . . . .
> How could she know?
>
> One had my Mother's eyes,
> Wistful and mild ;
> One had my Father's face ;
> One was a Child :
> All of them bent to me—
> Bent down and smiled ! "

Such simple words, and yet the eyes grow dim at reading
them, for their pathos is elemental and must touch everyone
who has loved and lost.

Austin Dobson's next volume of verse, *At the Sign of the
Lyre*, 1885, has its title preserved in the author's book-plate,

where in the foreground is an inn-like swinging sign-board bearing on it a lyre between the initials A. D.

Austin Dobson is more generally regarded as a poet than a prose writer, but, unlike George Meredith (who wished to be remembered as a poet rather than as a novelist), he was disposed to consider his prose his best work. He said on one occasion: " I have tried very hard to write prose, and I am always more pleased when I write a successful piece of prose than verse, though poetry comes easier to me. Dobson's prose work is notable for its wealth of allusion, presented in an attractive manner and with no suggestion of instructing his reader. But it is always clear how wide is the author's acquaintance with his subject and its illustrative references, in short, with its entire detailed archæological basis. As a brief example may be quoted his picture of the alfresco pleasure resorts on the outskirts of London in the eighteenth century : —

" The pleasure-loving 'prentice of the last century, when, in Cheap or Fleet, he put up his shutters and put on his sword, can seldom have been at a loss for amusement. Not only had every inn on the outskirts of the sign-haunted City its skittle ground, or bowling green, or ninepin alley, where he might doff his tarnished gala-dress, perch his scratch wig upon a post (as he does in Mr. Abbey's charming pictures), and cultivate to his heart's content the mysteries of managing a bowl with one hand and a long ' churchwarden ' with the other, but nearly every village within a mile or two of Paul's boasted its famous summer garden, presenting its peculiar and specific programme of diversions—diversions which included the enviable distinction of rubbing elbows with the quality, and snatching for a space the fearful joy of ' Bon Ton.' At Pentonville there was the White Conduit House, upon whose celebrated cakes and creams Dr. Goldsmith had once the misfortune of entertaining a party of ladies, and then finding himself, like Señor Patricio in Le Sage, without the wherewithal to pay the reckoning ; at Islington, where you might not only genteelly discuss the ' Killibeate ' (as Mr. Weller's friend called it), but regale yourself with the supplementary recreation of ' balance-masters, walking on the wire, rope dancing, tumbling, and pantomime entertainments.' At Bagnigge Wells, in what is now King's Cross Road, you might, after being received at the Assembly Room by a dignified Master of the Ceremonies in a cocked hat, enjoy, to the sound of an organ, the refreshment (with gilt spoons) of tea, which would be handed to you by a page with a kettle, like Pompey in Plate II. of Hogarth's *Harlot's Progress;* at Cuper's (*vulgo* ' Cupid's ') Gardens, over against Somerset House, on the Surrey side of the water, you might witness the noted fireworks, listen to Mr. Jones, his harp-playing, and assist at various other amusements, some of which, it is to be feared, were more suited to Thomas Idle than Francis Goodchild. Then—as time-honoured as any, since they dated from Pepys and the Restoration, and survived until Chatterton could write their burlettas—there were, at the bottom of Harley Street, the renowned gardens of Marybone, which in addition to the pyrotechnic displays of Torré or Caillot, and the privilege of having your pockets emptied by the notorious George Barrington, or some other equally quick-handed artist, offered the exceptional attractions of ' fine Epping butter,' ' almond cheesecakes, and ' tarts of a twelvepenny size,' made by no less a personage than the sister of the illustrious Dr. Trusler, author of that popular didactic work, *The Blossoms of Morality*. All of these, however, were but the shadows of the two greater rallying places of Vauxhall and Ranelagh, both of which were on the Thames. . . .''

Dobson was the author of excellent monographs on Henry Fielding, Horace Walpole, Fanny Burney and Samuel Richardson. His greatest achievement in prose was the admirable book on Hogarth, the man who was the touchstone or pre-eminent factor of his literary life, for it was his interest in the work of the great pictorial moralist that led Mr. Dobson to the study of the life and art of the eighteenth century. He related of his biography of Hogarth : '' My interest in the subject is of long standing, since it dates from the hours in which, as a boy, I used to wonder over Jackson's wood-cuts from the old *Penny Magazine*.'' The Hogarth book first appeared in 1879, and enlarged editions followed in 1891, 1898, 1902, and 1907.

Austin Dobson was naturally interested in Hogarth's house at Chiswick, and so was I. This was the link which brought about my acquaintance with Mr. Dobson, and I had the pleasure of visiting him several times at Ealing. In addition to the eighteenth century, we had many mutual interests in the bypaths of literature and in bygone, half-forgotten authors. I have related elsewhere how, when I was preparing a memoir of Frank Smedley and mentioned the matter to Mr. Dobson, he surprised me by quoting scenes and portions of dialogues from Smedley's *Frank Fairlegh*—a book he had read in his boyhood and not seen for over fifty years. I mention this as an example of Austin Dobson's extraordinary and retentive memory, wherein everything was mentally endorsed and pigeon-holed, so to speak, in a most orderly manner, his information and recollections being withdrawn from their resting-place, when required, by mere volition.

To revert to Hogarth, when the great painter's house at Chiswick was in danger of being pulled down and the site built over in 1901, Austin Dobson wrote in the first letter he addressed to me : '' I fear it is not possible to save Hogarth's house, nor, were it possible to save it now, would it be possible to save it long. I took a friend there last year, who would have paid five hundred pounds for it, but he found that nearly four times that amount would probably be asked for the house and site. There are plenty of rich people, too, in the neighbourhood who should be able to buy it.''

Happily the last suggestion was realised, for in the following

year Hogarth's house was saved by the rare public spirit and
generosity of Lieutenant-Colonel Robert Shipway, of Grove
House,who purchased the property and presented it to the nation.
After its restoration there was an inaugural dinner in the house,
in May, 1904, when Austin Dobson made one of his few public
appearances, but he did not join in the subsequent speeches.
Among the other guests were Sir Lawrence Alma-Tadema (who
presided), Lord George Hamilton, Sir Charles Holroyd, Mr.
E. A. Abbey, R.A., and the late President of the Royal
Academy (Sir Aston Webb).

Another house Mr. Dobson and I were keenly interested in
was Fordhook, Ealing, the last home in England of Henry
Fielding, and where in later years Byron's daughter was married.
We both lived in the neighbourhood of Fordhook, and we deeply
regretted its ruthless demolition at the hands of the speculative
suburban builder. I wrote an article, in 1913, on the house and
its associations for the now defunct *English Illustrated Magazine*,
to which periodical, twenty years earlier, Austin Dobson had
contributed his delightful article on Ranelagh Gardens, an
example of his prose style at its best.* On the subject of my
article on Fordhook and Fielding he stated : —

" All that I know of Fordhook is contained in my ' Men of Letters,'
Fielding, last edition, 1907; in the *Journal of a Voyage to Lisbon*,
' World's Classics,' and in the article, *A Fielding Find, National Review*,
August, 1911. From these it appears that he is first heard of at Fordhook in May, 1754, and that he left it on June 26th, 1754. There is no
evidence I know of that he was at Ealing before, though he may have
been there. There is no mention of him in the rate-books, or of his
bailiff, Richard Boor. He made his will at Ealing. He held some farm
land, compare *A Fielding Find*. This last article will be reprinted, with
additions, in October (1912). There is a view of Fordhook in Jackson's
Ealing, 1898, p. 214, from a sketch in the Guildhall Library : it is
wrongly called ' Ealing Grove.' I think *Amelia* was written at the
Bow Street of which it reeks.

" May I say that if this information be new to you I hope you will
give me credit for it. I don't for a moment suppose you will not ; but the
old and good fashions of writing are not now always observed, and
everything printed is regarded as public property without any regard
to the painful excavator who first dug it up. I am often, from America,
asked for information which is not even acknowledged in writing. Please
do not regard these remarks as personal. They are not. But your letter
makes a peg for a *boutade*."

I duly incorporated his information and acknowledged the
source. He was pleased with the article and wrote to me : —

" Many thanks for your paper, which I have just been reading with
interest and profit. I wished it longer. It seems impossible to find out
any more about Fordhook. . . . Could you not do some more of these

* See *ante* page 217.

topographical articles? They are always interesting and valuable, since they preserve fugitive things. I shall preserve this one carefully.''*

I merely quote these brief extracts from many letters to demonstrate Mr. Dobson's kindly interest in the work of others. I found him a kind and sympathetic friend, always ready to help with detailed information from his great store of knowledge: yet he was singularly unassuming and modest regarding his own accomplishments in the art of letters. I imagine his was a very sensitive nature; his manner in conversation was a curious blend of old-world courtesy and shyness—for, as he said, he was a recluse. I look back with real pleasure to my intercourse with him, and recall how he would show me the treasures of his library apropos of some subject we were discussing, and his collection of Hogarth engravings, which were kept in portfolio.

As for his own books, as I have said, he was always modest about them, though they were of outstanding merit in their own particular style. Mr. Owen Seaman well expressed Austin Dobson's special and peculiar position in modern literature in the parodic tribute he offered twenty years ago:—

> " You keep your courtly pride of place
> Within the circle's charmed space,
> You rest unchallenged, as of old,
> At sixty years.

> " Not time, nor silence sets its trace
> On golden lyre and voice of gold;
> Our Poet's Poet, still you hold
> The laurels got by no man's grace—
> At sixty years.''

But the advancing years all too soon affected Mr. Dobson's health. As far back as 1913 I find he wrote, in response to an invitation of mine: " Many thanks for your very kind proposal. But week-ends, alas! are now entirely out of my line. I got influenza last year, and have never quite got rid of it, and seldom go out anywhere. You know, since it is idle to conceal it, that I am no longer young." Eighteen months later he told me he was suffering much from arthritis, and henceforth he was practically confined to his house and garden. But he was still able to write, and despite his pain and inactivity, voiced his serene and high philosophy and joy of life:—

> " Yes. For it still was good,
> Good to be living;
> Buoyant of heart and blood;
> Fighting, forgiving;

---

* The article on *Fordhook* will be found at page 222 of this book.

> Glad for the earth and sky;
>   Glad for mere gladness;
> Grateful, one knew not why,
>   Even for sadness;
> Finding the ray of hope
>   Gleam through distresses;
> Building a larger scope
>   Out from successes;
> Blithe to the close, and still
>   Tendering ever,
> Both for the good and ill,
>   Thanks to the Giver."

Austin Dobson died at 75, Eaton Rise, Ealing, on September 2nd, 1921, and he was buried in the Westminster Cemetery at Hanwell. His was a well-spent life, and he had the satisfaction of writing nothing of which he need be ashamed. His most beautiful poem was this:—

> " In after days when grasses high
> O'er-top the stone where I shall lie,
>   Though ill or well the world adjust
>   My slender claim to honoured dust,
> I shall not question or reply.
>
> I shall not see the morning sky;
> I shall not hear the night-wind sigh;
>   I shall be mute, as all men must
>   In after days !
>
> But yet, now living, fain were I
> That some one then should testify,
>   Saying—' He held his pen in trust
>   To Art, not serving shame or lust.'
> Will none?—Then let my memory die
>   In after days."

Surely his aspiration will be fulfilled. It will be long years hence before the memory of Austin Dobson and his artistic achievement fades.

FORDHOOK,

And Some Other Memories of Acton and Ealing.*

When once a London suburb is invaded by the Army of Progress —as represented by speculative builders, aspiring vestries, prancing municipalities, and tramway promoters—the changes effected in a few years in the aspect and social conditions of rural, quiet localities are truly amazing; and for those persons who have known such districts before the Progressive invasion, it is fully possible to enact the regretful, reminiscent rôle of " ancient inhabitant " and *laudator temporis acti* when only half-way through the Psalmist's allotted span.

Some twenty years ago that portion of the highway from London to Uxbridge which lies between Acton and Ealing was distinctly countrified, with a few fine old houses standing in large grounds: now it is lined with suburban villas and shops, past which rush motor 'buses and clanging trams in never-ceasing noisy procession, where of yore one old, yellow horse-'bus wended its leisurely way from Acton to Ealing. Let us, in imagination, mount that long-vanished 'bus (whose driver's vast hat was suggestive of even an earlier Wellerian mode) and note from its box-seat the aspect of the route in those pleasant days we recall and regret.

Starting from the North London Railway Station, at the junction of Churchfield Road with Horn Lane stood, on the right, Acton House, a dull yellow brick mansion of the type so frequently erected in Middlesex at the close of the eighteenth century. It was formerly occupied by the Selbys and Kellys, Roman Catholic families, and a subterranean passage led from the house, under Horn Lane, to an additional garden in King Street, whence access was obtained to a small house (on the site now occupied by the Post Office) adapted for the purposes of a chapel.

Horn Lane being off the route of the old 'bus, there is no excuse to expatiate at length on its vanished charms, pre-eminent of which was the great garden wall—seventeenth century work undoubtedly, of mellow red brick with foxgloves growing from the top—of Derwentwater House. The house itself was of more recent date, 1804, standing on the site of the original mansion built by Sir Henry Garway in 1638, and subsequently occupied by the Cromwellian General Skippon. Still later it was the

* *The English Illustrated Magazine*, February, 1913.

residence of Lady Derwentwater, widow of the gallant Earl who sacrificed fortune and life for the cause of his King and cousin in 1715-1716. Many long-established, picturesque traditions of the unfortunate Derwentwater lingered about the place; his body was said to be buried temporarily in the garden, pending removal to Dilston in Northumberland, and his headless ghost "to walk." House and garden and grave are gone, and in their place are small suburban dwellings—certainly the most unghostly situation the mind could picture—and it is best to believe that this brave spirit long ago found rest and oblivion. Springfield House, occupied for the last thirty-six years by Mrs. Stewart, has a vague tradition that one of Cromwell's sisters once resided there. It is the only survivor of the old houses of Horn Lane. Gone is its neighbour, The Lodge, long the residence of the Scott-Turner family; gone is Shalimar; and gone Friars Place, which in the early days of the nineteenth century one of its occupants, Dr. Robert Wake, found " almost painfully lonely," so remote and unfrequented were the country lanes of Acton.* Even about thirty years ago that portion of Horn Lane now covered by Shalimar Terrace and Nemoure Road was extremely rural. Here was a great meadow, fronted by fine trees and a raised footpath (said to be " haunted ") divided by a hawthorn hedge from Horn Lane. The little house, now in pathetic ruins, at the south corner of Creffield Road was occupied by Mrs. Payne, who had been housekeeper to Mr. Antrobus, of Springfield Park adjoining—a truly beautiful sylvan estate before it was cut up for building purposes.

A little way up Creffield Road on the left was a small farm-stead—" Blake's Farm "—reached by *descending* steps, where milk and eggs were to be had at any time. The residence of Springfield Park still stands, much altered, and was until recent years the home of the late Dr. Lingham, a medical man of the old school. The house was very small for such a large park, and the situation at an extreme corner of the estate was curious, as it practically adjoined The Steyne, a poor quarter of the village. The Steyne, however, was exceedingly picturesque before the ancient inns were rebuilt and its grass railed in and beshrubbed, and even now some old red-tiled cottages preserve a memory of its former aspect. And so, passing the Rectory of 1728, we regain the High Street. And what a change is here. Gone are the ancient houses on the left-hand side, Baxter's reputed dwelling and the Cock and Crown Yard of dubious notoriety (our

---

* East Acton still retains its village aspect, with green and ancient houses, and small shop.

local Clare Market), and all the quaint inns turned into alcoholic palaces. And the whole block of buildings, between the Church and King Street, with the curious raised pavement and steps completely cleared away. We come to the foot* of Acton Hill, and this long row of shops on the left has succeeded the houses and large gardens of Woodlands and The Oaks. The Red Lion, at the top of Acton Hill, was a famous coaching inn in former days. Adjoining it was a large meadow, well remembered by those who were children twenty odd years ago as the location of Sanger's Circus and other travelling shows. At the western boundary of this meadow stood East Lodge, then occupied by Mr. and Mrs. Beauchamp, and consequently the early home of their daughter, Miss May Beauchamp, now the Countess von Arnim,† who, as the author of *Elizabeth and her German Garden* and other delightful books, has won such a notable position in contemporary literary life. An earlier occupant of the house, about 1842, was Frederick Tyrrell, a celebrated oculist. East Lodge has succumbed to the crush of more modern bricks and mortar: but its smaller neighbour, West Lodge, still stands, though bereft of gardens.

On the right hand side of Acton Hill was Hill House, a square, white building only recently demolished, and next to it The Elms, the only survivor of all the fine old houses that were situated between Acton and Ealing. It is a stately building still, and, standing back from the noisy highway, seems to brood upon former occupants who played out the drama of life there, amid such different surroundings, in the days long gone. Formerly the extensive gardens of The Elms reached back to Springfield Park, and what looks like a Maze is marked in a map of 1741, when Sir Joseph Ayloffe was in possession. The house was also for some period the abode of the Wegg family, who gave their name to the adjoining Wegg Avenue, more familiarly and appositely known as Green Lane. Before this lane of lofty elms and oaks was metamorphosed into the

---

* Here, earlier, on the right hand side, stood Bank House, the former residence of the Adair family from the eighteenth century until about 1830. It was surrounded by large gardens, and the estate covered the site bounded by the Steyne and the backs of the houses in King Street and High Street. The house itself was somewhere near the present Nelson Place, facing the "Rising Sun" public-house, but the Steyne was shut off from view by the high garden wall, lined with closely-set poplars. The grounds on the High Street frontage (immediately east of the late offices of the Local Board) were high, with sloping terrace and steps, and here was an additional and more modern entrance. One of the last occupants of Bank House, in 1866, was Mr. H. M. Coules, who told me it was substantially built, with a stone staircase and very large kitchen; and on the first floor were five rooms, all communicating with each other.

† Now the Countess Russell.

residential " Twyford Avenue," its entrance in the Uxbridge Road was truly rural; on the right was a large pond, belonging to The Elms, with swans; on the left was another pond, and then a beautiful range of meadowland—open country to Hanger Hill—whose fragrance in the haymaking season scented the whole stretch of highway. Yet another large pond, surrounded by white palings, and adjoining a market garden, was situated on the other side of the Uxbridge Road (just before reaching Ealing Common Station), and immediately facing this pond was the picturesque ivy-covered lodge giving admittance to Fordhook.

Fordhook, which possessed some of the most interesting associations of this favoured locality, was probably first erected early in the eighteenth century, but its most memorable year was 1754, when it became the last home in England of Henry Fielding. Broken in health, victim of asthma, gout, and dropsy, the once robust, dashing author of *Tom Jones* in May, 1754, moved to Fordhook, the " little house " at Ealing he had taken on account of the salubrious air of this district of Middlesex, then considered " far superior to that of Kensington Gravel-Pits " (which comprised that portion of Notting Hill, by Bayswater, adjoining the north side of the Uxbridge Road).

There seems to be no proof of the statement, made elsewhere, that Fielding wrote *Amelia* at Fordhook, for Mr. Austin Dobson (himself long a resident of Ealing), who has so industriously studied and admirably recorded Fielding's life, informs me that " he is first heard of at Fordhook in May, 1754, and that he left it on the 26th June, 1754. There is no evidence I know of that he was at Ealing before, though he may have been there. He held some farm land. . . . I think *Amelia* was written at the Bow Street of which it reeks."*

At Fordhook, Fielding was surrounded by his daughter Harriet, his second wife, Mary Daniel, and her young children. These latter comprised William Fielding, then a boy of six, Sophia, and Allen, an infant of four weeks. The dying novelist made his will at Ealing, and on June 26th, 1754, he set out on that sad last voyage to Lisbon, in the vain search for lost health, from which he was never to return. Fielding was only forty-seven years of age, but he bravely faced his fate and did not shrink from

---

* Mr. Charles Jones, C.E., of Ealing, by means of the old parish rate books has established the fact that Fielding paid rates for Fordhook until September, 1754. In February, 1755, they were paid by Fielding's half-brother John, and John Ranby (Serjeant-Surgeon to George II), who is alluded to in *Tom Jones* (Book VIII, Chapter XIII). Ranby evidently took over Fordhook altogether, as he solely paid the rates in September, 1755. He later became Surgeon to Chelsea Hospital, and died in 1773. See letter from Mr. J. P. de Castro, *The Times Literary Supplement,* July 3rd, 1924.

approaching death. The words, in his *Journal of a Voyage to Lisbon*, wherewith he recorded his farewell to Fordhook have become, as Mr. Dobson says, classic, and to repeat them yet again cannot rob them of their pathos : —

" *Wednesday, June 26th,* 1754. On this day, the most melancholy sun I had ever beheld arose, and found me awake at my house at Fordhook. By the light of this sun, I was, in my own opinion, last to behold and take leave of some of those creatures on whom I doated with a mother-like fondness, guided by nature and passion, and uncured and unhardened by all the doctrine of that philosophical school where I had learnt to bear pains and to despise death.

" In this situation, as I could not conquer nature, I submitted entirely to her, and she made as great a fool of me as she had ever done of any woman whatsoever : under pretence of giving me leave to enjoy, she drew me to suffer the company of my little ones, during eight hours ; and I doubt not whether, in that time, I did not undergo more than in all my distemper.

" At twelve o'clock precisely my coach was at the door, which was no sooner told me than I kiss'd my children, and went into it with some little resolution. My wife, who behaved more like a heroine and philosopher, tho' at the same time the tenderest mother in the world, and my eldest daughter followed me ; some friends went with us, and others here took their leave ; and I heard my behaviour applauded, with many murmurs and phrases to which I well knew I had no title ; as all other such philosophers may, if they have any modesty, confess on the like occasions."

The coach rumbled away through the country to Acton and thence to London and Rotherhithe, whence the party sailed for Lisbon, and there, a little more than three months after the departure from Fordhook, Fielding died.* He was buried at Lisbon.

---

* The following advertisement from an old newspaper of 1754 was contributed to *The Times Literary Supplement* of June 26th, 1924, by M. Dorothy George, who thus establishes the fact that " exactly six months after the tragic leave-taking, Fielding's farm, his household goods, and the coach in which he travelled so expeditiously (in two hours) the twelve miles from Ealing to Rotherhithe were advertised for sale " :
" To be Sold by Auction
By Mr. Langford
(By order of the Administrator) This and the following Days, The Lease of the Dwelling House, Out-houses and Gardens with about Forty Acres of Land thereunto belonging, situated at the hither end of Ealing Common, a little beyond Acton, of   Henry Fielding, Esq.,
Late of Bow Street, Covent Garden, deceased;
Together with all the Stock of the Farm consisting of Two large Ricks of Hay, Two of Wheat, One of Oats, and One of Pease; about Eighty Sheep, Seven Cows (four of them Alderney), Five Hogs, Three Sows, Three Asses, A Monkey, Seven Coach and Cart-Horses, Two Saddle Horses, three Carts, and other farming Utensils. As likewise all the genuine Household Furniture, his Landau and Harness, Plate, Wines and other Effects.
" All which will be exhibited to public View every Day (Christmas Day excepted) till the Time of Sale which will begin each Day punctually at Twelve o'clock.
" Catalogues of which may be had gratis at the Place of Sale, and at Mr. Langford's in the Great Piazza, Covent Garden.
" Printed Particulars of the Estate may be had at both the Places above-named."—*Public Advertiser,* December 26, 1754."

FORDHOOK

[*Page 226.*

Before the following year, 1755, Fielding's young family had been removed from Fordhook; and it was, presumably, after this date that the Atlee family—a name associated with Ealing for a very long period—acquired the property. In the south aisle of St. Mary's Church, Acton, there is a tablet, bearing the family arms, inscribed as follows: "In memory of those members of the Atlee family, of Fordhook, who are buried in the middle aisle of this church, this tablet is erected by descendants in America."

Fordhook was subsequently occupied by Sir A. Denton, Judge of Common Pleas; the Misses Crowcher (in 1811); and then by another very notable resident, Anne Isabella, Lady Byron, widow of the poet. Lady Byron first resided at Hanger Hill, Ealing, probably in Hanger Vale House, situated at what is now the south-west corner of the Golf Links. It was from here that she wrote her "Remarks," dated February 19th, 1830, on Moore's *Life of Byron*, which related particularly to her separation from her husband. The only child of the marriage, Augusta Ada, then aged fourteen, was, of course, with her mother, and the two removed to Fordhook, 1831-2. Here, then, it was that Ada Byron passed her brief spell of happy girlhood.* All too soon for her it came to an end, and in the after years of pain and trouble she must often have regretted the peaceful Ealing days, in Fordhook and its beautiful garden. Ada Byron was married at the age of nineteen to Lord King, created, three years later, Earl of Lovelace. The ceremony was performed in the upstairs drawing-room at Fordhook, by special license, on July 8th, 1835, in the presence of the bride's mother; her cousin, Lord Byron (the poet, her father, had been dead eleven years); Viscount Ebrington (afterwards second Earl Fortescue), the bridegroom's uncle; the Hon. Hester and the Hon. Charlotte King, sisters of the bridegroom, and Lady Olivia Acheson (daughter of the second Earl of Gosford) who, no doubt, comprised the three bridesmaids.

Lady Lovelace's married life was sorrowful, her death appalling. Of her last days Miss Mitford gives a terrible picture.

"Ada, Lady Lovelace, died of a frightful form of internal cancer. While she was dying her death of martyrdom, Mrs. Sartoris (Adelaide Kemble) went to sing to her. Through the open door she saw poor Lady Lovelace crouching on her hands and knees, on the floor which was covered with mattresses, this being the only posture she could bear in her agony."

This was at 8, Great Cumberland Place, and the end came on

---

* See *ante*, page 78.

November, 29th, 1852, when she was but thirty-six. The funeral, Miss Mitford adds, " was very ostentatious, escutcheons and silver coronals everywhere—the taste of Lord Lovelace, and not Lady Byron's, which is perfectly simple." Lady Lovelace was buried at Hucknall Torkard in the same vault with Byron, although she had " been brought up in entire ignorance of all that regards my father," as she once told Colonel Wildman, the owner of Newstead Abbey, and she had never read a line of her father's poems till towards the end of her short life.

Lady Byron remained at Fordhook after her daughter's marriage. She was engaged in much philanthropic work at Ealing, and was particularly interested in an Industrial School for Boys, which she founded in 1833 at Ealing Grove House. The large grounds of this estate stretched from Ealing Green to the Common, and here the pupils worked in a practical way at gardening and its allied labours; others spent part of their working day with the village carpenters, shoemakers, and various tradesmen, to whom the boys were severally apprenticed as their abilities or tastes suggested. In 1848, when there were about eighty pupils, the school was transferred to the headmaster, Mr. C. N. Atlee, who carried it on in new premises (now known as Byron House, The Park) until his death in 1866.

Lady Byron, who died in 1860, left Ealing in 1841, when Fordhook was purchased by Captain Tyrrell, R.N. (brother of Mr. Frederick Tyrrell, of East Lodge), the place remaining his residence until his death in 1872. His daughter, Miss Elizabeth Tyrrell, became the wife of Mr. Hilliard, Vicar of Christ Church, Ealing, and his son, Captain Tyrrell, prominently associated with the early days of the Volunteers in the district, the next owner of Fordhook, died there in 1887. His widow, subsequently Mrs. Mansel-Jones, was its last occupant; she left in 1903, and two years later this old house of many memories was ruthlessly razed to the ground to make room for shops and villas. No attempt was made in the district to preserve Fordhook and appropriately adapt it to the purposes of a local museum and subsidiary public library, and no private benefactor came forward to save it for the public as, most happily, was the case with Hogarth's House at Chiswick through the generosity of Colonel Shipway. So Fordhook disappeared, and with it a visible, intimate link with two great names in English literature—Fielding and Byron.

In these progressive days one must be thankful for qualified mercies, so it is pleasant to add that a few of the great houses which made Ealing and Acton notable in earlier years are still in existence. In particular, Gunnersbury Lane is scarcely

changed; and East Acton yet retains its Green and other
picturesque features—a quiet oasis off the bustling high-road,
surrounded by that queer, indeterminate country which is so
vividly pictured by Mr. Arthur Machen in the latter part of *The
Hill of Dreams*. East Acton Manor House, though empty and
sadly gone to ruin, is a beautiful example of a Jacobean residence;
it might have been the very *Covering End* of Mr. Henry James
when in repair: now it images *The Haunted House* of Hood.*

About 1765 East Acton was the resort of people of rank and
fashion, who came to drink the cathartic waters of its three wells,
which were similar to those of Cheltenham. An assembly room
was built, and the adjoining inn of Mr. Gardner provided more
material necessities. The wells were situated on Old Oak
Common, to the east of the present North London Railway line.
The name was perpetuated in Wells Farm and Wells House
Farm, which stood, until recent years, further south in Old Oak
Lane. But the district has now been entirely changed by building
operations.

It was the proximity of the wells that caused the building of
so many good houses at East Acton, and among the temporary
residents was Sir Lucas Pepys, Bart., who was often visited here
by his brother, Sir William Pepys, Bart., and members of the
" Bas Bleu " coterie.

NOTE.—In the spring of 1842 Lady Byron lent Fordhook for
some weeks to Mrs. Augustus De Morgan. Her son, William
De Morgan, the future artist and author, was then a little boy
not yet three years of age. Extracts from his mother's journal
relating to Fordhook will be found in *William De Morgan and
his Wife*, by A. M. W. Stirling.

---

* The Manor House was demolished in 1912.

THE NEW BYRON LETTERS.*

INTEREST in Byron the man is perennial, and transcends the attention now given to his poetry. *Childe Harold, Don Juan* and some of the shorter poems are, of course, for all time; but it is doubtful if his poetical dramas, such as *Manfred* and *Cain*, are very widely read in these latter days. The drama of the poet's actual life, however, remains vivid and alive, for, though nearly a hundred years have elapsed since his death, controversy still rages (mildly now, it is true) around the complicated story of his relations with his half-sister and the separation from his wife. Any new light on these matters is welcomed by those acquainted with the literary and social history of Byron's period, and the strange story also appeals to students of pathological psychology.

For these and other reasons the new Byron letters,† now at this late date edited and published by Mr. Murray, are an important contribution to a right understanding of the poet's life. They were known to exist, and copies were in the possession of Byron's grandson, the late Lord Lovelace. But he could not publish them, as they were the property of Byron's executor, John Cam Hobhouse (Lord Broughton); and by the strange and illogical law which governs executorship, the documents—and, more important, the copyright in them—passed to the alien possession of Hobhouse's daughter, the late Lady Dorchester. She at one time intended to leave these family papers to their rightful possessor, Lord Lovelace; but after the publication of his book, *Astarte*, in 1905, Lady Dorchester changed her mind, for she disapproved of this work, in which the poet's grandson expressed and endeavoured to prove his belief in the charge of incest against Byron. Lord Lovelace died before Lady Dorchester, but as his widow shared his views, Lady Dorchester eventually left the documents to Mr. Murray, who, it may be granted, as the grandson of Byron's publisher, was the most fitting depositary in view of the circumstances that guided her decision.

The letters in question number about five hundred. They were addressed mainly to Hobhouse himself, to the Hon. Douglas Kinnaird, and—most interesting of all—a long series to

* *The Fortnightly Review*, April, 1922.
† *Lord Byron's Correspondence.* Edited by John Murray. Illustrated. In 2 vols. (London : John Murray.)

Lady Melbourne during 1812-1815. There are also various letters included in these volumes written to Byron by Shelley and other friends. The correspondence covers the period of Byron's life from the age of twenty, in 1808, to his death in 1824. The first instalment to Hobhouse, 1808-1811, is not the most attractive of the collection, for the style is spasmodic, and in the absence of the complementary letters from Hobhouse the meaning of allusions is not always very clear. However, there are many characteristic touches. Thus, when he was abroad in 1810, and staying at The Convent, Athens, Byron set the boy pupils to box, and recovered his own boyhood in their society : —

" We have nothing but riot from noon to night. . . . But I am vastly happy and childish. . . . I am learning Italian, and this day translated an ode of Horace, ' Exegi monumentum,' into that language. I chatter with everybody, good or bad, and tradute prayers out of the mass ritual; but my lessons, though very long, are sadly interrupted by scamperings, and eating fruit, and peltings and playings; and I am in fact at school again, and make as little improvement now as I did there, my time being wasted in the same way."

And then in the following year, when he was recalled to England by business worries connected with his estates, came the sudden death of his mother, and the hysterical, morbid side of his temperament finds expression : —

" My dwelling you already know is the house of mourning, and I am really so much bewildered with the different shocks I have sustained, that I can hardly reduce myself to reason by the most frivolous occupations. My poor friend, J. Wingfield, my mother, and your best friend (and surely not the worst of mine) C. S. M. [Matthews] have disappeared in one little month since my return. . . . There is to me something so incomprehensible in death that I can neither speak nor think on the subject. . . . I have neither hopes nor fears beyond the grave. . . . In the room where I now write (flanked by the *skulls* you have seen so often) did you and Matthews and myself pass some joyous unprofitable evenings, and here we will drink to his memory, which, though it cannot reach the dead, will soothe the survivors, and to them only death can be an evil. . . . I am very lonely, and should think myself miserable were it not for a kind of hysterical merriment, which I can neither account for nor conquer; but strange as it is, I do laugh, and heartily, wondering at myself while I sustain it. I have tried reading, and boxing, and swimming, and writing, and rising early, and sitting late, and water, and wine, with a number of ineffectual remedies, and here I am, wretched, but not ' melancholy or gentlemanlike.' . . . I fear the more we see of life, the more we shall regret those who have ceased to live—we will speak of them no more."

He was at this date devoted to his beautiful ancestral home, Newstead Abbey, and was resolved not to sell it, however pressing the embarrassments of the estate : —

" I *will not;* and though I have in more than one letter to you requested you to corroborate and assist this negative, I beg in this, and all subsequent communications, to entreat you to tell him [Hanson] and all whom it may concern, that I will not sell my patrimony."

Unhappily his financial difficulties compelled him to part with Newstead in 1817, the purchaser, at the price of ninety-four thousand five hundred pounds, being his former school friend at Harrow, Colonel Wildman.

In 1811, too, there is an interesting allusion to Byron's first meeting with Thomas Moore, destined to become his intimate friend and unsatisfactory biographer. They had been near to fighting a duel, arising from an idea of Moore's that Byron had accused him of falsehood. Byron tells Hobhouse : —

" I neither *retracted* nor would *apologise,* never having seen ye address in question, and told him in answer to his *demi-hostile, semi-amicable* epistle (for it began with a complaint and ended with a hope that *we* should be ' intimate '), that I was ' willing ' to adopt any ' conciliatory proposition that should not compromise my own honour, or failing that to give him satisfaction.' . . . Now that is settled, Mr. Rogers (whom I never saw) has sent me an invitation to meet the Irish Melodist on Monday."

The meeting duly took place, and Byron decided that " Rogers is a most excellent and unassuming soul, and Moore an epitome of all that's delightful. . . . Rogers said his behaviour was rather Irish, and that mine was candid and manly. I hope it was, at least the latter."

With 1812 comes a greatly increased value in the correspondence, for this was Byron's *annus mirabilis*, the year of *Childe Harold* and fame meteoric, and the formation of new friendships. Most eventful of the latter was that with Lady Melbourne, for it was mainly owing to this clever woman, formerly Miss Elizabeth Milbanke, that he contracted his disastrous marriage with her niece, Anne Isabella Milbanke, three years later. But that was only one of the curious events resulting from the familiar confidences which soon subsisted between Byron, a young man of twenty-three, and Lady Melbourne, a woman of sixty. She was more than old enough to be his mother, and, as he said, " if she had been a few years younger, what a fool she would have made of me had she thought it worth her while—and I should have lost a most valuable and agreeable friend." Or, as he expressed it to her : " You know I have obeyed you in everything. . . . You have been my director, and are still, for I do not know anything you could not make me do or undo."

Lady Melbourne became Byron's most intimate *confidante*, to whom he wrote, for a time, almost daily, detailing his most delicate concerns, particularly his amatory experiences, for he was obsessed with sex—his " demon," as he termed it—and passed from one entanglement to another as soon as he wearied of the object of pursuit or became satiated by success. At the period in question, the first matter of the kind was the intrigue with Lady Melbourne's daughter-in-law, Lady Caroline Lamb: it was ended, it is true, but the dismal echo of the affair sounds all through the letters to Lady Melbourne like an ever-recurring *motif*. As is well known, this episode ran a rapid and fiery course. Byron was soon weary of it, but the lady would not accept the painful truth that her charm and influence had waned. She pursued him with such a lack of dignity and self-respect, and acted in public towards him in such an outrageous way, that the only excuse to be offered for her behaviour was insanity.   Thus, she carried out an *auto-da-fé* of her Byronic keepsakes with incantations of hate, and another day she cut herself at a dance. Lady Melbourne thus describes the latter scene to Byron : —

" She is now like a Barrel of Gunpowder, and takes fire with the most trifling spark. . . . With her, when the fermentation begins there is no stopping it till it bursts forth, she must have gone to Lady Heath- cote's determined to pique you by her waltzing, and when she found that fail'd, in her passion she wish'd to expose you. . . . She broke a glass and scratched herself, as you call it, with the broken pieces . . . . she had a pair of scissors in her hand when I went up, with which she was wounding herself, but not deeply."

How Byron's attitude of tired resignation changed to hate by reason of Lady Caroline Lamb's conduct can be illustrated by a few extracts from his letters to Lady Melbourne : —

September, 1812.   " If, after all, ' it is decreed on high ' that, like James the fatalist, I *must* be hers, she shall be mine as long as it pleases her, and the circumstances under which she becomes so will at least make me devote my life to the vain attempt of reconciling her to herself. Wretched as it would render me, she should never know it ; the sentence once past, I could never restore that which she had lost, but all the reparation I could make should be made, and the cup drained to the very dregs by myself, so that its bitterness passed from her.   In the mean- time, till it is irrevocable, I must and may fairly endeavour to extricate both from a situation which, from our total want of all but selfish con- siderations, has brought us to the brink of the gulf. Before I sink I will at least have a swim for it, though I wish with all my heart it was the Hellespont instead, or that I could cross this as easily as I did ye other."

October, 1812.   " And now this must end. If she persists I will leave the country.   I shall enter into no explanations, write no epistles, softening or reverse, nor will I meet her, if it can be avoided, and certainly never but in society. . . . In short, I am not her lover, and would rather not be her friend, though I never can nor will be her enemy."

April, 1813.   " I give up pictures, letters, etc., to her tender mercies ; let that satisfy her.   The detestation, the utter abhorrence I feel at part of her conduct I will neither shock you with, nor trust myself to express. That feeling has become a part of my nature ; it has poisoned my future existence.   I know not whom I may love, but to the latest hour of my life I shall hate that woman. . . . To her I do not express this, because I have no desire to make her uncomfortable; but such is the state of my mind towards her, for reasons I shall not recur to, and beg to be spared from meeting her until we may be chained together in Dante's Inferno."

June, 1814. " I would sooner, much sooner, be with the dead in purgatory than with her, Caroline (I put the name at length as I am not jesting), upon earth. She may hunt me down—it is the power of any mad or bad woman to do so by any man—but *snare* me she shall not: torment me she may; how am I to bar myself from her? I am already almost a prisoner; she has no shame, no feeling, no one estimable or redeemable quality. . . . If there is one human being whom I do utterly *detest* and *abhor* it is she. . . ."

Such was the bitter aftermath of the harvest of passion. Lady Caroline Lamb had been succeeded in the affections of Byron by Lady Oxford during the autumn of 1812, when Hobhouse was informed : —

" You will infer that the connection with Lady Caroline Lamb is completely broken off—it is. I have formed another which, whatever its advantages or disadvantages, is at least less troublesome and more to my taste. . . . I leave you to your brilliant conjectures and usual laugh at my *égaremens.*"

The poet paid long visits to Eywood, Lord Oxford's estate. The husband seems to have been a very unsuspicious or complaisant person. His family name was Harley, and Lady Oxford's children were wittily known as " The Harleian Miscellany." Byron was very fond of one of the daughters, Lady Charlotte Harley, whom, he said, he " should love for ever if she could always be only eleven years old, and whom I shall probably marry when she is old enough and bad enough to be made into a modern wife." She was the " Ianthe " of *Childe Harold.*

A footnote should have been included in these volumes of letters stating that Lady Oxford was the daughter of the Rev. James Scott, vicar of Itchen, Hampshire, and that she married the fifth Earl of Oxford in 1794. Her portrait by Hoppner is in the National Gallery. Probably Lady Oxford set out to entrap Byron. Her methods are described by Lady Charlotte Bury,* the occasion being a party at Kensington Palace in 1810 : —

" Lord G——r was forcibly seized upon by Lady Oxford. Altogether, in my quality of looker-on, I could not but think that lady was no honour to society : and it was only surprising to remark in her instance, as well as that of many others, how well impudence succeeds, even with the mild and the noble, who are often subdued by its arrogant assumption of command. . . . If ever Lord G——r was in such ignoble thrall it could not hold him long. He was too high, too noble, too much above the coarseness of manner and mind of that lady, to become for any length of time ensnared."

---

* *Diary of the Times of George the Fourth* (1838).

Lady Oxford's power over Byron was of short duration—about six months. He relates the end in May, 1813 : —

" Lady Oxford arrives in town to-morrow, which I regret—when people have once fairly parted. How do I abhor these partings ! I know them to be of no use, and yet as painful at the time as the first plunge into purgatory."

And in June : —

" Lady Oxford sailed yesterday, and now, my dear Lady Melbourne, without pretending to *affect* or *effect,* will you not mention her name to me for the remainder of my weeks in England? To tell you the truth, I feel more *Carolinish* about her than I expected."

Before dealing with Byron's paramount attachment, mention must be made of the full reports he sent to Lady Melbourne of his attempted seduction of Lady Frances Webster, a daughter of the Earl of Mountnorris (Viscount Valentia). She was only twenty years old, and married to a very jealous husband. Byron visited them at Aston Hall, Rotherham, and later the party returned with him to Newstead Abbey. The impressions of this time are obviously presented in the Thirteenth Canto of *Don Juan,* which contains the description of Newstead and the arrival of a house-party there. Lady Frances Webster would seem to be

" The Lady Adeline Amundeville,
    The fair most fatal Juan ever met
Although she was not evil, nor meant ill ;

    .   .   .   .   .

Chaste was she, to detraction's desperation. . . ."

Byron did not succeed, though Lady Frances was much in love with him. There were embraces and exchanges of notes under the very eyes of the jealous husband. Byron related to Lady Melbourne : —

" The most amusing part was the interchange of notes, for we sat up all night scribbling to each other, and came down like ghosts in the morning. I shall never forget the quiet manner in which she would pass her epistles in a music-book, or any book, looking in Webster's face with great tranquillity the whole time, and taking mine in the same way. One she offered me as I was leading her to dinner at Newstead, all the servants before, and Webster and sister close behind. To take it was impossible, and how she was to retain it, without *pockets,* was equally perplexing."

But when the supreme crisis came, Lady Frances was saved by her gentleness and by the fact that Byron's better angel was for once in the ascendant. He thus describes the scene in his amazing confessions to Lady Melbourne : —

" You were right. I have been a little too sanguine as to the *conclusion*—but hear. One day, left entirely to ourselves, was nearly fatal—another such victory, and with Pyrrhus, we were lost—it came to this. ' I am entirely at your *mercy.* I own it. I give myself up to you. I am not *cold*—whatever I seem to others; but I know that I cannot bear the reflection hereafter. Do not imagine that these are mere words. I tell you the truth—now act as you will.' Was I wrong? I spared her. There was a something so very peculiar in her manner—a kind of mild decision—no scene—not even a struggle; but still I know not what, that convinced me that she was serious. It was not the mere ' No,' which one has heard forty times before, and always with the same accent; but the *tone,* and aspect—yet I sacrificed much—the hour *two* in the morning—away—the Devil whispering that it was mere *verbiage,* etc. And yet I know not whether I can regret it—she seems so very thankful for my forbearance—a proof, at least, that she was not playing merely the usual decorous reluctance, which is sometimes so tiresome on these occasions.''

Byron could never be held for long by any one woman, and he was now fully involved in the most debatable and peculiar of his love affairs, that with his half-sister, Augusta Leigh. This unpleasant matter was lately brought into prominence again by a new edition last year of *Astarte*, wherein it is directly stated that Mrs. Leigh's child by Byron, named Elizabeth Medora Leigh, was born on April 15th, 1814, and that confirmation would be found in Byron's letters (then unpublished, of course) to Lady Melbourne. That statement proves to be correct. In the present volumes there is a letter dated April 25th, 1814—ten days after the birth of the child—with this undeniable allusion to the event :—

" Oh ! but it is ' worth while,' I can't tell you why, and it is *not* an ' Ape,' and if it is, that must be my fault; however, I will positively reform. You must, however, allow that it is utterly impossible I can ever be half so well liked elsewhere, and I have been all my life trying to make someone love me, and never got the sort that I preferred before. But positively she and I will grow good and all that, and so we are *now* and shall be these three weeks and more too.''

Mr. Murray has not provided a footnote suggesting any other interpretation of this " Ape " passage, though presumably he believes—or tries to believe—in Byron's innocence in the matter of this particular accusation, for in his Preface he quotes from Hobhouse's *Recollections of a Long Life* the phrase that " Byron had not been guilty of any enormity." But the context shows that Hobhouse was speaking of offences committed after Byron's marriage, and most students of the affair believe that Byron's guilty relations with his half-sister were not continued after his marriage, or at any rate only for a short time. Unfortunately, there are many other incriminatory passages relating to Mrs. Leigh and himself in Byron's letters to Lady Melbourne :—

" You are quite mistaken, however, as to *her*, and it must be from some misrepresentation of mine, that you throw the blame so completely on the side least deserving, and least able to bear it. I dare say I made the best of my own story, as one always does from natural selfishness without intending it, but it was not her fault, but my own *folly* (give it what name may suit it better) and her weakness, for the intentions of both were very different, and for some time adhered to, and when not, it was entirely my own—in short, I know no name for my conduct. Pray do not speak so harshly of her to me—the cause of it all.

" Really and truly—as I hope mercy and happiness for her—by that God who made me for my own misery, and not much for the good of others, *she* was not to blame, one thousandth part in comparison. She was not aware of her own peril till it was too late, and I can only account for her subsequent ' *abandon* ' by an observation which I think is not unjust, that women are much more *attached* than men if they are treated with anything like fairness or tenderness.

" It is true she married a fool, but she *would* have him; they agreed, and agreed very well, and I never heard a complaint, but many vindications, of him. As for me, brought up as I was, and sent into the world as I was, both physically and morally, nothing better could be expected, and it is odd that I always had a foreboding, and I remember when a child reading the Roman history about a *marriage* I will tell you of when we meet, asking *ma mère* why I should not marry X.*

" All that you say is exceeding true; but who ever said, or supposed, that you were not shocked, and all that? You *have* done everything in your power; and more than any other person breathing would have done for *me*, to make me act rationally; but there is an old saying (excuse the Latin, which I won't quote, but translate), ' Whom the Gods wish to destroy they first madden.' . . . I will not persuade *her* into any *fugitive* piece of absurdity, but more I cannot promise."

It is evident that Lady Melbourne had remonstrated with Byron, and begged him to pause in this wild adventure. Yet the psychology of their friendship remains a truly amazing problem, for at the very time she was receiving Byron's intimate confidences about his incestuous intrigue, Lady Melbourne was doing her best to get him to marry her niece, Annabella Milbanke. He accepted her recommendation, and conducted his proposal through the confidential aunt. Miss Milbanke had refused him in October, 1812, and he met his rejection philosophically:—

" She is perfectly right in every point of view. . . . I should have preferred a woman of birth and talents; but such a woman was not at all to blame for not preferring me; my *heart* never had an opportunity of being much interested in the business, further than that I should have very much liked to be *your relation*."

However, a correspondence with Miss Milbanke commenced in the spring of 1814 (soon after the birth of Medora Leigh), which gradually developed on Byron's side into an epistolary courtship. Finally, he proposed again, by letter, and was accepted, in September. In announcing the news to Lady Melbourne he said:—

" May I hope for your consent, too? Without it I should be

---

* Byron used the symbol X to designate his half-sister. Presumably in the endeavour to gloss over this affair, the editors of the poet's correspondence at times changed " X " into " I," thus making certain sentences meaningless. See *The London Mercury*, May, 1922.

unhappy, even were it not for many reasons important in other points of view. . . . In course I mean to reform most thoroughly, and become ' a good man and true,' in all the various senses of these respective and respectable appellations. Seriously, I will endeavour to make your niece happy. . . . I will settle on her all I can . . . and my property, such as it is, shall go as far as it may for her. I will do almost anything rather than lose her now. . . .

" As to Annabella, you cannot think higher of her than I do. I never doubted anything but that she would have me. After all, it is a match of your making, and better had it been had *your* proposal been accepted at the time. I am quite horrified in casting up my moral accounts of the two intervening years, all which would have been prevented, and the heartache into the bargain, had she—but I can't blame her. . . . My pride (which my schoolmaster said was my ruling passion) has in all events been spared. She is the only woman to whom I ever proposed in that way, and it is something to have got into the affirmative at last.

" I quite agree with you, that it were best over; but I have several previous arrangements that must take place before I can even go down there. I shall make no limitation about settlements, as far as my property will go, nor did I pay my addresses to her with the notion of her being a very considerable *parti.*"

It will be observed that Byron was very generous in the matter of settlements, but the rather tardy suitor did not arrive at Seaham until November : —

" Annabella's meeting and mine made a kind of scene; though there was no acting, nor even speaking, but the pantomime was very expressive. She seems to have more feeling than we imagined; but is the most silent woman I ever encountered; which perplexes me extremely. I like them to talk, because then they *think* less. Much cogitation will not be in my favour. . . . However, the die is cast; neither party can recede; the lawyers are here—mine and all; and, I presume, the parchments once scribbled, I shall become Lord Annabella. I can't yet tell whether we are to be happy or not. I have every disposition to do her all possible justice, but I fear she won't govern me; and if she don't it will not do at all."

A week after there was indication of some of the troubles which were destined, in part, to wreck the marriage later on : —

" Her disposition is the very reverse of our imaginings. She is over-run with fine feelings, scruples about herself and her disposition (I suppose, in fact, she means mine), and to crown all, is taken ill once every three days with I know not what. . . . A few days ago she made one scene, not altogether out of Caroline's style. . . . I can only inter-pret these things one way, and merely wait to be certain, to make my obeisance and ' exit singly.' I hear of nothing but ' feeling ' from morning till night. . . . I don't think her temper *bad* at any time, but very *self* tormenting and anxious, and romantic. In short, it is impos-sible to foresee how this will end, any more than two years ago; if there is a break, it shall be her doing, not mine."

Miss Milbanke did not cause a " break "; and preparations for the wedding were hurried on. Byron returned to London for a few weeks. He spent Christmas of 1814 with Mrs. Leigh at Newmarket (hardly a good omen for the coming marriage), on his way back to Seaham, where he was married to Annabella Milbanke on January 2nd, 1815. Hobhouse, who was present, noted: " Byron was calm, and as usual. I felt as if I had buried a friend." The next day Byron wrote to Lady Melbourne: —

" We were married yesterday at ten upon ye clock, so there's an end of that matter, and the beginning of many others. Bell has gone through all the ceremonies with great fortitude, and I am much as usual, and your dutiful nephew. . . . You would think we had been married these fifty years. Bell is fast asleep on a corner of the sopha, and I am keeping myself awake with this epistle."

Miss Milbanke's attributes as a wife can be traced in *Don Juan*: —

" There was Miss Millpond, smooth as summer's sea,
    That usual paragon, an only daughter,
Who seemed the cream of equanimity,
    Till skimm'd—and then there was some milk and water,
With a slight shade of blue, too, it might be,
    Beneath the surface; but what did it matter?
Love's riotous, but marriage should have quiet,
And, being consumptive, live on a milk diet."

The sequel is well known. Lady Byron's daughter, Augusta Ada, was born in December, 1815, and Mrs. Leigh was invited to come on a visit to 13, Piccadilly Terrace during the confinement. In January the world of London was startled by Lady Byron's sudden departure with her child for her father's house, while Mrs. Leigh remained with Byron for two months. Lady Byron never returned, and henceforth her husband regarded her with hatred, and spoke of " that devil " in terms of the most violent obloquy. The causes of the separation have ever since remained a subject of controversy. One result was the abrupt cessation of Byron's correspondence with Lady Melbourne. Whether he was indignant with her for having persuaded him into a disastrous marriage, or whether she felt remorse for having brought it about, the fact remains that, apparently, no letters between Lady Melbourne and Byron exist after the date of February, 1816.

Byron went abroad in April, and the remainder of the letters in this collection, addressed chiefly to Hobhouse and Douglas Kinnaird, deal with his life in Switzerland and Italy and Greece —the last phase. Those from Venice are of particular value. He relates, of course, his new amatory adventures with Marianna Segati and the Countess Guiccioli and others, for the " *besoin d'aimer* " was rarely in abeyance. The letters from the Shelleys are also of great interest, and some of them deal with Elise Foggi's allegations about Shelley and Clare Clairmont. All through Byron's letters his characteristic, terse style remains as delightful as ever.   Here is a pleasant little bit of self-appreciation : —

" As to *Don Juan*, confess, confess you dog, and be candid, that it is the sublime of *that there* sort of writing.   I have written about a hundred stanzas of a Third Canto, but it is damned modest; the outcry has frightened me.   I had such projects for the Don, but the benefit of my experiences must now be lost to despairing posterity.   After all, what stuff this outcry is.   *Lalla Rookh* and Little are more dangerous than any burlesque poem can be.   Moore has been here; we got tipsy together, and were very amicable.   He is gone on to Rome.   I put my life (in MS.) into his hands (*not* for publication).   You, or anybody else, may see it at his return.   It only comes up to 1816."

Byron died in 1824; his autobiography was unfortunately destroyed, and a really complete and satisfactory biography of the poet has yet to be written.   When that desirable consummation is practicable, these additional letters will form an important contribution to a right appreciation of Byron's wayward but supremely interesting personality.*

---

* *Byron* by Miss Ethel Colburn Mayne is an admirable and sympathetic presentation of the poet's life; but it does not contain full quotations from Byron's letters and journals which so vividly reveal the man.

BYRON AND HIS SISTER.*

FOR over a hundred years the world has taken a keen interest in the matrimonial and amatory affairs of Byron. Interest to a certain extent was—and is—expressed in the similar adventures of Shelley; in Keats's relations with Fanny Brawne; in the unhappy marriages of Bulwer-Lytton with Rosina Wheeler and of George Meredith with the daughter of Thomas Love Peacock. But the attention devoted to these and similar cases is far transcended by the notoriety and publicity that have ever attended what should have been the private aspects of Byron's life. His grandson, the late Lord Lovelace, was justified in the protest he made against the excessive number of publications concerned with the poet's sexual life. He said: —

" It has been more and more ignored that Lord Byron's own descendants have some feelings or even rights in connection with the affairs of their own family. They cannot regard their concerns as a provision or a playground for press and public, publicists and publishers. There is an extreme point for personalities and misrepresentations, whether laudatory, damnatory, or predatory. The time comes at last when some measure of truth preservation is forced upon the victims. "

It was in view of these unauthorised and unwanted activities, more or less literary, that Lord Lovelace was constrained to publish sixteen years ago, his remarkable book, *Astarte*,† which is now reissued, in a more accessible form, with new matter and letters, under the editorship of his widow Mary, Countess of Lovelace. The title of the work is derived from the spirit Astarte in Byron's drama of *Manfred*—a story of incest and remorse. And it was with the charge of incest against Byron that his grandson had to deal and, unfortunately, in the interests of Lady Byron, prove.

When, in 1816, English Society was startled by the separation of the much-discussed poet from his young wife after only a year of marriage, it was whispered that the cause was Byron's incestuous relationship with his own half-sister, Augusta Leigh, a married woman four years his senior. Their amour is supposed to have begun in 1813, when the poet was twenty-five years old. In the following year, with his characteristic delight in outraging

---

* *The Saturday Review,* July 16th, 1921.
† *Astarte,* by Ralph, Earl of Lovelace. New edition, with many additional letters. Edited by Mary, Countess of Lovelace. (Christophers, 18s. net.)

public opinion and acting in a perverse manner, Byron spoke
openly in society of indulging in a love affair within the prohibited
degree. He would say: "Oh! I never knew what it was
before. There is a woman I love so passionately—she is with
child by me, and if a daughter, it shall be called Medora." And
at a party at Holland House he advanced the most startling
theories concerning the fitting relationship between brothers and
sisters. Attention was naturally directed to Mrs. Leigh, the only
sister of Byron, and further confirmation of suspicion was
discovered in the recent poem of *The Bride of Abydos*.

In June, 1813, Mrs. Leigh came on a prolonged visit to
Byron, and their child, duly named Elizabeth Medora, was born
on April 15th, 1814.

In January, 1815, Byron married Anne Isabella Milbanke, and
his daughter by her, Augusta Ada (subsequently Countess of
Lovelace) was born in December of the same year. Lady Byron,
very curiously, invited Mrs. Leigh to come on a visit to 13,
Piccadilly Terrace, during her confinement, although she afterwards stated that from a very early period of her marriage her
suspicions were aroused as to the real relationship that had
existed between her husband and his sister. Even when her
fears were confirmed, and she left Byron for ever in January,
1816, whilst Mrs. Leigh remained for two months longer, and
alone, with Byron her brother, some degree of affection still
existed between the two women and lasted to the end of life.

Rumour was naturally clamant for confirmation of its theory
concerning Lady Byron's sudden flight from husband and home,
but the injured wife would never make any public statement,
though from the outset she began to collect the evidence for
proving her case. She conducted an affectionate correspondence
with Mrs. Leigh by means of which she gradually extracted from
that erring lady a confession of guilt in September, 1816. She
further persuaded Mrs. Leigh to send on to her Byron's love
letters, which he was writing from abroad in ignorance that they
also were read by his wife.

Lady Byron was an inscrutable character, an implacable
nature which loved domination, while at the same time she
possessed all the Stoic's power of enduring suffering without
noisy complaint. She was one of those hard, good women who
seek the spiritual salvation of persons who have injured them.
Nevertheless she bided her time and planned her Old Testa-
mentary revenge, submitting to public obloquy and misrepresentation for over forty years—for there was a general
impression that it was Lady Byron who by her incompatibility

and temper had helped to wreck the poet's marriage, and driven him abroad to seek solace in sexual excesses in Venice and an early death in Greece.

Byron died in 1824, and Mrs. Leigh in 1851. Lady Byron survived until 1860, and she left directions for her papers dealing with her marriage and separation to be made public in 1880. But during her lifetime she had related the facts by word of mouth to certain friends. One of these was Mrs. Beecher Stowe, who amazed the reading world in 1869 by her article entitled *The True Story of Lady Byron's Life*, which was published simultaneously in *The Atlantic Mcnthly* and *Macmillan's Magazine*. It was by no means " the true story," but a furious controversy was aroused among the partisans of the ancient contention of 1816. The friends of Mrs. Leigh engaged Abraham Hayward to present her side of the case in *The Quarterly Review*. One of the best and fairest examinations of the baffling mystery appeared in *The Saturday Review*, in a series of articles from September 4th to December 25th, 1869. They were written by the Rev. William Scott,* one of the original founders of *The Saturday Review;* but he, like everyone else, was unable to explain how Lady Byron, believing her sister-in-law guilty of incest, could at the same time continue on affectionate terms with her—except on the hypothesis that Lady Byron was a morbidly virtuous subject, who was prepared to go to any extreme to save a lost soul.

Such were the tangled and unpleasant problems that Lord Lovelace felt it to be his peculiar duty to solve and explain in *Astarte*. He had been brought up by his grandmother, but even he could not interpret satisfactorily the influences which moved Lady Byron's strange mind to action. He very fairly admits the faults and curiosities of her nature, but he cannot unravel the complex motives of her brain.

The author was quite successful in proving the painful fact that Byron was guilty of incest. The poet's letters to his sister cannot be controverted, especially that passionate epistle of May 17th, 1819, wherein he says:—

" I have never ceased, nor can cease, to feel for a moment that perfect and boundless attachment which bound and binds me to you— which renders me utterly incapable of *real* love for any other human being—for what could they be to me after *you?* My own . . . we may have been very wrong—but I repent of nothing except that cursed marriage and your refusing to continue to love me as you had loved me. . . . It is heartbreaking to think of our long separation—and I am sure more than punishment enough for all our sins. . . . They say absence

---

* Father of Clement Scott, the dramatic critic.

destroys weak passions and confirms strong ones—alas! mine for you is the union of all passions and of all affections."

Unfortunately this book is not well arranged, or use made in the right place of the valuable new letters it contains. The whole work is overweighted with too many footnotes, many of them unnecessary, and there is no index. Nevertheless, it is a very interesting and curious contribution to the roll of biography, and essential for a true understanding of Byron's mysterious and sex-ridden life.

THOMAS HARDY: HIS LYRICS.*

A NEW book by Thomas Hardy must ever be an event of literary importance. True, he no longer offers novels, since he brought to a close, now over a quarter of a century ago, the wonderful series of Wessex romances. It was the decision of a great and conscientious artist—to complete his fictional work when still in the lofty heights of his powers: there was certainly no declension of art and creative power in the last two novels, *The Well Beloved* and *Jude the Obscure*. In fact, for some of his readers, the latter story may be the greatest and most poignant of all.

Fortunately, since 1895 Mr. Hardy has given us several volumes of short stories, epic dramas, and poems—three art forms in which he is as distinctive and uncommon as in his novels. This is not the occasion to consider the short stories (though some of them, such as *The Three Strangers*, *The Withered Arm*, and *Fellow Townsmen*, are among the finest in the language) or *The Dynasts*. Mr. Hardy's new book,† as the title adumbrates, contains a diversified collection of poems. Some have been written recently, and others date back as far as his London days at 16, Westbourne Park Villas, in 1867, when he was a young man studying architecture—particularly the Gothic form—under Sir A. Blomfield. The earlier poems, it is stated, were overlooked in arranging previous collections. Mr. Hardy is right in believing, as he puts it, that " those readers who care for my poems at all—readers to whom no passport is required—will care for this new instalment of them, perhaps the last, as much as for any that have preceded them ": but he need not at this period of his career and fame feel " the natural disinclination of a writer whose works have been so frequently regarded askance by a pragmatic section here and there, to draw attention to them once more," even though, as he humorously adds, they contain " little or nothing in technic or teaching that can be considered a Star Chamber matter or so much as agitating to a ladies' school." I am quoting from the Preface—or " Apology," as he terms it—which is not the least interesting portion of the author's latest volume.

In the course of this characteristic pronouncement, Mr.

* *The Fortnightly Review*, October, 1922.
† *Late Lyrics and Earlier, with many other Verses,* by Thomas Hardy, (Macmillan & Co., 7s. 6d. net.)

Hardy is at some pains to consider and deny—or justify—what is generally called his "pessimism." The *cliché* has become duly stereotyped in most of the critical appraisements of the literary achievements of the poet-novelist : but again the question arises, Is it necessary or worth while for Mr. Hardy to bother about such a trivial and, in my opinion, incorrect misnomer of his work as a whole? His position in the World of Letters is above effective assault, and unique as long as Literature endures. Still, as Mr. Hardy has chosen to present an Apologia (partly with his tongue in his cheek, I fancy), it must be considered. As he very rightly claims, pessimism underlies the Gospel scheme and permeates Greek drama—if any excuse be needed to use it as a literary weapon. He defines his own indulgence in the vice as " Questionings . . . concerning existence in this universe, in attempts to explain or excuse the presence of evil and the incongruity of penalising the irresponsible "; to him it is " the exploration of reality, and is the first step towards the soul's betterment, and the body's also "—in short, as he expressed it in a poem written many years ago : " If way to the Better there be, it exacts a full look at the Worst."

This is getting on to a high and rather precious plane of definition, and I prefer to consider pessimism in the ordinary accepted sense of the word—" a depressing view of life, the doctrine that on the whole the world is bad rather than good." A cynic would say that is an obvious truth. But it does not sum up the literary gospel or philosophy of Mr. Hardy. It may be a recurring suggestion in his work, both prose and poetry, but the point I maintain is that Mr. Hardy finds the world—that is Life—*sad* rather than bad. That is the explanation of his " pessimism," and it is an irrefutable truth. Life is sad—its brevity and impermanence alone must make it so, for, despite all the sorrow and pain, there is much of infinite beauty and joy, to say nothing of material pleasures. As Shelley cried : —

> " This world is the nurse of all we know,
>   This world is the mother of all we feel ;
> And the coming of death is a fearful blow
>   To a brain unencompassed with nerves of steel,
> When all that we know or feel or see
> Shall pass like an unreal mystery."

All imaginative and sympathetic and sensitive people must be oppressed by the facts of life and death. Mr. Hardy has faced them, and his work reflects and expresses his regret, and resignation to the inevitable. But these cogitations do not affect his conversation or personal aspects, which are bright and

humorous—despite statements to the contrary by "interviewers."
It does not come within the scope of this article to set out to
prove that the Wessex novels are not " pessimistic," but rather
faithful and true presentments of Life, which, after joy and
sorrow, inevitably ends in Death. But the same argument
applies to Mr. Hardy's new volume of verse. I think only five
of the poems might be called pessimistic in reality—*Where Three
Roads Joined, The Wedding Morning, Drawing Details in an
Old Church, The Wanderer*: —

> " There is nobody on the road
>   But I,
> And no beseeming abode
>   I can try
> For shelter, so abroad
>   I must lie.
>
>   .   .   .
>
> Yet it's meet—this bed of hay
>   And roofless plight;
> For there's a house of clay,
>   My own, quite,
> To roof me soon, all day
>   And all night."

And most of all *A Drizzling Easter Morning*: —

> " And He is risen? Well, be it so . . .
> And still the pensive lands complain,
> And dead men wait, as long ago,
> As if, much doubting, they would know
> What they are ransomed from, before
> They pass again their sheltering door.
>
> I stand amid them in the rain,
> While blusters vex the yew and vane;
> And on the road the weary wain
> Plods forward, laden heavily;
> And toilers with their aches are fain
> For endless rest—though risen is He."

So much for the accusation; and for the defence I would
advance numerous poems—the great majority of this collection
—in which only sings a wistful regret for the happy past,
memories of old times with loved ones and friends long dead.
*In the Small Hours, The Little Old Table, The Last Time, Read
by Moonlight, Welcome Home, The Garden Seat*—all these
are concerned with happy memories of the past, *The Best
Times*: —

> " We went a day's excursion to the stream,
> Basked by the bank, and bent to the ripple-gleam,
>   And I did not know
>   That life would show
> However it might flower, no finer glow.
>
>   .   .   .   .   .

And that calm eve, when you walked up the stair,
After a gaiety prolonged and rare,
　　No thought soever
　　That you might never
Walk down again, struck me as I stood there."

And in *The Selfsame Song* : —

" A bird bills the selfsame song,
　With never a fault in its flow,
　That we listened to here those long
　　Long years ago.

．　　．　　．　　．　　．

—But it's not the selfsame bird—
No : perished to dust is he ．．．．．．
As also are those who heard
　That song with me."

Sad, yes, all sad, but not pessimistic. " Joy once lost is pain "—that is the note which echoes through these poems, and not least in the beautiful tribute to a favourite white cat, " Snow-dove " : —

" Pet was never mourned as you,
Purrer of the spotless hue,
Plumy tail and wistful gaze,
While you humoured our queer ways,
Or out-shrilled your morning call
Up the stairs and through the hall—
Foot suspended in its fall—
While expectant you would stand
Arched, to meet the stroking hand ;
Till your way you chose to wend
Yonder, to your tragic end.

Never another pet for me,
Let your place all vacant be ;
Better blankness day by day
Than companion torn away.
Better bid his memory fade,
Better blot each mark he made,
Selfishly escape distress
By contrived forgetfulness
Than preserve his prints to make
Every morn and eve an ache.

From the chair whereon he sat,
Sweep his fur, nor wince thereat ;
Rake his little pathways out
'Mid the bushes roundabout ;
Smooth away his talons' mark
From the claw-worn pine-tree bark,
Where he climbed as dusk embrowned,
Waiting us who loitered round.

．　　．　　．　　．　　．

As a prisoner, flight debarred,
Exercising in a yard,
Still retain I, troubled, shaken,
Mean estate by him forsaken;
And this home, which scarcely took
Impress from his little look,
By his faring to the Dim
Grows all eloquent of him.

Housemate, I can think you still
Bounding to the window-sill,
Over which I vaguely see
Your small mound beneath the tree,
Showing in the autumn shade
That you moulder where you played."

Mr. Hardy once pointed out to me that little grave beneath the shrubbery trees at Maxgate..

Mr. Hardy feels to a poignant degree what the late William De Morgan used to term The Sentiment of Place—particularly of old houses. For him, every dwelling, of any age, is peopled with the ghosts of those who lived out the drama of their lives there in the long ago, and the house retains the influences of the joy and pain that its former occupants experienced. In *The Strange House* he pictures his own home, Maxgate, eighty years hence in the possession of strangers, one of whom is dimly conscious of echoes from the past:—

" I hear the piano playing—
Just as a ghost might play."
" —O, but what are you saying?
There's no piano to-day;
Their old one was sold and broken;
Years past it went amiss."
" —I heard it, or shouldn't have spoken:
A strange house, this ! "

.   .   .

" Seek my own room I cannot—
A figure is on the stair ! "
" —What figure?   Nay, I scan not
Anyone lingering there.
A bough outside is waving,
And that's its shade by the moon."
" —Well, all is strange !   I am craving
Strength to leave soon."

" —Ah, maybe you've some vision
Of showings beyond our sphere;
Some sight, sense, intuition
Of what once happened here?
The house is old; they've hinted
It once held two love-thralls,
And they may have imprinted
Their dreams on its walls?

.   .   .

> Some folk can not abide here,
> But we—we do not care
> Who loved, laughed, wept, or died here,
> Knew joy, or despair.''

And in *The Two Houses,* the old house tells its brand-new neighbour : —

> '' You have not known
> Men's lives, deaths, toils, and teens
>
> .　　　.　　　.　　　.　　　.
>
> . . . I am packed with these,
> Though, strangely, living dwellers who come
> See not the phantoms all my substance sees !
>
> Visible in the morning
> Stand they, when dawn drags in ;
> Visible at night. . . .
>
> Babes new-brought forth
> Obsess my rooms ; straight-stretched
> Lank corpses, ere outborne to earth. . . .''

In the Apology before mentioned, Mr. Hardy makes admission that the philosophy of some of his poems may appear '' queer ''; the adjective is not of his own choosing. Two of the poems might come under this designation— *The Wood Fire* and *Surview*—and no one but their author could have conceived them. The former pictures the curious fancy of a fire made from the wood of the three crosses used at the Crucifixion.

> '' Though only three were impaled, you may know it didn't pass off
> So quietly as was wont? That Galilee carpenter's son
> Who boasted he was king, incensed the rabble to scoff :
> I heard the noise from my garden. This piece is the one he was on. . .
> Yes, it blazes up well if lit with a few dry chips and shroff ;
> And it's worthless for much else, what with cuts and stains thereon.''

The philosophy of this is somewhat elusive. *Surview* seems to be a paraphrase of the Psalmist's '' While I was musing the fire burned; then spake I with my tongue '' : —

> '' A cry from the green-grained sticks of the fire
> Made me gaze where it seemed to be :
> 'Twas my own voice talking therefrom to me
> On how I had walked when my sun was higher—
> My heart in its arrogancy. . . . .''

It is a beautiful and remarkable fancy, and needs to be read in its entirety. Mr. Hardy retains all his old power of conjuring up a picture with a word or two. Thus in *A Night in November* : —

> '' I marked when the weather changed,
> And the panes began to quake,
> And the winds rose up and ranged,
> That night, lying half-awake.''

It visualises in a moment a great stretch of open country,* with a wan moon peeping through a murky sky, and the wind rising in ominous gusts and wails. Only a master of words can do these things.

---

* The country spreading from the front of Maxgate to the sea—the country of *The Trumpet Major*—I like to think.

RICHARD MIDDLETON.*

RICHARD MIDDLETON, who committed suicide eleven years ago at the age of twenty-nine, was born, one feels, a decade too late. Instead of 1882, he should have come to this world in 1872, and so would have been one of the band of those brilliant young men of " The 'Nineties " who have left so vivid an impress on the Art and Literature of their time. His work, his way of life, and his untimely end so much resembled theirs. Aubrey Beardsley, Ernest Dowson, Lionel Johnson, all died in their youth; Hubert Crackanthorpe and John Davidson (like Middleton) ended their own lives. All too soon, alas! these bright spirits were extinguished; and to others of their company, who have survived to middle-age, Fate has proved none too kind.

Richard Middleton distinctly had a touch of genius. His fantastic stories—*The Ghost Ship, On the Brighton Road,* and *The Coffin Merchant*—will always stand in the van of bizarre literature; his rather morbid studies of himself as a boy—*A Drama of Youth* and *The New Boy*—are marvels of introspection; and much of his poetry has beauty and charm. We were indebted to Mr. Henry Savage for collecting and supervising the publication of Middleton's work in prose and verse— five volumes, which commenced to appear a year after the young author's mournful death. The same devoted and enthusiastic friend has now come forward as the biographer of Richard Middleton.†

Mr. Savage's book is more a consideration and appreciation of Middleton's literary work than a biography. Mr. Savage is an able and sympathetic critic, but he lacks another equally essential quality in a biographer—the presentation in an interesting, yet accurate, way of prosaic but very necessary facts. He boasts in fact (alas! the tautophony) that during the period of his friendship with Middleton he had " an excessive contempt for facts in general." As he supposes, his memoir does suffer accordingly. For biography cannot be written without facts, and such facts as are adduced need to be related correctly, otherwise the work is valueless as biography. It is

* *The Fortnightly Review,* October, 1922.
† *Richard Middleton, The Man and his Work,* by Henry Savage. (Cecil Palmer, 12s. 6d. net.)

a pity that this otherwise excellent book should be marred by such elementary errors as that which speaks of the author of *The Ingoldsby Legends* as the Rev. *Thomas* Barham: a minute's research would have obviated this careless and faulty reference to Middleton's distant relative. When mentioning Middleton's schools, Mr. Savage says: " In London he seems to have gone both to St. Paul's and Merchant Taylors', the *former* of which was probably the scene of *A Drama of Youth.*" It is quite apparent from the story itself that Middleton describes Merchant Taylors', which is located in the old Charterhouse buildings near the Meat Markets of Smithfield:—

" For some days school has seemed to me even more tedious than usual. The long train journey in the morning, the walk through Farringdon Meat Market, which æsthetic butchers made hideous with mosaics of the intestines of animals, as if the horror of suety pavements and bloody sawdust did not suffice. . . . I saw the greasy, red-faced men with their hands and aprons stained with blood. I saw the hideous carcases of animals, the masses of entrails, the heaps of repulsive hides; but most clearly of all I saw an ugly, sad little boy, with a satchel of books on his back, set down in the midst of an enormous and hostile world. The windows and stones of the houses were black with soot, and before me there lay school, the place that had never brought me anything but sorrow and humiliation."

However, Mr. Savage might be justified in claiming that the facts of Middleton's life are unimportant, for beyond his literary work and tragic end it was singularly uneventful. After leaving school, he was, from the age of nineteen, a clerk in the Royal Exchange Assurance Corporation for six years. Clerking could hardly be expected to form a congenial career for such a brilliant, erratic spirit, whose mind during office hours was occupied with the composition of blank verse plays in the Elizabethan manner. In 1907 he resigned his position and resolved to earn his living by journalism. Two years earlier he had become a member of that literary-bohemian coterie known as " The New Bohemians," which met at " The Prince's Head " tavern, in the region of the Strand and the Street of Adventure. Here he formed his friendships with Mr. Savage, Mr. Arthur Machen, and Mr. Louis McQuilland—the trio who have consolidated his posthumous fame. On one occasion Lord Alfred Douglas came to dine with the band; owner and editor then of *The Academy*, it was he who gave Middleton the first chance of mounting the literary ladder. He accepted both articles and reviews, and, as Middleton said: " Oh, but the reviewing is great fun, an' the man Douglas is a peach with a stone in it to let me do it." Middleton established himself in two rooms at 7, Blackfriars Road, and wrote in the first flush of his aspirations:—

" My name is Richard Middleton, I'm living at Blackfriars,
Two stories up, above the street, to chasten my desires;
I have no purple heather here, no field, nor living tree—
But every night when I look out God lights the stars for me.

.   .   .   .   .

I am not rich nor hope to be, but mine are day and night,
And all the world to look upon, and laughter, and the light,
Where I can set my torch ablaze to make the beacon burn,
And show to God that in Blackfriars, two stories up, I yearn."

Mr. Savage draws a delightful picture of the days—or rather
nights—of " The New Bohemians," and, though he writes but
of sixteen years ago he is already *laudator temporis acti.* The
symposia at " The Prince's Head " would last until closing hour
(half-past twelve in those spiritual times), and the boon companions would then continue their carouse at the rooms of one of
the party until dawn. Sometimes there were walks to Hampstead,
and on one occasion two of the company tore down the moonlit
hill chanting Swinburne's *A Ballad of Life,* " and wholly at one
in our ecstasy "—much like Swinburne himself, forty years
earlier, when he declaimed, with Meredith, on The Mound at
Copsham, the newly discovered version by FitzGerald of *Omar
Khayyám.* Another adventure was in the best style of Theodore
Hook. A party of the roysterers invaded the sacred precincts of
the National Liberal Club, where one of them posed as a member
and ordered drinks for his " guests." They were served, but a
polite attendant came up to the " host," and said, " I beg your
pardon, sir, but your name does not appear to be on our list of
members." The visitor expressed his regret, and explained that
he had mistaken the premises for those of the Athenæum. He
and his friends then made as dignified an exit as was possible.
Youth will have its fling.

Middleton's attitude to love—sexual love—how much he
experienced it, and how far it influenced his literary work, would
provide an interesting theme of speculation. At the end of his
life he wrote of a book he was contemplating : " Love I mean to
leave out altogether if I possibly can, because I won't accept their
damned convention. It has helped me to make a mess of things
sometimes, but I don't know that it has had any great spiritual
influence on my life." His biographer states that " Middleton
was a man of strong passions, but what of natural desire was
in him seems, so far at least as these girls were concerned, to
have turned inward to be expressed in song." The girls in
question, Lily and Christine, were merely commonplace young
persons, apparently chorus girls of the humbler class, who were

idealised by the poet. They inspired some beautiful things, pre-
eminently *The Silent Lover*:—

> " I cannot sing, I have no words
> To love you, hate you, make you mine—
> To win your ear like mating birds,
> To brim your veins with wanton wine;
> But all my longing senses cry
> Their faltering, broken oratory.
>
> .   .   .   .   .
>
> I have no words, but Time shall prove
> This song of mine the best of all,
> My lips shall be as Love's, for love
> Shall make their silence musical;
> And on some rapt, enchanted night
> They shall reveal my heart's delight."

A wonderful thing that a plebeian girl like Lily (who, as Mr.
Savage relates, married the lover of her choice, a news-boy, and
became " the stout mother of very many children ") could
generate such passionate poetry as this: but, of course, she was
only a symbol to the poet. Middleton wrote of his poems
suggested by Lily: " I wonder whether I love Lily or youth,
or is it only compassion for the little boy I never was that moves
me? The doubt does not prevent my writing good verses. I
want to love something or other anyhow: love kills the ego
with a surfeit of egoism, and I appreciate but do not like mine."

He was right; he could write " good verses." *The Last
Serenade, To Mélisande, Irene, Hylas*, are beautiful. And he
was right about his " surfeit of egoism," " the arrogance of his
culture," as he called it in another place. He suffered from
neuralgia, and too much alcohol at times, but his real complaint,
which killed him at the last, was his morbid introspection.
Shortly before his death he wrote: " Indeed, it is not hard to put
a name to my disease; but one man is an egoist just as another is
a negro."

> " Having the thought of death
> Eternally to perplex me "

he had said in one of his poems, and in another (not mentioned by
Mr. Savage, though full of beauty), *Night on Hungerford
Bridge*, he voiced the lure of suicide and oblivion:—

> " Lights on the water, lights on the tide,
> And the white stars a-shiver.
> ' Here is your resting, here by my side
> Forever, forever,
> And they shall forget that you lived or died.'
> Thus sang the river."

In his last message to Mr. Savage, before the fatal dose of chloroform, he wrote, " I am going adventuring again." He died, in Brussels, penniless. His books, still unpublished, were going the round of publishers for rejection. *The London Magazine* had declined his finest short story, *The Ghost Ship*, though a week after the author's death a cable arrived to say it had been accepted by *The Century Magazine*, the payment being £25. The pity of it all resembles the tragedy of Chatterton.

GEORGE MOORE: HIS CELIBATES.*

MR. GEORGE MOORE is becoming the Apostle of the Unexpected. Hitherto he has written, in the main, of normal sexual relations and passion. In his new book† he offers five studies of people who would be classed by pathologists as abnormal—though their manifestations are common enough. As may be gathered from the title, *In Single Strictness*, the protagonists of these five stories are all celibates, and though the narratives are distinct and separate, they form a cohesive whole for the interpretation of the author's subject and intention—the consideration of chastity.

The principal characters of these tales are peculiar people, lonely in their lives but chaste—though in two instances they are near to falling from their high status, one to prostitution and the other in a manner which requires some delicacy of narration. These two stories are the most important, and reveal Mr. Moore's new power of probing and interpreting, with unexpected gentleness and sympathy, the psychology of those who are generally regarded as moral pariahs.

Sarah Gwynn relates how a peasant girl from County Down comes to Dublin to find work. She falls in with another girl, Phyllis, a factory worker, who helps her to the same employment, and the two girls live together. But their wages are only eight shillings a week each, and Sarah Gwynn soon discovers that her friend procures the additional money needed for adequate food, clothes, and so on, by promiscuous prostitution. Then ensues a long struggle between conscience and innate chastity. Sarah feels she cannot continue to live mainly on the money earned by Phyllis at night, while she herself stays at home in peace and sinlessness. She must take her own share of the wages of sin. She is on the point of going on the streets of Dublin, when she hears of a convent in Wales where a working lay sister is required. But how to find the money for the necessary clothes and journey? A " gentleman friend " of Phyllis's, hearing the story, provides the money. Despite his sexual lapses, he " was really a very religious man," and the only return he asked from Sarah was that she would pray for him when she reached her convent. That she earnestly does for him and Phyllis. For ten long years she

* *The Fortnightly Review*, October, 1922.
† *In Single Strictness*, by George Moore. (Heinemann.)

R

worked in the convent, feeling at times that she ought to return
to her friend and lead her life : —

" There was always in my heart the pain that I had left Phyllis to a
life of sin and gone away myself to a life of comfort and ease, with the
hope of Heaven at the end. . . . Yes, Phyllis is a good girl. There
never was a better one, so good that it seemed to me that I was the
wicked girl. . . ."

Eventually Sarah quarrelled with the nuns, and came back
to Dublin, taking a situation as parlourmaid. She sought long
and vainly for Phyllis, but never found her again. A respectable
young man wishes to marry her, but Sarah refuses; and when
she has saved enough money from her wages to return to another
convent, she goes there, to spend the remainder of her days in
prayer for the souls of the girl and the man who had saved her
from prostitution by the wages of sin. It is a remarkable and
complex study, which only Mr. Moore can make probable. In a
way, this sad little saga of a girl whose hard life is bounded by
convent walls, with an interval of adventure before and between
her periods of existence there, reminds us of the author's earlier
creation, Esther Waters, whose life was bounded by the
house called " Woodview ": there she had gone as a young
girl, and thither, after worldly experience, she returned a broken
woman. And the same supreme artistry which irradiates that
great tale of the commonplace is found in the shorter story of
Sarah Gwynn.

In *Hugh Montfert* Mr. Moore presents an even more acute
problem. Hugh is a young man of twenty-two, an only child,
and heir to a fine property and great wealth. His widowed
mother ardently desires his early marriage, so that the family line
may continue. But Hugh, a Roman Catholic, is obsessed with
the idea of personal purity and chastity. He debates the idea of
becoming a priest, and has an aversion to women in a sexual
sense. So, some time passes in a conflict with the wishes of his
mother, Hugh withdrawing into an inner mental life of his own—
dreams of mediæval romance and spotless knights *sans peur et
sans reproche.* Speaking of the Middle Ages, he said : —

" I seem to have known them always. . . . I am but the shadow of
a knight who lived eight hundred years ago. . . . I can only love the
beautiful. . . . The mediæval world is nearer to me; it is my present,
the Greek world is my past; in the world around me I am an exile."

A new influence comes into his life. He meets Percy Knight,
a youth of seventeen, talented and compact of artistic aspirations.
The two become friends at once by affinity of tastes, and Hugh
soon loves the boy very devotedly—as is the way with solitary
individuals of romantic temperament. The friends go off on a

wild expedition, partly on foot, which eventually leads them to Wales, to St. David's and Ramsey Island. This itinerary gives Mr. Moore scope to introduce numerous adventures, experiences, and incidental tales, such as were found in a previous book of his, *A Story Teller's Holiday*. It is impossible to quote at any length beyond a word or two, such as these which bring to mind in a moment the great grey cliffs of the Fishguard coast—" Cliffs towering hundreds of feet above the sea, and about whose base the sea prowled like a savage beast, though the day was calm, almost windless." And these, which picture so exquisitely the coming of evening at the old Hall in Essex:—

" The conversation was brought to a pause suddenly by a little wind laden with the fragrance of a blossoming lime; and then another wind went by impregnated with the pungent odour of lavender, and looking whence the winds came they saw the shrubs in bloom in the narrow beds between the paved paths and the walls of the house . . . the rooks returned through the overhanging night, the old birds leading the young ones to their roosts, their soft cawing speaking of rest, of the weariness of the day ended at last. A vague sound came across the meadows; it might be the rumble of a passing cart. The pea-fowl gathered under the cedars . . . the swans with their grey brood climbed out of the ponds to hide themselves among the reeds. . . ."

The two boys return. Percy has a sister, Beatrice Knight, who much resembles him in physical appearance, and she professes to share the tastes in Art and Literature of the friends. The girl is invited on a visit by Mrs. Montfert, and thrown much into the society of Hugh. He hears that local gossip couples their names together, and, worn out by the importunities of his mother that he should marry, he suddenly proposes to Beatrice, and is accepted. They are married, and Hugh finds he is unable to consummate the union. He leaves his wife, and the reasons are best told in Hugh's confession to a priest:—

" I did not leave my wife because of impotence; I am not impotent. It would be better, perhaps, if I were, for then I should be out of reach of temptation. . . . I was attracted to Beatrice not for herself but for her likeness to her brother; her voice, her figure, her gait, in a thousand ways she reminded me of him, and I mistook the nature of my affection. I was deceived: it was not until I took Beatrice in my arms that I knew I could never love a woman. . . . Percy knows nothing of my love. How could he, for I did not know it myself until last night."

All the advice and suggestions of the Church are in vain. Hugh refuses to return to Beatrice, who obtains a nullity of the marriage. He resumes his life of mediæval dreams and dilettantism. He builds a Roman Catholic Church, and designs for stained glass windows and the revival of music by Palestrina Vittoria and Orlandi Lasso occupy his lonely days. Then comes the crushing news of Percy's sudden death:

" Nothing makes any difference now. . . . Percy is gone for ever and I am left . . . the spring of life is gone for ever out of me. . . ." And he is left with his unchanging grief for his friend, and his unsullied chastity. Mr. George Moore has found his way through a briary bypath of human psychology with infinite skill, and his treatment of a difficult subject merits the highest praise.

LYTTON STRACHEY*

MR. LYTTON STRACHEY is in the happy position of having any new book he may issue received with *éclat* and impressive respect. This desirable state of things is owing to the fame he won deservedly with his *Eminent Victorians* and *Queen Victoria.* Had he not those two works to his credit, the present production† would not, probably, have appeared, for it is a reprinting of articles and reviews which Mr. Strachey wrote in his 'prentice days when he was forming his distinctive style. Though not a new work in the literal sense, that is not to say the collection of these articles is unnecessary. For there is much that is good and worthy of preservation in this literary survey which alights on such diverse personalities as Shakspere and Creevey, Voltaire and Thomas Beddoes, Henri Beyle and Lady Hester Stanhope.

The best article is that on Thómas Lovell Beddoes, whom the author styles " The Last Elizabethan . . . a star which had wandered from its constellation, and was lost among alien lights." Beddoes was an eccentric, who wrote two remarkable plays, *The Bride's Tragedy* and *Death's Jest Book*, and he is as unknown to the general reader as an actual minor Elizabethan poet, though he died as recently as 1849. But he has his own select band of appreciators, headed by Mr. Edmund Gosse, who has supervised editions of Beddoes's poems and letters. Mr. Strachey's succinct and sympathetic little memoir of Beddoes provides an excellent source of information for those who care to learn something of the life and work of a very uncommon and gifted man.

The essay on Henri Beyle (Stendhal) is also illuminating. In speaking, however, of the unfamiliarity of English people with Beyle's work, Mr. Strachey seems unaware that an early disciple over here of the French novelist was George Meredith, who sixty years ago was recommending Beyle to his friends as an aid to form a good literary style. As far back as 1861 Meredith wrote: " I think de Stendhal very subtle and observant. He goes over ground that I know." In the course of his article Mr. Strachey says: —

---

* *The Fortnightly Review*, October, 1922.
† *Books and Characters, French and English,* by Lytton Strachey. (Chatto & Windus, 12s 6d. net.)

" Perhaps the best test of a man's intelligence is his capacity for making a summary. Beyle knew this, and his novels are full of passages which read like nothing so much as extraordinarily able summaries of some enormous original narrative."

This statement might be applied to the author himself. Mr. Strachey's memorable final paragraph in his *Queen Victoria* is a case in point, for that sentence summarised what were, very likely, the memories of a long life. It is interesting to find that in his earlier work Mr. Strachey was experimenting in and perfecting his gift for a long picturesque peroration. Thus, how excellent is the close of his article on *Racine* : —

" To hear the words of Phèdre spoken by the mouth of Bernhardt, to watch, in the culminating horror of crime and of remorse, of jealousy, of rage, of desire, and of despair, all the dark forces of destiny crowd down upon that great spirit, when the heavens and the earth reject her, and Hell opens, and the terrific urn of Minos thunders and crashes to the ground—that indeed is to come close to immortality, to plunge shuddering through infinite abysses, and to look, if only for a moment, upon eternal light."

And how delightfully he ends the essay on *Sir Thomas Browne* : —

" But, after all, who can doubt that it is at Oxford that Browne himself would choose to linger? May we not guess that he breathed in there, in his boyhood, some part of that mysterious and charming spirit which pervades his words? For one traces something of him, often enough, in the old gardens, and down the hidden streets ; one has heard his footstep beside the quiet waters of Magdalen ; and his smile still hovers amid that strange company of faces which guard, with such a large passivity, the circumference of the Sheldonian."

That expresses a real comprehension of the elusive Spirit of Place. Mr. Strachey is constantly picturesque, even in unexpected places. Thus, in the review of *Mr. Creevey*, how good is his conceit of Clio, the stately Muse of History, in her pompous robes and buskins, accompanied in her march down the ages " by certain apish, impish creatures, who run round her tittering, pulling long noses, threatening to trip the good lady up, and even sometimes whisking to one side the corner of her drapery, and revealing her undergarments in a most indecorous manner "—these indiscreet attendants being the memoir and letter writers, such as Pepys, Horace Walpole, Greville, and Creevey. It might be invidious to suggest that, in future ages, Mr. Strachey will be reckoned a member of this gay subsidiary band of ironical historians, who have torn the mask of majesty or dignity from kings (and queens) and famous men, reducing all to the level of commonplace, erring, but human, beings.

A. E. HOUSMAN.*

In all the annals of English literature there is no analogy to the case of Mr. A. E. Housman's intermittent spring of pure poetry. Other poets, such as Keats and Chatterton, have left but a small volume as evidence of their genius, but the reason is generally to be found in the fact that they died young, before consummating (or exhausting) their powers:—

> " Cut is the branch that might have grown full straight,
>   And burnèd is Apollo's laurel bough. "

But, on the other hand, these have escaped the fate of their choicest poems being engulfed and lost in the dreary wastes of " Collected Editions," compact of superfine binding and unreadably small print.

Mr. A. E. Housman's bequest to posterity and fame is two small books. Over a quarter of a century ago—in 1896—he offered, without any preliminary flourishes of trumpets or Press puffings, a slim little book of verse entitled *A Shropshire Lad.* Beyond its title, which was, perhaps, unusual for a work emanating from a Professor of Latin at University College, London, there was no hint before perusal that this was a unique book—one that was to strike a new note of music in English poesy, to be a literary influence for all time, to have numerous imitators. It appeared, and critics and general readers (at once, for a marvel, in agreement) instantly realised that here was something fresh, a song that sang what had never been heard so poignantly before—" the long, long thoughts " of a boy, and more, the intense sadness of regret for lost youth, friends long dead, and all the beauty and the brave days that are no more:—

> " Into my heart an air that kills
>   From yon far country blows :
> What are those blue remembered hills,
>   What spires, what farms are those?
>
> That is the land of lost content,
>   I see it shining plain,
> The happy highways where I went
>   And cannot come again. "

There was something about the haunting cadences of these little songs that touched the very spring of tears—like the sad, wan notes of the shepherd's fluting pipe heard by the dying Tristan, left with only memories of life and love; something far

---

* *The Fortnightly Review,* January, 1923.

and remote and elusive like " the horns of Elfland faintly
blowing." They expressed the Soul of Memory:—

> " Far in a western brookland,
>   That bred me long ago,
> The poplars stand and tremble
>   By pools I used to know.
>
> .   .   .   .
>
> There, by the starlit fences,
> The wanderer halts and hears
> My soul that lingers sighing
>   About the glittering weirs."

Now, after twenty-seven years, and again unheralded, Mr.
Housman has provided a little pendant to *A Shropshire Lad*.*
It is described as Last Poems, and the author states " it is not
likely that I shall ever be impelled to write much more."   There
is hope, in that reservation, for his readers that some or a few
" more " poems may yet be written, despite the melancholy little
song which ushers in the present collection:—

> " We'll to the woods no more,
> The laurels are all cut,
> The bowers are bare of bay
> That once the Muses wore;
> The year draws in the day,
> And soon will evening shut. . . ."

The new book is smaller than its predecessor, and, therefore,
does not contain quite so many exquisite things.   The theme and
the setting are, happily, the same as found expression in *A
Shropshire Lad*: it is the continuation of a familiar song, not a
new melody.   Once more the poems voice the memories of youth
and sad regret for the beauty of the past that is dead—youth
that was spent and beauty that was realised amid the vales and
hills of Shropshire:—

> " When summer's end is nighing,
>   And skies at evening cloud,
> I muse on change and fortune
>   And all the feats I vowed
>   When I was young and proud.
>
> The weathercock at sunset
>   Would lose the slanted ray,
> And I would climb the beacon
>   That looked to Wales away,
>   And saw the last of day.
>
> From hill and cloud and heaven
>   The lines of evening died;
> Night welled through lane and hollow
>   And hushed the countryside,
>   And I had youth and pride."

---

* *Last Poems,* by A. E. Housman.   (Grant Richards, 5s. net).

But the summers come hasting and the years go by, and the
winter of life draws in with the dreams of youth unfulfilled : —

> " So here's an end of roaming
>   On eves when autumn nighs :
> The ear too fondly listens
>   For summer's parting sighs,
>   And then the heart replies."
>
> .   .   .   .
>
> " Too fast to yonder strand forlorn
> We journey, to the sunken bourn,
> To flush the fading tinges eyed
> By other lads at eventide."

A new generation arises and dreams the old visions of love
and beauty like those that went before, and like an eternal
treadmill the tragedy is repeated. The facts of life kill romance,
and loveliness fades in the glare of sordid disillusion. Mr.
Housman again expresses his brooding melancholy for the
frequent untimely fate of youth cut off by some act of passion : —

> " Think I, the round world over
>   What golden lads are low
> With hurts not mine to mourn for
>   And shames I shall not know."

Three consecutive poems, *The Deserter, The Culprit, Eight
o'Clock*, picture lads on the eve of execution, and are touched
with a note of understandable pessimism : —

> " Oh let not man remember
>   The soul that God forgot,
> But fetch the county kerchief
>   And noose me in the knot,
>   And I will rot."

The poet voices bravely the lawless claims of youth and hot
blood : —

> " The laws of God, the laws of man,
> He may keep that will and can ;
> Not I : let God and man decree
> Laws for themselves and not for me ;
> And if my ways are not as theirs
> Let them mind their own affairs.
> Their deeds I judge and much condemn,
> Yet when did I make laws for them ?
> Please yourselves, say I, and they
> Need only look the other way.
> But no, they will not ; they must still
> Wrest their neighbour to their will,
> And make me dance as they desire
> With jail and gallows and hell-fire . . ."

In a previous article I endeavoured to demonstrate that the
work of Mr. Thomas Hardy was not, to an excessive degree,
pessimistic in the ordinary and accepted sense of the word. It

would be more difficult to establish the same contention in the case of Mr. Housman, for he is frankly pessimistic in many of his poems, though, perhaps, fatalistic would be the more correct word to use. One of the most melancholy of his songs, by a graveside, faces the painful truth that memory and love of the dead will fade:—

> " The rain it streams on stone and hillock,
>   The boot clings to the clay.
> Since all is done that's due and right
> Let's home ; and now, my lad, good-night,
>   For I must turn away.
>
> Over the hill the highway marches
> And what's beyond is wide :
> Oh soon enough will pine to nought
> Remembrance and the painful thought
>   That sits the grave beside.
>
> But oh, my man, the house is fallen
>   That none can build again;
> My man, how full of joy and woe
> Your mother bore you years ago
>   To-night to lie in the rain."

Truly, it is the saddest thought in the world—that the passing years will inevitably bring forgetfulness of the lonely dead, however dearly they once were loved and however poignant was the grief that broke over their grave. Surely, some echo of that intense sorrow and emotion should linger there for ever : but no, the years pass, the flowers wither, the weeds are triumphant, and the headstone sinks down. Who can forget Swinburne's wonderful but terrible lines :—

> " Love deep as the sea as a rose must wither,
>   As the rose-red seaweed that mocks the rose.
> Shall the dead take thought for the dead to love them?
>   What love was ever as deep as a grave?
> They are loveless now as the grass above them
>   Or the wave."

All sincere poetry is the conscious or unconscious expression of momentous personal experience, even though it may appear sometimes as but the reflection of a passing mood. Mr. Housman has never revealed or hinted how far his poems may reflect his own experiences. He states that *A Shropshire Lad* was mainly written when the author was in a state of " continuous excitement," and presumably the same words apply to his later work. That must suffice for his present readers. But, inevitably, in years to come, the world will want to know more. Poets, like Byron, Shelley, and Keats, who wrote of great passions and

emotions, cannot escape this posthumous curiosity which asks
to what extent they lived their poems and if they found " the
lover's crown of myrtle," if not better, at least equal to " the
poet's crown of bays."

In the same way it will be matter for future speculation
whether the author of *A Shropshire Lad* once worked on a farm
and went ploughing

> " When smoke stood up from Ludlow
> And mist blew off from Teme,"

and it will be matter for wonder how a college don came to know
so much about the call of the drum and the life of the recruit.
Whatever the facts may be, we are not concerned to elucidate
them. Mr. Housman is a poet, and, as in his first book, he
continues to be the pre-eminent poet of the young soldier*—a
sad one, it is true, for his vision looks to after the battle. *Illic
Jacet, Grenadier, I 'listed at Home for a Lancer, Wake not,
Soldier from the Wars Returning* are in the category. Finest
of all is this : —

> " In valleys green and still,
>   Where lovers wander maying,
> They hear from over hill
>   A music playing.
>
> Behind the drum and fife,
>   Past hawthornwood and hollow,
> Through earth and out of life
>   The soldiers follow.
>
> The soldier's is the trade :
>   In any wind or weather
> He steals the heart of maid
>   And man together.
>
> The lover and his lass,
>   Beneath the hawthorn lying,
> Have heard the soldiers pass,
>   And both are sighing.
>
> And down the distance they,
>   With dying note and swelling,
> Walk the resounding way
>   To the still dwelling."

Twenty lines, and what a train of imagery and thought they
kindle with strange subtlety of suggestion—every line a picture

---

* " The street sounds to the soldiers' tread,
>   And out we troop to see :
> A single redcoat turns his head,
>   He turns and looks at me.
>
> .   .   .   .
>
> What thoughts at heart have you and I
>   We cannot stop to tell;
> But dead or living, drunk or dry,
>   Soldier, I wish you well."

for the imagination. This new book contains an even more powerful imaginative poem, *Hell Gate*—a vision of a soldier in the Inferno which must be read in its longer completeness. It is different from any other poem of Mr. Housman's in its bizarre detail, for generally he only suggests. But it resembles the others in that it concerns friendship—in this case, friendship triumphant. Mr. Housman is the poet of infinite sympathy for the fallen; no sinner is beyond his understanding and compassion. Even a flower plucked at the grave of the suicide by the crossways moves him to exquisite comprehension : —

> " It seemed a herb of healing
> A balsam and a sign,
> Flower of a heart whose trouble
> Must have been worse than mine. "

Beautiful Shropshire has won its own distinctive poet; and Ludlow, Wenlock, Bredon Hill, Clun, and Teme have now as gracious a literary significance as Grasmere, Ayr, Onley, Abbotsford, and Newstead.

ARTHUR MACHEN.*

MR. ARTHUR MACHEN is now, at long last, acknowledged to be one of the most arresting and distinguished writers of our time. It has been his fate, like so many of his genius, to experience bitter disappointment and neglect; the way of his literary pilgrimage has been long and stormy—nay, by his own relation, at times of a soul-searing horror. I think I am right in saying that his finest book, *The Hill of Dreams*, was rejected by most of the publishers in London. It is well that recognition has at length come in his life-time, and that his works are already being issued in collected editions both here and in America. Posthumous fame, after all, is but naught: better a jug of wine for a live man to drink than a centenary dinner eaten by his admirers when he is dust and oblivious.

Mr. Machen has written a fragment of autobiography†—by no means complete, for it is confined to the first twenty-one years of his life, 1863-1884, or thereabouts. He is right in affirming that these years of youth are the most important of all in the growth and development of the imagination. In agreeing with Hazlitt's dictum that the man of genius spent his whole life in telling the world what he had known himself by the time he was eighteen, Mr. Machen adds: " He who has any traffic with the affairs of the imagination has found out all the wisdom that he will ever know, in this life at all events, by the age of eighteen or thereabouts."

It is only children, with some few exceptions, who have the power to enter Fairyland and convert the land of make-believe into a mental reality. A few rare spirits have been permitted to reserve their gifts of imagination and awe with which they entered the realms of Faery in childhood, and these, added to the creative powers of age and experience, produce a genius like Barrie or Fiona Macleod. Such as these have seized and quaffed the magic goblet of Edenhall.

It is in youth we glean and garner, unconsciously, impressions of beauty and ugliness, joy and sorrow, which, in the case of an artist, find expression in terms of music, painting or sculpture, and literature, in later years. Mr. Machen is a case in proof

* *The Fortnightly Review*, January, 1923.
† *Far Off Things*, by Arthur Machen. (Martin Secker, 7s. 6d. net.)

with his own literary work, which is the reflection of the beauty and sombre grandeur of the countryside where he spent his boyhood. He says:—

" I shall always esteem it as the greatest piece of fortune that has fallen to me that I was born in the noble, fallen Caerleon-on-Usk, in the heart of Gwent. My greatest fortune, I mean, from that point of view which I now more especially have in mind, the career of letters. For the older I grow the more firmly am I convinced that anything which I may have accomplished in literature is due to the fact that when my eyes were first opened in earliest childhood they had before them the vision of an enchanted land."

And he goes on to describe the mountain ranges, the mystic tumuli, the high woods and forests, the gleam of the wide Severn, which were visible from the windows of his native Llanddewi Rectory:—

" And hardly a house in sight in all the landscape. Here the gable of a barn, here a glint of a white-washed farmhouse, here blue wood smoke rising from an orchard grove, where an old cottage was snugly hidden. . . . And of nights, when the dusk fell and the farmer went his rounds, you might chance to see his lantern glimmering a very spark on the hill-side. This was all that showed in a vague, dark world; and the only sounds were the faint distant barking of the sheep dog and the melancholy cry of the owls from the border of the brake."

Daylight, too, had its equal enchantment, for the country-side was illuminated " by suns that rose from the holy seas of Faery and sank down behind magic hills." But there were also formidable and malignant aspects in this romantic land. One day, in his boyhood ramblings, he came upon a lonely and weird-looking house between the dark forest and the silvern river Usk. Years later he wrote *The Great God Pan* in the endeavour to translate or pass on the vague sense of awe and mystery and terror with which this old house had invested him, and to it he added an influence of evil.

Such, then, were the conditions of Mr. Machen's youth—a lonely time (for he was an only child) spent amid the suggestive beauty and solemnity of hills and woods and waters. In this autobiography he gives many glimpses of now vanished aspects of rural life; and his father, the Rector, and the quiet life of the Rectory, its books and its furnishings, are all depicted with a true and affectionate fidelity. These things played their part in the development of the boy's psychology. Mr. Machen has ever had a keen perception of the virtues (and also, I admit, of the vices) of houses and place. He gives here a vivid realisation of the comfort and security of home when the great storms of winter range over the hills:—

" The green shutters are close fastened without the window, the settle is curved about the hearth, and that great cavern is ablaze and glorious with heaped wood and coals, and the white walls golden with the light of the leaping flames.   And those within can hear the rain dashing upon shutter and upon closed door, and the fire hisses now and again as stray drops fall down the chimney ; and the great wind shakes the trees and goes roaring down the hillside to the valley, and moans and mutters about the housetop.   A man will leave his place, snug in shelter, in the deepest glow of the fire, and go out for a moment and open but a little of the door in the porch and see all the world black and wild and wet, and then come back to the light and heat, and thank God for his home, wondering whether any are still abroad on such a night of tempest.''

That passage pictures the same acute contrast of storm without and warmth within which is presented in the scene in *Pickwick* when Wardle and his guests are gathered round the blazing fire at Dingley Dell on Christmas Eve—" How it snows ! " said one of the men. . . . " Rough, cold night . . . . and there's a wind got up that drifts it across the fields in a thick, white cloud." And the wind rumbled in the chimney.

Mr. Machen relates but little of his school life in Hereford. He passes on to his first visit to London with his father in the year 1880, and his impressions are of interest.   I agree with him that, despite the modern increase of luxury and ostentatious extravagance, arising from a new plutocracy, the outward aspect of social life in London was far more splendid even thirty years ago than it is to-day.   This is primarily owing to the supersession of the horsed carriages by the motor-car, the disappearance of the Opera as a social function, and the passing of the great mansions such as Devonshire House, Stafford House, Grosvenor House, and Montagu House.   When entertainments on a large scale were given in houses like these the neighbouring streets would be packed with ornate family coaches drawn by magnificent horses, prancing and champing their bits, and attended by men-servants with powdered hair and elaborate livery.   The same in the Park.   A stream of the most expensive of motor-cars, gliding rapidly along, and affording but a momentary glimpse of their occupants, cannot compare for a moment as a spectacle with the procession of high barouches and high-stepping horses in the old days.   Then people drove in the Park to see and be seen. The Opera House presented a scene of authentic splendour on the great nights of the Season, with the rows of boxes filled with beautiful women blazing with magnificent jewels.   Like the London Season, the Opera, as a social function, ceased to exist after the death of Edward the Seventh and the retirement of his widow.   Their successors, though able to carry out ceremonial when occasion demands it, have not the same capacity for enjoying State display, pagentry, and social gaieties.*

To return to the London of 1880, Mr. Machen heaves a sigh of regret, like many another, for the changed aspect of the Strand and the vanished picturesque squalor of the Clare Market district. The sincere *laudator temporis acti* would sooner have one of those old houses, of the time of Charles the Second, such as stood in Wych Street and Holywell Street, than all the American glories of Aldwych and Kingsway.† During the next few years Mr. Machen passed his time between Monmouthshire and London, where he lodged variously in the suburbs at Wandsworth, Turnham Green, Shepherd's Bush, and Clarendon Road, Notting Hill, At one period he worked in a publisher's office, and at another had some pupils, but ever the call to write was urgent. Poetry was tried first, but with no success. Incidentally, Mr. Machen offers the suggestion that " almost every literary career, certainly every literary career which is to be concerned with the imaginative side of literature, begins with the writing of verses." I doubt if that holds good as a general rule. It is true that many of the more romantic novelists, such as Scott, Fielding, Smollett, Bulwer, Ainsworth, Meredith, and (to a certain extent) Thomas Hardy and Kipling, commenced their literary work with poetry or plays; but, on the other hand, Dickens, Thackeray, Trollope, William De Morgan, Joseph Conrad, Marryat, Arnold Bennett, H. G. Wells, and many others, did not.

Mr. Machen draws a terrible picture of his early days in London, a boy of twenty, alone and friendless, vainly trying to earn his living. In his room, under the roof in Clarendon Road, ten feet by five, there was no fireplace—" I would sit in my shabby old great-coat, reading or writing, and if I were writing I would every now and then stand up and warm my hands over the gas-jet, to prevent my fingers getting numb." It was at this period he acquired his peculiar knowledge of the western outskirts of London, those recondite districts which so often form the scenes of his stories. Weary of his cold and desolate little room, he would wander forth to Wormwood Scrubs, Shepherd's Bush, Gunnersbury, and even as far as Brentford

---

* They evidently do not care for music, as they did not attend a single performance of the Covent Garden Opera season of 1924, which was a laudable attempt to revive the Opera on the old lines, and deserved encouragement.

† Since this was written we have witnessed the disastrous destruction of Regent Street. Future generations will certainly condemn the Bœotian municipal " authorities " who, all unmindful of their responsibilities and trusts, permitted the gracious lines and dignity of the old street to be supplanted by buildings suitable only for a second-rate American town.

and Hounslow. When he went north of Clarendon Road, generally he found his footsteps arrested by Kensal Green Cemetery, which possessed for him a malignant influence—" a terrible city of white gravestones and shattered marble pillars and granite urns, and every sort of horrid heathenry . . . it added new terror to death. . . . I would break off by way of Portobello Road and entangle myself in Notting Hill, and presently I would come upon the goblin city; I might wander into the Harrow Road, but at last the ghost-stones would appal me. Maida Vale was treacherous, Paddington false—inevitably, it seemed, my path led me to the detested habitation of the dead." Beyond this Golgotha lay Harlesden, synonymous with Horror. Here were then arising, amid the green fields, the outposts of those legions of suburban villas and shops which have since laid waste and devoured the once rural beauties of the Willesden countryside, beloved forty years earlier by Harrison Ainsworth and his frequent guests, Dickens, Forster, and Maclise. That quartette found joy and rest and inspiration there " at a picturesque cottage in a green lane somewhere in the country of *Jack Sheppard* . . . in pastoral Willesden," as Maclise described it. A few years bring many changes, and Mr. Machen found inspiration of a different sort in the red villas which had replaced the white cottage of the Early Victorians. He transmuted the horrid apparition of the crude new houses into the pith of his tale, *The Inmost Light*: —

" The man in my story, resting in green fields, looked up and saw a face that chilled his blood gazing at him from the back of one of those red houses that once had frightened me, when I was a sorry lad of twenty, wandering about the verges of London. The doctor of my tale lived in Harlesden."

Mr. Machen is also, as we have seen, acutely sensitive to the decaying aspect and sombre influences of an old, dying house. There were, some years ago, of necessity, many old farmhouses and once rustic dwellings in the outer suburbs of London which fell into disuse and ruin at the advent of a new population of people employed in the city, who required a different kind of abode. In that great romance, *The Hill of Dreams* (which, curiously enough, the author does not mention in his present book, although it is in many respects an earlier form of his own autobiography), Lucian, like his prototype, wanders forth from his dismal lodgings in Shepherd's Bush across Wormwood Scrubs and by East Acton towards Harlesden. And he comes upon a desolate and decaying old house, all stained and damp from the drippings of the great elm tree which overshadowed

it. The place becomes to him like *The Haunted House* of Hood
—" under some prodigious ban of excommunication "; a
symbol of very horror and dread. It haunts his dreams, and
to the moment of death the impress of the drear old house is
upon him, and the sound of the beating and the moaning branches
of the great elm. I always think this fateful house was suggested
by Old Oak Farm and Friar's Place Farm—a sort of composite
picture of two lone houses beyond Wormwood Scrubs. But,
as Mr. Machen observed to me, years ago, when we took a
ramble together to revisit these two old farms, the house of
The Hill of Dreams was a thing of fantasy, and does not need
too close an identification.

I am glad to find that Acton and Ealing have some pleasanter
memories for Mr. Machen than unhappy Harlesden in his days of
the wilderness. He relates : —

" Acton used to do me good; it was then more like a country town
than a modern suburb. On the right hand, as you came up from the
Uxbridge Road under the railway bridge, there were then some grave
and dignified houses of the Early Georgian period, with broad lawns
before them and big gardens behind them.* On the left was the Priory,
with spacious and park-like grounds and many greeny elms. Legends
about the first Lord Lytton hung about the Priory, and it was whispered
that the old lady who kept the lodge-gate had in her day written daring
poetry, of the erotic kind."

Rumour was indeed a lying jade about Mrs. Bourne, of the
Priory Lodge, " The Acton Poetess," whose " daring " poetry
was in the following gentle vein : —

" Hark the village bells at evening
Gaily chiming ' Farewell day '—
Some are changed, and all are changing,
Softly sing time's parting lay."

The only sense in which the word " erotic " could be
associated with her would lay in the fact that she first came to the
Lodge in the service of George Trafford Heald, when he established that exotic lady, Lola Montez, as his wife in Berrymead
Priory, in the year 1850. But the marriage seems to have been
bigamous; Lola Montez and her youthful Cornet of the Life
Guards were not long in Acton, though Mrs. Bourne remained
there till her death in 1906.

Like all sincere and great artists, Mr. Machen has cherished
the vision of writing a supreme and perfect book—for, alas!
realisation on paper so often falls short of the original conception
of the brain. His intention of " high fantasies " is linked, like

---

* Some of these old houses still exist behind shop fronts, but the gardens
are gone, of course.

so much of his work, with the western outskirts of London, where Fate placed his youthful, imaginative years equally with Gwent on the romantic Welsh borders. In a beautiful passage, very characteristic of his vivid style, he describes how he took the thoughts of his great book to Ealing Common one autumn evening : —

" The work was drawing to a close, and I stood meditating the matter, looking from the height down towards Brentford. There was a wild sunset, scarlet and green and gold, and, as it were, gardens of Persian roses, far in the evening sky. I stood by an old twisted oak, and thought of my book as I would have made it, and sighed, and so went home and made it as I could."

JOHN ST. LOE STRACHEY*

In the book I have been considering overleaf, Mr. Machen draws attention to the acute contrast between his own early Via Dolorosa of literature—its loneliness, desolation, difficulty, and pain—and the luxurious, Rolls-Roycean swiftness with which many a young man nowadays glides along the road of success in letters—" he drops so easily, so pleasantly, so delightfully into a quite distinguished place in literature before he is twenty-five . . . . and is almost a classic in a year or two." But luck plays a large part in securing the prizes in letters, as in other vocations, and there have been the same sharp contrasts between success and the reverse at all periods of literary history. This is aptly illustrated by another autobiography which has appeared almost simultaneously with Mr. Machen's and is the self-expression of Mr. John St. Loe Strachey.† The two men are contemporaries, and but a year or two marks their difference in age.

In the early 'Eighties, when Mr. Machen was experiencing failure and privation and loneliness in dismal suburban lodgings, Mr. Strachey, an Oxford undergraduate with influential relatives and friends, was already contributing " middle articles " to *The Saturday Review*. This was followed by work for *The Pall Mall Gazette* and *The Academy*. In 1885 he became a leader-writer and reviewer for *The Spectator*, and in the following year, at the age of twenty-six, he had become the right-hand man of the two editor-proprietors, Meredith Townsend and Hutton, attaining also the reversion of the sole editorship and proprietorship of the paper he has now so ably conducted for the last quarter of a century.

Mr. Strachey was born under a lucky star. He has never known privation or failure, and success has crowned all his endeavours in youth and middle-age. And he looks forward serenely to old age, with no fear of death and the hereafter—" I may have a pleasant thrill of dread of what is there, but not of fear. The tremendous nature of that splendid unknown may send a shiver through my limbs, but it is stimulating, not paralysing." Truly, a happy state of mind, and in the exposition

---

* *The Fortnightly Review*, January, 1923.
† *The Adventure of Living*, A Subjective Autobiography, by John St. Loe Strachey, editor of *The Spectator*. (Hodder & Stoughton. Illustrated. 20s. net.)

and history of the growth of his mind the author has found the *raison d'être* for a most interesting book, which has no concern with the gossip and personalities of the usual autobiography.

The son of an admirable and cultured father, incidentally a baronet, Mr. Strachey had the supreme advantage of being brought up in an English Manor House, Sutton Court, in the beautiful country of the Mendip Hills. Here, in a home of many memories, he was free of a good and diversified library. Reading as he listed, and, further, being educated privately and hearing much conversation of his elders, he developed in the individual and self-assertive manner generally found in a boy who escapes the public-school system, which aims at turning out a uniformity of type whatever the original ingredients cast into the mould. Thus, Mr. Strachey, although a good rider and sportsman, knew nothing of the fetish of cricket and football; and when he went up to Oxford he amazed the dons by his ignorance of Greek, Latin, and the usual school curriculum, and irritated them by his vast fund of general and literary knowledge on matters of which they were, in many cases, ignorant.

In addition to the invaluable influence of his father's culture and sapient sayings and his mother's social circle (which included Frances Lady Waldegrave, the owner of Horace Walpole's Strawberry Hill, where she gave notable entertainments), Mr. Strachey owed a great deal of his early acquaintance with English literature to a most remarkable nurse, Mrs. Leaker. A girl from a poor and illiterate home in Devonshire, she taught herself to read before reaching womanhood. As a young housemaid, dusting the books in a library, she opened *The Letters of Junius*. She read a page or two, and the glowing style went to her head " like brandy." As time went on she became familiar with the works of Shakspere, Milton, Coleridge, Wordsworth, Johnson, Byron, Moore, Browning, and Tennyson. As nurse to the Strachey children, she imparted to them her literary tastes, together with a store of wise rustic sayings, ghost legends from Devonshire, and memories of her youth there in the days of the Press Gang and Waterloo. Mr. Strachey relates of this wonderful nurse : —

" She was quite prepared to read us to sleep with the witches in *Macbeth* or the death-scene in *Othello*. . . . I see her now, with her wrinkled, brown face, her cap with white streamers awry over her black hair beginning to turn grey. In front of her was a book, propped up against the rim of a tin candlestick shaped like a small basin. In it was a dip candle and a pair of snuffers. That was how nursery light was provided in the later sixties, and even in the early seventies. As she sat, bent forward, declaiming the most soul-shaking things in Shakespeare, between nine and tea at night, we lay in our beds, with our chins on the counterpanes, silent, scared, but intensely happy."

Mrs. Leaker was, of course, a unique example of her class in the matter of her " book learning." Splendid women as the Victorian domestic nurses were, they were also, as a rule, illiterate, for they had gone out to work in childhood in days when education was not compulsory. In my own example, our nurse lived in my mother's service for over forty years. She was proficient in every domestic art, from nursing, cookery, and all branches of house-maidery, through tailoring, valeting, and upholstering, to papering and whitewashing and gardening (if these last named be domestic arts), but she could not read a word, and but hardly sign her name. Like Mrs. Leaker, she had a fund of legend, superstition, and old rustic distiches, added to a vast vocabulary of obsolete East Anglian words, such as lummock, golder, and housen. She was also famous for many quaint malapropisms of her own invention. Some of these were adopted by our friends, particularly " deplorious," which was infinitely more descriptive than " deplorable "; to treat an offending person " with cool content " showed a wealth of philosophy not to be found in " cool contempt "; and perchance someone with a nasty " cask of countenance " would be " hit dummy (dumb-y)," i.e., not spoken to or "knowledged," because he or she (" the mawther ") was " the low of the low," and lived or dressed in a " mean and miserbel " manner.

Mr. Strachey passed on to Balliol, where, as already indicated, his frank and unabashed egotism, his stores of out-of-the-way knowledge and literary proficiency, his dislike of school games and dull academic learning, caused him to be misunderstood and disliked by the dons and pundits. Thus he found one erudite classicist ignorant of Marlowe's *Dido and Æneas;* and Jowett himself, who evidently suffered much from " Stracheyphobia," only showed to the brilliant, eager young undergraduate as one who treated him with attempted sarcasm, and as a snob with a partiality for " dukes and marquesses, and even of the offscourings of Debrett," and a blind eye for *their* peccadillos. Mr. Strachey is absolutely right in his condemnation of the unfortunate habit many schoolmasters and tutors have of treating their pupils with cheap attempts at sarcasm and superciliousness. He says : —

" Sarcasm is the one weapon which it is never right or useful to use in the case of persons who are in the dependent position when compared with the wielder of the sarcastic rapier—i.e., persons *in statu pupillari*, persons much younger than oneself, persons in one's employment, or, finally, members of one's own family. Sarcasm should be reserved for one's equals, or, still better, for one's superiors. The man who is treated with sarcasm, if he cannot answer back either because it is half true, or he is stupid, or he is afraid to counter-attack a superior, is filled, and naturally filled, with a sense of burning indignation."

The feeling of antagonism thus created in the pupil destroys all chance of sympathy with the tutor, and therefore any prospect of success resulting from their mutual work. The self-respect (or dignity) of a boy is a very sensitive thing, and to wound it is a cruel and fatuous act. The sure way to win the heart of a boy is to treat him as an equal. To digress again personally for a moment, I recall a private tutor—an Oxford man, I think—whose classes I, as a youth, attended for a short time. At our first meeting he offered me in greeting two fingers to shake, to which I naturally responded with one, for I remembered my Becky Sharp and George Osborne. Of course, after that, the atmosphere was tense. I disliked him, and, no doubt, he disliked me. He did not succeed in teaching me anything, and our paths soon separated.

The dons excepted, Mr. Strachey found nothing but joy in Oxford and the friendships he formed there with men of his own age. He pays a fine tribute of love to his *alma mater* " for her beauty and her quietness, and for the golden stream of youth which runs a glittering torrent through her stately streets and hallowed gardens, her walks between the waters, and her woodlands."

I have no space left to follow Mr. Strachey through his later years in London and his impressions of life and people there. The outstanding quality of his autobiography is its superlative egotism. He has never found himself a failure. Greatly daring, he quotes the verse he wrote as a young boy, and says that it is good; he says, as a young leader-writer for *The Spectator*, that his chiefs knew that he had written good stuff; and when he looks back over the long miles of articles he has written during forty years, he paraphrases the Duke of Wellington : " Damned good! " But, of course, a real autobiography must be egotistic, and Mr. Strachey disarms all criticism by the frank revelations he gives of the workings of his mind and the consequent growth of his personality. He is a clever, brilliant man, and knows it; and having found life pleasant and successful by reason of his own gifts and merits, he rightly records the facts.

W. B. YEATS.*

MR. W. B. YEATS opens his reminiscences† with the somewhat unusual admission that, of the friends of his earlier years, " I have said all the good I know and all the evil: I have kept nothing back necessary to understanding." That frank statement certainly clears the air for a captious reviewer, or, rather, puts him in the position of finding his occupation gone; for, if, in a final attempt to assert himself, he objects to the publication of intimate revelations of the minds and characters of Mr. Yeats's famous contemporaries of the 'Nineties, he will, in most cases, be gagged by the memoirist's undeniable contention that over the dead he has an historian's rights.

Mr. Yeats is, of course, pre-eminently the poet of the mystic isles of the West of Ireland, of lake and legend—

> " A dim, green, well-beloved isle
> Where people love beside star-laden seas."

But most of his youth and memories find their location in a then new suburb of London, far from " lake water lapping with low sounds by the shore," and where the most insistent sounds would be the grinding wheels of the old District railway trains, in their days of steam, as they drew up at Turnham Green Station.

A lengthy dissertation might be penned on how far poets are affected or not by environment. *A priori*, a singer would claim, with Miltonian plea:—

> " Let my lamp, at midnight hour,
> Be seen in some high lonely tower."

Scott had his towers of Abbotsford; Byron his Gothic glories at Newstead; Wordsworth his Lake beauties; Tennyson his " garden of roses and lilies fair on a lawn "; Meredith his Green Hill; Thomas Hardy his spacious Wessex. But, on the other hand, Shakspere had no particular setting; Shelley was a homeless wanderer; Swinburne passed from uncomfortable town lodgings to the solid suburban comforts of Putney; Austin Dobson, the singer of Romance and the graces of the eighteenth century, conceived his best work in a modest and modern Ealing villa; Roden Noel, the passionate adorer of Beauty, was content with the flatness of Hove; Ernest Dowson wrote most of his

---

* *The Fortnightly Review*, April, 1923.
† *The Trembling of the Veil*, by W. B. Yeats. (Privately printed for subscribers only by T. Werner Laurie.)

exquisite and wan little songs by Limehouse Dock; John Payne, full of the glow of the sensuous East and Moslem metres, lived and died in the unsuggestive atmosphere of Kilburn.

Given a poet and a suburban dwelling, Mr. Yeats was so far fortunate in the assignment of his adolescent years to Bedford Park (near Chiswick), which was certainly the most picturesque community of its kind to be found in the outskirts of London at the period in question. In its early days it possessed an authentic artistic culture, and was the legitimate offspring of the Pre-Raphaelite Movement. Perhaps its genesis was, to some extent, due to the propinquity of William Morris at Hammersmith Mall, and Burne-Jones (in Samuel Richardson's former house) at The Grange, North End Road. Anyway, it was about 1877 that certain orchard land lying between Turnham Green and Acton Vale was acquired by a Mr. Carr, who proceeded to erect little red houses in the style of Queen Anne, many of them being designed by Norman Shaw. A church, club-house, stores, and inn were added in the same fashion of architecture. Unfortunately, the archæological sense of the projectors went astray when they named the inn " The Tabard," for it is difficult to see what possible association Chaucer and tabards could have with an Augustan community: " The Peruke " or " The Clouded Cane," or even " The Coffee-House," would have been better appellations for the hostelry.

In those first years Bedford Park was really very pleasant. The houses were built in small groups, literally in the midst of orchards of apples, pears, and plums, and there was a stretch of open fields to the north. The original inhabitants tried to live up to their Pre-Raphaelite reputation; the men were mostly artists, and the ladies wore the flowing gowns of rich colour associated with Mrs. Morris, and were of the " greenery-yallery, Grosvenor Gallery " type. In fact, as W. S. Gilbert again put it, the aim of Bedford Park was to " convince 'em if you can that the reign of good Queen Anne was Culture's palmiest day."

Mr. Yeats's parents were among the earliest settlers in Bedford Park, and the future poet, as a boy of twelve or thirteen, attended Godolphin School, Hammersmith. The family went to Dublin for a time, but returned to Bedford Park (3, Blenheim Road, I think) when Mr. Yeats was about twenty-one. He says :—

" At the end of the 'eighties my father and mother, my brother and sisters and myself, all newly arrived from Dublin, were settled in Bedford Park, in a red-brick house with several mantelpieces of wood, copied from marble mantelpieces designed by the brothers Adam, a balcony and a little garden shadowed by a great horse-chestnut tree. Years before we had lived there, when the crooked ostentatiously picturesque streets with great trees casting great shadows had been a new enthusiasm : the Pre-Raphaelite Movement at last affecting life. . . . I remember feeling disappointed because the co-operative stores, with their little seventeenth-century panes, had lost the romance they had when I had passed them still unfinished on my way to school ; and because the public-house called *The Tabard* after Chaucer's Inn was so plainly a common public-house ; and because the great sign of a trumpeter designed by Rooke, the Pre-Raphaelite artist, had been freshened by some inferior hand. . . . I could not understand where the charm had gone that I had felt, when as a schoolboy of twelve or thirteen I had played among the unfinished houses, once leaving the marks of my two hands, blacked by a fall among some paint, upon a white balustrade. Sometimes I thought it was because these were real houses, while my play had been among toy-houses some day to be inhabited by imaginary people full of the happiness that one can see in picture books. I was in all things Pre-Raphaelite."

So much for early influences. His father, John Butler Yeats, was an artist with many friends, among the most intimate at Bedford Park being John Todhunter (doctor and poet) and York Powell. Artists of various ability were clustered around—one, of modest temperament, was wont to say : " I, myself, and Sir Frederick Leighton are the greatest decorative artists of the age."

To digress a moment from Mr. Yeats's narrative, Bedford Park ten years later was still the resort of artists—the Blair Leighton and Dollman families, Cecil Aldin, L. Pissarro, and others. It was also the favoured retreat of theatrical people, such as William Terriss (at 2, Bedford Road), Sydney Brough, Henry Lytton, Louis Bradfield, J. A. E. Malone, and Harry Nicholls (who was at 2, Rupert Road, and one of the last representatives of the old days). Other denizens included Sir Edward Thackeray, Mr. J. Penderel-Brodhurst, Mr. Beresford Chancellor, and Mr. Charles Elkin Matthews.

Bedford Park had a little theatre attached to its red-brick club-house, and here was produced Dr. Todhunter's *Sicilian Idyll.* " The little theatre was full for twice the number of performances intended, for artists, men of letters, and students had come from all over London." The chief female rôle was played by Florence Farr, who lived in lodgings, not distant, at Brook Green. She was destined to become a close friend, and a definite influence in Mr. Yeats's life. She produced his *Land of Heart's Desire* at the Avenue Theatre in 1894.

Many notable people came to the Yeatses' house in Bedford Park. I like the description of the arrival, by hansom, of Maud Gonne in the little colony of apple blossom.

" In that day she seemed a classical impersonation of the Spring, the Virgilian commendation ' she walks like a goddess ' made for her alone. Her complexion was luminous, like that of apple blossom through which the light falls, and I remember her standing that first day by a great heap of such blossoms in the window. In the next few years I saw her always when she passed to and fro between Dublin and Paris, surrounded, no matter how rapid her journey and how brief her stay at either end of it, by cages full of birds, canaries, finches of all kinds, dogs, a parrot, and once a full-grown hawk from Donegal. . . . It was years before I could see into the mind that lay hidden under so much beauty and so much energy."

Mr. Yeats came early under the influence of W. E. Henley, then living a short distance away on the high road to Kew and Richmond. Mr. Yeats was in no sense one of " Henley's Young Men," for they disagreed about everything. Henley derided Pre-Raphaelitism and all it stood for, and Mr. Yeats disliked Henley's poetry, with its details of physical pain and hospital wards. I think Mr. Yeats is a trifle lax in his judgment here. Henley did write a few beautiful and lyrical things, such as : —

" On the way to Kew,
By the river old and gray,
Where in the long ago
We laughed and loitered so,
I met a ghost to-day,
A ghost that told of you,
A ghost of low replies
And sweet inscrutable eyes,
    Coming up from Richmond,
As you used to do."

Henley's volcanic energy, sardonic invective, and—strange combination—appreciative tact seem to have hypnotised his youthful friends, despite antipathy of views. " I did not dare," Yeats writes, " and I think none of us dared, to speak our admiration for book or picture he condemned, but he made us feel always our importance, and no man among us could do good work, or show the promise of it, and lack his praise." But it was a nerve-wracking curriculum—" I cannot go more than once a year, it is too exhausting," as even the Nihilist Stepniak had to admit—Stepniak, who, a few years later, I think I am right in saying, met his death beneath a train at a level crossing of the railway line which encircled Bedford Park to the north and east.

At Henley's, Mr. Yeats met George Wyndham, Oscar Wilde, and many others. He has much to relate of Wilde, whose heredity and temperament he judges very acutely. Premising that the Wilde family was of the variety so often pictured by Charles Lever in his novels—wild, dirty, untidy, drinking, brave, clever, and imaginative, he says Oscar " lived, with no self-mockery at all, an imaginary life, perpetually performed a play which was in all things the opposite of all that he had known in childhood and early youth; never put off completely his wonder at opening his eyes every morning on his own beautiful house, and in remembering that he had dined yesterday with a duchess . . . the dinner-table was Wilde's event and made him the greatest talker of his time, and his plays and dialogues have what merit they possess from being now an imitation, now a record, of his talk . . . he hated Bohemia. ' Olive Schreiner,' he said once to me, ' is staying in the East End because that is the only place where people do not wear masks upon their faces, but I have told her that I live in the West End because nothing in life interests me but the mask.' " All of which is uncannily true about Wilde and his work, if one thinks it out.

The literary and artistic potentialities of the Bedford Park locality were wonderful in those days, for Mr. Yeats was also a frequent visitor to William Morris at Kelmscott House, where, after the debates of the Socialist League in the adjoining stable, he would remain for supper. " We sat round a long unpolished and unpainted trestle table of new wood in a room where hung Rossetti's ' Pomegranate,' a portrait of Mrs. Morris, and where one wall and part of the ceiling were covered by a great Persian carpet." Here the guests included Walter Crane, Emery Walker, Bernard Shaw, and H. M. Hyndman. Mr. Yeats seceded from the coterie on a question of religious difference. His own genius was now finding expression. He had already written *The Wanderings of Usheen*, and this is the genesis of *The Lake Isle of Innisfree* : —

" I had still the ambition, formed in Sligo in my teens, of living, in imitation of Thoreau, on Innisfree, a little island in Lough Gill, and when walking through Fleet Street very homesick I heard a little tinkle of water and saw a fountain in a shop-window which balanced a little ball upon its jet, and began to remember lake water. From the sudden remembrance came my poem *Innisfree,* my first lyric with anything in its rhythm of my own music."

He was now acquainted with most of the poets of his generation, and, in conjunction with Mr. Ernest Rhys, founded The Rhymers' Club, which met in an upper room of " The Cheshire Cheese." Among the prominent members were Lionel Johnson, Ernest Dowson, Richard Le Gallienne, John Davidson, Victor Plarr, Selwyn Image, and Arthur Symons; rarer visitors were Francis Thompson and Wilde. Mr. Yeats rightly speaks of this band as The Tragic Generation, for it is terrible to recall how many of these brilliant men ended in tragedy and pain. His accounts of the ruin by alcohol of Lionel Johnson and Ernest Dowson make painful reading, and the close of Aubrey Beardsley's life is equally sad. The tragedy of Oscar Wilde is here enlivened by some grim humour concerning the idiosyncrasies of his brother, Willie Wilde, at the time of the *débâcle*.

I fear I have but little space left to refer to the history of Mr. Yeats's most important literary gesture—his conception of a National Movement in Ireland allied to and sustained by a symbolical and mythological literature. The growth of this ideal can be traced all through his memoirs, despite his early question, " Does cultivated youth ever really love the future, where the eye can discover no persecuted Royalty hidden among oak leaves ? " His profession of Faith is well defined in a very suggestive passage, which ends : —

" We had in Ireland imaginative stories, which the uneducated classes knew and even sang, and might we not make those stories current among the educated classes, rediscovering for the world's sake what I have called ' the applied arts of literature,' the association of literature, that is, with music, speech, and dance ; and at last, it might be, so deepen the political passion of the nation that all, artist and poet, craftsman and day-labourer, would accept a common design? Perhaps even these images, once created and associated with river and mountain, might move of themselves and with some powerful, even turbulent life, like those painted horses that trampled the rice fields of Japan."

But it would be impertinent for an Englishman to attempt to review any Irish National-Literary ideal, for how can he interpret the antithetical tear and smile in Erin's eye? When is an Irishman serious and sincere? Mr. Yeats relates how a member of Parliament, who had fought for Parnell's policy after the leader's death, much against his own interest, refused to attend a meeting in opposition to the Boer War, because he believed " England was in the right " : yet a week later he sided with the Dublin mob, advised Irish soldiers to shoot their officers and join President Kruger. And how pregnant is the story of the Irish enthusiasts who were resolved to clothe themselves nationally with Connemara cloth. Mr. Yeats dressed according to the patriotic encyclical, until, alas ! his tailor informed him : " It takes such a long time getting Connemara cloth, as it has to come all the way from Scotland." Perhaps the most significant allegory of Irish troubles and Home Rule will be found in a legend related to Mr. Yeats by another Irishman, Oscar Wilde : " If you carve a Cerebus upon an emerald and put it in the oil of a lamp and carry it into a room where your enemy is, two heads will come upon his shoulders and devour one another."

Politics do not interest me much, but the occult, visionary

side of Irish Nationalists is full of allure. When in Sligo with his uncle, George Pollexfen, Mr. Yeats had some curious experiences of vision and mental suggestion. To free himself from nightmare he forced himself to imagine he was guarded by four watch-dogs, one at each corner of his room. He did not mention the conceit to anyone, but his uncle said: "Here is a very curious thing: most nights now when I lay my head upon the pillow I hear a sound of dogs baying; the sound seems to come up out of the pillow." Mr. Yeats tells a somewhat similar story about William Sharp and an hallucination set up by seeing a death symbol, which ended in his throwing himself into the Seine: —

"The story had been created by the influence but it had remained a reverie, though he may in the course of years have come to believe that it happened as an event. The affectionate husband of his admiring and devoted wife, he had created an imaginary beloved, had attributed to her the authorship of all his books that had any talent, and though habitually a sober man, I have known him to get drunk, and at the height of his intoxication, when most men speak the truth, to attribute his state to remorse for having been unfaithful to Fiona Macleod."

But again the question, is a Celt ever serious or sincere about anything? Even on the subject of the supernatural he will be flippant, as witness this delightful, if reprehensible, *bon mot* of Macgregor Mathers: —

"Macgregor is much troubled by ladies who seek spiritual advice, and one has called to ask his help against phantoms who have the appearance of decayed corpses and try to get into bed with her at night. He has driven her away with one furious sentence—'Very bad taste on both sides.'"

There is something in that of the deft, brutal humour of *The Play Boy of the Western World;* and I, for one, prefer to read the works of Mr. Yeats and his gifted friends, J. M. Synge and Lady Gregory, as essays in romance and fantasy and humour without any political-allegorical alloy.

JOHN GAY AND LONDON.*

THIS is, indeed, the era of the recrudescence of Mr. John Gay. His two plays with music, *The Beggar's Opera* and *Polly*, are running simultaneously in London with immense success, moving erudite income-tax collectors to send in pressing demands to the prosperous author for some share of the rich proceeds. This theatrical *éclat* has caused attention to Gay's other literary work, and one result is a new and beautifully produced edition of his almost forgotten metrical essay, *Trivia: or the Art of Walking the Streets of London.*† It preceded *The Beggar's Opera* in composition by more than ten years, being published first in 1716, though it was not the author's first work.

John Gay, born at Barnstaple in 1685, was originally a shop assistant to a mercer in the Strand. He was next in the service, as steward and secretary, of the Duchess of Monmouth (widow of Charles the Second's son) at the time she lived in Lawrence Street, Chelsea. Gay's delightful *Fables*—which by claim of local tradition were written mainly in a summer-house by the Thames at Petersham, between Richmond and Ham—first brought him fame. Some plays, *The Mohocks*, *The Wife of Bath*, and *The What d'ye Call It* were not so successful.

Trivia was a new venture altogether. It was intended originally as a satire on the conventional eighteenth-century verses which eulogised various " Arts," from Painting to Pleasing in Conversation. Gay intended a burlesque—" The Art of Walking the Streets of London "—but he was not equipped with either the vigour or venom essential to a satirist of that period; and *Trivia*, happily, soon shed its original prospectus—just as *Joseph Andrews* discarded the trappings of *Pamela*—and became instead an inimitable and valuable commentary in verse on the life of the London streets when Queen Anne was but lately and literally dead. *Trivia* presents the same social scenes, the modes and morals, which a few years after were limned pictorially for all time by Hogarth—

" Whose pictur'd Morals charm the Mind,
And through the Eye correct the Heart."

All down the ages, writers and artists have delighted in

* *The Fortnightly Review*, April, 1923.
† *Trivia: or the Art of Walking the Streets of London,* by John Gay. With Introduction and Notes by W. H. Williams, M.A. (Daniel O'Connor, £2 2s. net.)

walking the streets of a city, noticing the buildings and watching the ever-changing panorama of its life—an epitome of Humanity. Ever since the Psalmist walked about Zion telling the towers, marking the bulwarks, considering the palaces for purpose of narration " to the generation following," and those glorious jewelled verses were written to picture how " the mourners go about the streets or ever the silver cord be loosed," the literary observers have been active. From Horace and Juvenal, through Lydgate and Pepys to " Rainy-Day " Smith and Charles Dickens, they have walked the streets and recorded what they beheld with results as valuable as " looks commercing with the skies." And London, more than any place, has presented the most fruitful field of observation, for, as Johnson said, " When a man is tired of London he is tired of life, for there is in London all that life can afford."

Trivia was immediately preceded by T. D'Urfey's *Collin's Walk Through London and Westminster* (1690) and *The Works of Mr. Thomas Brown, Serious and Comical, in Prose and Verse* (1715), but Gay surpassed them both in quaint phrasing and human interest. At the outset of the Walk ·he prescribes the clothes most fitting to withstand the conditions and possible accidents of the streets. Incidentally, we find that London shoeblacks and umbrellas were already institutions in 1715, when George the First was but newly arrived from Hanover and Jacobites were suffering on Tower Hill—

> " When the *Black Youth* at chosen Stands rejoice,
> And *Clean your Shoes* resounds from ev'ry Voice;
> Then let the prudent Walker Shoes provide,
> Not of the Spanish or Morocco Hide;
> Let firm, well-hammer'd Soles protect thy Feet
> Thro' freezing Snows, and Rains, and soaking Sleet.
> Good Huswives all the Winter's Rage despise,
> Defended by the Riding-hood's Disguise;
> Or underneath th' *Umbrella's* oily Shed,
> Safe thro' the Wet on clinking Pattens tread."

We start with Mr. Gay on his Walk, and it is interesting to find that many things he advises us to avoid are still causing annoyance in these enlightened days of Police and County Council regulations :—

> " When *Small-coal* murmurs in the hoarser Throat,
> From smutty Dangers guard thy threaten'd Coat;
> The Dustman's Cart offends thy Cloaths and Eyes,
> When through the Street a Cloud of Ashes flies;
> Where Porters' Hogsheads roll from carts aslope,
> Or Brewers down steep Cellars stretch the Rope,
> Where counted Billets are by Carmen tost;
> Stay thy rash Steps, and walk without the Post."

The London gamin, too, is ever the same and a terror to
nervous pedestrians with his snowballs, slides, and footballs : —

> " In harden'd Orbs the Schoolboy moulds the Snow,
> To mark the Coachman with a dextrous Throw.
> Why do ye, Boys, the Kennel's Surface spread,
> To tempt with faithless Pass the Matron's Tread?
> How can ye Laugh, to see the Damsel spurn,
> Sink in your Frauds and her green Stocking mourn?
> Where Covent Garden's famous Temple stands,
> That boasts the Work of Jones' immortal Hands,
> Columns with plain Magnificence appear,
> And graceful Porches lead around the Square :
> Here oft my Course I bend, when lo ! from far
> I spy the Furies of the Foot-ball War :
> The 'Prentice quits his Shop, to join the Crew,
> Encreasing Crouds the flying Game pursue.
> Thus as you roll the Ball o'er snowy Ground,
> The gath'ring Globe augments with ev'ry Round ;
> But wither shall I run? the Throng draws nigh,
> The Ball now skims the Street, now soars on high."

Then, as now, it would be useless to protest, for the London
boy would but respond with " a long nose "—" the 'Prentice
speaks his disrespect by an extended finger." Mr. Williams,
the editor of this edition of *Trivia*, in one of his valuable notes,
mentions how Thomas Brown compares the citation of the
Fathers in support of truisms to " sending for the Sheriff to come
with the *Posse Comitatus* to disperse a few Boys at Foot-ball."
Just the same difficulties, centuries later, attend the Civic Fathers
of to-day. Thus, on some waste land near Kew Bridge the
authorities, for an unknown and presumably inadequate reason,
erected notice boards prohibiting football to be played there.
All in vain. The local youth continued " to chase the rolling
circle's speed, and urge the flying ball " near where " wanders
the hoary Thames along." As a last resource, the authorities
were reduced, ignominiously, to piling up heaps of earth
and rubbish on the sward as the only means of preventing football
on " their " land.

To return to Mr. Gay, he warns the pedestrian to " pass by
the Meuse, nor try the Thimble's Cheats." The Mews (formerly
the King's Falconry) was on the site of the present National
Gallery ; and Thimble's Cheats, or thimble-rigging, was an early
form of The Three Card Trick, " Find the Lady." This varia-
tion of sleight of hand was played with a pea and three little cups
or thimbles, and the victim staked his money on which thimble
he thought covered the pea ; the ethics of the sport and " a
bonnet " will be found in the fifty-third chapter of *Lavengro*.

Passing on to St. Giles's, Mr. Gay points out some things no

T

longer to be seen there—the Pillory with a poor wretch the target of the mob, and the column which formerly stood where Seven Dials converge.

> " Where elevated o'er the gaping Croud,
> Clasp'd in the Board the perjur'd Head is bow'd,
> Betimes retreat; here, thick as Hail-stones pour
> Turnips and half-hatched Eggs (a mingled Show'r).
> Where fam'd Saint Giles's ancient Limits spread,
> An inrail'd Column rears its lofty Head,
> Here to sev'n Streets, sev'n Dials count the Day,
> And from each other catch the circling Ray."

The column or pillar which gave the name to Seven Dials was adorned with only six dials, despite its name. It dated from the end of the seventeenth century, for Evelyn notes in his Diary, October 5th, 1694 :—" I went also to see the building beginning neere St. Giles's, where 7 streets make a star from a Doric pillar plac'd in the middle of a circular area; said to be built by Mr. Neale, introducer of the late Lotteries, in imitation of those at Venice."

Mr. Williams does not mention in the Notes that in 1774 the column and dials were taken down in a vain search for treasure reputed to be hidden under the site. They were never replaced, and were stored away somewhere until their purchase in 1822 by a stonemason, who, in turn, sold them to the parish of Weybridge. The column was erected on the Green there as a memorial to the Duchess of York, who died at Oatlands Park in 1820, and the dial stone found a base use as a stepping-stone at the neighbouring " Ship " inn.

In 1715 the dangers of robbery in the street were much greater than now. Even the periwig was liable to be snatched from the head of the wearer by a small boy carried in a basket on the shoulder of a senior thief :—

> " Nor is thy Flaxen Wigg with Safety worn;
> High on the Shoulder, in the Basket born,
> Lurks the sly Boy; whose Hand to Rapine bred,
> Plucks off the curling Honours of the Head.
> Here dives the skulking Thief, with practis'd Slight,
> And unfelt Fingers make thy Pocket light.
> Where's now thy Watch, with all its Trinkets, flown?
> And thy late Snuff-Box is no more thy own.
> But lo! his bolder Thefts some Tradesman spies,
> Swift from his Prey the scudding Lurcher flies;
> Dext'rous he scapes the Coach, with nimble Bounds,
> While ev'ry honest Tongue *Stop Thief* resounds.
> Breathless he stumbling falls : ill-fated Boy!
> Why did not honest Work thy Youth employ?

> Seiz'd by rough Hands, he's dragg'd amid the Rout,
> And stretch'd beneath the Pump's incessant Spout :
> Or plung'd in miry Ponds he gasping lies,
> Mud choaks his Mouth, and plaisters o'er his Eyes. "

At night, Lincoln's Inn Fields was not to be visited, for ungrateful mendicants here converted their crutches into weapons of assault : —

> " Where Lincoln's Inn, wide space, is rail'd around,
> Cross not with vent'rous Step; there oft is found
> The lurking Thief, who while the Day-light shone
> Made the Walls echo with his begging Tone :
> That Crutch which late Compassion mov'd shall wound
> Thy bleeding Head, and fell thee to the Ground. "

Drury Lane presented dangers of another sort : —

> " O ! may thy Virtue guard thee through the Roads
> Of Drury's mazy Courts and dark Abodes,
> The Harlots' guileful Paths, who nightly stand
> Where Katherine Street descends into the Strand. "

Catherine Street is gone now, and for this generation of the old or middle-aged it mainly lives in memory as the place where one waited outside the pit door of the old Gaiety Theatre; there were no queues in those days, and in the intervals between rushes and crushes one had the prospect on the other side of the street of such activities as attended the newspaper offices of *The Echo*. It is often stated that the present Gaiety Theatre was rebuilt on the site of its predecessor. That is incorrect, and it may be well to record that the old Gaiety stood some little distance west of the present building; it extended nearly to Wellington Street, and, in fact, the stage door faced the portico of the Lyceum Theatre. There is one other association for Catherine Street; from its east side once opened the entrance leading to the wretched dwellings called " Tom-all-alone's " in *Bleak House*.

Gay concludes his *Trivia* with some mock heroic lines which come very near the truth in view of *The Beggar's Opera*.

> " And now compleat my gen'rous Labours lye,
> Finish'd, and ripe for Immortality,
> Death shall entomb in Dust this mould'ring Frame,
> But never reach th' eternal Part, my Fame. "

* * * * *

MRS. ASQUITH'S MEMOIRS*

MRS. ASQUITH'S second volume† is of considerably more historical value than the first, and she has been well advised to continue the publication of her reminiscences despite the adverse and captious criticism which was aroused by her previous book. She now sums up in her Preface this journalistic abuse: " I should not have written about the living; it was unpardonable to criticise the dead; bad taste to publish letters; worse to mention love; and, to crown the crescendo, egotistical to write about myself. As these criticisms were directed more against myself than my art, I was not discouraged from finishing this second and final volume."

If the objections specified by the reviewers were indeed germane, it would be difficult to write an autobiography at all. The wide-spread personal animus against Mrs. Asquith and, in a lesser degree, her husband, is very difficult to fathom. It was in the main an artificial product of the least worthy section of a party propaganda, which during the war was manured with every possible scandal and lie. It was one of the most discreditable and noxious emanations from the war fever, and it is matter for amazement that so many otherwise sane and good people should have succumbed to the epidemic of credulity and promulgated so much falsehood and guile culled from their diurnal and weekly newspapers. Mrs. Asquith is, of course, partly responsible for the vulgar misconception of her character by reason of her own reckless disregard of public opinion‡ and her freedom of speech, which has created many enemies. But Gladstone liked her; and she is the valued friend of such men as Lord Grey of Fallodon, Lord Morley of Blackburn, and Lord Balfour; and by the evidence of her friends she is a clever and brilliant woman, and beloved by her step-children—a pregnant test of amiability of character. Mr. Asquith's nobility of nature scarcely needs reiteration. Sir Henry Campbell-Bannerman, his former chief, pronounced him as a colleague " so loyal, so disinterested, and so able," and added to Mr. Morley: " We have never served with a greater gentleman." He has always remained

---

  * *The Fortnightly Review,* April, 1923.
  † *The Autobiography of Margot Asquith,* Volume II. (Thornton Butterworth, 25s. net.)
  ‡ In a subsequent letter to me, Mrs. Asquith said whatever little respect she had for public opinion was shattered after the Election of 1918.

a gentleman in politics—a rare phenomenon in these days—and has never retorted on his calumniating foes with their own coin. I am not concerned with the political controversies that arise in Mrs. Asquith's book; but every reader must be constrained to admit that when she does allude to the ingratitude and treachery of those who succeeded her husband in power, and bit the hand that fed them in earlier years, she exercises great restraint in view of the provocation endured.

The great and outstanding value, in my opinion, of Mrs. Asquith's records lies in that portion which describes certain episodes of the life and Court of King Edward the Seventh. Here the narrative is as vivid and engrossing as that of Greville or Creevey relating scenes in the private life of George the Fourth. The brief and brilliant era of the seventh Edward is fast becoming as shadowy and legendary as that of his grand-uncle. And there were many points of resemblance between the two men. Both were gifted with tact, the Grand Manner combined with graciousness, and a sincere, if perhaps superficial, appreciation of Art and Beauty. Both succeeded to the Throne late in life—George the Fourth at the age of fifty-seven and Edward the Seventh at fifty-nine; both followed a parent who had reigned for sixty years or more; and their own reigns, in consequence, were short—ten and nine years respectively. Both had very human failings. Edward the Seventh realised and carried out his public duties more conscientiously than George the Fourth, and his lamentably short reign was memorable for the splendour of its Court functions and hospitality. Unlike the present *régime*, the Court was then much at Windsor. George the Fourth, too, loved Windsor, and his last years were passed there in seclusion at The Cottage in the Park. He would drive out, accompanied by his last favourite, Lady Conyngham, through the green Rides (then kept strictly private) to the Sandpit Gate and inspect his aviary and menagerie, or proceed to Virginia Water for a picnic and water excursion in his barge on that most picturesque of lakes (evolved from the Great Swamp of Herne the Hunter's time). Huish, Greville, and other memoirists have recorded these scenes of a hundred years ago; and Mrs. Asquith's vivid picture of Windsor Castle in the time of Edward the Seventh will have equal historical interest in future ages for those who wish to reconstruct mentally a vanished era. One incident she relates is full of illumination on various temperaments : —

" Our Dane informed me that we were to join their Majesties in the Castle Courtyard at 4 o'clock, to motor first to the Gardens and then to

Virginia Water, where we were to have tea. On my arrival in the Court-yard the King came up to me and said, ' Where is the Prime Minister? ' Curtsying to the ground, I answered, ' I am sorry, Sir, but I have not seen him since lunch : I fear he cannot have got your command, and may have gone for a walk with Sir Edward Grey.' HIS MAJESTY (angrily turning to his gentlemen-in-waiting, Harry Stonor and Seymour Fortescue : ' What have you done? Where have you looked for him? Did you not give him my command? ' The distracted gentlemen flew about, but I could see in a moment that Henry was not likely to turn up, so I begged the King to get into his motor. He answered with indigna-tion, ' Certainly not ! I cannot start without the Prime Minister.' He looked first at his watch and then at the Castle clock, and fussed crossly about the yard. Seeing affairs at a standstill, I went up to the Queen and said I feared there had been a scandal at Court, and that Henry must have eloped with one of the Maids of Honour. I begged her to save my blushes by commanding the King to proceed, at which she limped up to him with her amazing grace, and in her charming way, tapping him firmly on the arm, pointed with a sweeping gesture to his motor, and invited Gracie Raincliffe (Lady Londesborough) and Alice Keppel to accompany him : at which they all drove off. . . . When we returned to the Castle we found that Henry had gone for a long walk with the Hon. Violet Vivian, one of the Queen's Maids of Honour, over which the King was jovial and even eloquent.''

An inimitable picture, and worthy to rank with one of Lord Hervey's entertaining and amazing glimpses of the domestic side of the Court of George the Second and Queen Caroline of Anspach. Mrs. Asquith has, indeed, all the equipment of a gossiping historian and more, for she can sketch a character most deftly. Her estimate of Edward the Seventh is very just : —

'' Our King devotes what time he does not spend upon sport and pleasure ungrudgingly to duty. He subscribes to his cripples, rewards his sailors, reviews his soldiers, and opens bridges, bazaars, hospitals, and railway tunnels with enviable sweetness. He is fond of Henry, but is not really interested in any man. He is loyal to all his West End friends, female admirers, Jewish financiers, and Newmarket bloods : and adds to fine manners rare prestige, courage, and simplicity.''

The courage of the King at the advent of Death was superb. He loved life and all the pleasures it provided in his eminent position. Yet he met the end with amazing fortitude, and fought every step through the darkening shadows with intrepid bravery. He gave audiences the day before he died, and even on the day of his death: '' It is practically over; he is unconscious. He sent for Sir Ernest Cassel this morning and insisted on sitting up in his clothes although breathless and unable to speak; his courage is amazing.'' George the Fourth also died bravely, although Thackeray suppressed all mention of the fact when cataloguing his vices and failings; for some days before the end he could only sleep sitting up at a table with his head supported on his hand, for he could not breathe lying down. And at the last, when the King fell forward into the arms of his little page, Sir Wathen Waller, all he said was : " My boy, *this is death*."

On the night of the death of Edward the Seventh, Mrs. Asquith dined with Mrs. George West, " and met Winston Churchill, the Crewes, and the Harcourts. At the end of dinner Winston said, ' Let us drink to the health of the new King.' To which Lord Crewe answered, ' Rather to the memory of the old.' " That was well said. Mrs. Asquith's picturesque accounts of the King's funeral; of her husband's succession to the Premiership; of the scenes in 1914 when the war clouds burst, are all of authentic value.

THE FARINGTON DIARY: THE FIRST VOLUME.*

The Farington Diary,† ever since it commenced to appear serially in *The Morning Post,* has been received with much interest and approbation—and deservedly so, despite its limitations. It is already the co-equal of Greville, Creevey, Crabb Robinson, and Evelyn on the bookshelf where stand the notable diarists, but it cannot claim to be a rival of Pepys, for Farington has little to relate or reveal of his own personality. His style is dull, and, in general, ungrammatical; his entries are restricted often to the baldest detail and destitute of any interest. Thus:—

" Rose this morning at 7. Breakfasted at a little past 8. Employed myself in washing my river views, while Sir George was painting. Dined at 4. Drank tea between 6 and 7—and went to bed at ½ past 10. "

But in acute contrast may follow an entry of great human interest:—

" Boswell told me it was not by advice of any medical friend that Dr. Johnson was induced to leave off drinking wine. A constant apprehension which he had of becoming insane made him fear the consequence of continuing the use of it. Yet he often declared he had never been known to have been intoxicated, though he said he once at College drank three bottles at a sitting. "

Farington has been extremely fortunate in finding a most painstaking and thorough editor in Mr. James Greig. No point in the text has been too small for his careful attention; but he might have furnished a more complete introductory memoir of Farington himself, and added a few additional elucidatory details to certain entries in the *Diary* which I may specify presently. Further, his method of introducing notes within brackets in the midst of the diarist's statements is not to be commended. For example:—

" I met G. Steevens [1736-1800] at the Shakespeare Gallery. He told me his library consisted of about 5,000 volumes. [His books realised £2,740 on May 13th, 1800.] He mentioned the library of Lord Spencer as being the most select in England and not worth less than £30,000. [In 1892 this splendid collection, greatly added to, was purchased by Mrs. Rylands, and is now in the Rylands Library, Manchester.]"

This kind of thing ruins all illusion of a personal, spontaneous narrative, and brings the deadening atmosphere of a museum catalogue. Perhaps, however, Mr. Greig adopted this form of

* *The Fortnightly Review,* September, 1923.
† *The Farington Diary,* by Joseph Farington, R.A. Edited by James Greig. Vol. 1 (1793-1802). (Hutchinson & Co., 21s. net.)

notes within the text after seing the vilely small type which the printers have used for his valuable footnotes. These latter are practically lost and useless; for only those blessed with the most powerful eyesight could endure the prolonged strain of deciphering frequent notes, often covering a third of the page, in the minute type which is called, I believe, " Diamond." The fact is, the book is too long for one volume. The present instalment of the *Diary*, with the constant notes, is of immense length, and should have been produced in at least two volumes.

So much for criticism, which I hope the editor will believe is offered in no captious spirit, but solely with the view that *The Farington Diary* will eventually be re-published in a form and types worthy of its importance. For it is a very valuable addition, as a whole, to the records of its period—from 1793 to 1802 in the present volume, though it is understood the entries continue until December 30th, 1821, the day of the diarist's sudden death. Joseph Farington was staying near Manchester, and had attended morning and afternoon service at Didsbury Church. Although seventy-five years of age, he went to the evening service too, and his niece relates in breathless detail, devoid of punctuation, the tragic sequel:—

" The Service concluded he was descending from the Gallery where his Brother's Pew was—but his hands encumbered with hat Umbrella and prayer book—His feet equally so with Golloshes he was unable to recover from a slip of his feet and went down the flight of stairs with great rapidity and force—such as to project him beyond the Stairs—so that his head came with heavy fall on the pavement of the Church floor—the vital spark was gone. He neither looked spoke moved—or breathed again. Such was the WILL OF GOD—and *doubtless all in Mercy.*"

Yes, no doubt; but, still, rather a peculiar death, and very disconcerting for all present, particularly the chief actor in the scene. It is so easy for the survivors to be resigned and philosophic about a death.

Joseph Farington was a Lancashire man. One branch of the family, of Worden Hall, Lancs., spelt the name ffarington. James Nowell ffarington married Sarah, daughter and co-heiress of John Touchet, of Broome Hall, Eccles, the last male representative of the ancient Lancashire family of Touchet, members of which had been Earls of Castlehaven and Barons Audley in earlier years. The John Touchet mentioned above was offered the revival in his favour of the title of Earl of Castlehaven in 1837, but he declined the honour, having no male heir. The maternal grandmother of Harrison Ainsworth, the Lancashire novelist, was Ann Touchet, and I happen to possess a copy of *Sir John Chiverton*, an early romance written by J. P. Aston, of

Manchester, with the collaboration of Ainsworth, which is inscribed to a member of the Farington family.

Joseph Farington, the diarist, was the son of a clergyman, the rector of Warrington, and formerly of Leigh, where the future Royal Academician was born in 1747. He was apprenticed as a boy to Richard Wilson, and when he became a student at the Royal Academy Schools he endeavoured to emulate the fine performances of that excellent scenic artist. Some of Farington's topographical drawings are very good, particularly one of Edinburgh Castle, executed in 1778.

Joseph Farington was elected an Associate of the Royal Academy in 1783, and he attained to the full degree of a Royal Academician two years later—quite a rapid promotion in view of the fact that he was but thirty-eight years of age and by no means in the front rank of contemporary artists. But he was a good man of business, and useful to the Council of the Royal Academy. Much of his *Diary* relates to the affairs of the institution and the election of new members and officials.

Farington settled in London at 35, Upper Charlotte Street, Fitzroy Square, in 1780, but it was not until thirteen years later that he commenced to make notes in a journal concerning the eminent (and sometimes unimportant) people he met or heard particulars of from his friends. As I have said, *The Farington Diary* is no intimate revelation of the writer's personality; and, unlike his most famous diarian rivals, he is not particularly interested in the gossip and scandals of his time: rather is it a plodding, conscientious record of the (to him) interesting things the diarist heard and saw and did—a sort of petty cash ledger translated into terms of social doings and conversation and the affairs of the Royal Academy.

Just as Farington excelled as a topographical artist, so the chief charm, to me, of his *Diary* is to be found in its frequent and unexpected topographical details of London at the close of the eighteenth century. Like J. T. Smith in *Nollekens and his Times* and *A Book for a Rainy Day*, Farington is meticulous in his details of where notable people lived. That is a matter of absorbing interest for those who believe that personality is influenced strongly by environment—particularly in early years— and that houses may retain the influences of great passions, joy and sorrow and crime, experienced or enacted there in the past. As the late William De Morgan used to say, the occupant of every house ought to write an account of his experiences and adventures therein and secrete the manuscript somewhere in the house, where it could be found in future ages for the benefit of students of humanity and history.   To proceed, Farington notes on August 28th, 1797 : —

" Marchi called.   He dined yesterday with Mr. and Mrs Radcliffe the authoress.   She is daughter to Mr. Ward who was a bookseller at Bath.   Mrs. Radcliffe is 27 or 8 years old, a pretty face.   Marchi told her of Johnson and Goldsmith coming to Sir Joshua Reynolds, she said, those were fine times.   Mr. Radcliffe was educated at Oxford. . . . He is about 30 years old and democratically inclined.   They reside at No. 7, Medina Place—St. George's Fields.''

Now, such an entry as this has both biographical and topographical value.   1797 was the year in which Mrs. Radcliffe published *The Italian*, and it has not hitherto been recorded where she wrote this romance.   Possibly, also, *The Mysteries of Udolpho* (1794) was conceived during her residence in St. George's Fields, which was then a rural district situated between the Borough and Kennington Road.   Villas had just begun to be erected on this lonely marshland, hitherto only occupied by dubious resorts such as the Apollo Gardens and " The Dog and the Duck ''—plebeian imitations of Ranelagh and Vauxhall, and the haunts of St. Giles's roughs and Drury Lane nymphs : —

" St. George's Fields, with taste of fashion struck,
Display Arcadia at ' The Dog and Duck,'
And Drury misses here, in tawdry pride,
Are there ' Pastoras ' by the fountain side.''

So Garrick wrote in 1774.   In 1780, St. George's Fields were the scene of the assembly of the Gordon Rioters.   But the hand of the builder was busy in the two following decades, and by 1812 the authors of *Rejected Addresses* were able to write : —

" St. George's Fields are fields no more,
The trowel supersedes the plough ;
Huge inundated swamps of yore
Are changed to civic villas now.''

A few more years, and the " civic villas '' vanished before the Robotian onrush of sordid streets and commercial undertakings, and St. George's Fields are but a name in what is now St. George's Circus.

Farington was able to commence his journal in July, 1793, with interesting accounts of two visits to Horace Walpole at Strawberry Hill, where on each occasion the host showed, and discoursed upon, the treasures of his " Gothic Vatican,'' and on each evening Mr. Berry and his two daughters came over to dine from Little Strawberry Hill, which was on the Teddington side of Walpole's property.   Mr. Greig does not point out that the Berrys had taken up their residence at Little Strawberry Hill in 1791, and that Walpole subsequently bequeathed the house to Mary and Agnes Berry for life. They survived until 1852, and thus linked up the centuries in a remarkable way, for, as Thackeray observed in a well quoted passage, Mary Berry had known Johnson and Fox and all the brilliant society of the eighteenth century, and had been asked in marriage (as was her sister also) by Horace Walpole, " who had been patted on the head by George the First."

Previously, Little Strawberry Hill had been occupied by another of Walpole's fair friends, Kitty Clive, the actress, who died here in 1785. A later resident was Alderman Matthew Wood, the doughty civic champion of Queen Caroline in 1820, and twice Lord Mayor of London. Wood was the father of Lord Hatherley, the Lord Chancellor, and the grandfather of Sir Evelyn Wood, the late Lady Barrett-Lennard, and Mrs. O'Shea, who subsequently married Parnell. Such are the vagaries of genealogy.

When Farington visited Strawberry Hill, Walpole alluded to the number of French *emigrés* of high distinction then living in Richmond and the neighbourhood owing to the Revolution in France. Some illumination on this subject will be found in the memoirs of the Marquise de la Tour du Pin* This lady, born a Dillon, and a near relative of Lord Dillon, Lord Kenmare, and the Jerninghams, had been brought up in France, and married the Comte de Gouvernet, who, after the death of his father by the guillotine in 1794, succeeded to the title of de la Tour du Pin. With the aid of Tallien they came to England, and in 1798 secured a little house on The Green at Richmond—evidently it was situated in what is now called Old Palace Terrace. The place was leased at a rent of £45 from a former actress at Drury Lane Theatre:—

" This little house, which was a real jewel, was only fifteen feet wide. On the ground floor was a hall, a pretty salon with two windows, and then a stairway which was hardly visible. The first floor comprised two charming bedrooms, and the floor above, two other rooms for servants. At the end of the hall, on the ground floor, was a nice kitchen which looked out on a miniature garden, with only a path and two flower-beds. There were rugs everywhere and fine English oilcloth in the passage-ways and upon the staircase."

So really, except for the rent, things in 1798 were much as to-day when Russian princes and princesses, exiled from their country, so bravely face the problem of existence in England, and are content with a little house in the suburbs of London in

---

* *Recollections of the Revolution and the Empire,* by La Marquise de la Tour du Pin. Edited and translated by Walter Geer. (Jonathan Cape, 30s. net.)

lieu of their former palaces by the Neva. Next door to Madame de la Tour du Pin at Richmond was "a rich Alderman of London," but as she proceeds to note:—

"England, where there are fortunes so immense, existences so luxurious, is at the same time the country in the world where poor people can live in the most comfortable manner. For instance, there is no necessity for going to market. The butcher never fails a single day to come at a fixed hour crying 'Butcher' at your door. You open the door and tell him what you want. Is a leg of lamb? He brings it all arranged ready to put it upon the spit. Is it lamb chops? They are arranged on a little wooden platter which he calls for the following day. On a slip of paper are written the weight and the price."

So, again, the ways of the conservative butcher remain as they were one hundred and twenty-five years ago.

Another French *emigré* at Richmond was Monsieur de Poix, and Madame de Duras was at Teddington. Madame de la Tour du Pin formed an intimate friendship with Lydia White, the famous "Blue-Stocking," who was then living temporarily at Richmond with her sister:—

"She had conceived for me a kind of romantic passion. . . . One of these ladies sang well, and we enjoyed our music together. Their books were at my disposal. When I went to visit them in the morning they kept me with them the whole day, and, when the evening arrived, I was only able to tear myself away by promising to return before the end of the week. Having formed the plan of passing a week at London, they implored Monsieur de la Tour du Pin to permit me to accompany them. This little trip to London with Miss Lydia White and her sister put me somewhat in touch with Society. We went to the Opera and they also took me to a large assembly at the house of a lady whom I hardly saw. There were people on the stairway, and no one was able to sit down. We had great difficulty in leaving the house, the crowd of guests was so numerous. At the end of the week, which appeared to me long and tiresome, I returned with pleasure to Richmond. . . . Towards the end of the winter Miss White left Richmond. This was a real grief to me, not because we had formed a durable friendship, but because she had been so kind to me that I had found her sojourn in our neighbourhood very agreeable."

I think this is one of the earliest references in print to Lydia White. In 1808, Walter Scott makes amusing mention of her visit to Scotland in a letter to Lady Louisa Stuart: "Pray don't triumph over me too much in the case of Lydia. I stood a very respectable siege; but she caressed my wife, coaxed my children, and made, by dint of cake and pudding, some impression even upon the affections of my favourite dog; so, when all the outworks were carried, the main fortress had no choice but to surrender on honourable terms. To the best of my thinking, notwithstanding the cerulean hue of her stockings, and a most plentiful stock of eccentric affectation, she is really at bottom a good-natured woman, with much liveliness and some talent." Eighteen years afterwards Scott went to see her at 113, Park Street, Grosvenor Square, where she had held her famous *salon* for so many years. Now the shadows were drawing in, and Sir Walter relates: " Went to poor Lydia White's, and found her extended on a couch, frightfully swelled, unable to stir, rouged, jesting, and dying. She has a good heart, and is really a clever creature, but unhappily, or rather happily, she has set up the whole staff of her rest in keeping literary society about her. The world has not neglected her. . . . She is wealthy, to be sure, and gives *petit* dinners, but not in a style to carry the point *à force d'argent.*" Two months later she died, living her chosen life to the end, for on January 28th, 1827, Scott notes in his Journal: " Hear of Miss White's death. Poor Lydia! She gave a dinner on the Friday before, and had written with her own hand invitations for another party. Twenty years ago she used to tease me with her youthful affectations—her dressing like the Queen of Chimney-sweeps on May Day morning, etc.; and sometimes with letting her wit run wild. But she *was* a woman of wit, and had a feeling and kind heart. Poor Lydia! "

So passed the last of the Bas Bleu, although one other of the coterie survived until 1840 in the person of old Lady Cork (Mary Monckton), who claims a moiety of being the original of Lady Kew in *The Newcomes*. But Lady Cork was not the hostess of highly cultured society in the sense Lydia White was to the last. Lydia White was the Miss Diddle of Byron's " Literary Eclogue," *The Blues*: —

> " Miss Diddle invites us to sup.
> Then at two hours past midnight we all meet again,
> For the sciences, sandwiches, hock and champagne."

She had no successor, for though Lady Holland held a famous *salon* and Lady Blessington was a delightful hostess and charming in conversation, their dinner parties did not claim to be more than reunions where brilliant men of all professions and arts talked at their best on general subjects; the converse at Holland House and Gore House never soared to the cerulean empyrean as it did at 113, Park Street, in the days—or, rather, nights—of Lydia White.

MR. BARING-GOULD'S MEMOIRS.*

THE REV. S. BARING-GOULD has much to be thankful for. He has lived, at the present time, until nearly ninety years of age, and has ever found life set in pleasant places and full of varied interests. He had the privilege of being born a member of a notable Devon family and, after his twelfth year, having for home a beautiful Devonian Manor House, Lew Trenchard, which had been in the possession of his forebears since the early seventeenth century; so here was an inheritance of tradition and romance. Further, Mr. Baring-Gould had the advantage as a boy of much travel on the Continent during the period 1837-1851, and he must be one of the last survivors who can remember Europe in those distant days. His parents travelled in the old pleasant way of leisurely comfort in their own carriage and with their own horses and servants. The life they led was much like that described by Charles Lever in *The Daltons* and *Davenport Dunn*, and by Dickens in the Continental portion of *Little Dorrit*.

In later life Mr. Baring-Gould presents an admirable example of the Squarson—for he is both Squire and Parson of Lew Trenchard—and he has had the joy of restoring both his Church and Manor House, as he resolved to do when he was but a youth of seventeen. He formed a third purpose at the same age—the moral and spiritual improvement of the parish of Lew, and no doubt that has been accomplished also since he presented himself to the benefice forty-two years ago.

Mr. Baring-Gould is the author of such well-known hymns as *Onward, Christian Soldiers* and *Now the Day is Over*, and of quite a hundred books since his first appeared in 1854, when he was twenty. The titles of his volumes adumbrate his extraordinarily diversified interests. All kinds of literature are represented—history, biography, poetry, topography, religion, folklore, church history, fairy tales, ghosts, and many novels. All through his literary output runs the thread of his love for old legends and customs and ghostly lore, and these are the subjects I find of most interest in his latest book†—the records and beliefs of a past or fast vanishing rustic order in the English countryside. Mr. Baring-Gould laments the disappearance of the fairies and pixies as a result of a new alleged superior knowledge of the peasantry : —

---

* *The Fortnightly Review,* September, 1923.
† *Early Reminiscences,* 1834-1864, by S. Baring-Gould. (John Lane, The Bodley Head. Illustrated. 16s. net.)
303

" How noticeable in the progress of mankind in knowledge is the fact that before the opening of a door hitherto shut, another door that has swung wide for generations should be slammed and double bolted. For untold ages our ancestors had believed in a fairy world. The little soulless people had been seen by men of good report, their songs had reached wondering ears, their good deeds and their malicious tricks were commonly related; but almost suddenly, that is to say in my life-time, belief in the existence of pixies, elves, gnomes, has melted away; and in its place a door has been opened, disclosing to our astonished eyes a whole bacterial world, swarming with microbes, living, making love, fighting; some beneficial and others noxious. . . . Now all the spiritual world has vanished out of sight and is lost to the mind. Not a child knows aught now of its occupants. We have cast aside Oberon, Titania, Robin Goodfellow, the Brownie, Wag at the Wa', and the Wild Huntsman with the Gabelrachet. Their place has been usurped by the Bacilli, by Schizophyta, and Sphæro bacteria, Micro bacteria, Desmo bacteria, and Spiro bacteria. What Shakespeare of the future will think of giving us a Bacteriological Midsummer Night's Dream? "

But I am not so sure that a belief in the supernatural world has altogether vanished from the English countryside (it survives, of course, in Ireland and the Scottish Highlands). I fancy the older denizens round Pendle Hill still cherish a belief in the occult—a legacy from their ancestors in that district when it was the particular location of the Lancashire witches in the time of James the First, those lonely heaths and ravines and hills, the site of : —

> " Malkin's Tower . . . where
> Report makes caitiff witches meet to swear
> Their homage to the devil, and contrive
> The deaths of men and beasts."

In Suffolk, too, the generation that is now old certainly believe in many superstitions and ghostly manifestations. My own nurse in childhood was firmly persuaded she had seen the East Anglian " Shuck Dog "—a spectral black hound, with flaming eyes, which came suddenly upon a belated pedestrian in lonely lanes at night. It was not actively offensive, but ran silently, the great paws soundless on the road, beside the affrighted victim until human aid or distant lights materialised. " The Shuck Dog " is, or was, I opine, in the same ghostly category as " The Gytrash," the Northern spectre which Charlotte Brontë mentions in that wonderfully vivid scene where Jane Eyre first meets Rochester on a winter's evening as the daylight waned and the moon rose. She is sitting on a stile, and she hears the clang of an invisible horse's hooves approaching on the frozen road :

" As this horse approached, and as I watched for it to appear through the dusk, I remembered certain of Bessie's tales, wherein figured a North-of-England spirit, called a ' Gytrash '; which, in the form of horse, mule, or large dog, haunted solitary ways, and sometimes came upon belated travellers, as this horse was now coming upon me."

The invisible horse was the portent of the Unknown, the Footsteps of Fate riding into her life, bringing tragedy and romance. The Unknown, the supernatural, the fear of what lies beyond the shadows—these are the causes of the original belief in ghosts and midnight terrors. Poor Humanity lives, with amazing bravery, under a perpetual Sword of Damocles, which may fall at any moment without the slightest warning—the incredible and inevitable horror, *Death*, perhaps attended by pain and agony. Most of us forget this appalling foe, who ever lurks near, when we are in good health and happy; but for the imaginative and those cognisant of the beauty and joy of this world it is an ever-present and fearsome reality. If there had been no Death there would be no belief in ghosts and spectres, for these last are but emanations from the terrors of the tomb. It is conclusive proof of man's belief in the finality and irrevocableness of Death that he has ever recoiled from any spectral visitant in the guise of a living being, whether human or merely animal. If from a room where a corpse has been left alone there should be heard sounds of knocking or footsteps what amazement and terror would be caused among the living: there would be no joyful anticipation that he who was reputed dead had returned to life. All the stories of those who have returned to consciousness and movement from a state of cataleptic trance relate that they were received with horror and shrieks of fear on the part of their relations and friends. No, Death creates an irremovable barrier, and those who have gone over can no more be visible, without fear and dread, to mortal eyes; and anything in the semblance of a shadow from the unknown land is correlated to both ghosts and the grave.

When dealing with legends and superstitions, Mr. Baring-Gould makes some mention of *The Corpse Candle*—which the hoary-headed eld asserted took the form of a pale blue flame flickering over the site of a future grave in the churchyard; the light would then travel to the house of the person about to die. After the death had occurred, two lights flickered along the lanes, side by side, back to the churchyard. One evening the Rev. Dr. Bussell, a former Vice-Principal of Brasenose College, Oxford, was dining with Mr. Baring-Gould, and after he had left he soon returned, because he had seen a blue flame dancing above a grave in the churchyard. It would, of course, be easy to evoke some cheap wit about this post-prandial occurrence; but Mr. Baring-Gould advised his guest to return home by another route and

U

avoid the churchyard, and Dr. Bussell did so.   Mr. Baring-Gould
has written a ballad on this subject wedded to an old Devonshire
air.   It commences : —

> " All under the stars, and beneath the green tree,
> All over the sward, and along the cold lea
>   A little blue flame
>   A-fluttering came,
> It came from the churchyard for you or for me."

This reminds me of Harrison Ainsworth's ballad *The Corpse
Candle*, in *Rookwood* : —

> " Through the midnight gloom did a pale blue light
> To the churchyard mirk wing its lonesome flight :
> Thrice it floated those old walls round—
> Thrice it paused—till the grave it found.
> Over the grass-green sod it glanced,
> Over the fresh-turned earth it danced,
> Like a torch in the night breeze quivering—
> Never was seen so gay a thing !
> Never was seen so blithe a sight
> As the midnight dance of that pale blue light.
>
> Now, what of that pale blue flame dost know?
> Canst tell where it comes from, or where it will go?
> Is it the soul, released from clay,
> Over the earth that takes its way,
> And tarries a moment in mirth and glee
> Where the corse it hath quitted interr'd shall be?
> Or is it the trick of some fanciful sprite,
> That taketh in mortal mischance delight,
> And marketh the road the coffin shall go
> And the spot where the dead shall be soon laid low?
> Ask him, who can answer these questions aright ;
> I know not the cause of that pale blue light !''

Mr. Baring-Gould has a very impressive ghost attached to
his family place in the similitude of his great-great-grandmother,
Margaret Gould, *née* Belfield, and known as " Old Madam,"
who died in her great high-backed chair in 1795.   She haunts
both the gallery at Lew Trenchard and the surrounding avenues
and orchards.   Her very first appearance as a ghost has
remarkable proof attached to the story.   A young man from a
neighbouring village had gone to America in Madam Gould's
life-time.   After some years he returned, and hiring a horse a
Tavistock he rode to his home.   It was a clear, moonlit night
and as he passed through the Lew Valley he noticed to the lef
of the road a plough on which was seated the figure of Madan
Gould.   He recognised her at once, as the moon shone full o:
her uplifted face, and taking off his hat he called out, " I wis
you a very good-night, Madam."   She bowed in return, an
waved her hand, on which, the man observed, sparkled diamon

rings. On reaching Galford, after greeting his relatives, he said, " What do you think? I have seen that strange old Madam Gould sitting on a plough, this time of the night, looking at the moon." All who heard him stared with a blank expression. Then said one: " Madam was buried seven days ago in Lew Church."

I have dwelt overlong, perhaps, on the ghostly records in Mr. Baring-Gould's book, and left myself no space in which to consider other aspects of his very entertaining reminiscences. He has much to relate of Devonshire life in mid-Victorian times, of his own early travels on the Continent, of his experiences at Cambridge, and as a young priest, the whole interspersed with many good stories of a by no means rigidly clerical nature. One concerns the late Baron de Stern (later Lord Michelham) when he stood as Parliamentary candidate for a Kentish constituency. He was being heckled as to his Austrian antecedents, and someone shouted: " Who and what are you? " Stern replied: " I am a Baron, and mein fader was Baron, too." To which his interlocutor responded: " Pity your modder was not barren also! "

One is also pleased by the story of the Baring-Goulds's Devonshire coachman, Pengelly, who accompanied them to the Continent. At St. Jean-de-Luz, on one occasion being very hungry he entered a restaurant, and expressed his desire for immediate food, thus: " *Je suis fameux.*" " *Je le crois bien, monsieur!* " said the *restaurateur*, bowing, but without making any movement to supply Pengelly's wants. He, convinced that he had made some mistake, rectified his assertion, by saying: " *J'ai une femme grosse.*"

" *Ah! monsieur, je suis charmé de l'entendre: j'espère qu'elle aura des couches heureuses.*"

Pengelly, feeling that he was again misunderstood, in a loud and important tone declared: " *Mossoo! Je suis femme.*" " *Mais c'est incroyable—et avec de si beaux favoris!* " Pengelly's whiskers were of a sandy colour.

Mr. Baring-Gould's *Early Reminiscences* comprise the first thirty years of his life; he must soon publish the second series, which will bring him to sixty years of age; and I hope he will accomplish the record of the third thirty years, for never before has an octogenarian—nay, nonagenarian—plied such a lively and active reminiscent pen, or looked back over the long vista of life with such fresh and perennial interest.

The FARINGTON DIARY: THE SECOND VOLUME.*

THE second volume of *The Farington Diary*† proves to be a better book in form than the first, for it is not so abundant, and is consequently more convenient to handle. The contents, too, suffer no diminution of interest, because the period, 1802-1804, this second instalment covers was an eventful and memorable one. It commences with a very interesting account of Farington's visit to France during the brief Peace of Amiens—that curious little interval in the Napoleonic saga of storm, when, for a year, the Drums of War were silent, and every English person who could rushed over to Paris, and various French people of distinction came to London. Among the latter was Madame Récamier, who presented to astonished English eyes the first glimpse of the coming scanty modes of the Empire. Emma Sophia, Countess Brownlow, noted in her *Reminiscences of a Septuagenarian* that Madame Récamier " appeared in Kensington Gardens *à l'antique*, a muslin gown clinging to her form like the folds of the drapery on a statue; her hair in a plait at the back, and falling in small ringlets round her face, and greasy with *huile antique;* a large veil thrown over the head completed her attire, that not unnaturally caused her to be followed and stared at."

But over all the restless, laughing " General Post " game of social movement and reunion between France and England there was a tension—a conviction that these diversions were but a lull in the storm, and that the Dogs of War would again be unleashed as soon as it suited the ambitious plans of Napoleon. And so it proved. Farington saw the First Consul several times. On the first occasion it was a review of six thousand troops—horse, foot, and artillery—in the great Court of the Tuileries:—

" At 10 minutes past 12 a body of officers rushed hastily out of the great entrance of the Palace and mounted their horses, and were followed by Buonaparte, who was upon his white horse almost as soon as seen, and advanced forward, followed by a cluster of Generals, among whom were Berthier and Murat and aides-de-camp, along the first line of troops. He was dressed in Blue with White waistcoat and Breeches. His Hat, quite plain, with a very small Cockade. After passing along the front of every line He took his stand in the front of the Thullieries before the great entrance, where I had a constant and full view of him,

---

* *The Fortnightly Review*, November, 1923.
† *The Farington Diary*, by Joseph Farington, R.A. Edited by James Greig. Volume II (1802-1804). (Hutchinson & Co., 21s. net.)

and had the opportunity I wished to consider his appearance and manner.
. . . As all circumstances are remarkable about an extraordinary man,
I noticed that He picked His nose very much—sometimes took Snuff,
and would take off His Hat and wipe his forehead in a careless manner.
. . . the Troops were passing before him in a state of the highest
display, and the most exact order, with Trumpets and musick, which
had a very military effect.''

Farington in this passage is quite at his best, for, despite his
careless grammar and spelling, he paints a picture which vividly
conforms with the scene as one has mentally fixed it from
numerous paintings and the illustrations Phiz furnished for
Charles Lever's *Tom Burke*—the figure of Napoleon, plainly
dressed, on his white horse at the head of a cluster of generals
in brilliant uniforms, the curveting horses, the parading troops,
with the crash of their bands and rolling drums, the dust, and
the roar of the saluting cannon of the Invalides—it is all as real
as an actual memory.

The review over, Farington, in the company of Samuel
Rogers, proceeded to the first landing of the grand staircase of
the Palace in order to get a near view of Napoleon :—

" He passed me so close that I could have touched him. His eye
having glanced upon strangers, when He came opposite to me He looked
me full in the face, which gave me an opportunity to observe the colour
of his eyes which are lighter, and more of blue grey than I should have
expected from his complexion. . . I thought there was something rather
feverish than piercing in the expression of his eyes, but his general aspect
was milder than I had before thought it. . . . His person is below the
middle size. I do not think more than 5 feet 6, I rather judge him to be
less than that measure. . . . He is not what can be called thin. Rogers
stood a little way from me and had an equally good opportunity of seeing
him, and observed that He looked us both full in the face. Rogers
seemed to be disappointed in the look of his countenance and said it was
that of a little Italian. That he had no eye-brows or eye-lash to
give strong expression, and that his eye was rather weak. . . . His
general appearance from his dress (Blue and White) bore some resemblance to the Uniform of the Officers of the English Navy,* and while
I endeavoured, while viewing him, to consider what I should think of
him simply as a man, I thought he would be a very passable figure upon
an English quarter deck. The Physiognomist might perhaps write a
dissertation upon the form of his head and his countenance ; to do that
I am not qualified. What struck me was that there are points of *determination* in the formation of his head and in his features. It would be
extravagant to say that there is that expressed about him which denotes
that such a man must be superior to others in an eminent degree, but I
certainly felt no disappointment on seeing him after all I had heard of
his character, unless it was that his deportment was more easy and open
than I had pictured to myself.''

It is interesting to compare these accounts with the more

---

* Farington notes in another entry that he saw a bust of Nelson (executed
by Mrs. Damer) in one of Napoleon's private rooms in the Tuileries.

sentimental one of Lady Brownlow, to whom I alluded just now, for she witnessed apparently this same review before the Tuileries on October 7th, 1802. She says Napoleon " was attended by Rustan, his favourite Mameluke, in his national costume; and le Prince Eugène de Beauharnais, the son of Josephine, was there, commanding, I think, the light cavalry; but my eyes and attention were riveted on Buonaparte. He was then thin, and his figure appeared to be *mesquin;* but how grand was his face, with its handsome features, its grave and stern and somewhat melancholy expression ! A face once seen never to be forgotten. It fascinated and acted upon me like a rattlesnake, for, though a mere child, I felt all the English horror of the man, and yet could not look at him without admiration and awe." Lady Brownlow's *Reminiscences of a Septuagenarian,* by the way, received the distinction of a special review by George Meredith in *The Fortnightly Review* on February 1st, 1868.

When in Paris, Farington visited the Tivoli Gardens in the Rue de Clichy, and witnessed a scene which might well be one of to-day in a modern " Palais du Danse " in England :—

" It is a Vauxhall, but upon a larger scale. It appeared to me that some thousands of persons were assembled, and all was gaiety and pleasure. The dancing was to me a very agreeable sight, for I then saw the French in their element. There are large spaces near the Orchestra covered with boards, answering the purposes of stages on which the people assemble and dance, hundreds of couples being in motion at the same time. The effect was very gratifying to see them striving at their favourite exercise who should be most alert or most graceful. The woemen were light, airy, and easy in their motions, and their persons, in general, well formed for the purpose. The men appeared in comparison to much disadvantage; inelegant in their dress, and as below the class and rank of their woemen, and ill-suited to them as partners.

" One tune seemed to have a magical effect upon them, it was that to the ' Walse Dance.' It was no sooner played than a Couple began to turn round, which is the whole figure of the dance, and as they moved forward, proceeding in this circular motion, they were followed by other couples, that never ceased to advance while the music of the Orchestra continued. I observed that in this dance the man makes a Circle with his arms, within which the woman continually turns round. Many of the woemen assumed attitudes while turning to appear easy and graceful, and those who were most perfect in it seemed to receive scarcely the touch of a finger from the man. A few that were clumsy made a rolling, awkward business of it. . What particularly surprised me was that no giddiness appeared to be caused by it, which shews what practice and habit will do. On observing this multitude I could not but be sensible that beauty among the woemen is much more rare than it is in England in large assemblies, but in form, and more particularly in carriage, the French woemen cannot be looked upon without much interest."

Farington's editor, Mr. Greig, might have added a note about the history of the waltz. It would seem that the steps have changed somewhat since Farington wrote of " the walse " that " the man makes a Circle with his arms, within which the woman continually turns round." The origin of the waltz is a favourite subject for dispute among quidnuncs. The Germans claim it as their national dance, and the Austrians brought it to melodic perfection in the flowing rhythms of the Strauss family. (" The Blue Danube " dates from 1867, and Mr. John Drinkwater, or his producer, was, therefore, historically incorrect when he caused that waltz to be played in the ballroom scene of his play, *Robert E. Lee*, which portrays events in 1861-1862). In all probability, the waltz is a direct descendant of La Volte, danced at Paris as early as 1178, and later known in England as the Lavolta of the sixteenth and seventeenth centuries. Sir John Davies wrote of this dance in 1596 : —

> " Where arm-in-arm two dancers are entwined
> And while themselves with strict embracements bound,
> And still their feet an anapest do sound."

An anapest represents three syllables, the last being accentuated.

All books of reference seem to repeat the error that the waltz was first introduced into England in 1813—that is, eleven years after Farington saw it danced in Paris. But it certainly was known and practised over here much earlier. Mary Russell Mitford related she learned the waltz in 1801; and a *Domestic Encyclopædia* of 1802 heavily propounded : —

> " In the heavy days of autumn and winter, when the atmosphere is loaded with humid particles, when a sedentary life disposes the human body to hypochondriacal affections, dancing is an admirable amusement. . . . . But these maniacal turnings and gesticulations which have lately become fashionable in this country under the appellation of German Vaults (or rather, *walsen,* i.e., performing a circular motion, like that of a man on the eve of intoxication) are attended with very different effects. . . ."

And so on, until the Encyclopædist finally and alarmingly advances " that avenging disease, *Consumption,*" as the penalty of violent dancing.

Byron's " Apostrophic Hymn," *The Waltz*, was written in 1812, and published the following year. In this poem the date of the arrival of the waltz craze in England is placed contemporaneously with the news of Austerlitz, namely, 1805 : —

> " O Muse of motion ! say,
> How first to Albion found thy Waltz her way? . . .
> While unburnt Moscow yet had news to send,
> Nor owed her fiery exit to a friend,
> She came—Waltz came—and with her certain sets
> Of true despatches, and as true gazettes :
> Then flamed of Austerlitz the blest despatch . . ."

Byron, of course, in this pseudonymous production assumed
a mock virtuous attitude of reprobation of the waltz and the
intimate contact its exponents enjoyed : —

> " Hot from the hands promiscuously applied
> Round the slight waist, or down the flowing side,
> Where were the rapture then to clasp the form
> From this lewd grasp and lawless contact warm?
>
> . . . . .
>
> Approach the lip which all, without restraint,
> Come near enough—if not to touch—to taint ;
> If such thou lovest—love her then no more,
> Or give—like her—caresses to a score ;
> Her mind with these is gone, and with it go
> The little left behind it to bestow."

There exactly, from the words of a hundred and ten years ago,
we have the gravamen of the charges against the dancing of to-
day. Contemporary bishops, moral censors, and critics in tilting
at the immodest dances of 1923 and the scanty costumes of
the damsels who fox-trot (and fall, as represented nightly at
Wyndham's Theatre) imagine a vain thing if they believe they
wage war against new sins. Such laxities as they reprobate are
ever the aftermath of a great social convulsion like the recent
war. Let these grim judges study the feminine fashion plates of
the first fifteen years of the nineteenth century, and ponder over
this little paragraph from a paper dated June 8th, 1812 : —

" A young lady of rank and high condition, in the warmth of her
dancing heart, thus addressed her partner at the late Lord Mayor's
Ball : ' God bless you, take care and don't tread upon my muslin gown,
for you see that I have nothing under it.' "

In December, 1802, Stothard told Farington he had recently
been at Burleigh House executing some paintings for the first
Marquis of Exeter. He was much pleased with Lady Exeter, the
third wife, and formerly Elizabeth Duchess of Hamilton, " who
appears to conduct herself in a very domestick and proper manner
in the family, paying great attention to his Lordship's children
by a former wife."

Again, the editor might have pointed out that these " children
by a former wife" were those by Sarah Hoggins, the daughter of a
small shopkeeper of Bolas Magna, Shropshire—she who became
the " peasant " Countess of Exeter and the idealised heroine of
Tennyson's *Lord of Burleigh*. " Three fair children first she
bore him, then before her time she died." The children became
the second Marquis of Exeter, Colonel Lord Thomas Cecil, and
Lady Sophia Cecil, who married a member of the Pierrepont
family, and has the present Duke of Wellington for one of her
grandsons. Historians shatter all romances now, and when Mr

Vicary Gibbs published the fifth volume of *The Complete Peerage* he rather tarnished the Tennysonian idyll by pointing out that the eldest child of the " village maiden she " was born four months after the marriage with " John Jones," Lord Exeter. He had divorced his first wife the same year, 1791. The " peasant " Countess only lived for five years after her marriage, for she died in giving birth to her second son. Despite her uneuphonious name of Hoggins, her romantic story has attracted many poets and artists. In 1875 an oratorio—or rather cantata—based on her career was performed at the Birmingham Musical Festival.

A footnote on page 72 of *The Farington Diary* relating to an earlier Elizabeth Duchess of Hamilton—wife of the sixth Duke, and one of the beautiful Gunning sisters—contains an error which should be corrected in future editions. Maria Gunning is spoken of as " Lady Maria Coventry ": she was, of course, Maria Countess of Coventry. On page 150 the date of the marriage of Charles Townshend, Chancellor to the Exchequer, needs to be corrected from 1775 to 1755; and on page 59 the caption " Dieppe's One Pretty Street " is misleading: what Farington wrote was " Dieppe has one pretty long street," which is quite another thing to " pretty."

Farington has a reference to Mrs. Fitzherbert when she was present at the Royal Academy in 1804, on the occasion of the Prince of Wales's visit, and looked, according to Benjamin West, the President, like a "Mother Windsor "—meaning, presumably, an ungraceful, bunchy figure such as Queen Charlotte presented. The editor has gone astray in his footnote about Mrs. Fitzherbert in stating she " married first Thomas Fitzherbert, and then in 1774 Edward Weld." The facts were that she married first Edward Weld, in 1775, and he died the same year; his widow married Thomas Fitzherbert in 1778, and the Prince of Wales in 1785.

In 1803 Farington makes many interesting references to the expected invasion of England by Napoleon. All sorts of quidnuncs, as in 1914-1918, came forward with ideas of how the enemy would advance on London and how he should be met. At a meeting of the Deputy-Lieutenants of Middlesex, Lord Cathcart described his plan of defence when the Napoleonic hordes should approach London by the river Lea; and the mother and sisters of Halls, the artist, were removed from Colchester on the advice of General Sir J. Craggs. " The General said that if, unluckily, the French were to succeed in their first attack, they might in a few hours be in possession of Colchester, which is but ten miles

from the sea." On July 19th the motion of the Secretary of War
for arming all persons between the ages of seventeen and fifty-
five passed without opposition, but two weeks later, when
Farington took an agreeable walk through rural Chelsea he
noticed the crowds of people strolling about and enjoying the
fine weather—" The apprehension of Invasion has certainly at
present very little effect upon the public mind." By the autumn
there was more amateur bellicose activity to be seen in the fields
then existing north of the New (now Marylebone) Road:—

" October 16th (1803). Military preparations abound. On my way
to the (Fitzroy) Chapel I saw the large Corps of the Duke of Bedford's
workpeople drawn out and performing their exercises. The St. Pancras
Corps was also out this morning. . . . Then walked to Chalk Farm,
where many Volunteers were firing at a target."

All over the country it was the same. Worthy tradesmen,
like Melchizedek Meredith, reversing the Scriptural aphorism
about swords and ploughshares, resigned their shears and other
implements of business, and blossomed out as officers of
" yeomanry cavalry." All round the coast useless forts, such
as those still to be seen on Portsdown, near Portsmouth, were
erected. The procedure was repeated during the recent war,
when little " pill-box " forts were put up on the East Coast.
There was only room for a few men in them, and what such
flimsy toys were to do in the face of the advancing Teuton
legions, with their heavy artillery, is not clear.

Farington notes that in 1803 William Gifford, author of *The
Baviad*, told him that " the name of the French Physician who
refused to poison the French troops who were sick in an Hospital
in Egypt, which Buonaparte proposed to him to do, the name
was Des Genets. . . . Des Genets was a prisoner to Lord
Hutchinson, to whom he told the circumstance. After he refused
to do it, Buonaparte prevailed on one of His (the Physician's)
mates to mix opium with their food. Out of upwards of five
hundred, about twelve or fourteen had strength of constitution
which enabled them by means of emetics to get the better of the
poison. The particulars, fully authenticated, were transmitted
to France, and are in many hands, but the interest and power of
Buonaparte has prevented the publication of them." Curiously
enough, in this same conversation, Gifford mentioned to
Farington that he sometimes saw William Combe, author of
Doctor Syntax, who was still within the rules of the King's
Bench Prison. Combe, in his " Hudibrastic Poem," *The Life of
Napoleon*, thus describes the alleged poisoning of prisoners at
Jaffa by the order of Napoleon:—

" Another great thing Boney now did,
With sick the hospitals were crowded,
He therefore planned, nor planned in vain,
To put the wretches out of pain ;
He an apothecary found—
For a physician, since renowned,
The butchering task with scorn declined,
Th' apothecary, tho' was *kind*.
It seems that Romeo met with such a one,
This is a mournful theme to touch upon,
Opium was put in pleasant food,
The wretched victims thought it good ;
But in a few hours, as they say,
Almost six hundred breathless lay."

Mr. Greig is to be congratulated on the continuation of his valuable work in editing so industriously *The Farington Diary*. The third volume will be awaited with interest.

WALBURGA, LADY PAGET'S MEMOIRS.*

WALBURGA, LADY PAGET has gazed upon an extensive and varied panorama of life for eighty-four years. She was born in Saxony, and spent her early and impressionable days there and in other parts of Germany. Fate decreed that her middle years should pass at the capitals of Europe—Berlin, London, Copenhagen, Rome, and Vienna—by reason of Court and diplomatic duties. And in serene old age she lives at Newnham, by the wide Severn. It follows that her long and intimate associations with many of the highest and most influential persons of Europe during the period 1858-1893, and the confidences many of them entrusted her with, would provide material for a most interesting book.† *Embassies of Other Days* proves to be eminently that, and, further, it is often of historical value, although the author has been compelled to omit much that is still of too private a nature for publication at present. In consequence, the narrative is at times rather formless and vague, for, as the writer herself says, " the book is like a string of beads with many gaps between them, for I have not tried to change or arrange things, such as is generally done in memoirs written years after the events have happened." But it records faithfully the first impressions of events and people and experiences as they appeared at the time to Lady Paget.

It is a pity her book has not been more carefully edited and corrected, thus obviating many errors in the spelling of proper names. For example, " Longleate " occurs always instead of " Longleat," and the title of Lord Ingestre, who was drowned in a pond in the Prater at Vienna, is perpetrated as " Ingestry " at least eight times. By the way, according to *Burke*, Lord Ingestre's death happened in 1820, at the age of nineteen, and not in 1826 as reported by Lord Churchill to Lady Paget. Further, the account of the three ladies, dressed in conventual-like black, seen at Rudolstadt in Thuringia in the 'Forties, needs some genealogical explanation : " They were the Duchess of Angoulême . . . the Comtesse de Chambord, her niece by marriage, and the Duchess of Parma, Madame de France, the sister of Henry the Fifth. I was deeply impressed, and remember their poor, plain, dignified appearance to this day."

* *The Fortnightly Review*, November, 1923.
† *Embassies of Other Days,* by Walburga, Lady Paget. In two volumes, with sixteen illustrations. (Hutchinson & Co., 42s. net.)

Now, as the Duchesse D'Angoulême was the daughter of Louis the Sixteenth and the daughter-in-law of Charles the Tenth, the Comtesse de Chambord, whose husband was a grandson of Charles the Tenth, would at best be but a niece by marriage of the Duc D'Angoulême. The Comte de Chambord (son of the Duc de Berri) *would* have been Henry the Fifth had he succeeded as King of France.

To pass from carping to praise, Lady Paget can paint a word-scene most picturesquely. She has a vivid imagination together with the artistic temperament, and a deep appreciation of history and legend and romance and the influences of ancient buildings and impressive scenery. As a daughter of Count Hohenthal-Puechau and granddaughter of Field-Marshal Count Gneisenau, the author of this book had wide acquaintance with many of the romantic, legend-haunted castles in the land of wild mountain peaks, pine forests, and rushing streams; and she deduces her own name of Walburga or Walpurga from Walpurgis Nacht, the great Sabbath of the Witches, May the First—" On that night the young ones mount broom-sticks, the old ones goats, and they fly storm-driven through sulphurous clouds till they land on the Blocksburg, the highest peak of the Hartz Mountains. There they perform their unholy rites upon the big stone, which is reddened by the heart-blood of little children and the flames of sacrifice." In later years the Princess Royal and Lady Paget's children were solicitous that she should reach the Brocken appropriately, and so on every May the First at night she would find on her bed a new broom-stick decked with gay ribbons and flowers! Not the least attractive of Lady Paget's pages are those which describe the German castles of Gothic romance. Of Puechau, her home, built by Henry the Fowler in the ninth century, she writes:—

" Below lay the village, overshadowed by secular oaks, here and there only a white wall, a steep red roof, or a bit of thatch would show between the green leaves; but the thing which enthralled my imagination, and for hours filled my mind with vague and wondrous thoughts, were the mossy, dark green old orchards behind the peasants' houses. My eye dived down into them from the heights, and I was fascinated by the deep silent pools overhung by the large white flowers of the ancient elders, out of which on a still summer's evening came the saddest of sounds, the call of the ' Unke.' I used to listen to that cry breathless and thrilled, kneeling by my mother's side and looking at her graceful and stately form in her white dress as she sat on the raised seat of the deep window. I believed the old German fairy tale that if unseen I could slip out of my bed on midsummer eve and spread a deep blue kerchief on the margin of the pool, the little ' Unke '—this strange creature which never dies and which no eye has ever seen—would leave a tiny golden crown upon it, which in the morning I should find."

That is a passage full of descriptive power and suggestion; it is like one of the old graceful engravings illustrating a romantic story in *The Keepsake* of ninety years ago. Another of Lady Paget's descriptions is also very characteristic. This time it is the castle of Sommerschenburg, the home of her mother's family: —

" This delightful old place on the last spurs of the Hartz mountains, with its solid square towers and long, dead walls, charmed my romantic soul, and I was not indifferent to the comfort and luxury with which my uncle had furnished it. He had lived in England, especially at Belvoir, from which he had copied a good deal. His fruit gardens were those of the Hesperides, with strawberries like plums, currants as big as cherries, and apricots which defy description, and which I gathered myself on the sun-steeped terraces, on which the castle sat. These terraces, piled high one above the other, looking south, filled me with longing for lands unknown, and the wilderness of fragrant, old-fashioned flowers and aromatic herbs, which shrouded them in mystery, called up in my mind elusive memories of things and days long vanished in the mists of many centuries."

This is the old Germany of romance which George Meredith pictured in his early and undeservedly forgotten poem, *Pictures of the Rhine*: —

> " The Spirit of Romance dies not to those
> Who hold a kindred spirit in their souls.
>
> Beauty renews itself in many ways;
> The flower is fading while the new bud blows;
> And this dear land as true a symbol shows,
> While o'er it like a mellow sunset strays
> The legendary splendour of old days.
>
> The mountains on each other climb,
> With spaces for rich meadows flowery bright;
> The winding river freshening the sight
> At intervals; the trees in leafy prime;
> The distant village roofs of blue and white,
> With intersections of quaint fashioned beams
> All slanting crosswise, and the feudal gleams
> Of ruined turrets, barren in the light.
>
> To dream of fairy foot and sudden flower;
> Or haply with a twilight on the brow,
> To muse upon the legendary hour.
>
> Rare is the loveliness of slow decay,
> With youth and beauty all must be desired,
> But 'tis the charm of things long past away,
> They leave, alone, the light they have inspired."

Through some marriage connections the young Countess Walburga Hohenthal was brought early into contact with royal circles. Her kinsman, Count Alfred Hohenthal Koenigsbrueck, was married to Marie, Princess of Holstein, sister of King Christian the Ninth of Denmark and aunt of Queen Alexandra; and her uncle, Count Adolph Hohenthal, married the Countess of Bergen, widow of William the Second, Elector of Hesse Cassel, and a very prominent figure in Berlin and Dresden society. It was through this latter royal relative that at the age of eighteen the Countess Walburga went to England to take up the duties of Lady-in-Waiting to the Princess Royal on the occasion of her marriage, in January, 1858, with Prince Frederick of Prussia (he did not become Crown Prince until two years later).

The Countess gives an amusing account of life at Windsor Castle and Buckingham Palace in those days. One is surprised to find that dinner was as late as 8-30; in most houses in England the dinner-hour then might be anywhere between 4 and 7 o'clock. Queen Victoria, the Princess Royal, and all the ladies wore coloured woollen petticoats; a glass of lemonade or water was served before the company retired to bed; and at a State Ball the Countess Walburga danced with the Duke of Brabant (later King Leopold the Second of Belgium), " who the whole time squeezed my hand in the most peculiar way." But it transpired later that all the dance partners that night of the royal life-long philanderer had the same unflattering experience.

These memoirs bring out strongly the fact how much more easily and simply people were amused sixty-odd years ago. The foreign visitors for the Royal Wedding were entertained at several State functions and went to a few dull plays, where the ladies were frozen with cold and could not put on even a mantilla, because the Queen never felt the cold and dressed accordingly. Then there were the hectic excitements of visits to the " Sydenham Palace " (how little the young Countess Walburga thought then this building, years later, would be preserved for the public by the exertions and financial aid of her son-in-law of the future, the late Earl of Plymouth), the Chamber of Wax Horrors, and a Polytechnic School, where a diver remained ten minutes under the water. And yet, as the author points out, though she was but eighteen and associating mainly with people double her age, she was perfectly happy.

In due time she proceeded with the Princess Royal, now married, to Germany, and had to participate in the prodigious life of the Prussian Court—dinner in full dress between 2 and 5 o'clock, and tea and supper at 8; a great scarcity of water and washing utensils; huge beds in mysterious vast rooms; and a prospect of seeing the ghostly White Lady of the Hohenzollerns'

Schloss. The Maid of Honour was eighteen, the Royal Bride seventeen, and the former had been requested by Queen Victoria to write once a week and report all that her daughter was doing. This was an unpleasant task, naturally, for there was no desire to tell tales, and the Princess Royal sometimes said " Don't tell Mamma this " : —

" I confess that these letters cost me many sighs. . . . The Queen was beginning to be anxious, for the Princess had been married three months and yet there were no prospects of an heir, when in April she slipped on a staircase and was laid up for three weeks with a sprained ankle, after which, to Her Majesty's great satisfaction, it was announced that the Princess was in an interesting state."

A curious topic for a youthful Maid of Honour to be required to report progress on. But Queen Victoria was the High Priestess of Philoprogenitiveness, and as soon as the members of her family were out of the school-room they were married off at once, preferably to cousins, without much thought for the suitability or prospects of future happiness of the victims of her decisive matrimonial arrangements. Thus her next two daughters, the Princesses Alice and Helena, were both married at the age of nineteen to impoverished German princelings. The granddaughters shared the same early marital fate, and in the case of the Duke of Edinburgh's second daughter, Princess Victoria Melita, with most disastrous results. Lady Paget relates a conversation she had with the Emperor Francis Joseph of Austria when the Duke of Edinburgh's eldest daughter, Marie, now the truly regal and beautiful Queen of Roumania, was but lately married, æt. eighteen, in 1893. The Emperor said: " You sent something much too beautiful to Roumania. I don't understand how the Duchess of Edinburgh could make up her mind to do so."

The Princess Royal married and the mother of the infant destined to become the ex-Kaiser, she and Queen Victoria now resolved to find a wife for the youthful Prince of Wales, then but seventeen years of age. The young Maid of Honour was called into consultation, and she wisely represented that the Prince " was much too young, not only in age but also in disposition; but the Queen and the Prince Consort thought it would keep him out of mischief." So the Princess Royal and the Countess Walburga set forth on a scouring of Germany to find a future Queen of England. Every available German princess was paraded at a huge supper-party at Düsseldorf. Princess Elizabeth of Wied, later to be Carmen Sylva, the literary Queen of Roumania, was the only one worthy of a second thought—

but she " looked insignificant then. She was hardly pretty—
beauty in my own mind I had settled on as a *sine quâ non* for the
Prince of Wales's wife. We therefore returned to Berlin, having
mercifully done nothing."

This was indeed fortunate, because two years later the writer
was able to play a very important part in finding the right wife
for the Prince of Wales. It came about through the Countess
Walburga's own marriage, in October, 1860, with Augustus
Berkeley Paget, of the Diplomatic Service, and a son of Sir
Arthur Paget, who was a brother of the first Marquis of
Anglesey, the gallant leader of cavalry at Waterloo. Augustus
Paget was Minister at Copenhagen, and there his young wife
met her connections, Prince and Princess Christian of Denmark
and their beautiful daughter Alexandra, who she rightly resolved
was the fitting bride for the Prince of Wales. The story of the
negotiations for the marriage, and how the Prince first saw his
future wife, and how the Princess Alexandra set out for England
(where she has been beloved as no Queen Consort ever was
before)—all this must be read in Lady Paget's book. In her
own way, she has proved as distinguished a diplomatist as
her husband, and England owes her many thanks for Queen
Alexandra.

I wish I had space to follow Lady Paget's records of official
life in Copenhagen, Rome, and Vienna, where she has much of
interest to relate concerning the ill-fated Empress Elizabeth and
the tragedy of Meyerling. In England, too, the narrative is
ever interesting and amusing for the sidelights it throws on
innumerable people of distinction. The account of Ouida's visit
to the second Lord Lytton cries out for quotation : —

" In the evening I came here to Knebworth. I had promised dear
Lytton to chaperon him in the train, for Ouida had insisted upon his
coming to London to fetch her, and he fears her love much more than her
hate. Lord Salisbury got into the carriage where I was sitting with Sir
Ashley Eden, and said he did not wish to know Ouida. At that moment
she appeared, be-furred and be-velveted, on Lytton's arm. Nobody
volunteered an introduction, and I felt she must never know she had
missed this long-coveted opportunity of making Lord Salisbury's
acquaintance. . . . Fortunately it was dark and Lord Salisbury kept
his face turned to the window. When he got out at Hatfield he shook
hands with us, and Ouida quickly asked : ' And who was that? ' Lord
Lytton turned to me in the most disgracefully-comic way and said,
opening his green eyes very wide : ' Yes, who was that? ' I said :
' Yes, I know his face,' and Sir Ashley Eden added : ' I think some
local man.' "

The book is a notable contribution to the literature of
Memoirs.

THE GHOST STORY AND ITS EXPONENTS.*

THIS being the month of December and the season of Christmas, it may not be inappropriate to consider two recently published volumes of stories of the supernatural and their correlation to the history of the ghost story and tale of terror in this country.

The art of the ghost story—and that surely is an art which can create sensations of very real, and at the same time pleasurable, fear and disquiet in the mind of the hearer or reader—has passed through many mutations of form in England. From the earliest days ghostly legend and tales of horror have been told. The Bible has its apparitions. Shakspere, in *Macbeth*, *Hamlet*, and elsewhere, made effective use of the ghost. The early romance writers, such as Horace Walpole, Mrs. Radcliffe, " Monk " Lewis, and Maturin, were admirable in their settings and scenic accessories. They followed the German tradition, and rightly so, for no country has been so prolific as Germany in evolving through the ages supernatural and romantic legends allied to, or arising from, wild mountain scenery, mysterious forests, rivers and lakes, and ancient buildings—a national characteristic which found supreme expression in the great music dramas of Wagner.

Consequently we find in the pages of the early romancers I have just mentioned the castle of mystery set amid towering crags or the glooms of a vast forest. Walpole and " Monk " Lewis were content, when they came to supernatural appearances, to present the orthodox conventional demon, complete with talons and horns and hooves and tail, such as can be seen in George Cruikshank's illustrations to *The Ingoldsby Legends*—the demons, in short, created by the imaginations of monkish chroniclers and mediæval painters. Unfortunately these picturesque fiends are liable to become funny in a supernatural story. Their antics in *The Castle of Otranto* engender mirth; and the final horrific scene in *The Monk* is ruined by the fact that the demon talks persistently in the manner of an old-time villain of transpontine melodrama :—

" ' Miscreant, prepare for death ; you have not many hours to live ! '

" On hearing this sentence, dreadful were the feelings of the devoted wretch. He sank upon his knees, and raised his hands towards heaven. The fiend read his intention and prevented it.

" ' What ! ' he cried, darting at him a look of fury, ' dare you still

* *The Fortnightly Review*, December, 1923.

implore the Eternal's mercy? Would you feign penitence, and again act
a hypocrite's part? Villain, resign your hopes of pardon ! Thus I secure
my prey ! '

" As he said this, darting his talons into the monk's shaven crown,
he sprang with him from the rock.   The caves and mountains rang with
Ambrosio's shrieks.   The demon continued to soar aloft, till, reaching
a dreadful height, he released the sufferer.   Headlong fell the monk
through the airy waste; the sharp point of a rock received him, and he
rolled from precipice to precipice. . . ."

Mrs. Radcliffe differed from her contemporaries in the tale of
terror.   All her effects were obtained by suggestion of the
unknown—hollow groans and low sighs heard behind the arras,
flitting lights and shadowy forms seen in the distance of
labyrinthine dungeons or forest aisles, the while the wind soughed
eerily or the advancing thunder rumbled warningly among the
hills.   She was magnificent in her *mise en scène;* but no terrible
apparitions ever materialise, however imminent they appear,
because, alas ! all the mysteries and horrors are explained in the
end to have occurred by human agency.   That is the great blot
on the artistry of Mrs. Radcliffe.   She trifled with the supernatural.   She summoned spirits from the vasty deep, and then,
alarmed by her own temerity, she dismissed her potential spectres
and substituted puppets and unsatisfactory explanations.

Mrs. Radcliffe's influence upon literature, as I have demonstrated elsewhere,* was very great and lasting; and her inartistic
way of solving the ghost story was followed by many of her
successors in fiction—that is to say, the lesser ones, for, as we
shall see presently, the great artists in literature (with the
exception of Thackeray and Meredith) have treated the ghost
story seriously and impressively.   But the immediate effect of
Mrs. Radcliffe's method descended upon G. P. R. James, who in
The Castle of Ehrenstein (1847) provided at the outset one of the
finest supernatural romances, with an admirable scenic setting.
But all is ruined in the end by the fatuous " explanations."

Happily other writers developed the ghost story on the right
lines.   Walter Scott in *The Tapestried Chamber* (1829) and
Wandering Willie's Tale (in *Redgauntlet,* 1824) reached the
supreme heights.   What superb artistry permeates *Wandering
Willie's Tale;* every sentence and detail has its place in the
cumulative effect.   As Ruskin said, " It is as natural as the best
of Burns, with a grandeur in its main scene equal to Dante."
Following, and inspired by, this great example came W. Harrison
Ainsworth.   Supernatural events are effectively introduced into
most of his early books, and in *The Lancashire Witches* (1848)

* See *ante,* page 19.

he achieved a masterpiece, despite some faults of contemporary style, for this, in my opinion, is the greatest of all romances dealing with the occult and the combined influences and " atmosphere " of wild and suggestive scenery. James Grant, the military novelist, was excellent in *The Phantom Regiment* and other ghostly tales.

Sheridan Le Fanu, meanwhile, was developing with his own peculiar art another line of the supernatural tale. For thirty-five years, 1838-1873, he wrote stories of mystery, but his pre-eminent method did not deal with apparitions visible to several persons, but rather with terrible spectres generated in the brain of the haunted. Le Fanu's greatest stories, *The House by the Church-yard, Green Tea, Carmilla, Uncle Silas*, and others, are accessible to a certain but not great extent. Several of his short stories were contributed, in most cases anonymously, to *All the Year Round, Temple Bar, Belgravia, London Society*, and *The Dublin University Magazine*. Twelve of these unknown or forgotten tales have now been collected and published,* with a preface and bibliographical notes by Dr. M. R. James, the Provost of Eton, who is himself the most distinguished living writer of ghost stories. The book is very acceptable at this season, and the stories most worthy of rescue from oblivion. They are also of collatable interest for those who desire to consider Le Fanu's work as a whole. One of his peculiarities was to present and rewrite a tale several times; generally commencing as a short story it would appear later in longer form, and finally as a full-length novel, with the setting and, sometimes, the details and period changed. Thus the famous *Uncle Silas* had two preliminary canters on a shorter course—to use an equine metaphor. In the present volume Dr. James provides us with *Some Strange Disturbances in Aungier Street*, which is the earlier form of the well-known story of *Mr. Justice Harbottle*, one of the five tales in the volume called *In a Glass Darkly*. I am inclined to think the early version the most impressive; at any rate, it is more of a ghost story than *Mr. Justice Harbottle* is. The spectre is malignant, and this is another aspect of Le Fanu's work which is distinctive. In the majority of ghost stories, both authenticated and fictional, it rarely occurs that the apparition has any power to harm human beings physically: the ghostly activities are confined to inspiring terror by sight mainly, and it is only occasionally that an actual malign touch is recorded.

---

* *Madam Crowl's Ghost*, and other tales of mystery, by Joseph Sheridan Le Fanu. Collected and edited by M. R. James. (G. Bell & Sons, 7s. 6d. net.) See *ante*, page 150.

I recall one such authenticated case at a house near Bandon, in Co. Cork, where the apparition touched a woman's arm, which immediately became paralysed and remained useless for two weeks after. But Le Fanu's ghosts are very actively malignant. There is his terrible *Familiar (The Watcher)*, and in this new volume the tale of *Dickon the Devil* relates how the spectre carried off a boy in its arms, and when the lad was eventually discovered he was an idiot and so remained to the end. " No one could ever get him to sleep under roof-tree more. He wanders from house to house while daylight lasts . . . and folk would rather not meet him after nightfall, for they think where he is there may be worse things near." *Squire Toby's Will* is also an awe-inspiring ghost story; in this case a dead person returns in the semblance of a great dog.

In all these collected tales I find Le Fanu's particular art of creating the right " atmosphere " of melancholy and mystery by a preliminary picture of some direly foreboding old mansion and its gloomy park seen in the twilight of an autumn or winter eve. He gets his artistic effect with a word or two.

" The Park-wall was grey with age, and in many places laden with ivy. In deep grey shadow, that contrasted with the dim fires of evening reflected on the foliage above it, in a gentle hollow, stretched a lake that looked cold and black, and seemed, as it were, to skulk from observation with a guilty knowledge."

As I have said, several of Le Fanu's stories, including the truly awful *Green Tea* (1869), were first issued in *All the Year Round*, for Charles Dickens was ever intensely interested in the supernatural, and wrote of it admirably, as everyone knows, in the stories of *The Bagman's Uncle* and *The Goblins who Stole a Sexton* in *Pickwick;* in *A Christmas Carol;* and in the short stories called *The Signalman* and *The Bride-Chamber*, and elsewhere. In *Household Words* and *All the Year Round*, both under Dickens's editorship, are to be found some of the best ghost stories ever written, including *The Old Nurse's Story*, by Mrs. Gaskell—another triumph in the presentation of scenic " atmosphere "; *The Phantom Coach*, by Amelia B. Edwards; the very fine anonymous *Ghost Story; The Haunted Organist of Hurly Burly*, by Rosa Mulholland; and many other tales of the supernatural and horror—such as *The Spare Bed*, by Wilkie Collins, who was also author of a very successful full-length ghost story, *The Haunted Hotel*. It was Dickens who asked Bulwer-Lytton to write a serial tale for *All the Year Round*, and this proved to be *A Strange Story* (1861)—a pioneer in the metaphysical branch of the ghost tale.

Dickens, then, may be said to have consolidated the modern taste and appreciation for the supernatural story. The magazines which sprang up in imitation of *All the Year Round*—*Tinsley's Magazine*, *Temple Bar*, *Belgravia*, and *London Society*—all provided the ghost story. Those in *Tinsley's Magazine* were truly good, and before leaving this period of the 'Sixties and 'Seventies I must mention the work of Mrs. Riddell. Her ghost stories in *Weird Tales*, as examples of the old-fashioned Christmassy kind, have never been excelled, and she also wrote a story of death called *The Haunted River*, which has a tense atmosphere of brooding horror settling over it like a pall. I still treasure the 1891 Christmas Number of *The Whitehall Review* for its collection of delightful ghost stories by Lady William Lennox, John K. Leys, Lady Alexandra Egerton, William Le Queux, Lady Harris, and other writers.

In later years Rudyard Kipling, W. W. Jacobs, E. F. Benson, H. G. Wells, R. L. Stevenson, Marion Crawford (author of *The Upper Berth*), Mrs. Molesworth, Fergus Hume, William De Morgan, Evelyn Nesbit, Miss Violet Hunt, Clark Russell, Barry Pain, Elliot O'Donnell, Perceval Landon, John Buchan, Miss Marjorie Bowen, the Rev. E. G. Swain, Mrs. Campbell Praed, and many others, have written excellent ghost stories. Henry James advanced the prominence of the metaphysical ghost story with his arresting and terrible tale, *The Turn of the Screw*, and another in lighter vein, *The Way it Came*. I have always regretted that Mr. Thomas Hardy has not written more extensively of the supernatural, for he showed in *The Withered Arm* that he was master of this branch of his craft, as well as of those he has so pre-eminently made his own.

To-day, two writers stand out as specialists in the art of the ghost story and tale of terror—Dr. M. R. James, the Provost of Eton, and Mr. Algernon Blackwood. Dr. James has created a style entirely his own, for his horrific events are narrated with scholarly erudition amid an authentic archæological and antiquarian "atmosphere." He has produced three volumes of tales of this description, and the next is awaited with pleasurable anticipation. Mr. Algernon Blackwood in his first three books, *The Empty House*, *The Listener*, and *John Silence*, presented a collection of supernatural stories of particular merit, subtle and suggestive of ulterior trains of thought. Unfortunately, in my view, he later wandered away into metaphysical spaces and pantheistic groves, where I do not follow him with the same enjoyment as of yore. I would sacrifice all the Starlight Expresses and Centaurs and Men that the Trees

Loved for some more stories in the style of *A Case of Eaves-dropping, The Listener,* and *Secret Worship. On y revient toujours,* and I trust to see Mr. Blackwood back in his haunted houses.

I have glanced lightly through the notable band of men and women who have written ghost stories and tales of terror, and to the list must now be added the name of Miss May Sinclair. In her new book* she offers seven stories which in turn illustrate the various types we have been considering; they range from the tales in the old fashion of an apparition in a haunted house, through mental hallucinations, to a metaphysical state. To the first category belong *The Token; If the Dead Knew;* and *The Victim,* which is an amazingly vivid study of temperament and murder. In a lonely house on the Yorkshire moors an old man is murdered by his manservant from mistaken motives of jealousy. The description of the crime is painfully realistic and very minute. For after insensibility by strangulation the victim is hung over the edge of a bath and his arteries cut, the blood draining away with the hot water which is running into the bath with the waste-plug out. Miss Sinclair here condenses into one or two pages all the horror of many famous murder stories—the pig-like slaughter of Weare by Thurtell and the victims of Jack-the-Ripper; the unusual end of the Brides in the Bath; the butcherly cutting-up of the body of her mistress by Kate Webster at Richmond, and of Mrs. Crippen by her husband; and all the mystery of Dougal at the Moat Farm after the disappearance of his victim. For the murderer in Miss Sinclair's o'er-bloody tale lives on in his master's house, and the psychology of the criminal and his precautions to avoid detection are presented with the most subtle skill. So, too, is his terror when the apparition of the murdered man appears to him, or is heard shuffling, as in life, along the flagged passages of the house. Here the story should have ended with the suicide of the murderer down the pit in the moor into which he had cast the remains of his victim. But having written one of the most gruesome murder-cum-ghost stories in existence, Miss Sinclair, with a sudden failure of artistic sense, chooses to end her tale with humorous bathos. The apparition has merely returned to thank the murderer for removing him to a far more delightful plane, and he—or it—proceeds to chaff his " benefactor " upon the comic appearance he presented when engaged upon the business in the bath and the subsequent use of chopper and saw

---

* *Uncanny Stories,* by May Sinclair. With illustrations by the Chevalier ean de Bosschère. (Hutchinson & Co., 7s. 6d. net.)

in disposing of his body. Miss Sinclair should have studied the effective ending of a somewhat similar tale to hers—*The House with the Brick-Kiln*, by Mr. E. F. Benson—before she decided to ruin her own clever work.

Happily there are no further attempts at comic relief, and Miss Sinclair's six remaining stories are treated seriously, though one of them unintentionally comes perilously near to being funny This is *The Nature of the Evidence*, the sad tale of a chaste deaa wife, who, strongly disapproving of her successor, so effectually haunts the bridal couple that they can neither get to bed nor consummate their marriage. The husband is conjured away from his living sensual wife, and joins the spirit of his deceased first wife in the library, where such wonderful experiences occurred as caused him ever after to say that no mortal woman could know what passion is really like. I hope I am not flippant with this particular story, which may possess some finer spiritual essence that has eluded me. Frankly, I think it nonsense and unpleasant. The recondite depths of such a union between a living being and a spirit were explored twenty years ago by Lord Kilmarnock in his story of *Ferelith*, and he even provided an infant half-human and half-ghostly as the result. But *cui bono?* Miss Violet Hunt has also touched upon the subject in *Love's Last Leave (The Ghost of Suvla Bay)*.

Miss Sinclair's cleverest story is *The Flaw in the Crystal*, which may be taken as a parable of the dangers of psycho-analysis and other forms of mental and physical healing accomplished by the will and suggestions of another person. Agatha Verrall in this story has " The Gift," and she uses her psychic power—" You could think of it as a current of transcendent power, hitherto mysteriously inhibited. You made the connection, having cut off all other currents that interfered . . . you tapped the Power, as it were, underground at any point you pleased, and turned it on in any direction."

She turned it on to cure a man of a terrible form of recurrent insanity which compelled him to hide in darkness from " It "—a mental horror such as Le Fanu or Dr. M. R. James might have conceived. His eyes were those " of a terrified thing, a thing hunted and on the watch, a thing that listened continually for the soft feet of the hunter." Agatha cures her friend, but—in curing him his madness passes into her, and *she* becomes a hunted, furtive thing, seeking darkness from the terror of " It "; and her ears of insanity are opened to all the hitherto inaudible voices of Nature and Life on the earth and under the earth. The Pursuer is upon her, and she is

> " Like one that on a lonesome road
> Doth walk in fear and dread,
> And having once turned round, walks on
> And turns no more his head ;
> Because he knows a frightful fiend
> Doth close behind him tread."

Miss Sinclair works out her thesis very ably—how the spiritual operation of " The Gift " obliged Agatha, in getting at Harding to cure him, " to destroy, not only the barriers of flesh and blood, but those innermost walls of personality that divide and protect, mercifully, one spirit from another. With the first thinning of the walls Harding's insanity had leaked through to her, with the first breach it had broken in." And the Flaw in the Crystal was that she had not been absolutely pure in thought, for absolute purity was the touchstone for the success of the experiment. Happily for her she retains the power to " cut off " Harding spiritually and to repair the breaches in the walls of her own personality. And, finally, by a great renunciation of self and of the man she loves (not Harding), the madness is cast out from her and " It " returns to Harding.

Where Their Fire is not Quenched is also a powerful story conducive to thought. It propounds the idea that Hell will provide an eternal repetition and re-enactment of the original sin that caused damnation with all its monotony, sordid detail, and nausea—for passion had died in life long before nominal "death " came to the unhappy protagonists of this tale—an unmarried woman and a married man. In the course of their affair they had gone to Paris and stayed at a dingy hotel. After death, years later, all through the æons of eternity, they continually come upon that Hôtel Saint Pierre, and the old nauseating sin has ever to be repeated. " In the last death we shall be shut up in this room, behind that locked door, together. We shall be here together, for ever and ever, joined so fast that even God can't put us asunder. We shall be one flesh and one spirit, one sin repeated for ever and ever; spirit loathing flesh, flesh loathing spirit; you and I loathing each other."

It will have been obvious from this extract that the modern metaphysical tale of terror has changed a good deal in method and thesis from the early examples by Bulwer-Lytton. In his *Haunted and the Haunters* (1857) and *A Strange Story* the malignant beings he imagined continued to live on in *this* world, far past the allotted span, by the power of will. The terrible punishment of Vanderdecken and the Ancient Mariner consisted in the fact that they were compelled to wander for ever on the sea and land of *this* earth. The old tellers of ghost tales never took their victims to Hell—or to Heaven either, for that matter. They were concerned with hapless spirits tied to earth by reason of crime or sorrow in their time of flesh. In Oscar Wilde's exquisite fantasy, *The Canterville Ghost*, the apparition only desires rest and oblivion. The other world or plane has no terrors for these earth-bound spirits. They long for it.

If the modern teller of tales of terror is to take us to Hell for the purposes of his story that will not be so pleasant and cosy as the old way. As Byron put it—

> " 'Twas as the watchmen say, a cloudy night :
> No moon, no stars, the wind was low or loud
> By gusts, and many a sparkling hearth was bright
> With the piled wood. "

That is the right setting in which to hear a ghost story. We must keep our spectres to our plane, and not let them entice us to metaphysical infernos.

NOTE.—In a former article in *The Fortnightly Review* (September, 1923) I made some allusion to the East Anglian spectre, " The Shuck Dog " (related to " The Gytrash " of the northern counties)—a great black hound with flaming eyes, seen by belated pedestrains in lonely lanes at nightfall.* I have since learned that " The Shuck [or ' Shock '] Dog " apparently arrived in East Anglia in the sixteenth century, when he behaved, at the outset, in a very malignant and rabietic manner. By the courtesy of the Vicar of St. Mary's Church, Bungay, the Rev. Joseph Wood, I am enabled to quote the following account from ancient records : —

" Sunday, being the 4th August, 1577, to the amasing and singular astonishment of the present beholders and absent hearers, at a certain town called Bungay, not past ten miles [really fourteen] distant from the City of Norwich, there fell from Heaven an exceeding great and terrible tempest, sudden and violent, between 9 o'clock in the morning and 10 of the day aforesaid. This tempest beginning with a rain, which fell with a wonderful force . . . the church did as it were quake and stagger, which struck into the hearts of those that were present such a sore and sudden fear. . . . Immediately, hereupon, there appeared in a most horrible similitude and likeness to the congregation, then and there present, a dog as they might discern it, of a black colour; at the sight whereof, together with the fearful flashes of fire which then were seen, moved such admiration in the minds of the assembly that they thought Doomsday was already come.

This black dog, or the devil in such a likeness (God he knoweth all who worketh all), running all along down the body of the church with great swiftness, and incredible haste, among the people in a visible form and shape, passed between two persons, as they were kneeling upon their knees, and occupied in prayer as it seemed, wrung the necks of

* See *ante* page 304.

them both at one instant clean backward, inasmuch that even in a moment where they kneeled they strangely dyed.

There was at the same time another wonder wrought, for the same black dog still continuing in one and the self-same shape, passing by another man in the congregation in the church, gave him such a gripe in the back, that therewith all he was presently drawn together and shrunk up as it were a piece of leather scorched in a hot fire, or as a mouth of a purse or bag drawn together with a string. . . .

Now for the verifying of the report . . . there are remaining in the stones of the church, and likewise in the church door, which are marvellously rent and torn, the marks as it were of claws and talons. . . . .''

The picturesque language and apt simile of this old story make it strangely vivid—it is almost biblical in style. The great storm of 1577, whether accompanied or not by the supernatural visitant in canine guise, must have made a great impression upon the denizens of East Anglia for its echo to be heard in the Victorian period.

(a) THE LAST LORD HOLLAND.*
(b) UNCENSORED RECOLLECTIONS.

THE continuity of Holland House and its preserved associations with one notable family are facts that should be appreciated keenly, for, as Macaulay observed, Holland House " can boast of a greater number of inmates distinguished in political and literary history than any other private dwelling in England." With the exception of Syon House, Chiswick House, and Ken Wood at Hampstead, Holland House is the last survivor of the great country mansions that once were ranged numerously on the outskirts of London, and its survival is the more remarkable because its situation was ever much nearer to 'the ceaseless growth of the town westward than the other three houses mentioned, and the land consequently more to be desired by the speculative builder. A hundred years ago it stood in rural privacy, far more reserved than the neighbouring Palace of Kensington; and a few years earlier, at the close of the eighteenth century, the high road to London was very lonely, and travellers in danger from attack by robbers. Writing from Kensington Palace to the Duchess of Argyll, Mrs. Burgoyne relates:—

" We live here (I mean the female part of the family) as retired as if we were at a country place forty or fifty miles from London. . . . Mrs. L . . . was stop'd by two highwaymen between one and two in the morning about Kensington Gore, coming from Lady Holland's; one of them stood by the footman, and the other, after having drawn his pistol out to the coachman to stop, put it up again, and then asked Mrs. L. for her purse, which she gave them (the one she has had so long ready for them). He then asked for her watch, which she likewise gave; then for her pocket-book. . . ."

In 1828, when Sir Walter Scott had stayed a night at Holland House, he noted in his Journal:—

" May 18th. The freshness of the air, the singing of the birds, the beautiful aspect of nature, the size of the venerable trees, gave me altogether a delightful feeling this morning. . . . We (i.e., Rogers and I) wandered into a green lane, bordered with fine trees, which might have been twenty miles from a town. It will be a great pity when this ancient house must come down and give way to rows and crescents . . . one is chiefly affected by the air of deep seclusion which is spread around the domain."

The advancing tide of London duly swept up to Holland House, but it resisted the attack with a sacrifice of a large portion

* The Fortnightly Review, April, 1924.

of the grounds on the north side (which reached originally to the Uxbridge Road); the " rows and crescents " were erected to north and east and west, leaving Holland House secluded amid its gardens and roseries. There it still stands, and still in the possession of a direct descendant (the Earl of Ilchester) of Sir Stephen Fox, whose youngest son, Henry Fox, first Lord Holland, was the original purchaser of Holland House in the reign of George the Second, and the father of Charles James Fox, who spent his boyhood here. It was in the time of the third Lord Holland (1773-1840) that Holland House attained its greatest fame by reason of the memorable *salon* of his wife, Elizabeth Vassall Lady Holland, when, as Brougham says, it was " the resort not only of the most interesting persons composing English society, literary, philosophical, and political, but also to all belonging to those classes who ever visited this country from abroad."

The archives of Holland House seem inexhaustible. For over twenty years Lord Ilchester, aided by his mother Mary Countess of Ilchester, has been editing and publishing a series of the letters and journals, preserved in the library there, written by distinguished members or relatives of the Fox family, such as the first and third Lords Holland, Lady Sarah Lennox, and that arrogant Elizabeth Vassall Lady Holland, whose famous *salon*, as I have just indicated, was the most memorable social feature of the first half of the nineteenth century. The latest volume,* now published, is the most interesting of all, I think, for in addition to its record of the life of the writer and his family, it offers a running commentary on the social or fashionable life of the period (1818-1830), and, further, it is as intimate a personal revelation of character and temperament as the diaries of Pepys or Creevey, despite the fact that Henry Fox only kept up his journal for twelve years, and in a desultory manner.

Henry Edward Fox (1802-1859), fourth and last Lord Holland, was the son and heir of the third Lord Holland and Elizabeth Vassall Lady Holland. He was a curious, precocious boy in a mental sense by reason of his heredity and a constitutional weakness of the hip, which prevented him from going to a public school. He consequently received his education from private tutors, and was ever from early childhood in the company of the brilliant adults who formed the circle of Holland House. A boy who is brought up in this way always develops into an uncommon

---

* *The Journal of the Hon. Henry Edward Fox (Fourth and Last Lord Holland),* 1818-1830. Edited by the Earl of Ilchester. (Thornton Butterworth, 25s. net.)

youth, self-opinionated and with an assurance beyond his years
disdainful of his juvenile contemporaries and averse to activ
sports. It was doubly so in the case of Henry Fox, with hi
exceptional environment and temperament. By the time he wa
sixteen he was accustomed, as his Journal now shows, to form
very decided views, and express critical, caustic observation
about his friends and relatives. As he said, it was his " ar
always to see the worst first," which may perhaps account, fo
example, for his youthful disapproval of poor Campbell, the
poet : —

" Campbell sat next to me. His voice is sharp and querulous, hi
ideas vulgarly conceited. He took all my bread and all my glasses
spilt half his dinner into my lap, and then fished for a compliment fo
his *New Monthly Magazine,* which I was determined he should no
extract. He admired, praised, or was pleased with no place, book, o
person that was mentioned during dinner, except an idea of his own
which he most particularly eulogised, and from which, he says, Lor
Byron has taken the notion of his poem, *Darkness.* . . . How odiou
all authors are, and how doubly so to each other."

From the time he was a small boy, Henry Fox was much
liked by Byron, who records in his Journal, 1813, that he took
him to see a drama called *Nourjahad.* Byron's subsequen
references to Henry Fox illustrate the boy's temperament and
appearance so aptly in a few words that I am surprised Lord
Ilchester has not quoted them. The first passage refers to the
celebrated persons present at a typical assembly at Holland
House, when Henry Fox was eleven years old : —

" Little Henry Fox, a very fine boy, and very promising in mind
and manner—he went away to bed before I had time to talk to him.
I am sure I had rather hear him than all the *savans.*"

The second reference is ten years later (in a letter to Moore),
when Henry Fox visited Byron at Genoa on March 31st, 1823 : —

" I have also seen Henry Fox, Lord Holland's son, whom I had not
looked upon since I left him a pretty, mild boy, without a neckcloth, in
a jacket, and in delicate health, seven long years agone, at the period of
mine eclipse. . . . I think that he has the softest and most amiable
expression of countenance I ever saw, and manners correspondent. If
to those he can add hereditary talents, he will keep the name of Fox in
all its freshness for half a century more, I hope. I speak from a
transient glimpse—but I love still to yield to such impressions ; for I
have ever found that those I liked longest and best, I took to at first
sight ; and I always liked that boy—perhaps, in part, from some resemblance in the less fortunate part of our destinies—I mean, to avoid
mistakes, his lameness. But there is this difference, that *he* appears a
halting angel, who has tripped against a star ; whilst I am *Le Diable
Boiteux.*"

Fox gives an interesting account of this visit to Byron : —

" He received me most kindly, and, indeed, his good-nature to me has always been most marked and flattering. His figure is shorter than I recollected. . . . In face he is not altered. A few grey locks scattered among his beautiful black locks are all that announce the approach of that age that has made such an impression on his mind, and of which he talks so much. However, he is only thirty-five. . . . . Rogers he talked of in terms of deep-rooted dislike. He talked a great deal about Lady Byron, and asked if I knew anything about her or the child. He said it was an odd fact, and perhaps one I should not believe, but that his recollection of her face is so imperfect, that he is not sure he should know her again. The child he means to leave entirely under her guidance, for if it was to pass a month, a week, or a day with him alone, whatever it might do wrong afterwards would be ascribed to that unfortunate time. . . . He says he now is taking to be fond of money, and he has saved £3,000. . . . The tones of his voice are as beautiful as ever, and I am not surprised at any woman falling in love with him. Lady C. Lamb, he says, has the power of imitating his hand to an alarming perfection, and still possesses many of his letters which she may alter very easily."

Perhaps I ought to point out that Fox's statement that Byron was annoyed by the simultaneous arrival of the Blessingtons and their " impertinence " in " forcing their way " into the villa at Albaro is not confirmed by Byron's report of them as " very agreeable personages "—with whom, indeed, he at once formed an intimate friendship, with the result that Lady Blessington was later enabled to publish her *Conversations with Lord Byron*. An account of this first meeting with Byron will be found in Lady Blessington's *The Idler in Italy*, where she relates how the poet hurried out hatless to her carriage and begged her to enter the villa, where " our visit was a long one . . . he so warmly urged our stay."

Byron, of course, died just a year later, and how little he imagined that his young friend, Henry Fox, was destined to be his immediate successor in the affections of the Countess Guiccioli. Fox met her first on December 30th, 1824, at the apartment in Rome of the wife of Sir Humphry Davy, and he was not much impressed. " She is coarse and far from being, to my taste, the least attractive. Her hair is nearly red, her figure squat, and her eyes have no expression but what with study and affectation she contrives to throw into them." He met her again at Naples in July of the following year, and his victory was a rapid affair : —

" I observed Teresa rather sought than shrunk from proffered civilities, but I was not prepared for the extreme facility of the conquest, which (such is the perverseness of one's nature) scarcely gave me pleasure. She is too gross and carnal. As Lord Byron says, there is nothing like the moon for mischief.[*] It was on Sunday evening, the 7th of August, that she listened and consented at her balcony as we

---

[*] *Don Juan,* Canto the First, cxiii.

were gazing at chaste Dian's beams. Sentiment or caprice would not permit her to yield then, but appointed me the next night, and received me as those females receive one who make such occupations not their pleasure, but their trade. Her sentiment is ridiculous. . . . She tries and believes she is in love for a short time, but it is alarming when she talks and expects a constancy of five years. She has a pretty voice, pretty eyes, white skin, and strong, not to say *turbulent,* passions. She has no other attraction. . . . We had several agreeable evenings together, especially one night we went to Nisida and landed in my little favourite bay. It was a beautiful night and the moon was splendid, besides the heavens were brightly illuminated by summer lightnings. I grew to like her better as I knew more of her."

The intrigue continued, with many quarrels and many reconciliations, until October, 1825. Teresa Guiccioli then left Naples, and Fox was prevented from following her by a riding mishap. This accident occurred as he was about to pay a call on Lady Blessington at the Villa Gallo, and he was, in result, laid up there for some days. Originally he had disliked both the Blessingtons and Count D'Orsay, terming Lady Blessington vulgar and D'Orsay a coxcomb. But they were so kind to him during his enforced visit that, for a time, he recanted his former strictures. He grew to like D'Orsay very much—" He has a thousand merits, many talents, and a very warm heart . . . he has great frankness, generosity, and sincerity "—but with Lady Blessington he was never able to feel in sympathy, which was curious, as she possessed, usually, the peculiar art of winning the sincere friendship of men of the most diversified talents and temperaments. It may be of interest to quote from Lady Blessington's diary her very acute observations of Henry Fox's character at this same date, when she saw a good deal of him in Naples at the Villa Gallo in 1825 :—

" Mr. Henry Fox, the son of Lord Holland, has been our inmate for some days. He is a most agreeable companion, lively, playful, and abounding in anecdote, with just enough of what the French term *malice* to render his remarks very piquant, and just sufficient good nature to prevent their being too satirical. The French term, *malice,* must not be taken in the sense of the broader and stronger one of the word malice in our own language. The French phrase means simply a roguishness or slyness that induces a person to play tricks and draw out and exhibit the follies of his acquaintance for the sake of exciting a laugh without being impelled by any desire of injuring them. Henry Fox gives such admirable imitations of the peculiarities of his absent acquaintances that those present are infinitely amused, forgetting that they in turn will furnish subjects for the talent they are now admiring. Henry Fox is just such a forced plant, as might be expected from the hot-bed culture of Holland House, where wit and talent are deemed of such importance that more solid qualities are sometimes, if not sacrificed to their growth, at least overlooked in the search for them. Accustomed from infancy to see all around him contributing to the amusement of the circle they compose, by a brilliant persiflage, a witty version of the *on dits* of the day, epigrammatical sallies, which, though pungent, never violate *les bienséances de société,* and remarks on the literature of the day, full of point and tact, it cannot be wondered at that he has become what he is—a most agreeable companion. As, however, he possesses no inconsiderable portion of the sweet temper and gaiety of spirits of his father, he may yet attain the more worthy distinction of becoming an estimable man."

At Naples, Henry Fox was destined to die thirty-four years later. Such work as he accomplished in his life was, fittingly, in the Diplomatic Service. But that and his marriage in 1833 with Lady Mary Augusta Coventry do not come within the range of his Journal. But his numerous previous love affairs are fully recounted, and in one case he came very near to marrying the clever Miss Villiers, afterwards to be well known as Lady Theresa Lewis. Politics Henry Fox always frankly disliked, and they find but little mention in his Journal, and in that respect it differs from the contemporary diary of his friend, Charles Greville; but, as regards gossip and details of society, the two records often suggest comparison, as when both writers picture the close Court of George the Fourth and the wonderful jewels (some of them Crown property inherited by the King from the Cardinal Prince, the last of the Stuarts) worn by the Royal Favourite, Lady Conyngham. Such details are the authentic garniture of history.

.   .   .   .   .

It will be granted, then, that books of gossip and even scandalous memoirs have their fitting and useful purpose or place in the future presentation of history and the social life of an epoch. We could not do without Gramont and Sévigné, Creevey and Pepys, Horace Walpole, and fifty others. But it is imperative and essential that the gossip be authentic and the recollections correct before books of this description are admitted to the important office of attending the Muse of History. In a recent volume of reminiscences,* which has been read widely, it is contended on the " jacket " or paper cover that this " is probably *the* best Book of Gossip that has been published during the last twenty years." If that be so, it may be of interest to examine how far such a claim is justified and point out where the recollections fail in accuracy or pervert real facts. The author chooses to be anonymous. He is apparently a septuagenarian, who has resided mostly in Paris since early childhood (perchance his father was British Ambassador there), and who in later years held some office at the British Embassy in the same city at the time Lord Lyons was Ambassador

---

* *Uncensored Recollections,* Anon. (Nash & Grayson, 12s. 6d. net.)

(1867-1887). Perhaps his anonymity is wise when he has such startling " recollections " to publish as those which pronounce the late Empress Eugénie to have been the illegitimate daughter of her (admitted) mother, Madame de Montijo (*née* Kirkpatrick), by the fourth Earl of Clarendon (1800-1870), the diplomat, who was later British Ambassador at Madrid.

The suggestion is that Madame de Montijo, who, it is agreed, was a person of dubious character, emulated Catherine the Second of Russia, so that when she saw a pretty youth she fancied she spared no pains to get him. The young men whom she desired were kidnapped and borne off to La Granja, and disappeared from mortal ken, like Hylas stolen by the nymphs of the stream. But, unlike Hylas, they were restored to their friends when the lady had done with them. Presumably, however, Madame de Montijo's wooing of Lord Clarendon (he would have been George Villiers, aged twenty-six, at the time of the birth of Eugénie, the future Empress) did not involve his forcible abduction. And the proofs of the story? The author of this book says he was told by a man named Coleman that the Empress frequently stayed incognito as Madame de Guzman at his house near Watford, where she was visited daily by Lord Clarendon, whose seat, of course, was The Grove, near Watford; that Lord Clarendon had ever taken a great interest in the lady before her marriage, and arranged with a certain Mrs. Gould to lend her apartments in the Champs Elysées for Louis Napoleon there to meet Eugénie de Montijo, and so conduct his courtship in private, and that in return the future Emperor and Empress were godparents to Mrs. Gould's youngest boy, named Louis Eugene, and Lord Clarendon subsequently procured for the fortunate youth a clerkship in the English Foreign Office. Finally, it is advanced that the Empress's beautiful golden-red hair was peculiar to the Clarendon Villiers family (though hitherto it has been accepted as an inheritance from her mother's Scottish family, the Kirkpatricks of Closeburn). Such is the story. It may be true, of course; but who can disprove it now all the parties concerned are dead? A legend of this kind might be fitted in after years to the origin of anyone, and it is not a pastime to be encouraged.

The most valuable portion of this book is contained in the amazingly vivid picture it gives of the gay, irresponsible society of the Second Empire. No breath of scandal ever touched the Empress, but apparently everyone else about the Court was vicious. The French aristocracy had learned nothing from the fate of their predecessors in the Great Revolution, and life and prodigal excesses were much the same under Napoleon the Third and Louis the Fifteenth. Here is a picture of Cora Pearl, the ugly but well-made courtesan, with her red hair and profusion of diamonds and pearls, when she gave an entertainment to her friends at the Théâtre des Bouffes. She " appeared as Cupidon, almost nude; that is, with no clothing worth mentioning, but covered from head to foot with jewels—literally so, for in one last extravagant gambol she threw herself flat on her back and flung her legs up in the air to show the soles of her shoes that were one mass of diamonds." Again, there is another picture of the young Duc de Mouchy dancing naked before the soldiers in the Pépinière Barracks; and a second youthful Duc— he of Gramont Caderousse—seems to have graduated in the school of Monsieur the Marquis in *A Tale of Two Cities* to a certain extent : —

" As he stepped out of his carriage the young Duke let fall a louis, and the gold coin rolled into the mud. A half-starved man in rags was passing. Caderousse stopped him : ' Do you see that louis there? Well, if you'll pick it up with your teeth, not touching it with your hands, I'll give it you." The man frowned, hesitated, but then knelt down, pushed his face about in the mud, caught the coin with his lips, and then stood and faced Caderousse with it between his teeth. The duke smiled and nodded, but seeing the scowl on the man's face, said ' That's all right for the louis; of course, you've won it. But I can see you hate me for making you win it in that way, don't you? ' ' Of course, I do,' growled the man. ' You're a brute, a *cochon*, you ought to be killed.' ' Quite right,' said the Duke, ' only I don't want to die just yet. But I'll tell you what I will do for you, just to relieve your feelings. I'll just give you this,' and he held up a thousand franc note, ' if you'll hit me as hard as you possibly can, right in the face. I deserve it.' The words were hardly out of his mouth before he found himself sprawling in the gutter with both lips bleeding. ' Thanks ! ' he gasped, as he struggled to his feet, and gave the man the note. Then, bowing low, he said : ' *C'est parfait. Bonsoir et bon appetit, mon ami.' "*

Such things are invaluable as pictures of the manners of a time. The Duc de Gramont Caderousse had his contemporary English double over here in the person of the Marquis of Hastings, who, after a few years of wild escapades and the squandering of a vast fortune, died at the age of twenty-six. His French rival also died young and staged a theatrical end, as can be read in this book.

Unfortunately, many statements by the anonymous author are inaccurate, as he himself might have ascertained by consulting authentic records and books of reference. For example, he says, after describing the Court of Napoleon the Third and Eugénie, that the Emperor was reluctant to receive his old friend and benefactor, Lady Blessington, because " the young and prudish

Y 2

Queen Victoria was looking critically and carefully at all that was taking place at the new Court in Paris." But poor Lady Blessington died in 1849, and Louis Napoleon did not become Emperor or marry until 1852 and 1853 respectively, so when Lady Blessington arrived in Paris the Prince was merely President, and when he asked her if she expected to remain long she replied, " *Non, monsieur* " (and not " Sire," as stated in this book): " *Et vous?* "

The author has a good deal to say about the Duke of Brunswick : —

" The wicked old duke (he lived to a very great age) I remember well in Paris. When still very young his reputation was so abominable that when he came to try and marry George IV.'s only child His Majesty sent him about his business. . . . Once my father met him at a reception of the Duchesse Pozzo di Borgo, and one of the ladies of the Torlonia family happening to be standing near, my father called the old villain's attention to some splendid emeralds she was wearing. ' They're not so fine as these,' said the old duke (he was nearly eighty then), and calmly revealed the magnificent emeralds he was using as buttons for his pants. He used to . . . drive every afternoon in the Bois in a glass coach drawn by a pair of cream-coloured Hanoverian horses. I remember him well, for he was a very small, shrivelled-up man, and wore a spun glass wig; and the way he would wriggle and squirm to bow to my mother always amused me. He was nearly a hundred when he died."

As a matter of historical fact, the Duke of Brunswick (1804-1873) was only eleven years of age when his first cousin, Princess Charlotte (daughter of George the Fourth) married Prince Leopold in 1816. So far from the Duke of Brunswick attaining to " nearly a hundred " years, he was but sixty-nine at the time of his death. These kind of blunders emphasise a point I am continually urging in reviews of books of this nature, namely, that when elderly people write memoirs their pages should be submitted to a competent editor for correction and revision before the publication of palpable errors is perpetrated. In many cases the incorrect statements are never overtaken; they pass as facts, are quoted as such in subsequent books, and the mischief is irremediable.

This particular author's memory has also come to grief in his recollections of G. P. R. James, the novelist. He must have been a small boy when he saw James in Paris, because the last time the novelist visited that city was in 1858. He says amongst other things which are incorrect : —

" His name was George Payne Rainsford James, but he was called George Prince Regent James because he was so extravagant. He had been brought up by the Duchess of Kent with the Princess Victoria, and the Queen was very fond of him, was a true friend to him in every way, and was constantly writing to him. I used as a child to see lots of her letters to him, beginning, ' My Dear George,' and ending, ' Affectionately yours.' In fact, the sale of those Royal autographs was an important financial help to his family, when he finally drank himself to death in Venice, where the Queen had had him made Consul (he got into the habit of drinking when Consul in Norfolk, Virginia)."

Well, in the first place, when James was chaffingly called George Prince Regent James it was because his father held the appointment of physician to the Prince Regent (George the Fourth). The novelist was born in 1801, and Queen Victoria in 1819, so if the Duchess of Kent chose a young man eighteen years older than her daughter to be " brought up " with the little girl, she must have been a greater fool than her brother-in-law, King William the Fourth, was wont to designate her. I can assure the author of this book that G. P. R. James never spoke to Queen Victoria in his life, and the letters he saw signed " Affectionately yours," were most certainly *not* from Her Majesty. James was appointed Consul in Venice by that same Lord Clarendon to whom the author assigns the honour of the paternity of the Empress Eugénie. It does not err on the side of kindness or veracity to say James " drank himself to death." It is true that he drank more than was wise or necessary in his last months, but his health had been ruined by the unhealthy climate of the swamps of Virginia, and he was a martyr to many complaints. The actual cause of his death was paralysis—a stroke.

I also question the statement in this book that James brought Charles Lever to the Paris house of the author's parents; it was not in 1858, anyway, because Lever was then in Italy. Lever and James were on the Continent together in 1845, but this, I imagine, would be before the recollection of the anonymous memoirist. He attributes, by the way, to Charles Lever a scatological anecdote worthy of a place in *Les Contes Drolatiques* of Balzac.

The author has a story to tell of the war of 1870, on the authority of Lord Lyons, which is of some historical interest. It has always been a matter of argument how much, if at all, the Empress Eugénie was responsible for the precipitation of the conflict with Germany, or if she ever did term it " Ma Guerre " : —

" Now Baron Alphonse de Rothschild (who himself told this to Lord Lyons) being anxious to know exactly how matters stood and what were the chances of an amicable arrangement with Prussia, decided to go himself to the Emperor direct and ask him. The Court was at that time at St. Cloud. . . . The Emperor received him at once . . . and taking his hand in his, His Majesty said very earnestly, ' *C'est ne pas la guerre, mon cher Baron, foi de gentilhomme.*' Of course, the Baron was greatly relieved and delighted, and after a few words of thanks and congratulations took his departure. But in the corridor leading to the Emperor's private rooms he met the Empress going to see her husband. Of course, he stopped and had a few words with Her Majesty, but only on ordinary and trivial topics; and then, bowing low, rushed to his carriage and was driven post haste to his bank in the Rue Lafitte, the Empress proceeding to the Emperor's room. The Baron had not been back two hours when an estafette, his horse reeking, as he had galloped all the way from St. Cloud, dashed up to the bank with the laconic message—the words written in pencil to save time—' *Tout est changé; C'est la guerre, N.' "*

The author was an intimate friend, it would seem, of the Prince of Wales (Edward the Seventh), and he gives a very frank presentation of the Prince's character—his *bonhomie* and tact and, on the other side, his failings and the rather ruinous influence he had upon young men, not wealthy, who were admitted to the honour of his friendship. The Prince was not above tolerating introductions to himself of rich parvenus if his friends who arranged the matter were to benefit by a high monetary commission. In one case £15,000 was to be paid for the incredible privilege. The Duke of Edinburgh, it is alleged, was willing to take money himself in affairs of this nature (for, unlike his elder brother, he was of a thrifty disposition), and on a certain occasion £30,000 reached him for arranging the introduction of a wealthy but dubious Russian to his Imperial father-in-law, the Tsar Alexander the Second.

The author takes some effective shots to explode the reputations of several of his friends, including the late Duke of Fife and Lord Randolph Churchill. In dealing with the latter he achieves his best passage in a literary sense—when he compares Lord Randolph's rudeness to Gladstone in the House of Commons as a discharge of " broadside after broadside of the roughest Blenheim ammunition at the stately flagship."

Errors apart, this is a very entertaining book and of value as a social panopticon of the second half of the nineteenth century.

FORREST REID.*

Mr. George Moore in his last book poured contempt upon the actual names of popular novelists in Great Britain. Scott and Trollope suggest to him dull, commonplace respectability, and the sound of Thackeray and Dickens merely convey the clatter of the pantry. But, as a critic of cognomen, Mr. Moore would no doubt admit that his brilliant compatriot, Forrest Reid, possesses the appropriate name to suggest exactly the kind of books he writes. I know for a fact several people who think Forrest Reid an assumed name—an alliterative and picturesque pun, so to speak, conveying an image of the reeds by a forest pool. It is a justifiable supposition, for Mr. Reid's romances have ever a sylvan background of forest and mountain; a pool or stream is an essential adjunct to some important incident in all his stories; through ever one of them murmurs " the wind among the reeds." In short, Pan is Forrest Reid's presiding deity. But his names are his own—from birth and baptism.

He is a member of a well-known family in the north of Ireland, the son of Robert Reid, a merchant of Belfast. Two of his uncles were Dr. Seaton Reid, Materia Medica Professor at Queen's University, Belfast, and Sir Edward Reid, a former Mayor of Derry. An avuncular relative of an earlier generation was Dr. James Seaton Reid, Professor of Ecclesiastical and Civil History at Glasgow University and Presbyterian minister at Carrickfergus. The name of Forrest came through the marriage of a Reid with a member of that family.

Mr. Forrest Reid's mother was a Parr of Shropshire: but he was born in Belfast, and educated there at the Royal Academical Institution—a school which is described in two of his books, *Following Darkness* and *The Pirates of the Spring*. His experiences as an apprentice in the tea trade of Belfast are reflected in *At the Door of the Gate*. Mr. Reid completed his education at Christ's College, Cambridge, where he took his degree. Since then he has lived almost entirely in County Down and Belfast. His has not been an adventurous or romantic career apparently, though these are the qualities which permeate his books. If an inspiring cause for his literary work be sought, it might be found in the beautiful scenery and the wild sea coast

* *The Bookman*, May, 1920.

of his native province. Particularly has he been influenced by the Mourne Mountains, the very spirit of which he has grasped and interpreted.

I have said Pan is Mr. Reid's god. But his Pan is not the altogether malignant Pan of Mr. Arthur Machen, for instance: He is a more gracious and youthful deity, Pan as a boy, but nevertheless equally fatal to those mortals who meet him face to face. If Mr. Reid needs a goddess, it is the Moon, and she often plays a baleful part in the lives of his creations. Youth is the *motif* of his romances. The protagonist of his story is generally a slim brown boy, with dark eyes and coarse black hair, suggestive of a faun. Sometimes his characters reach the wan land of the occult and the supernatural, the realms of fantasy; and all those who cross the dividing line from normal life find tragedy and death beyond.

It will be seen that Mr. Reid's art is mystic and peculiar. He has the Celtic realisation of the unseen world as near at hand, and the Greek belief in inevitable fate. Consequently his stories can never be popular successes in the usual sense, for they do not end happily to the sound of wedding bells as per the usual formula. But, contradictory as it may seem, they are concerned alike with the grim realities, the beauty and sadness of life, and that lone dreamland of mystery and terror beyond the veil.

His earliest work, *The Kingdom of Twilight*, was published as No. 9 of Fisher Unwin's First Novel Library in 1904. It dealt incidentally with moon-influence. It was read and much appreciated by Henry James, who wrote a kindly letter to the young author. This led to the dedication of Mr. Reid's next book, *The Garden God* (1905), to Henry James. But the author now considers both these books hopelessly jejune and immature, and he does not include them in the list of his published works. The adjectives mentioned are not those I should apply to the books in question: to *The Garden God*, at any rate, rather should I venture to suggest " precious " or what used to be termed " *fin de siècle*."

The Bracknels (1911) is the work which Mr. Reid regards as the foundation stone of his literary career. It is a remarkable study of an abnormal boy, a moon-worshipper, who is obsessed and haunted by the malignant influences of an old house, his home, reputed in earlier times to have been the scene of a murder. Just as in the case of the boy in Henry James's finest supernatural story, *The Turn of the Screw*, Denis Bracknel is killed by the forces of evil that have reached him from another plane. Individual opinion may object to the manner in which the final tragedy occurs; but the whole story is bathed in that sense of terror and impending doom which Sheridan Le Fanu could so portentously convey, and compels admiration.

Following Darkness (1912) was an even greater achievement, for it was the first of those minute dissections of a boy's psychology which have since become so frequent and successful. It pre-dated by a year Mr. Compton Mackenzie's *Sinister Street*, which is generally taken to be the pioneer of this class of book. There were also, of course, earlier " revelations " of public-school life than Mr. Alec Waugh's *The Loom of Youth*. *Jaspar Tristram*, by A. W. Clarke, and *The Puppets' Dallying*, by Louis Marlow, both dealing with Radley, respectively appeared as far back as 1899 and 1905. *Following Darkness* was to a certain extent autobiographic, for the author drew the mentality of Peter Waring from himself, changing or altering all externals of course, except the dominating background of the Mourne Mountains, the seascape of County Down, and some incidents in Belfast.

In *The Gentle Lover* (1913) Mr. Reid struck an entirely new note, and this book is the exception to the general rule of his stories. It is not overshadowed by tragic fate, the whole aim being to produce an atmosphere from which all harshness, cruelty, and ugliness should be excluded. *At the Door of the Gate* (1915) is a kind of compromise in style. It is rich in humour, but ends in a mist of tragedy. The terrible struggle and murder on the grey sea cliffs of Antrim is an unforgettable picture of stark realism. But in " the vision " which comes to the murderer, wherein he finds God, I confess I do not follow the author: it is the one instance where his intention and meaning, actual or symbolical, eludes me.

In 1915, also, Mr. Reid published his critical and very able study of his fellow countryman, W. B. Yeats, with whom of course he has much in common, both in mental outlook and mystical literary expression. Three years later he collected his short stories and some other pieces in a volume entitled *A Garden by the Sea*. In this, *The Accomplice* and *An Ulster Farm* are grim little masterpieces; *Kenneth* is extremely funny; *A Boy and His Dog* full of pathos; whilst *An Ending* is a remarkable presentation of the Spirit of Bruges by means of a character, morbidly sensitive, within whose mind the ancient and picturesquely crumbling city is mirrored as in one of its own canals.

Mr. Reid reached the most typical expression of his art in *The Spring Song* (1916). It is impossible to give an idea of this uncommon book in a few words. It is not a novel; it is a picture of the Spirit of Youth as personified by a party of jolly boys and girls on holiday in, perchance, the Ballinderry district of County Antrim. But one of the boys is a dreamer; he hears the Pipes of Pan—the Spring Song. He also comes under the influence of a man, a homicidal maniac, who suggests terrible things to his acutely sensitive mind. Then ensue supernatural experiences, in one of which the boy is saved by his faithful dog; but in the end Death again claims its toll from one who, in pursuit of Pan, had parted the curtain of the unknown. It is a fantastic tale and, as the author has said, it belongs to the land where memories end and dreams begin.

In his latest book, *The Pirates of the Spring*, Mr. Reid has reintroduced two of the characters from *The Spring Song;* but it is in much lighter vein. There is no tragedy and nothing occult. It is a very subtle and sympathetic study of boyhood as represented by several contrasted types, and displays an extraordinary insight into the psychology of youthful friendships, affections, jealousies, and that spirit which generates adventures. The author's aim is to bring out the deeper and spiritual qualities that often lay hidden beneath a commonplace and unemotional exterior. Thus by means of their experiences his four principal characters progress and change—each in his own way, though the movement may be hidden, comes to life in a finer spiritual sense. It is a clever piece of analysis, but one ventures to hope that in his next book Mr. Forrest Reid will return to that plane of supernatural romance which is peculiarly his own, for he has dared to gaze through " magic casements opening on the foam of perilous seas."*

---

* Mr Reid has since written *Pender Among the Residents* (1922), which presents some supernatural features.

MISS MARY L. PENDERED.[*]

It seems to be a pleasant practice of women novelists, who study country life, to depict some particular county or district well known to them as the background and setting of their stories. Probably the fashion was instituted by Jane Austen, more than a century ago, with her delicate studies of Hampshire and Bath. The Brontës followed with their more vivid pictures of the moorlands of Yorkshire, and George Eliot with her charming presentments of Warwickshire. At the present day this specialisation, so to speak, of county novels is very marked. Sussex, in particular, is highly favoured in possessing three such literary artists as Mrs. Henry Dudeney, Miss Violet Simpson, and Miss Sheila Kaye-Smith.

Miss Mary L. Pendered is pre-eminently—nay solely—the living novelist of Northamptonshire, one of the most typical of English counties. Its situation in the heart of England has left it primitive and unspoiled in the rural districts away from the towns. What strikes a visitor to Northamptonshire most, in spring and summer, is the intense green of the countryside—a land of lush meadows, rich vegetation, wild straying hedges, grass-bordered roads, and waving woodlands which descend from the forests of Whittlebury and Rockingham. This, too, is the aspect which Miss Pendered has conveyed to her best novels and transcribed again and again with never failing charm—a picture of rich green country and Arcadian delights, of picturesque thatched cottages set in old-world gardens ablaze with flowers and scented with lavender, and always woods beyond. She draws from the actual scene, for, although born in London, Miss Pendered has, since the age of seven, lived practically all her life in Northamptonshire (with the exception of a few years spent at Beltinge, Herne Bay). Her girlhood was passed at an old house in Wellingborough, but later her family removed to a pleasant property, named Redwell, outside that town, and this is still her home. Wellingborough and the country round is consequently the district of her novels.

But though the scene of her novels may be local and peaceful, their subject matter is sometimes very different, for human passions are not slaked by a draught of green pastoralism and

---

[*] *The Bookman,* October, 1919.

innocence is not indigenous to a cottage.   Miss Pendered does
not shrink from the facts of life; she has on occasion presented
them with considerable courage for one of her sex, and has, in
result, not escaped the charge of " immorality " brought against
some of her books by inept persons.   The most remarkable fact
of her literary output is her extraordinary variety.   As I have
said, several of her novels have been stigmatised as " immoral
and too daring ": others have been termed " wholesome and
sweetly pretty."   This, perhaps, has militated against her work
becoming a popular success.   She has ever declined to write in a
groove.   The reading public which knows exactly what to expect
in the way of sentimental virtues or delicious vices from certain
popular lady novelists, who shall here be nameless, is a little shy
of a writer who runs up and down the whole scale in her books.
The unexpected is not desired by the great majority of novel
readers.   Those who liked Miss Pendered's " daring " studies
of the relations of the sexes were bored by her " wholesome "
pastorals, and those who liked the latter were shocked by the
former.   Consequently, the versatile author has missed the
particular following of the established favourite.   As she herself has described her variableness : —

" I cannot and don't want to write two books alike.   I cannot make
a name for a certain type of book, because my fancy pulls in so many
directions.   At one moment I long to write, like Herrick, ' of books, of
blossoms, birds and flowers, of April, May, of June and July flowers.'
At another time I feel impelled to write of poor, frail, fallen humankind.
At another I write of naughty people and their passions.   Or again I
have a sudden desire to recreate a once living man or woman in biography.   Or I feel sententious, and wish to spend myself in essays.   Or
a dramatic inspiration seizes me and I burn to write a play."

Miss Pendered's first novel, *Dust and Laurels*, published in
1893, was very well received by press and public, and went into a
second edition.   *The Literary World* observed that the author's
strength lay " in her smart Oscar Wilde paradoxes."   It was
followed by *A Pastoral Played Out*, which the critics decided was
an " immoral " book.   *The New York Times* gave it three
columns of violent abuse, which, however, failed to secure
popularity for the novel : the subject—the ruin of a young girl,
who eventually murders her illegitimate child—is painful.   The
book also gives some glimpses of stage life.

The author broke new ground with her third novel, *An
Englishman*, which Mr. W. L. Courtney described as " a
thoroughly wholesome, sympathetic, effective story . . . handled
with considerable adroitness and manifesting no inconsiderable
originality of characterisation " : he classed it as one of the best

books of the year (1899). Next came *Musk of Roses; The Secret of the Dragon;* and *Daisy the Minx*. The second of these—and the author's favourite work—was a remarkable romance: it dealt with alchemy and what *The Westminster Gazette* termed " the secret whispered through Keats's ' Magic Casements.' "

Miss Pendered now produced in sequence her three most characteristic novels of country life in Northamptonshire. *At Lavender Cottage* contains some excellent portraiture, in particular a very able and successful study of the psychology of a small boy. *Phyllida Flouts Me* describes the villages of the Cranfords near Kettering. *Lily Magic* interprets very finely the spirit of the lovely country of the midland county.

Plain Jill and *The Secret Sympathy* (which has been translated into Norwegian) were followed last year by *The Silent Battlefield*—a powerful novel which has brought the author an instalment of the recognition that is her due. It describes the career of an illegitimate boy and his struggle with the world: the title adumbrates his conflict with his own soul. The Eniborough of the story is, of course, Wellingborough. Miss Pendered has also written *The Book of Common Joys* (essays) and, anonymously, *All We Like Sheep* and *The Truth about Man* by " A Spinster," which ran through two magazines, and three editions in book form. She has written other works in collaboration, and contributed largely to magazines and newspapers. For nearly a year, in fact, she followed the calling of a journalist in London. But she now lives entirely in the country: no place can be too quiet for her. When not engaged in writing she devotes her time to gardening and music.

Mention must also be made of another book by Miss Pendered in quite a different vein to her novels. In 1910 she produced *The Fair Quaker*—an extremely painstaking and valuable study of Hannah Lightfoot and her relations with King George the Third, which shows considerable biographical skill and a *flair* for discovering evidence and the marshalling of salient facts. Miss Pendered's future career, both as biographer and novelist, will be watched with interest.*

---

* Miss Pendered has since written an excellent biography of *John Martin*, the Biblical painter (1923). See *ante,* page 74.

GEORGE SOMES LAYARD.*

Mr. George Somes Layard holds the belief that an author should never confine himself to one particular groove of writing or specialisation, and he practises what he preaches, for he is one of the most versatile of contemporary bookmen. Biography, novels, "queer" short stories, and expert dissertations on prints and book illustrations are all within his literary ambit, and he turns from one category of composition to another with equal ease and never-failing enthusiasm for the work in hand.

Mr. Layard is descended from the Huguenot family of Raymond de Layarde. His great-great-grandfather, Daniel Peter Layard, was physician to Augusta, Princess of Wales, and his great-grandfather became Dean of Bristol. He is a son of the Rev. C. C. Layard (a first cousin of Sir Henry Layard, the explorer), and received his education at Harrow and Trinity College, Cambridge. Mr. Layard is by profession a barrister of the Inner Temple, but he has ever preferred the pursuits of literature and art.

His first publication appeared during his University days, in *The Oxford and Cambridge Undergraduates' Journal*, his contribution taking the form of a skit on the Proctors. Later he wrote for *The Globe*, but it was not until 1890 that Mr. Layard established his literary reputation by the series of remarkable *Queer Stories*, which were published in *Truth* during the next three years. Some of the stories were reprinted in book form in two volumes entitled *His Golf Madness* (1892) and *Society Straws* (1897). It is curious that the rest of these *Queer Stories* have not been discovered by some enterprising publisher for reissue in a book, because they are in the front rank of merit as a peculiar combination of the sensational and bizarre. They can be read again and again with fresh delight in their ingenuity of action and originality of unexpected *dénouement*.

Mr. Layard entered a new field of literature by the publication of his finely produced monograph on *Charles Keene of "Punch"* (1892). It was followed by *Tennyson and His Pre-Raphaelite Illustrators* (1894); *George Cruikshank's Portraits of Himself* (1897); *Mrs. Lynn Linton* (1901); *Dolly's*

* *The Bookman*, July, 1922.

Governess (1904), a novel; *Kate Greenaway*, written in collaboration with H. M. Spielmann (1905); *Sir Thomas Lawrence's Letter-Bag* (1906); *A Great " Punch " Editor, Shirley Brooks* (1907); *Suppressed Plates* (1907); *Wax* (1909), a most original novel with the unusual setting of Madame Tussaud's for part of its action; and *Peter Clement Layard*, a memoir, with letters, of his son who was killed in the war (1919).

It will be apparent from the list of his books that Mr. Layard makes a perennial study of the work of artists, engravers, and book illustrators. He is also a keen and perceptive collector of fine engravings which he loves for their beauty and archæological interest, and not merely as prizes of monetary value. His collection is not secreted in portfolios but hangs upon the walls of his pleasant house in Pelham Place. As he has truly written of prints—or any other beautiful work of art:—

" Make friends of them, grow in intimacy with them, and they will never fail you. . . Holding in deepest loathing the dryasdust treatment of anything on God's beautiful earth, I am wholly out of patience with the ghoul-collector who gloats over the number of his victims embalmed in portfolios and coffined in solander-cases."

In connection with his zeal for print collecting, Mr. Layard tells an amusing story:—

" One day at Buxton I had been introduced to a lady with whom I had a long talk on art. The next day, in the Gardens, I saw her sitting with a man whom I did not know. She bowed to me, and as I raised my hat and approached her, I cudgelled my brains for an opening gambit. ' How do you do? ' I said. ' Are you very keen on prints? ' Her hitherto smiling face turned to thunder, and she snapped out, ' I beg your pardon, *what* did you say? ' I then explained that I had just been up the town and bought a fine mezzotint. She was then all smiles again, and it was not till the next day that I discovered that her companion's name was PRINCE ! "

Mr. Layard's latest book* is concerned with prints—an exhaustive study of the variations of the engraving by Pierre Lombart of a mounted horseman, whose face, in different states of the plate, has represented, in turn, Cromwell, Louis the Fourteenth, Cromwell again, Charles the First, and Cromwell yet again.

Lombart, a French engraver who was in London during the last years of the reign of Charles the First and most of the Commonwealth, borrowed the main details of his chameleon-like plate from the famous picture by Van Dyck, now at Windsor Castle, representing Charles the First on horseback, under an archway, and attended, on foot, by the Duc d'Espernon, who

---

* *The Headless Horseman.* Pierre Lombart's Engraving : Charles or Cromwell. By George Somes Layard, with twelve reproductions (Philip Allan.)

bears the King's helmet. In Lombart's engraving the figures of
the King and the horse have remained much the same during its
various mutations; but, as I have said, the face of the rider has
been altered again and again. Lombart also converted the figure
of the bearded duke into a youthful foot-page, who, however, still
and ever bears the rider's helmet; and the archway in Van
Dyck's picture is transformed into a view of a little castle on a
hill with a cavalry combat in progress at its base.

It has hitherto been believed by the experts that Lombart
originally intended his print to portray the features of Charles
the First, and that he changed the face to that of Cromwell as
a matter of political expediency when the regicide succeeded to
the position and power he had wrested from his royal victim.
Mr. Layard's theory is that Lombart from the outset, 1657,
engraved the portrait of Cromwell in his picture, but that the
first version of the face proved to be unsatisfactory to the artist,
who then burnished or hammered out the head, and substituted
another, which would account for the " halo " effect visible in
the first known Cromwell state of this print. Then, Mr. Layard
argues, came the Restoration, when a portrait of Cromwell would
naturally be an unpalatable drug in the market. Lombart erased
once more the head of the regicide, and the probably unique
print from the plate in this truncated state—showing the horseman actually headless—is in the British Museum.

Instead of presenting, as one would expect, a portrait of the
new king, Charles the Second, Lombart proceeded to engrave
on his plate the face of his own king, Louis the Fourteenth, and
two varying states of the engraving at this stage are in
existence. Now, accordoing to Mr. Layard, the plate passed
out of the possession of Lombart, who had returned to France,
and the new owner-engraver once more turned the picture into a
portrait of Cromwell—a curious thing to do in the reign of
Charles the Second, and which certainly could not expect to be a
profitable venture. Before seven years had passed the artist
discovered this fact, and about 1666 the engraving appeared with
the head of Charles the First. It became a good seller, yet,
marvellous to relate, within a year the beheaded king was again
beheaded in his portrait and Cromwell once more reappeared—
but this time in the guise of an older, weaker man.

How Mr. Layard establishes all this, how he notes and records
the varying differences of detail and accessory in the succeeding
stages of this Vicar of Bray-like print, and how he refutes the
beliefs of the experts who preceded him in the study of the
subject, must be read in his book, which is a brilliant, and beauti-

fully produced, contribution to the fascinating cult of print collecting. It is by no means a dry, technical treatise. Romance, the joys and humours of hunting and successful pursuit, run through its pages. Here is one excellent story. The author was inspecting the copy of Van Dyck's picture (the same which forms the basis of his book) hanging in the Middle Temple Hall, and conversed with the custodian thus:

" ' There's a curious legend attaching to that picture, sir,' he said. ' Cromwell, not content with beheading Charles the First, must needs command the Benchers of the Inn to behead his picture, too.' "

' Behead his picture? ' I said. ' What a vandal ! '

' No, sir,' he said, correcting me, ' a Van Dyck ! '

' Ah, yes,' I said, rather taken aback. ' I mean, but what did he want to mutilate the picture for? '

' He didn't exactly want them to cut up the picture, sir. He ordered the Benchers to take it down, get the king's face obliterated, and have his own painted in its place.' "

The story is curiously in agreement with the history of Lombart's engraving, and Mr. Layard has probed and related that history with a thoroughness worthy of the highest praise.

THE BOY JONES.*

THE recent successful invasion of Buckingham Palace by a midnight intruder† brings to mind similar incidents in March, 1841, which had for hero The Boy Jones, who succeeded in reaching the private apartments of Queen Victoria no less than three times. Probably the Palace was less securely guarded in those days. Raikes, in his *Journal*, relates : —

> " A little scamp of an apothecary's errand-boy, named Jones, has the unaccountable mania of sneaking privately into Buckingham Palace, where he is found secreted at night under a sofa, or some other hiding-place, close to the Queen's bed-chamber. No one can divine his object, but twice he has been detected and conveyed to the police-office, and put into confinement for a time. The other day he was detected in a third attempt, with apparently as little object. Lady Sandwich wittily wrote that he must be a descendant of *In-I-go* Jones, the architect."

After his third arrest The Boy Jones was detained, and Charles Dickens interested himself in the enterprising youth's future. He wrote this unpublished letter to Francis Smedley (father of Frank Smedley, the novelist), who, as High Bailiff of Westminster, presumably had the disposal of the youthful explorer in High Latitudes : —

" Devonshire Terrace,
" April the Nineteenth, 1841.

" My dear Sir,

" Unless you forbid me, I mean to call upon you next Monday between 12 and 1, and avail myself of your good offices in the matter of ' The Boy Jones,' as the Sunday newspapers denominate him in very fat capitals.

" Faithfully yours,

" CHARLES DICKENS.

" Francis Smedley, Esquire."

Eventually Jones was sent to sea. *Punch*, then newly-born, made great fun of the whole affair. In its first number there appeared a *Court Circular*, " Communicated exclusively to this Journal by Master Jones, whose services we have succeeded in retaining "; and soon after there was *The Boy Jones's Log*, with two woodcuts, from which the following extracts are taken : —

---

* *The Dickensian*, August, 1914.

† In 1914 a man named Pike climbed the railings separating the grounds of Buckingham Palace from Constitution Hill, and entered the Palace. He was discovered in the bedroom of one of the King's pages and given into custody. At the King's desire, when the case came before the magistrates, Pike was ordered to find a surety to keep the peace for six months, or alternatively serve one month's imprisonment.

" So soon as the fust aggytation of my mind is woar off, I take up my pen to put my sentiments on peaper . . . Halass, Sir, the wicktim of that crewel bluebeard, Lord Melbun, who got affeard of my rising poplarity in the Palass, and as sent me to *see* for my peeping, though, heaven nose, I was acktyated by the pewrest motiffs in what I did. The real fax of the case is, I'm a young man of an ighly cultiwated mind and a very ink-wisitive disposition, wich naturally led me to the use of the pen. I ad also been in the abit of reading *Jak Sheppard,* and I may add that I O all my eleygant tastes to the perowsal of that faxinating book. O ! wot a noble mind the author of these wollums must have !—what a frootful inwention and fine feelings he displays . . . when I read it fust I felt a thust for litterry fame spring up in my buzzem, and I thort I should be an orthor. . . . At last I resolved to rite, and I cast my i's about for a subject—they fell on the Palass ! Ear, as my friend Litton Bulwer ses, ear was a field for genus to sore into ; ear was an area for fillosophy to dive into ; ear was a truly magnificient and comprehensive desine for a great *nash*-ional picture. . . .—*Pencillings in the Palass; or A Small Voice from the Royal Larder,* with commick illustriations by Fiz. . . .''

It is almost certain that this *jeu d'esprit* was written by Thackeray. It is in his *Yellowplush* style of diction, and the supposition is confirmed by the allusions to Ainsworth and Bulwer-Lytton, two authors Thackeray always delighted to pillory in *Punch.* The Boy Jones thus has some literary interest attached to his exploits, for he employed the pens of both Dickens and Thackeray, and reached a niche in the Valhalla of *Punch.* Whether his rival of to-day will gain equal fame is doubtful.

THE LITERATURE OF RESURRECTION MEN.

MEMORIES of the case of Burke and Hare are revived by a recent publication.* Very unpleasant as the subject is, it yet has considerable interest and some literary associations. Even the word " Burke " has become an accepted adjective of the English language—signifying " to kill silently by suffocation, to put out of the way," for Burke and Hare generally murdered their victims by lying on them and closing the air passages of mouth and nostril, which was easily accomplished when the prey had been first stupefied with drink.

Burke and Hare were not, of course, Resurrection Men in the usual meaning of the words, for they did not dig up corpses from graveyards : they followed the far more criminal course of murder in order to obtain bodies to sell to the surgeons for purposes of anatomical research.

In old days the Company of Barbers and Surgeons had obtained sufficient material for research work in the bodies of malefactors who had been hung, and which were handed over to them for that purpose.† But during the first quarter of the nineteenth century new Medical Schools arose, and the consequent competition for bodies caused the rise of Resurrection Men to supply a want which was paid for at a handsome remuneration.

According to Dickens, in *A Tale of Two Cities*, Mr. Jerry Cruncher followed by night the avocation of a body-snatcher as early as what that worthy would have termed " Anna Dominoes " 1780. Twenty years later the fell profession was well-known in London. There is preserved in the Royal College of Surgeons a fragment of manuscript, covering sixteen leaves, presented to that institution by Sir Thomas Longmore. It was printed

---

* *Burke and Hare,* edited by William Roughead. Notable British Trials. (Hodge, 10s. 6d. net.)

† Sometimes condemned criminals tried to sell their bodies beforehand. The following letter was found among the papers of Mr. Goldwyr, a surgeon of Salisbury :—

" To Mr. Edward Goldwyr, at his house in the Close of Salisbury.

" Sir,—Being informed that you are the only surgeon in this city (or county) that anatomizes men, and I, being under the unhappy circumstances, and in a very mean condition, would gladly live as long as I can; but, by all appearances, I am to be executed next March, having no friends on earth that will speak a word to save my life, nor send me a morsel of bread to keep life and soul together until that fatal day; so, if you will vouchsafe to come hither, I will gladly sell you my body (being whole and sound), to be ordered at your discretion, knowing it will rise again at the general resurrection as well from your house as from the grave.

" Your answer, sir, will highly oblige.—Yours, etc.,

" JAMES BROOKE.

" Fisherton-Anger Gaol, October 3rd, 1736."

356

in 1896 under the title of *The Diary of a Resurrectionist*. The
date was 1811-1812, and the record concerned a gang of seven
men, who rifled many churchyards and sold their spoil to the
hospitals of London.   Their earnings were large—certainly near
£1,400 for one year alone.   A typical entry in the Diary is this : —
    " Tuesday, 4th.   Met at Bartholomew, settled each man's share,
£21. 9s. 4d.   Met at night, went to Guy's, got 3 adults.   Took them to
Bartholomew."

By 1822 the practice of body-snatching had become very pre-
valent, particularly in Scotland.   Mort-safes or strong iron
railings were placed over graves to protect them from outrage,
and iron or lead coffins came into use.   Robert Southey alludes
to these matters in his ballad of *The Surgeon's Warning*, which
relates how an anatomist feared that after his death his apprentices
would utilise his body in the way he had treated many a corpse
procured for him by resurrectionists : —

> " And my 'prentices will surely come
>   And carve me bone from bone,
> And I, who have rifled the dead man's grave,
>   Shall never rest in my own.
>
> Bury me in lead, when I am dead,
>   My brethren, I entreat,
> And see the coffin weigh'd I beg,
>   Lest the plumber should be a cheat.
>
> And let it be solder'd closely down,
>   Strong as strong can be, I implore,
> And put it in a patent coffin
>   That I may rise no more."

There are, of course, many references to body-snatchers by
authors of varied merit.   Samuel Warren in *A Diary of a Late
Physician* offers a chapter on the matter, entitled *Grave Doings*.
In *The Medical Times*, volumes one and two, there was a series
of articles written by Albert Smith, *The Confessions of Jasper
Muddle, Dissecting-room Porter*.   Bulwer-Lytton in *Lucretia*,
Mrs. Crowe in *Light and Darkness*, and David Moir in *Mansie
Wauch*, have all dealt with the subject of Resurrection Men.
And akin to this subject must be mentioned a terrible short story
entitled *The Secret of the Two Plaster Casts*, which appeared in
Tinsley's Magazine in the 'Sixties.   Tom Hood, of course,
treated it with his own characteristic whimsey in several of his
poems.   *The Dead Robbery* concerns one Peter Bunce : —

> " The Parish buried him !
>   Unwatch'd, unwept,
> As commonly a pauper sleeps he slept ;
> There could not be a better opportunity
> For bodies to steal a body so ill-kept,
>   With all impunity.

In fact, when night o'er human vice and folly
Had drawn her very necessary curtains,
Down came a fellow with a sack and spade,
Accustom'd many years to drive a trade
With that Anatomy more Melancholy
    Than Burton's.

The watchman in his box was dozing;
The sexton drinking at the Cheshire Cheese;
No fear of any creature interposing,
The human jackal work'd away at ease.
    He toss'd the mould to left and right,
    The shabby coffin came in sight,
And soon it open'd to his double-knocks . . . ."

The startling and humorous sequel* is too long to quote here,
for precedence must be given to another of Hood's ballads,
Mary's Ghost, wherein she relates to her earthly lover how her
anatomy had gone to various surgeons: —

" The body-snatchers they have come,
    And made a snatch at me;
It's very hard them kind of men
    Won't let a body be !

You thought that I was buried deep,
    Quite decent like and chary;
But from her grave in Mary-bone
    They've come and bon'd your Mary.

The arm that used to take your arm
    Is took to Dr. Vyse;
And both my legs are gone to walk
    The hospital at Guy's.

        .   .   .   .

I can't tell where my head is gone,
    But Dr. Carpne can;
And for my trunk, it's all packed up
    To go by Pickford's van.

I wish you'd go to Mr. P.,
    And save me such a ride;
I don't half like the outside place,
    They've took for my inside.

The cock it crows—I must be gone !
    My William, we must part !
But I'll be yours in death, altho'
    Sir Astley has my heart."†

---

* It is not within the scope of this article to relate examples of an allied
subject, namely, the desecration and rifling of tombs in order to steal jewels
buried with the corpse. In several of the stories the corpse comes to life as
the result of a finger being cut, with resulting flow of blood. A case, supposed
to be well-authenticated, occurred at Wyndham Park, Salisbury; a picturesque
account of it will be found in *The Spinster At Home in the Close of Salisbury*,
by Miss Child, 1844. Harrison Ainsworth introduced a similar incident in his
early comic-tragedy, *The Cut Finger*, 1822.
    † Several stories of Resurrection Men will be found in *The Life of Sir
Astley Cooper*.

Sir Walter Scott was always interested in murder trials.* He devoted particular attention to the case of Burke and Hare, possibly because in *Guy Mannering*, thirteen years earlier, he had made some mention of Helen Torrence and Jean Waldie, the only recorded instance of Resurrection Women, who were executed in 1752. Scott wrote two letters on the subject of Burke and Hare. One, very lengthy, to Miss Edgeworth, dated 4th February, 1829, will be found in Lockhart's *Life*, and the other, written three days later to John Stevenson, one of the publishers of the report of the trial, was embodied in a footnote to Buchanan's edition. He also witnessed the execution of Burke in the High Street, Edinburgh, sharing a window with Charles Kirkpatrick Sharpe and others. Scott noted in his diary that the mob was immense, and opined that a doggerel ballad upon Burke " would be popular, how brutal soever the wit." The want was well supplied in quantity if not in quality, for Mr. Roughead, the editor of the new volume on Burke and Hare, has compiled a whole bibliography of what he terms " the literary ' floral tributes ' " dedicated to the memory of the two murderers.

Finally, it may be recorded that the crimes of Burke and Hare were the inspiring cause of R. L. Stevenson's *macabre* romance, *The Body Snatcher*.

The last of the Resurrection Men in London were Williams, Bishop, and May, the two first named being executed in December, 1831, for the murder of an Italian boy of fourteen, whose body they attempted to sell at the dissecting room of King's College. Public opinion was so inflamed that legislation was immediately introduced in the House of Commons to provide by lawful means material for the study of anatomy; and when the Bill became law in August, 1832, the occupation of the body-snatchers, in the words of Othello, was gone.

---

* Scott, in May, 1828, on his journey north from London to Abbotsford, went out of his way specially to visit Gill's Hill, the scene of the famous murder of Weare by Thurtell four years previously. Sir Walter fully described the place and his views about the crime in his diary, May 28th, 1828. In view of this distinguished precedent, the recent public curiosity to see the bungalow associated with the Crumbles murder was, perhaps, too harshly condemned by pundits and Press.

TUTANKHAMEN AND CHARLES THE FIRST.*

SOME ENGLISH PRECEDENTS FOR
RIFLING ROYAL TOMBS.

IN view of Tutankhamen and the question of the moment,
" Where does scientific research end and violation of graves
begin ? " it may be of interest to recall that coffins of English
kings have not been kept sacred from the curiosity of investi-
gators. In the eighteenth century antiquarians inspected the
remains of Edward the First, and in March, 1789, the tomb of
Edward the Fourth, at Windsor, was opened. The royal
skeleton was measured, and found to be 6 feet, 3½ inches long;
some brown hair and a quantity of liquid were in the coffin, and
above it lay another coffin, containing the remains of a woman,
believed to be those of his Queen, Elizabeth Woodville.

Just one hundred and ten years ago the coffins of Henry the
Eighth and Charles the First were opened, also at Windsor.
There was some archæological excuse for identifying the grave
of Charles the First, because its situation was hitherto in doubt.
Evelyn, writing in 1654, five years after the King's murder, notes :
" We din'd at Windsor, and saw the Castle and the Chapell of
St. George, where they have laied our blessed Martyr King
Charles in the vault just before the altar."

But apparently the Republicans interfered with the vault and
disarranged the bodies, for at the Restoration great difficulty
was experienced in establishing where the King's body lay. This
doubt continued throughout the seventeenth and eighteenth
centuries. Pope, in his early poem of 1713, *Windsor Forest,*
wrote : —

> " Make sacred Charles's tomb for ever known
> (Obscure the place, and uninscribed the stone),
> Oh fact accursed ! . . . ."

A hundred years later, when the Duchess of Brunswick (sister
of George the Third, and mother of Caroline, Princess of Wales)
died, she was buried in the vault under the choir of St. George's
Chapel, Windsor, on March 31st, 1813. The opportunity was
then taken to find the body of Charles the First. A coffin was
discovered, bearing an inscription, " King Charles, 1648," on a
scroll of lead encircling it. Sir Henry Halford, who was present

---

when the coffin was opened and the King's body exposed, related : —

" The pointed beard was perfect. The shape of the face was a long oval ; many of the teeth remained. . . . When the head had been entirely disengaged from the attachments which confined it, it was found to be loose, and without any difficulty was taken up, and held to view. . . . The hair . . . which has since been cleaned and dried is of a beautiful dark brown colour; that of the beard was a redder brown. . . . An examination of the muscles of the neck clearly proved that the head had been severed from the body by a heavy blow with a very sharp instrument. . . . Neither of the other coffins had any inscriptions upon them. The larger one, supposed to contain the remains of King Henry VIII., measured six feet, ten inches . . . exposed a mere skeleton of the King. Some beard remained upon the chin."

The Regent (George the Fourth) was present at these investigations of the remains of his predecessors, and great play was made of the incident by the satirists of the time. Byron, whose sympathies were with the Regent's wife in their historic matrimonial infelicity, penned his *Windsor Poetics* : —

" Famed for contemptuous breach of sacred ties,
By headless Charles see heartless Henry lies ;
Between them stands another sceptred thing—
It moves, it reigns—in all but name, a king :
Charles to his people, Henry to his wife,
—In him the double tyrant starts to life :
Justice and death have mix'd their dust in vain,
Each Royal vampire wakes to life again.
Ah, what can tombs avail, since these disgorge
The blood and dust of both—to mould a George !"

There were many caricatures picturing the scene; one, by George Cruikshank, showed Sir Henry Halford cutting off some of the beard of Henry the Eighth, the while the Regent observes : " Aye ! There's Great Harry ! Great indeed ! ! for he got rid of many wives, whilst I, poor soul, can't get rid of one ! "

Unfortunately, it was only too true that the proceedings were of a ghoulish nature; " relics " were freely appropriated. The Regent actually presented Sir Henry Halford with a portion of the vertebræ of Charles the First. In 1887, Halford's grandson presented, in turn, the grim relic to the Prince of Wales (King Edward the Seventh), who, two years later, very rightly restored it to the coffin of Charles the First. In 1813, too, fragments of the inner and decayed wooden coffin of Charles the First were distributed to the Regent's friends. One portion, which I have seen, was given to Lord Stafford (later the Duke of Sutherland); it passed to his son, Lord Ronald Gower, who gave it to Oscar Wilde, and a son of the latter presented it to the present owner.

So, if Lord Carnarvon and his friends pursue their *macabre* delvings to the bitter or ceremental end, they can claim historical and royal precedents for their necroscopical proceedings.

NOTE.—The following letter appeared in *The Daily Graphic* of March 2nd, 1923 : —

" Sir,—Apropos of Mr. S. M. Ellis's article on ' English Precedents for Rifling Royal Tombs,' I think the following facts may be interesting.

" In 1832 a discussion arose as to whether Henry IV. was really buried in Canterbury Cathedral, according to tradition. My grandfather, the Hon. and Very Rev. Richard Bagot, then Dean of Canterbury (afterwards Bishop of Oxford and Bath and Wells), was present at the opening of the Royal tomb. This was done in the middle of the night by torchlight in the presence of some of the cathedral authorities and specially invited spectators. The body of the King was found wrapt in lead and leather. For a few moments after this covering was removed the face of the King was revealed in a state of perfect preservation. As the spectators looked, all crumbled away into dust. A portion of the King's beard, which was of a reddish colour, was cut off before the tomb was closed, and distributed.

" CECIL V. BAGOT.

" 25, Rusholme Road, Putney Hill."

MENKEN.*

MEMORIES of the remarkable and meteoric career of a theatrical star of sixty years ago are recalled by Mr. Richard Northcott's excellent little memoir of Adah Isaacs Menken. But few women have crowded such varied experiences of life and notoriety into the brief span of years that were hers.

Though regarded as an American, she was of near Irish descent, her father being James McCord, an assistant to a second-hand clothes dealer in Newcastle Street, Strand. Later he emigrated to Louisiana, to a village near New Orleans, where he married a Creole. The elder daughter of the marriage—the future Menken—was born on June 15th, 1835, and christened Dolores Adios.

The girl commenced her public career early as a ballet dancer at the Opera House of New Orleans. At the age of seventeen she joined a travelling circus as a rider of the *haute-ecole*, but soon returned to ballet, figuring as *première danseuse* at Mexico. Next, taking a holiday in Texas for buffalo hunting, she was captured by a band of Red Indians.

At the age of twenty she published her first poems—for Menken has literary associations as interesting as those which connect her with the stage. The name Menken came from the first of her four husbands—Alexander Isaac Menken, a Jew and musician, whom she married in 1856. Though she left him for ever two years later—because he reproved her for smoking cigarettes (she must have been a feminine pioneer in the practice) —she retained his name to the end of her life.

Her début as an actress took place in 1858 as Bianca in *Fazio*. She later impersonated male characters such as Macaire, Rob Roy, and Jack Sheppard. After a representation of Lady Macbeth, which she brought off successfully by a combination of impudence and the prompt-book, she appeared in the play with which her name will always be associated—*Mazeppa*—wherein, in the guise of a boy and scantily clothed, she was strapped to the back of the "fiery untamed steed."

After starring in this drama for three years in America, Menken produced it in London, at Astley's, in 1864. It was skilfully boomed and much was made of the lady's semi-nude

* *Sunday Evening Telegram,* July 3rd, 1921.

costume. One dramatic critic wrote: " We should hesitate about taking a sister just now to Astley's." Menken brought her literary gifts to the fray, and wrote a defence of herself and her lack of stage costume, in the course of which she said: " I have long been a student of sculpture, and my attitudes, selected from the works of Canova, present a classicality which has invariably been recognised by the foremost of American critics."

Mazeppa was a tremendous success and the talk of the town. Menken formed friendships with many of the literary men prominent at that period. With Swinburne, then about thirty years of age, she had a love affair. Menken had admired his poems, and arrived one day at Swinburne's rooms in London to say she was come " to love the poet." Many amusing stories are told of how poor nervous little Swinburne received this embarrassing argosy of flesh, for his lyrical amours were conceived mostly in his brain and not from actual erotic experiences. However, brandy proved helpful, and the next day, when Mazeppa showed an inclination to talk about poetry—her own probably—Swinburne said: " My darling, a woman with such beautiful legs should not bother herself about poetry."

Swinburne wrote to a friend in January, 1868: " I must send you in a day or two a photograph of my present possessor—known to Britannia as Miss Menken, and to me as Dolores (her real Christian name)—and myself taken together. We both come out very well."

It is not clear if Swinburne knew Menken before he published his *Dolores* in 1866: but he wrote another poem called *Dolorida* —*Mon Amour*—in her album.* It was in French. It was later translated by George Moore thus:—

> " How long canst thou be
> Faithful," she said to me.
> " For one night and a day,
> Mistress, I may.
> Love flatters us with sighs,
> And kisses on mouth and eyes,
> For one day and a night
> Before his flight."

A little volume of her own poems was dedicated to Charles Dickens, and his polite letter accepting the compliment was reprinted in facsimile. W. M. Rossetti included four of Menken's poems in an anthology he compiled. He rightly said they contained " touches of genius " and " they really express a life of much passion, and not a little aspiration, a life deeply sensible of loss." Here is an example:—

---

* Sold at Sotheby's, in the MacGeorge Collection, July 7th, 1924.

" Where is the promise of my years
  Once written on my brow ?
Ere errors, agonies and fears
Brought with them all that speaks in tears,
Ere I had sunk beneath my peers,
  Where sleeps that promise now ?

Myself ! alas for theme so poor—
  A theme but rich in Fear ;
I stand a wreck on Error's shore,
A spectre not within the door,
A houseless shadow evermore,
  An exile lingering here."

When in Paris, Menken was on intimate terms with the second Alexandre Dumas, and, as in the case with Swinburne, she was photographed embracing her lover.

Her second husband was John Heenan, the notorious prize-fighter known as " The Benicia Boy." She obtained a divorce from him on the grounds of ill-treatment in 1862, but, in the manner of modern American film stars, she " married " again some five months before the decree was granted. Her third husband was the humorist, Robert Henry Newell, known as " Orpheus C. Kerr."

Yet a fourth husband she took, James Paul Barclay, a New York broker. He spent thirty thousand pounds on her, left her within two months, and was soon after found dead in the street—penniless.

Menken's death was almost as sudden. She acted for the last time in London at Sadler's Wells, in her old part of Mazeppa, on May 30th, 1868. She was feeling ill, and left for Paris, where, after two months of intense suffering due to a malignant growth, she died on August 10th.

She was only thirty-three years old, but into those years had been crowded, as I have said, varied experiences, which, if related in a romance of fiction, would appear incredible.

DISRAELI: THE HUMAN SIDE.*

NEARLY forty years have passed since Disraeli's death, and it is remarkable that such a long period should have been necessary to achieve the consummation of his complete biography. But there have been valid reasons for the delay. The man who could most fittingly have essayed the task, Montagu Corry (Lord Rowton), the literary executor who inherited Disraeli's papers, did not do so. Eventually Mr. W. F. Monypenny commenced the great undertaking, and produced the first two volumes and part of the third. His failing health and death necessitated the transference of the work to Mr. G. E. Buckle, who duly wrote the fourth volume, and now completes this official biography by the publication of two more volumes.†

A vast canvas is required, of course, to portray the full and eventful life of one of the most remarkable and popular figures of the Victorian Era. A man who was eminent both as politician and author and was likewise distinguished in his friendships demands an uncommon biography, and in Disraeli's case it has arrived at long last thanks to the determination and skill of the writers. Particularly is Mr. Buckle to be congratulated, for it is no easy feat to carry on and complete the literary scheme of another man.

The period dealt with in these two concluding volumes comprises the last thirteen years of Disraeli's life—from 1868 to his death in 1881. In many respects it is the most important part of his career, because for more than half the period in question he was Prime Minister. It includes his great achievements in Eastern policy, the Suez Canal and the Indian Empire, and the Congress of Berlin. During these years he was the head and leader of the Conservative Party, particularly after his political victory in the election of 1874, and they witnessed his removal from the House of Commons to the House of Lords. On the literary side of his career there is only *Lothair* and *Endymion*, but these can claim to be his two greatest novels, even if they lack the sparkle and youthful audacity of *Vivian Grey*. In friendship the last phase was richest of all.

Mr. Buckle opens with the matter of the Disestablishment of

---

* *Plain English*, July 17th, 1920.
† *The Life of Benjamin Disraeli, Earl of Beaconsfield.* By George Earle Buckle. Volumes V and VI. (John Murray, 18s. net.)

the Irish Church, and the Premier's previous attempts to conciliate the leaders of the Roman Catholic Church in Ireland. Disraeli had long contemplated the founding of a Roman Catholic University in Dublin somewhat on the lines of Trinity College. On his accession to power, he was encouraged to persevere in the scheme by Manning, who had recently become Archbishop of Westminster. Unfortunately, the project was brought to nought by the exigent demands of the two prelates who were appointed by the hierarchy to negotiate with the English Government.

One of the most entertaining features of Disraeli's life was the pseudo-romantic attitude in which he stood to Queen Victoria. It will never be possible to diagnose exactly what his opinion of her was, or how far his behaviour was guided by expediency and self-interest. He was a courtier and a flatterer. He himself said that when in conversation with the Queen he followed a simple rule: " I never deny; I never contradict; I sometimes forget. It is true that I am a flatterer. Everyone likes flattery; and when you come to royalty you should lay it on with a trowel." Further proof is advanced by the story of how, after the publication of the Queen's *Leaves from the Journal of Our Life in the Highlands*, he would, when discussing literature with her, use the phrase, " We authors, ma'am." Disraeli inherited subtlety with his Oriental blood, and there is no reason to suppose he would reject any means to reach a desired goal. Mr. Buckle places his attitude to the Queen on a far higher plane : —

" Disraeli saw in the Sovereign not merely the Chief Magistrate of a self-governing nation—a magistrate sprung from a German stock which it had suited the Whigs to put upon the throne of England; but the heir to the historic monarchy of Alfred, of William the Conqueror, of the great Henrys and Edwards, of Elizabeth, of the Stuarts, and of the wrong-headed, but sturdy and national, George III. He realised that it was the Sovereign who, owing to historical and personal causes, was the chief unifying influence, not merely in the nation at home, but, even more, in an Empire of extraordinary diversity and extent. . . . It was after the romantic fashion of Raleigh's services to Queen Elizabeth that Disraeli conceived of his own service to Queen Victoria."

However that may be, there is ample proof in Disraeli's correspondence published here to show that he often alluded to his doting sovereign with his tongue very much in his cheek. Thus when the Queen, suffering from an attack of irritated nerves, went abroad incognita as the Countess of Kent, he wrote to Lord Cairns: " Our Peeress is very happy and, as yet, quite delighted. Her house is on a high hill, above the town, with a splendid view over the lake. . . . There has been rain and there is a grim world."

Again, when staying at Balmoral in 1868, he gives a cynical account of how the German Prince Christian had to be disguised as a Stuart and don the tartan: " The Duke of Edinburgh came . . . he wears the tartan and dined in it: and so did Prince Xtian, but it was for the first time; and the Duke told me he was an hour getting it on, and only succeeded in getting it all right by the aid of his wife and his affectionate brother-in-law."

Disraeli's nickname for Victoria was " The Faery." But in his personal relations with the Queen, he always preserved the attitude of the devout courtier. Endless supplies of flowers were sent to him by his Royal mistress, which he would acknowledge in high-flown, romancing style, terming them " an enchantment," " a Faery gift," " blessing the gracious tenderness that had deigned to fill his lonely home with fragrance and beauty."

Thus encouraged, the Queen would reply with one of her extraordinary ungrammatical letters in the third person singular, in the course of which, after expatiating on her worries caused by the hated Gladstone and his party, she would say, " The Queen sends a few more flowers for Mr. Disraeli. Really there never was such conduct as that of the Opposition. . . . The Queen trusts the Session will speedily be got to an end, for it is sure to be disagreeable as long as it lasts. Most grateful to Mr. Disraeli for the gift of his novels, which she values much."

Although Disraeli played on the weaknesses of the Queen, there is no doubt she was sincerely attached to him. When he died she pronounced herself " heart-broken," and, following her favourite habit, she erected a marble monument to his memory.

Most certainly the dominant factor of Disraeli's life was the influence of women. He craved for their society and sympathy. He did not favour girls. His women friends were generally older than himself, so much so that the Russian Ambassador observed that his society was *toutes grand'mères*. The main theme of his last novel, *Endymion* (finished but a short time before his death), was concerned with the immense and decisive influence women have in politics by directing and moulding the life of man.

Apart from his romantic relations with the Queen, Disraeli was in turn influenced by Lady Blessington and Lady Londonderry, and the aged Mrs. Brydges Willyams (who left him thirty thousand pounds). To his eccentric wife, who was some twelve years his senior, he was tenderly devoted. For thirty-three years she was his constant companion and confidant. She died in 1872, and it was this loss which brought about the most curious episode of his later life. Feeling the urgent need once more of intimate female society and sympathy, he turned to two sisters whom he had known in the far-away days of their youth and beauty. They were daughters of the first Lord Forester, and had become by marriage Anne, Countess of Chesterfield, and Selina, Countess of Bradford. In 1872 the former was seventy years of age and the latter fifty-five. Very soon they occupied a place in Disraeli's life such as the Misses Berry had filled in that of Horace Walpole. Disraeli's letters to these two ladies offer the most intimate revelation of his life, experiences, and aspirations. No less than sixteen hundred of his letters to them have been preserved, and extracts from the correspondence provide the most valuable new material of Mr. Buckle's concluding volumes.

Both the sisters were grandmothers, but this did not affect the ardent devotion of the senile widower. He, indeed, proposed marriage to Lady Chesterfield, the sister who was widowed. But she refused him, as it was Lady Bradford who really had the supreme place in Disraeli's affections. Lady Bradford was not free, and she had to keep her aged admirer in order with rather a firm hand. For her he suffered all the love-sick torments and jealousies of a youth. To her he wrote at the age of seventy: " To love as I love, and rarely to see the being one adores, whose constant society is absolutely necessary to my life, is a lot which I never could endure, and cannot. . . . I wonder if I shall see you to-morrow. Not to see you is a world without a sun. I wonder whom you will sit between to-day, and talk to, and delight and fascinate. I am always afraid of your dining at houses like Gerard's in my absence. I feel horribly jealous. I cannot help it."

A few years earlier in *Lothair*, his great novel of political life and the influences of the Roman Catholic Church, wherein figure so many characters drawn from well-known people, he stated his own case: " Threescore and ten, at the present day, is the period of romantic passions. As for our enamoured sexagenarians, they avenge the theories of our cold-hearted youth."

Truly the Sphinx was, pathetically, all human within.

A NOVELIST OF SUSSEX:
MISS SHEILA KAYE-SMITH.*

NOTE.—I reprint the following article as evidence that I may take some little credit to myself for discovering the superlative merits of Miss Sheila Kaye-Smith's work long before the majority of critics did likewise. The article was written eleven years ago to please myself (for it had no remuneration, or publication beyond that in a local Sussex newspaper), and I was moved to do this by the strange, uncommon charm I found in Miss Kaye-Smith's second novel, *Starbrace*, published in 1909. This book, coming from the pen of a young girl, was unique—for it is a virile, vital romance of highwaymen and great open spaces under the stars, of the elements of life, compact of scenes of infinite pathos, of human love and human cruelty, combined with a wonderful presentment of its scenic setting where Kent and Sussex unite.

Miss Sheila Kaye-Smith has only been recognised as a writer of the first rank during the last five years, and is now acclaimed as " the Hardy of Sussex " by reason of her later books, *Tamarisk Town*, *Green Apple Harvest*, and *Joanna Godden*. I still hold *Starbrace* to be Miss Kaye-Smith's best work: no doubt a peculiar opinion. Ten years ago the author told me *Starbrace* was the only one of her books which was not selling: " the sales stopped in 1913 ": it is full time for them to recommence, if they have not done so long since.

.   .   .   .

Sussex—county of woods and weald, downs and sea—has, with the exception of Yorkshire and Devonshire, inspired more poets and been the scene of more novels than any other portion of England. Especially has this been the case in recent years. Black, Kipling, Conan Doyle, Mrs. Dudeney, Miss Violet Simpson, E. P. H. Lulham, Marriott Watson, and Hilaire Belloc are but a few names that occur to memory from the long list of those who have voiced the charm of Sussex. That charm is apparent to all who know the district, and the secret of its lure may lie in the fact that Sussex is so typically and essentially English. Here are the farmsteads and meadows with woods beyond, grazing cattle and sheep-folds; here are the squires' manor houses and the little village churches, and beyond the great

* *Worthing Observer*, March 28th, 1914.

Miss SHEILA KAYE-SMITH

[*Page* 370.

downs is the sea, which is ever needed to complete a true conception of English life and history. As Hilaire Belloc sings:—

" The men that live in the South Country
    Are the kindest and most wise,
They get their laughter from the loud surf,
    And the faith in their happy eyes
Comes surely from our Sister, the Spring,
    When over the sea she flies.

I never get between the pines,
    But I smell the Sussex air,
Nor I never come on a belt of sand
    But my home is there;
And along the sky the line of the Downs
    So noble and so bare."

Within the last five years another Sussex novelist has arisen, one who has depicted the scenery and interpreted the " atmosphere " of the county very finely, for Miss Sheila Kaye-Smith, of St. Leonards, is pre-eminently a painter of the open road, of life in the open with the sky for roof—of the school, in short, of Borrow. In *The Tramping Methodist,* her first book, the author deals with the high road; *Starbrace* relates to highwaymen and outlaws; *Spell Land* concerns farming; and *Isle of Thorns* pictures the dear joys and pains of vagabondage.

Of the four books by far the finest is *Starbrace.* This work, although it failed—amid the torrent and welter of new novels— to receive the wide recognition and fame it so fully deserved, is of exceptional merit and originality, and, as the work of a woman, something in the way of a *tour de force.* Many of the book's reviewers laid stress on its " virility "—but that is scarcely the right word to use, for combined with virility *Starbrace* displays a delicate feminine sympathy with outlawry as symbolised by one who was misunderstood and unhappy throughout his short life, compelled by heredity and circumstances and friends to be an outlaw. *Starbrace* is the story of a boy, son of a gentleman by a plebeian wife, living in poverty with his father, both working as farm labourers in the Brede country of East Sussex, in 1735. His grandfather, a Kentish baronet, eventually adopts young Miles; but the atmosphere of his new home is one of repression and spirit breaking, and so the young rebel, meeting again an early acquaintance now become a highwayman, takes to " The Road." This leads to the most powerful portion of the romance, for here, amid the weird marsh-land between Rye and Romney, Miss Kaye-Smith has presented one of the most vivid and picturesque accounts in fiction of the highwayman. The free life, the customs, above all the language—half slang, half curses

aa 2

—are given with amazing fidelity. Here is all the romance of "The Road" and all its brutality and sordidness too, with Nemesis at the last. The scene of the capture of the highwaymen and the death of their leader, Michael Daunt, pulsates with reality and horror. It may be melodramatic, but life and death are often far more melodramatic than the most extravagant situations represented on the boards of Drury Lane.

Miles Starbrace escapes the gallows, but broken in spirit and disappointed again and again by the girl he loves—whose hard beliefs of right and wrong prevent her from consenting to marry him—seeks and finds death at Prestonpans, with his faithful horse, Pharisee. That last scene is of infinite pathos : —

"The dusk had fallen when Miles Starbrace opened his eyes and lifted them to the sky. Over the clear twilight green, dark masses of cloud were sailing peacefully. . . . He lay very still, his head pillowed on the roan's neck, and watched the sliding fold-star. How peaceful the sky was ! How softly the grasses rustled near his head. He must be at home in Sussex, in the fields. Were those sheep he saw yonder? Flocks of them, white and bleating. They touched his cheek with their faces, they were his father's sheep—his father must be folding them. He would soon pass that way, and carry little Miles home on his shoulder. . . . Here he is ! How kind his arms feel as they lift his tired child. The lambs are folded, and little Miles must come home. His bare legs feel the warmth of his father's breast as he sits on his shoulder, his arms round his neck, his cheek resting on the rough brown hair. . . . Our soul is escaped even as a bird out of the snare of the fowler; the snare is broken, and we are delivered."

In her latest work, *Isle of Thorns*, recently published, Miss Kaye-Smith, has evolved an intinerary of vagabonds by choice. It is primarily a romance of Ashdown Forest, with peregrinations as far as Selsey. The story and characters are all rather improbable, and the book—to take a motto from it—deals with "the ecstasies of common things," irradiated however by human love and endurance amid a setting of scenic beauty. Sally Odiarne, a London girl who had essayed literary work, throws aside the trammels of convention and casts in her lot with Stanger's Travelling Show. She becomes the spiritual—and, indeed, also corporeal—shuttlecock of two men who stand for the good and evil influences in her life. Virtue, Raphael Moore, is a priggish widower of High Church views, whom the girl meets by chance in a ruined cottage called *Isle of Thorns;* Vice, Andy Baird, is manager of the rifle range at the Fair. After some preliminary fights, the girl goes off with Andy on a vagabond *aventure à deux*, camping in copses at night, without, however, irrevocably giving herself to the man. She is pursued by her good genius, the widower, who, by a series of absurd adventures and the better to track the errant damsel by means of information from tramps and gipsies, adopts the guise of a vagabond, and endures the hardships of highway and dosshouse and nights in the rain. He wins in the end, of course, and incidentally his tramping experiences " save his own soul," for they purge him of much of his priggishness and conventional hypocrisy. It is somewhat difficult to understand the vagaries of the Puck-like heroine and her High Church lover, for both are compact of inconsistency and are as unstable as water. The author vouchsafes no hint as to the future of this ill-assorted pair; and one is compelled to think that so innate a little vagabond as Sally would never run long in double harness, but kick over the traces at the first new call of the wild and " go out into the high roads, to the commons, against the wind, under the stars," with any beloved vagabond that offered his society. On an earlier occasion " her retrospect rang with the thud of hoofs on frosty roads, the lurch and rumble of a cart, with wild words and kisses, screams and escapes—it smelled of bonfires, of half-frozen dew, of pungent leaf-strewn woods—it tasted of stream water, earthy and leafy, of rainy blackberries." Could she resist the future call of such things merely by means of a marriage tie with a man still somewhat of a prig? We doubt it.

Miss Kaye-Smith paints the joys of vagabondage inimitably, and equally realistic are her pictures of the Fair and caravan life —of more dubious pleasure far than that of the hedgerow. But the real charm of *Isle of Thorns* lies in its numerous little pen-pictures of Sussex scenery—particularly those when evening is at hand, and the mists rise and mingle with the scented smoke from burning leaves and wood fires. Here is an example:—

" Twilight came—but first of all the golden hour when the afternoon melts into the evening. A warm yellow kissed everything, hills, trees, cows, ponds, and cottage roofs. In the little houses of the bottoms, tables were spread for tea, and through the open doors Sally and Raphael smelled the wood-smoke, heard the cups rattle, and saw the loaf with the sunshine on it. . . . The sun had set; for a moment the fields had been swamped in gold, then the glory had mounted to the cottage roofs, then to the Down-tops, then to the sky—then it had gone, with a little gasp of the night wind in the hills. The mist was steaming up in the bottoms, and the southern meadow-valley was beginning to look like the sea, with here and there a star in the white waters, showing that lamp-time had come to some cottage far away."

Only a true literary artist could thus so finely transmute the ever-varying beauties of a Sussex landscape.

AN AUTHENTIC POET: LORD ALFRED DOUGLAS.

A TRUE poet in the real sense of the word is rare: Lord Alfred Douglas is indubitably one. As in the case of Marlowe and Keats, his literary output has not been large. His early poems, written before he reached the age of twenty-six, were published in Paris, 1896-1897, a volume that is now very scarce. *The City of the Soul* appeared in 1899, and the exquisite *Sonnets* in 1909. He does not coincide with the conventional idea of a poet as one who exudes rhyming rhetoric on every conceivable occasion (or excuse) and babbles new lines on every moonlit night. As he rightly says in the characteristic note appended to this new edition of his poems: —*

" Poets . . . do not pour out words like inspired gramophones. All good poetry is written slowly and cautiously, with great effort. . . It is forged slowly and painfully, and link by link, with sweat and blood and tears. The writing of a great poem leaves a poet exhausted. . . . The poet, therefore, is one who puts into a beautiful form the expression of an overpowering emotion, and it follows that his emotion must be exceptionally deep and sincere. . . ."

In this collected edition the author has omitted some of the poems which appeared in his earliest volume; but sufficient remain to illustrate how even in what the poet now regards as his immature work there was infinite beauty. Take *Plainte Eternelle*, where the metre pictures the slow, rhythmic motion of stately sailing ships floating with the tide: —

" The sun sinks down, the tremulous daylight dies.
(Down their long shafts the weary sunbeams glide.)
The white-winged ships drift with the falling tide,
Come back, my love, with pity in your eyes. "

And *A Winter Sunset*, which was an impromptu, and *Autumn Days*, and *The Sphinx*. One of the most beautiful, *Hymn to Physical Beauty*, is not included in this collection. Thus it began: —

" Sweet spirit of the body, archetype
Of lovely mortal shapes, where is thy shrine?
Long have I wandered over dales and hills
Seeking in vain, and now these eyes of mine
That were like stars, are like to running rills,
So sad am I; come, for the fruits are ripe,
The yellow fruits that wait thee, a white dove
For thee is caged, I have a thousand roses,
Both white and red; come, ere the hot day closes
Its languid eyes, and lead me to thy grove. "

* *The Collected Poems of Lord Alfred Douglas*. (Secker, 7s. 6d. net) 1919. Part of this notice appeared in *The Sunday Times*, November 2nd, 1919.

And ended:—

> " Come down and save us : let the world reborn
>   Be glad again.   Our hearts are barren fountains,
> Come down like rain.   Ah ! do I sleep or wake?
>   Methinks I hear thy feet upon the mountains ;
> And ere the red sun stoops and drinks the lake
>   Haply my aching eyes shall see thy dawn."

In later years of his poetical progress Lord Alfred pictures the same pursuit of Beauty : but it is now the mysticism of Spiritual Beauty that he seeks :—

> " Where lurks the shining quarry, swift and shy,
>   Immune, elusive, unsubstantial?
> In what dim forests of the soul, where call
>   No birds, and no beasts creep?   (The hunter's cry
> Wounds the deep darkness, and the low winds sigh
> Through avenues of trees whose faint leaves fall
> Down to the velvet ground, and like a pall
> The violet shadows cover all the sky.)
>
> .   .   .   .   .
>
> With what gold nets, what silver-pointed spears
> May we surprise her, what slim flutes inspire
> With breath of what serene enchanted air?—
> Wash we our star-ward gazing eyes with tears,
> Till on their pools (drawn by our white desire)
> She bend and look, and leave her image there."

Lord Alfred Douglas has written three superlative ballads in *Perkin Warbeck, Jonquil and Fleur-de-lys,* and *Saint Vitus*—which is like a series of superbly-coloured paintings in a mediæval missal—

> " For the room was filled with a soft sweet light
>   Of ambergris and apricot,
> And round the walls were angels bright
>   With lute and flute and angelot."

Colour and radiant imagery are ever the hall-marks of this poet; they are pre-eminent in *The City of the Soul,* wherein he reached the highest expression of his art : —*

> " Think how the hidden things that poets see
>   In amber eves or mornings crystalline,
>   Hide in the soul their constant quenchless light,
> Till called by some celestial alchemy,
>   Out of forgotten depths, they rise and shine
> Like buried treasure on midsummer night."
>
> .   .   .   .   .
>
> " Within my soul are some mean gardens found,
>   Where drooped flowers are, and unsung melodies,
>   And all companioning of piteous things.
> But in the midst is one high-terraced ground,
>   Where level lawns sweep through the stately trees
> And the great peacocks walk like painted kings."

---

* See also later, page 391.

How glorious these last three lines—a stately picture. For
me, they always bring back a memory of Warwick Castle, where
the great peacocks walked " like painted kings." Colour, again,
vivid colour, runs through all the *Sonnets,* as in the emblazoning
threads of a mediæval robe. Thus, *To Olive* : —

> " My thoughts, like bees, explore all sweetest things,
> To fill for you the honeycomb of praise,
> Linger in roses and white jasmine sprays,
> And marigolds that stand in yellow rings.
> In the blue air they moan on muted strings,
> And the blue sky of my soul's summer days
> Shines with your light, and through pale violet ways
> Birds bear your name in beatings of their wings.

> " I see you all bedecked in bows of rain,
> New showers of rain against new-risen suns,
> New tears against new light of shining joy.
> My youth, equipped to go, turns back again,
> Throws down its heavy pack of years and runs
> Back to the golden house a golden boy.
>   .   .   .

> " Now I have known the uttermost rose of love ;
> The years are very long, but love is longer ;
> I love you so, I have no time to hate
> Even those wolves without. The great winds move
> All their dark batteries to our fragile gate :
> The world is very strong, but love is stronger."

I have twice used the word mediæval in relation to Lord
Alfred's poems, and I think there is something mediæval in his
temperament (by reason of heredity) which responds to the
glowing colours and stately trappings of old romaunt and to the
pageantry of the old faith. Perchance he is a chivalric
troubadour born out of time, or an atavistic knight. Certain it
is, if he had lived in the old days he would have been a crusader
and the champion of lost—or, rather, desperate—causes in

> " Vanished years, unreal but sweet always . . .
> And mellow with old loves that used to burn
> Dead summer days ago, like fierce red kings."

NOTE.—Lord Alfred Douglas has this year, 1924, written a
series of seventeen Sonnets entitled *In Excelsis,* which he considers the best work he has done. It is evidence of his evolution
from the paganism of his youth to catholic mysticism, though
as he has stated to me, " Not that I claim to be a mystic in life :
I find it quite hard enough to be an ordinary practical Christian.
But, of course, being a poet, when I start to write I inevitably
gravitate to mysticism." The following Sonnets are the first
and (partly the) second of *In Excelsis;* fourteen of the sonnets

LORD ALFRED DOUGLAS
At the age of twenty-two.

[*Page* 376.

appeared in *The London Mercury,* October, 1924, and the complete work will follow in volume form : —

> " I follow honour, brokenly content,
> Though the sick flesh repine, though darkness creep
> Into the soul's unfathomable deep,
> Where fear is bred : though from my spirit spent
> Like poured-out water, the mind's weak consent
> Be hardly wrung, while eyes too tired to weep
> Dimly discern, as through a film of sleep,
> Squalor that is my honour's ornament.
>
> Without, the fire of earth-contemning stars
> Burns in deep blueness, like an opal set
> In jacinth borders underneath the moon.
> The dappled shadow that my window bars
> Cast on the walls is like a silver net.
> My angel, in my heart, sings ' heaven soon.'
>
> I have within me that which still defies
> This generation's bloat intelligence,
> Which is the advocate of my defence
> Against the indictment of the world's assize.
> Clutching with bleeding hands my hard-won prize,
> Immeasurably bought by fierce expense
> Of blood and sweat and spirit-harnessed sense,
> I keep the steadfast gaze of tear-washed eyes. . . ."

THEODORE WRATISLAW:
A POET OF THE 'NINETIES.*

THEODORE WILLIAM GRAF WRATISLAW is a member of a family settled in Rugby for four generations. His great-grandfather was a Bohemian noble, Count Marc Wratislaw von Mitrowitz, who came to England about 1770, and held the post of foreign language master at Rugby School until his death in 1796. Theodore Wratislaw, born at Rugby in April, 1871, is the son of Mr. Theodore Marc Wratislaw, for many years a solicitor practising in that town. He was educated at Rugby School, 1885-1888, and passed the final examination for solicitors in 1893; but in 1895 he entered the Estate Duty Office, Somerset House, where he still holds a position.

His earliest little volumes of poems, *Love's Memorial* and *Some Verses*, were published at Rugby in 1892. They were followed by *Caprices*, 1893, with a cover design by Gleeson White. Mr. Wratislaw was now a member of that talented coterie of writers and artists—including Oscar Wilde, Aubrey Beardsley, Ernest Dowson, Lord Alfred Douglas, Arthur Symons, Lionel Johnson, Victor Plarr, Gleeson White, Henry Harland, John Davidson, 'Hubert Crackanthorpe, Charles Condor, John Gray, and Max Beerbohm†—whose names will ever be associated with the last decade of the nineteenth century. Some of these men were called " decadent," but in the main their work was arresting, distinctive, and daringly original, and its characteristics are indelibly impressed upon the artistic history of the epoch in question.

The association of so many bright, if erratic, spirits was destined to last only for a few years. The younger men burned away their minds and bodies all too fiercely. It is sadly remarkable how many of them died in early manhood, some by violence. Hubert Crackanthorpe and John Davidson committed suicide, William Theodore Peters died of starvation in Paris. And with wiser living, Beardsley, Dowson, and Lionel Johnson need not have died so young. Time has since removed others, and of those who survive only one or two can be described as

---

* Part of this memoir appeared in the Warwickshire volume of *Poets of the Shires,* edited by Dr. C. H. Poole. (Ling & Co.) 1914.

† Two women poets, Olive Custance (Lady Alfred Douglas) and Nora Hopper (Mrs. W. H. Chesson), may be said to have been ex-officio members of the group.

prosperous : so it was not money, or even happiness, which was
the goal of the exponents of the " decadence."

Beardsley, of course, was the most outstanding and original
genius of this new movement in Art.   Born at Brighton in 1872,
and educated at that town's grammar school, he became, at
sixteen years of age, a clerk in an architect's office in London.
At twenty he was known as a new illustrator, and at twenty-one
he was famous.   And then after four more years of crowded life
he was dead, leaving as a legacy a new conception of black-and-
white and line drawing, which was to have a profound influence
upon Art and countless imitators.   During those last feverish
years he remained also a boy who sought to realise all the enjoyment life could offer.   Ernest Dowson, the exquisite poet, had
a fate as untimely.   But his was a more retiring, morbid nature,
given to mysterious solitudes.   He was the English Verlaine,
the sad singer of moonlight and shadows to the sound of muted
violins.   He voiced the beauty and brevity of life, and the
questionings of his group : —

> " When this our rose is faded,
>   And these, our days, are done,
>   In lands profoundly shaded
>   From tempest and from sun :
>   Ah, once more come together,
>   Shall we forgive the past,
>   And safe from worldly weather
>   Possess our souls at last."

Theodore Wratislaw's verse is characteristic of the literary
and artistic movement he allied himself with, or, as he put it, it
is " A shrine of loves that laugh and swoon and ache, a temple
of coloured sorrows ànd perfumed sins."   As this, *Plein Air*,
which Oscar Wilde always pronounced to be the best song of
" the poet Theodore " : —

> " Purple and white the pansies shone.
>   Tall stocks that stained the garden walk
>   With crimson, heard our amorous talk
>   And blushed to know that she was won.

> " The golden mirth of sunflowers eyed
>   Her bosom, and mauve heliotrope
>   Shed balmy breaths of scent in hope
>   Of her virginity untied.

> " So when the moon rose in the south
>   And trailed about the shadowy vine,
>   I felt her breasts pant under mine
>   And her breath sobbing in my mouth."

But I find something finer than this in many of his other poems
—a plaintive regret for the fleeting joys of life, and, further, an

interpretation of the sadness that underlies all earthly things and
the transient beauties of Nature dead too soon. Thus,
A Mood : —

> " The tide was weary as it came
> Towards the shore this autumn eve :
> It caught the sun's descending flame,
> And sighed and seemed too faint to grieve
> Because the summer hasted to be gone
> And all the days were done.
>
> " The sea heaved languidly and rolled
> Its purple breakers on the sand ;
> An infinite sadness manifold
> Fell on the deep and quiet land ;
> The seamews rested on the dipping foam
> And had no thought of home.
>
> " The poppies shivered as the breeze
> Went by and fell before it passed,
> And from the cliff I heard the sea's
> Faint requiem, the first and last,
> Above the tomb of pleasures that were sped
> And with the year lay dead.
>
> " One with the season's languor, I
> Lay long to watch the changing flight
> Of colours in the dreary sky
> Until the advent of the night,
> While banks of cloud above the sea-line rose
> And sorrow found repose."

And what a delicate, sad little threnody—worthy of Verlaine,
with whose poetry Wratislaw's may rightly be compared—is
this : —

> " So vague, so sweet, a long regret !
> So sweet, so vague, a dead perfume
> That lingers lest regret forget,
> A memory from an old-world tomb
> Where vainly sunshine gleams and vainly raindrops fret,
> And dying summer's wind-breath goes
> So lightly over petals of the fallen rose.
>
> Autumnal starlight, scents of hay
> Beneath the full September moon,
> And then, ah ! then ! the sighing tune
> That fades and yet is fain to stay :
> Ah ! weep for pleasures dead too soon,
> While like the love-song of an ancient day
> The distant music of the perfume dies away."

Theodore Wratislaw's last volume of verse, *Orchids*, 1896,
was produced by Leonard Smithers, the remarkable solicitor-
turned-publisher whose name is bound up with the uncommon
literature of this time. He has also written *The Pity of Love*, a
tragedy based on the dramatic love story of Sophie Dorothea

(wife of George the First) and Philip von Königsmarck; and *Algernon Charles Swinburne: A Study*, 1900, which is his best-known work. Mr. Wratislaw preserves his devotion to Swinburne, and only last year, 1923, he wrote the following beautiful tribute to the singer of the silvern voice: *At Bonchurch: In Memoriam, Algernon Charles Swinburne:*—*

> " Not long ago it seems—though long ago—
> Thy hand touched mine, Thou whom I loved so long.
> Yet here I stand and watch the roses blow
> Above thy grave, O Master of all Song.

> " In no diviner place may mortal sleep.
> But Thou who hast for time immortal years,
> Though summer burns with eyes that may not weep,
> Disdain not Thou, O Master, these swift tears."

---

* Here published for the first time by the courtesy of the author.

MRS. C. L. ANTROBUS.*

MRS. ANTROBUS, though possibly unknown to the great mass of readers of modern fiction, holds a very special and peculiar position among contemporary novelists. To class her with Thomas Love Peacock, she is read by those who possess a cultivated literary taste, and who appreciate her brilliant and humorous dialogue, giving constant evidence of wide and classical reading; her exquisite descriptions of scenery—particularly of woodlands; and, above all, her wistful presentment of the sad things of life, the delicate charm with which she transfigures sorrow and remorse, wan memories and death. Her literary qualities are thus often in startling antithesis: but the predominant traits are sorrow and tragedy. A reviewer in *The Times*, of one of Mrs. Antrobus's books compared her to George Eliot, and the late Justin McCarthy, in an appreciative letter, said her work reminded him of Nathaniel Hawthorne's. Both comparisons are apt, but Mrs. Antrobus's literary ambit is distinctly original, and she has a gift of poetical allusion entirely her own.

As is generally the case with imaginative writers, the early environment of Mrs. Antrobus had a strong influence in developing her gifts and shaping her career as a writer. Her father was Newcome Rogers, of Grantham, a very clever surgeon; and through her mother, Margaret Hunnings, she is descended from many prominent Lincolnshire families, including the Newcomens, Ludlows, and Dymokes, and the Yorkshire Fitzwilliams and Wentworths. The Hunnings family preserved the peculiar custom of burying their dead at midnight by torchlight; John Hunnings, the great-grandfather of Mrs. Antrobus, was the last to receive this picturesque form of sepulture, at Whaplode, in 1801.

Clara Louisa Rogers was born at Grantham in a romantic old house, oak-panelled, and with a diversity of rooms, to enter which one either went up or down a few steps. She was scarcely three years old when her parents removed to Bowdon, in Cheshire. Here she grew up, and Bowdon and the surrounding lovely woods of Dunham Massey were indelibly impressed upon her vivid mind, and became the background of some of her finest imaginative work in later years. As she says of this little town

* *The Bookman*, September, 1917.

on the Cheshire hill-side, " it was unique, an old-world place of
green peace, of legend, yet with a continuous stream of the outer
world's life flowing into it from Manchester." In the wonderful
woods she learnt her love of nature and wild life; and from the
natives of the countryside a vast store of legendary tales.
Her home in girlhood, up the hill of Bowdon, was a singularly
happy one. Her father was a most versatile man. He was both
a scholar and a sportsman, and a brilliant talker. He early
instructed his daughter in astronomy (a science which often peeps
forth in Mrs. Antrobus's stories), and long before she could
read made her familiar with the poetry of Scott. Milton, Byron,
Shelley, Keats, and *The Arabian Nights* were her favourite
reading in youth. Her mother was of artistic tastes and—that
rare conjunction—an excellent housekeeper. There was much
hospitality and much good conversation, for those were the days
of comfortable leisure when people had time to talk and consider
the great things of life and literature and art. This happy time
for the future novelist came to an end in 1869, when Mr. Rogers
died from injuries received in a railway accident. His daughter
married in 1871 Arthur John Antrobus, an old playmate of former
days, but she was left a widow in less than a year. She remained
in Bowdon for some time afterwards; but eventually came to live
in Fulham with her cousin, Miss Alice Hanslip, an artist, to whom
two of her books were dedicated. For twenty-five years this
devoted association continued, until broken by the death of Miss
Hanslip in 1907. Since then Mrs. Antrobus has lived alone with
memories.

Her first novel, *Wildersmoor*, was published by Bentley in
1895, and the locality of this grim story of moorland and murder
may be said to lie not far from the coast line of south Lancashire.
" Woffendale " is Manchester. There was a long interval before
Quality Corner appeared in 1901. In this, her finest novel, Mrs.
Antrobus describes with minute exactness her early home,
Bowdon, under the name of " Ringway," and the beauty of the
wild woods is limned with infinite art. *Quality Corner—A Study
of Remorse* is a sad and tragic story, illumined though it is by
scintillating dialogue and humorous observation. Mrs. Antrobus
has a fine gift of " atmosphere." She can bind the thunder and
the lightning to her purpose; a lowering and lurid sunset, a
spring dawn, moonlight on a forest pool, wind in the woodlands,
mist on the moorlands, are all intertwined and interplay with the
thoughts and actions of her characters. In *The Stone Ezel* (1910)
the author reached the height of her power in depicturing the
glamour and romance of forest scenery. Her topography is not

so exact here. The woods she describes are again those of Bowdon, but, more powerful than Canute, she has brought the sea to the edge of her valley. The little white house, "Lone Ends," she transplanted from Delamere Forest; the Ezel was compact of stories from other quarters; the legends were local; and all the characters were drawn from originals. There is an almost overwhelming sense of impending fate and tragedy in this book, for here again murder looms.

I have said it is the sad things of life that preoccupy predominantly the imaginative art of Mrs. Antrobus, and it is in her short stories that she is supreme in expressing the pathos of loss and regret, death and remorse, and wistful memories. Thirteen of her short stories were collected and published under the title of *The Wine of Finvarra* in 1902, and I have no hesitation in saying that they rank with the finest short stories in the English language. Five of them—the title tale, *The Two Twilights*, *The Man from Stalybridge*, *The Garden of Attalus*, and *The Lyke-Wake*—though all of sombre cast are masterpieces of description and construction, and a consummate short story is far more difficult to achieve than a long novel. If any comparison is needed, they can be compared with the short stories of Thomas Hardy.

Mrs. Antrobus's method of writing is unusual. She begins a story at the beginning or the end (which sounds Hibernian)—that is to say, the middle portion is always composed last. Sometimes she writes the first chapter or the commencement of a short tale, and then passes to the dénouement or close, working up from both ends till they meet in the middle, for, as she says, "I am most erratic as regards writing, and I cannot do it any other way. I have tried to be reasonable and go straight on—but I cannot." However, as the completed story is always a work of art, the means to the end are of little consequence.

Mrs. Antrobus preserves and practises the almost lost arts of conversation and letter-writing. Her letters and conversation possess many of the characteristics of her books—observation and descriptive power, particularly of Nature and scenery; they sparkle with allusive apt quotation and anecdote, reflect great classical knowledge, and express a personality of rare distinction and charm.

.   .   .   .   .

Note.—Mrs. Antrobus died in 1919. Her last years appear to me peculiarly sad. She lived alone (except for some intermittent domestic help from outside), with her dog, at 44, Chesilton Road, Fulham—a large and unsuitable house for one person.

Every day—whatever the weather, rain, snow, or intense heat—she went to the grave of her cousin, Miss Alice Hanslip, in the cemetery in Fulham Palace Road, to tend it and place fresh flowers. She continued this labour of love to the very end—when she was in a dying state herself and only able to move with difficulty and pain. In fact, I understand she died from the effects of a chill contracted at the graveside one bitter day of snow. It is one of the most pathetic cases in all the annals of human affection.

Mrs. Antrobus, in view of her exquisite tastes and appreciation of the beauties of Nature, should have lived in the country, but her mournful, self-imposed daily task tied her to Fulham, and I believe she never spent a night away during the last twelve years of her life, after Miss Hanslip's death in 1907. Consequently her visits to the country she loved so well were confined to a day's expedition to the outer suburbs of London. She particularly delighted in Petersham and the lovely surroundings of Richmond. I have happy memories of several visits she made to Kew Gardens. On one occasion it was in mid-winter, and the extracts from the following letters will illustrate her charming epistolary style :—

" December 8th, 1916.

" How perverse of sun and moon to wrap themselves in mist yesterday . . . yet the mist has its own fascination apart from sun and moon. I thought it most wonderful by that water—the colour of it —the entanglement of it in those tall, reed-like plants. I am inclined to think the Gardens more beautiful in winter than in summer because they have such mist effects . . . to feel the witchery of mist both trees and water are needed, and unexpected vistas, and woodlands not too dense, and open spaces not too open, and water that has curving shores—and so goes out of sight to reappear in yet stranger beauty. I am grateful to you for showing me all the ' fairyland forlorn ' of Kew Gardens in winter. Your fantastic semi-human trees are most remarkable. I forget in which book of Gogol's he describes the Gnome King, but instantly they reminded me of that."

Again, after a visit in spring :—

" May 12th, 1917.

" Thank you for a delightful afternoon in Fairyland. Assuredly Kew Gardens are a portion of Fairyland just now. One is inclined to say with Byron—is it not Byron?—

' We see
' What Eden was, what Paradise may be ! '

Though I always picture Paradise as a place of twilight peace and dark cedars—for it is only a waiting-place, and the separation of soul and body a most unnatural state and not to be desired save as an escape from worse things. . . . Yes, I am most grateful to you for showing me the Gardens in their winter witchery and their spring glory. The time of the blossoming is—well, there are no words wherewith to express it. I have been seeing it all in my mind's eye ever since. And the gracious silence —a lovely silence. . . .

"All that you say about my writings* makes me feel like the old woman who, on seeing her own portrait, asked in surprise, ' Be that really I? ' You are most kind, and I am most grateful—and I hope it is all true. Anyway, it makes me purr contentedly, as I used to purr over the praise I got from Justin McCarthy and Frederick Shields, the artist, and for the same reason—because they understood and looked at things from much the same standpoint, and had a sense of humour, which last, I think, is a most enlightening gift. *Are* my tales tragic? They must be, since you say so : but they seem to me just ordinary life."

True, indeed, tragedy and ordinary life are indissolubly entwined: "Joy cometh in the morning," but sorrow in the night. As Mrs. Antrobus wrote in one of the finest of her short stories—human dramas rather: "He had looked for the roses of life, and behold, they hung over a grave." Her own grave is in that sombre Fulham Cemetery which had exercised such a morbid influence during her latter years—far from the lovely woodlands and meres she had known in her youth and repictured in her books. And in those same books can be recovered her gracious personality, rare culture, and exquisite appreciation of natural beauty.

---

* In the article above.

HERBERT KENNEDY
[*E. S. Ball & Co., Cambridge.*

[*Page* 386.

Mrs. CLARA LOUISA ANTROBUS

A LOST POET: HERBERT KENNEDY

AND THE POETICAL ATTITUDE TO DEATH.*

By the death of Herbert Kennedy, at the age of eighteen, the world has lost a singer who might have been of the company of Keats and Shelley. Like them, and Chatterton, and Richard Middleton, and Ernest Dowson, and Francis Thompson, and Lionel Johnson, and Synge, he has all too early been claimed by jealous Death.

Born in 1892, the son of Gerald Kennedy, an actor, and great grandson of Benjamin Hall Kennedy, a former Head Master of Shrewsbury School and Regius Professor of Greek at Cambridge, Herbert Kennedy was educated at Brighton and Charterhouse. He essayed writing verse from the age of ten years, but was entirely exempt from the unpleasing qualities of the prodigy. His character was lovable, honest, and destitute of self-consciousness; he was not at all delicate, and he was proficient at football and rowing. He died at Charterhouse on November 7th, 1910, from a peculiar form of blood-poisoning, following measles. He had an only sister, to whom he was devoted.

How glorious was the promise of this young poet, when but scarcely seventeen he could give such perfect expression to his thoughts as this:—

> " Bright as the golden lily, ripple driven,
> Floating beneath the hawthorn flowers of June;
> So, stargirt, in the purple pool of Heaven
> Swam the low glory of the desert moon.
> And all the earth lay trembling in a swoon
> Of slumbering loveliness; until my brain
> Thrilled through with joy and the desire to weep,
> A perfect pleasure blent with perfect pain :
> And earth sank from me into sleep.
>
> Sweet music sounded; ghostly hands upraised
> My head, slow stealing from the shadowy vast;
> And through the moon-kissed veils of sleep I gazed
> Down the dim aisles of the forgotten past."

These lines may, and do, remind one of Keats, but it by no means follows that they are a conscious imitation. The finest similes of all the poets are drawn from Nature, and it is inevitable that some similarity of thought and word be apparent when the

---

* Part of this paper appeared in *The Poetry Review*, October, 1913.

great bed-rock foundations of Poetry are voiced by various
singers; and, even more so, when the poets don the panoply of
Allegory, there is nearly always a chink in the armour where
no defence can be made against a charge of unoriginality. It
can, therefore, be granted at once that Herbert Kennedy's
thoughts often follow subconsciously the pansy path where the
great have passed along before him. Take his exquisite picture
of Twilight : —

> " In that hour,
> At the dim gateways of the sunset, Day
> Kisses her sister Night, and side by side
> They lift together suppliant hands in prayer
> To Him Who is the King : and the low earth
> Lies faintly breathing in a silver sleep,
> Till far in Heaven the angel whispers die,
> And silent, slow, God's benediction falls,
> Through the blue veils of twilight, to the world.
>
> Thus 'twas I dreamed, while the slow roses swayed
> And little whispers whispered past my cheek,
> Whispered and wept and died : a nightingale
> Sang, till the night boughs trembled at her song,
> And sobbed themselves to sleep. The daylight died,
> Grey-green and tender, o'er the distant fields,
> And o'er the dreaming tree-tops sweetly swept
> The slender sickle of the maiden moon."

Compare this with Shelley's *To-Night* : —

> " Wrap thy form in a mantle grey
>   Star-inwrought,
> Blind with thine hair the eyes of Day
> Kiss her until she be wearied out."

And his lines in another poem : —

> " . . . . Pallid evening twines its beaming hair
> In duskier braids around the languid eyes of Day :
> Silence and Twilight, unbeloved of men,
> Creep hand in hand from yon obscurest glen."

Here we have the same beautiful fancies, but treated
differently. In his sombre moods Kennedy may remind us of
the magnificent horrors of Poe in vision—not metres.

> " How the wind moans !
>   The shadows leap and dance
> About my head, now stretching giant arms
> To crush me down, and plunge me in a gloom
> Of quivering shapes and sinuous hands that glide
> Along the dim, dark walls; then, swooping, fold
> Swift serpent fingers o'er my eyes.
>   The fire
> Dies flickering down and the red embers fall.

How the wind moans !
   The leafless branches lash
The shivering panes, and slow, sure, pitiless,
On the wan, winter world patters the rain.
Was it a dream—ah, God !—only a dream?
   .   .   .   .   .

But horror broods above me, and I stand
Dim in the graveyard of forgotten things.
The low white tombs gape open at my feet
And from the crumbling earth old ghosts arise.
Old fears, old griefs, old longings. . . .
   .   .   .   .   .

Like dead, white fingers tapping on a tomb,
The pitiless song of the cold autumn rain.''
   .   .   .   .   .

And, again, in his joyous moods may come reminders of Herrick, as in *Daffodils, April,* 1909, from which only a brief quotation is made here : —

  '' Blow, blow your golden trumpets,
     Ye dancing daffodils !
  Blow, blow your golden trumpets !
  For Spring is on the hills.
   .   .   .   .   .

  O ring it to the valleys
  And the hawthorn scented alleys ;
  O ring it out ye golden bells
  In sunshine or in rain ;
  O ring it out ye daffodils,
  Ye dainty dancing daffodils ;
  O ring it out across the world
  That Spring has come again.''

Very seldom, however, is Kennedy so blithe as this : his verse is generally permeated with pensive regret for the fleeting beauties and joys of Earth. Hear how he voices the beautiful brevity of Spring.

THE FIRST OF JUNE.

'' Sweetly smiles the sunset, through dark boughs golden gleaming,
  Tenderly to westward, faint and far away.
  Up into the glory of the sky my heart drifts dreaming,
  Dreaming in Earth's wonder hour at closing of the day.

Sadly sighs the sunset, as lost winds wander weeping,
  Weeping with the nightingales for the morns of May,
  May, whose fragrant loveliness in the grave is sleeping,
  Sleeping in that Heaven of dead, sweet things that cannot stay.
   .   .   .   .   .

Dead and gone the sunset : and, as night is falling,
  Faint with June's first sweetness, when the lilacs sway,
  Dim with far sweet memories, the voice of May is calling
  Sadly to my twilight heart at closing of the day.''

And of Summer : —

> " There's a song I would be ever singing,
> There's a strain that is for ever ringing
>   Sweet and low and lovely
>   In my heart.
> 'Tis the sound of Autumn breezes singing
> Whispering to Summer sunlit sleeping
>   That she from her children
>   Soon must part.
>
> 'Tis the song of Autumn blossoms crying
> O'er the rose-blown couch of Summer ; sighing
>   For their lovely Mother
>   Passed away.
> 'Tis the sound of Autumn breezes singing
> To the weeping flowers at even ; bringing
>   Comfort at the quiet
>   Close of day."

This boy's love of earthly loveliness was indeed soul-felt. To the end his longings were for it, and in his last poem, written about a fortnight before his death, he expressed his final aspiration : —

> " I know a quiet garden
> Where April violets blow,
> Where daffodils are golden,
> And blossoms burst in snow,
> Where summer brings her roses,
> And lilacs laugh in May,
> While chestnut boughs are lighting
> Their lamps along the way ;
> Paths where the lips of Autumn
> Have kissed the leaves to gold,
> And Christmas roses brighten
> In dim December's cold.
>
> .   .   .
>
> Oh ! I pray that when all is ended
> I may leave that land above
> Sometimes to walk through the twilight
> In the garden that I love."

As the shadows of Death drew near he had prayed that he might not die when the world was decked with spring and summer beauty : —

> " Let me not die in spring : I could not bear
> To leave the meadows where the breezes wake
> On wild March mornings : or the cowslips break
> About the feet of April frail and fair,
> The young year's maiden love : for whose sweet sake
> The primrose stars with tears of joy are wet,
> And daffodils their golden music shake
> To greet the winds that wake the violet.
>
> .   .   .   .   .

Let me not in the summer pass away,
When skies are warm, and all the world is sweet
With scent of roses round about my feet,
And glory of the jasmine's trailing spray
Above, as in the shadowed window seat
I lie and watch the swift-winged swallows dart
Through blue, bright air, till sunset shadows meet
To weave their web of peace about my heart.

.   .   .   .   .

Ah God ! I would not lie alone and cold
In the dark earth, while yet the world is fair,
While yet life's loveliness may softly fold
Mine eyes. . . . ."

His wish was granted, for he died on November 7th, 1910. Though he was resigned to the cruel decree of Fate, so doubly cruel " in that he died so young," he, like all true artists, longed to leave some record of his personality on the shifting sands of Humanity—or, as he phrased it, " To send some flash of light across the world, ere we pass back into the Great Unknown." Surely, this wish has also been granted.

.   .   .   .   .

The yearning of the artist that some token of his art may withstand the engulfing seas of Death and Time, and shine through the mists of the ages, has never been more poignantly expressed than in the words of Lord Alfred Douglas, a true poet : —

" O let us tell
In long carved line and painted parable,
How the white road curves down into the night.
Only to build one crystal barrier
Against this sea which beats upon our days ;
To ransom one lost moment with a rhyme ;
Or if fate cries and grudging gods demur,
To clutch Life's hair, and thrust one naked phrase
Like a lean knife between the ribs of Time."

In contradistinction to pictorial artists or painters, it is remarkable how literary expression by lyrical artists is confined to mundane glories and imagery. Putting aside Shakspere and Milton, and Wordsworth, Longfellow and Tennyson, how few of the great poets hymn the delights of Eternity, or, indeed, point to any hope of distinct existence beyond the grave. The pantheism of Shelley is the keynote for some; but the many regard Death as a blessed oblivion after life's fierce fever. Gray, in the splendid *Elegy*, promises the rustic labourer—as the best reward for life-long toil—eternal sleep. Thomas Hardy voices the same thought : —

" . . . . The weary wain
Plods forward, laden heavily;
And toilers with their aches are fain
For endless rest. . . ."

Swinburne rejoices:—

" That no life lives for ever;
That dead men rise up never,
That even the weariest river
Winds somewhere safe to sea.

　　　　　·　　　　·　　　　·

Only the sleep eternal
In an eternal night."

Byron cries:—

" When Time, or soon or late, shall bring
The dreamless sleep that lulls the dead,
Oblivion! may thy languid wing
Wave gently o'er my dying bed."

　　　·　　　·　　　·　　　·　　　·

Shelley blends his pantheism with some views of Death as a
beautiful sleep or dream:—

" The dead are sleeping in their sepulchres :

　　　·　　　·　　　·　　　·　　　·

Thus solemnized and softened, death is mild
And terrorless as this serenest night.
Here could I hope, like some inquiring child
Sporting on graves, that death did hide from human sight
Sweet secrets, or beside its breathless sleep
That loveliest dreams perpetual watch did keep."

Hood has, like Poe, rather a *macabre* interest in the grave
and dwells on the gloom of death; but in his happier moods
he certainly intimates a hope beyond, " I smell the rose above
the mould." Emily Brontë, despite her magnificent expression
of future egoism (" No coward soul is mine "), had her moods of
desire for oblivion:—

" Oh, for the time when I shall sleep
Without identity.
And never care how rain may steep,
Or snow may cover me !

No promised heaven, these wild desires
Could all or half fulfil;
No threatened hell, with quenchless fires,
Subdue this quenchless will ! "

For E. A. Poe, Eldorado is the Valley of the Shadow; Christina
Rossetti is content if there be no remembrance in the eternal
twilight "that doth not rise nor set"; and "Thomas Ingoldsby"
in his last lines, the exquisite " As I Laye a-thynkynge," forsook
his once merry muse, and worn by sorrow and pain only desired

rest after death. Of modern poets, many have expressed this view of Death as rest or oblivion in beautiful verse. Roden Noel wrote in " Dying " : —

> " They are waiting on the shore
> For the bark to take them home;
> They will toil and grieve no more;
> The hour for release hath come.
>
> ■   .   .   .   .
>
> Now the shadowy bark is come
> And the weary may go home.
>
> By still water they would rest,
> In the shadow of the tree;
> After battle sleep is best,
> After noise tranquillity."

Arthur Symons also lays stress on rest : —

> " If rest is sweet at shut of day,
> For tired hands and tired feet,
> How sweet at last to rest for aye,
>   If rest is sweet ! "

And Theodore Wratislaw, in more passionate vein, hymns oblivion : —

> " Somewhere, some day—I pray the day be soon !—
> Shall I lie dead, perchance when this green floor
> Of chequered grass beneath the sycamore
> Is burnt up by the fierce September noon :
> Some midnight when the sea's wan waters croon
> Their lullaby to the enchanted shore,—
> An ebb-tide with its vague and muffled roar,
> Past where the wet sands glisten to the moon.
> Then shalt thou gain at length thy great desire,
> O heart of mine, O heart of tears and fire !
> Thy life is troublous as the changing foam.
> Then shalt thou lie at peace and solemn rest,
> In calm attainment of thy life's long quest.
> The haven of thy wish, thine only home."

In perhaps his best short story, *The Canterville Ghost*, Oscar Wilde, in a few lines of lyrical, jewelled prose, gives an exquisite conception of Death as eternal oblivion and peace for the weary : —

" Far away beyond the pinewoods . . . there is a little garden. There the grass grows long and deep, there are the great white stars of the hemlock flower, there the nightingale sings all night long. All night long he sings, and the cold, crystal moon looks down, and the yew-tree spreads out its giant arms over the sleepers. . . . Death must be so beautiful. To lie in the soft brown earth, with the grasses waving above one's head, and listen to silence. To have no yesterday, and no to-morrow. To forget time, to forgive life, to be at peace."

This is indeed robbing the tomb of its terrors, and no doubt, with his superlatively imaginative mind, Wilde found this picturesque idealisation of the grave infinitely more consoling than the prospect of a problematical existence in another sphere for ever. And this seems to be the attitude of the greater number of his fellow-poets, those of the English tongue at any rate.

The fact, then, remains that the majority of lyrical artists have not been inspired by the thought of Eternity : it is the beauty of his world and the beauty of death as rest they have sung. And the reason ? Putting aside the flippant suggestion of some humorist that the conventional idea of Eternity—sitting, clothed in a halo, on damp clouds and playing the harp—is not sufficiently attractive, it is all too true that for those who are conscious and appreciative of natural and physical beauty in this world, and also of its mental and material pleasures, the unknown, unending vistas of Eternity present a stern and fearsome prospect. The things that poets delight to hymn—flowers, wine, the wonder and loveliness of earth, and sea and sky, the changing seasons, human love and pain and hate, physical beauty, the sweet sadness and regrets of memory—do these have their place in the future state ? We do not know. As Mrs. Marriott Watson so tenderly sings : —

" Shall we not weary in the windless days
 Hereafter, for the murmur of the sea,
 The cool salt air across some grassy lea?
Shall we not go bewildered through a maze
Of stately streets with glittering gems ablaze,
 Forlorn amid the pearl and ivory,
 Straining our eyes beyond the bourne to see
Phantoms from out life's dear, forsaken ways?

" Give us again the crazy clay-built nest,
 Summer, and soft, unseasonable spring,
 Our flowers to pluck, our broken songs to sing,
Our fairy gold of evening in the West;
 Still to the land we love our longings cling,
The sweet, vain world of turmoil and unrest."

For the reason, perhaps, that she was conscious that her life was to be cut off early, no poet has expressed so wistfully as Rosamund Marriott Watson this sad regret for the beauty of the world, its impermanence and joys and sorrows. It is the keynote of all her poems. And no artist ever realised so poignantly the crushing cruelty of Death and the sadness of remembering those loved and lost. How exquisite was her tribute to a little dog, *Heart of Gold* : —

" They've all gone out a-walking
   This day of blue and gold,
But you stay here behind with me,
   Just as of old.

" Just as of old—and yet not so
   I wander as I will
About the grassy garden-plot,
   But you lie still.

" You with the little eager feet,
   The eyes of tender brown,
The eyes and feet that followed me
   Aye, up and down.

" The sward lies smooth above you,
   Your gentle heart is cold,
And mine seems like to break for you,
   Dear Heart of Gold."

Another lyrical singer who died all too soon—Dora Sigerson Shorter—picturing the last sad journey only longed to see beyond the veil visions of dear life and home : —

" So on the far horizon I shall see
No alien land but this I hold so dear—
Killiney's silver sands, and Wicklow's hills,
Dawn on my frightened eyes as I draw near.

" And if it be no evil prayer to breathe,
Oh, let no stranger saint or seraphim
Wait there to lead up to the judgment-seat,
My timid soul with weeping eyes and dim.

" But let them come, those dear and lovely ghosts,
In all their human guise and lustihood,
To stand upon that shore and call me home,
Waving their joyful hands as once they stood—
   As once they stood ! "

Yes, it is Life, and its Beauty and Joys that the poets sing. James Thomson rising above *The City of Dreadful Night* could proclaim : —

" Let my voice ring out and over the earth,
   Through all the grief and strife,
With a golden joy in a silver mirth :
   Thank God for Life ! "

The later poets are more passionate in voicing the creed. Hear J. E. Flecker : —

" I know dead men are deaf, and cannot hear
The singing of a thousand nightingales. . . . .
I know dead men are blind and cannot see
The friend that shuts in horror their big eyes,
And they are witless—O I'd rather be
A living mouse than dead as a man dies."

And W. H. Davies : —

> " How sweet is life, how beautiful . . .
> Go, happy life, and say to death—
> ' I gave this man sufficient joy
> To last him for a thousand years.'
> Then ask him why my time's as short
> As one whose breath is full of tears."

And there is Rupert Brooke's sonnet *The Dead*, and many another poet to sing of the Beauty and Joys of this world. So it is, the poets are not inspired by Eternity, or Paradise, call it what you will, but confine their songs to what they can realise here, and that only for a short time, before the eternal sleep comes at the last. Poor Ernest Dowson sums up the poetical attitude to Life and Death in his delicate, plaintive song : —

> " They are not long, the weeping and the laughter,
> Love and desire and hate :
> I think they have no portion in us after
> We pass the gate.
>
> " They are not long, the days of wine and roses :
> Out of a misty dream
> Our path emerges for a while, then closes
> Within a dream."

But oh ! that the dream were longer. In the words of W. J. Linton : —

> " With flowers and love and wine and song,
> Oh ! Death, Life hath not been too long."

THE END.

INDEX

Index

ADDENDA

Page 204.

Note.—In *The Old Madhouse,* William De Morgan apparently described an old house actually existing in High Street, Upper Tooting. Some fifty or sixty years ago it was a school for boys, the headmaster being Dr. Batt, who, like Dr. Carteret in the tale, was a very heavy, big man. There was at one time a secret tunnel running from the old artesian well under the house to a small lake in the grounds, and one of the pupils, Frank Mainwaring (afterwards a famous general in the Indian Army), was traditionally said to have penetrated this tunnel for some distance one adventurous day. Evidently De Morgan heard the stories about this old house, and utilised them in his novel.

Page 362.

Note.—In 1876, certain repairs to the flooring of the Chapel of St. Peter ad Vincula on Tower Green involved the disturbance of the remains of the royal and distinguished persons buried under the chancel —all victims of the axe. The late Lord Redesdale, who was present at these excavations in his capacity as Secretary to the Office of Works, thus related the scene in his book, *A Tragedy in Stone*—an apt title for the Tower of London :—

" There was a thrill of emotion upon everyone present when, at two feet from the surface, we came upon the bones of a woman of from twenty-five to thirty years of age, as Dr. Monat certified. Anne Boleyn was twenty-nine years old at the time of her death. . . . The bones were .slender and beautifully formed—narrow feet and hands, delicate limbs in excellent proportion, the vertebræ very small, the atlas (the joint nearest the skull) tiny. Remember her laughing at her ' lyttel neck ' on the eve of her execution. . . . We spoke in whispers, tears were in our voices. . . . Sadly we carried the remains in a box, under lock and key, to the Governor's house, to be kept there until the chapel should be ready to receive them once more."

The body of Queen Katherine Howard was not found, the explanation being she was so young that the lime had entirely destroyed her immature soft bones. But the remains of the ambitious Duke of Northumberland (father-in-law of Lady Jane Grey), Lord Rochford (brother of Anne Boleyn), the Countess of Salisbury, and the Duke of Monmouth were all discovered where tradition had pointed.